Research Methodology

Methods and Techniques

Research Methodology
Methods and Techniques
(SECOND RESVISED EDITION)

C.R. Kothari

Former Principal, College of Commerce
University of Rajasthan, Jaipur
Rajasthan (India)

NEW AGE
TECHNO
PRESS

An Imprint of

NEW AGE INTERNATIONAL (P) LIMITED, PUBLISHERS

New Delhi • Bangalore • Chennai • Cochin • Guwahati • Hyderabad
Jalandhar • Kolkata • Lucknow • Mumbai • Ranchi
Visit us at **www.newagepublishers.com**

Copyright © 2004, 1990, 1985, New Age International (P) Ltd., Publishers
Published by New Age International (P) Ltd., Publishers
First Edition: 1985
Second Revised Edition: 2004
Reprint: 2008

Branches:

- 36, Malikarjuna Temple Street, Opp. ICWA, Basavanagudi, **Bangalore**. ✆ (080) 26677815
- 26, Damodaran Street, T. Nagar, **Chennai**. ✆ (044) 24353401
- Hemsen Complex, Mohd. Shah Road, Paltan Bazar, Near Starline Hotel, **Guwahati**. ✆ (0361) 2543669
- No. 105, 1st Floor, Madhiray Kaveri Tower, 3-2-19, Azam Jahi Road, Nimboliadda, **Hyderabad**. ✆ (040) 24652456
- RDB Chambers (Formerly Lotus Cinema) 106A, Ist Floor, S.N. Banerjee Road, **Kolkata**. ✆ (033) 22275247
- 18, Madan Mohan Malviya Marg, **Lucknow**. ✆ (0522) 2209578
- 142C, Victor House, Ground Floor, N.M. Joshi Marg, Lower Parel, **Mumbai**. ✆ (022) 24927869
- 22, Golden House, Daryaganj, **New Delhi**. ✆ (011) 23262370, 23262368

ISBN (10): 81-224-1522-9

ISBN (13): 978-81-224-1522-3

Rs. 200.00

C-08-09-3094

17 18 19 20

Printed in India at Dharmesh Art Process, Delhi.

PUBLISHING FOR ONE WORLD
NEW AGE INTERNATIONAL (P) LIMITED, PUBLISHERS
4835/24, Ansari Road, Daryaganj, New Delhi-110002
Visit us at **www.newagepublishers.com**

*In loving memory of
my revered father
(The fountain of inspiration)*

Preface to the Second Edition

I feel encouraged by the widespread response from teachers and students alike to the first edition. I am presenting this second edition, thoroughly revised and enlarged, to my readers in all humbleness. All possible efforts have been made to enhance further the usefulness of the book. The feedback received from different sources has been incorporated.

In this edition a new chapter on "*The Computer: Its role in Research*" have been added in view of the fact that electronic computers by now, for students of economics, management and other social sciences, constitute an indispensable part of research equipment.

The other highlights of this revised edition are (*i*) the subject contents has been developed, refined and restructured at several points, (*ii*) several new problems have also been added at the end of various chapters for the benefit of students, and (*iii*) every page of the book has been read very carefully so as to improve its quality.

I am grateful to all those who have helped me directly and/or indirectly in preparing this revised edition. I firmly believe that there is always scope for improvement and accordingly I shall look forward to received suggestions, (which shall be thankfully acknowledged) for further enriching the quality of the text.

Jaipur
May 1990

C.R. KOTHARI

Preface to the First Edition

Quite frequently these days people talk of research, both in academic institutions and outside. Several research studies are undertaken and accomplished year after year. But in most cases very little attention is paid to an important dimension relaing to research, namely, that of research methodology. The result is that much of research, particularly in social sciences, contains endless word-spinning and too many quotations. Thus a great deal of research tends to be futile. It may be noted, in the context of planning and development, that the significance of research lies in its quality and not in quantity. The need, therefore, is for those concerned with research to pay due attention to designing and adhering to the appropriate methodology throughout for improving the quality of research. The methodology may differ from problem to problem, yet the basic approach towards research remains the same.

Keeping all this in view, the present book has been written with two clear objectives, viz., (i) to enable researchers, irrespective of their discipline, in developing the most appropriate methodology for their research studies; and (ii) to make them familiar with the art of using different research-methods and techniques. It is hoped that the humble effort made in the form of this book will assist in the accomplishment of exploratory as well as result-oriented research studies.

Regarding the organization, the book consists of fourteen chapters, well arranged in a coherent manner. Chapter One is an introduction, presenting an overview of the research methodology. Chapter Two explains the technique of defining a research problem. Chapter Three dwells on various research designs, highlighting their main characteristics. Chapter Four presents the details of several sampling designs. Different measurement and scaling techniques, along with multidimensional scaling, have been lucidly described in Chapter Five. Chapter Six presents a comparative study of the different methods of data collection. It also provides in its appendices guidelines for successful interviewing as well as for constructing questionnaire/schedules. Chapter Seven deals with processing and analysis of data. Sampling fundamentals, along with the theory of estimation, constitutes the subject-matter of Chapter Eight. Chapter Nine has been exclusively devoted to several parametric tests of hypotheses, followed by Chapter Ten concerning Chi-square test. In Chapter Eleven important features of ANOVA and ANOCOVA techniques have been explained and illustrated. Important non-parametric tests, generally used by researchers have been described and illustrated in Chapter Twelve. In Chapter Thirteen, an effort has been made to present the conceptual aspects and circumstances under which various multivariate techniques can appropriate be utilized in research studies, specially in behavioural and social sciences. Factor analysis has been dealt with in relatively more detail. Chapter Fourteen has been devoted to the task of interpretation and the art of writing research reports.

The book is primarily intended to serve as a textbook for graduate and M.Phil. students of Research Methodology in all disciplines of various universities. It is hoped that the book shall provide guidelines to all interested in research studies of one sort or the other. The book is, in fact, an outgrowth of my experience of teaching the subject to M.Phil. students for the last several years.

I am highly indebted to my students and learned colleagues in the Department for providing the necessary stimulus for writing this book. I am grateful to all those persons whose writings and works have helped me in the preparation of this book. I am equally grateful to the reviewer of the manuscript of this book who made extremely valuable suggestions and has thus contributed in enhancing the standard of the book. I thankfully acknowledge the assistance provided by the University Grants Commission in the form of 'on account' grant in the preparation of the manuscript of this book.

I shall feel amply rewarded if the book proves helpful in the development of genuine research studies. I look forward to suggestions from all readers, specially from experienced researchers and scholars for further improving the subject content as well as the presentation of this book.

C.R. KOTHARI

Contents

1

Research Methodology: An Introduction

Research:- scientific & systematic search for pertinent information on a specific topic | *S²PT*

MEANING OF RESEARCH

Research in common parlance refers to a search for knowledge. One can also define research as a scientific and systematic search for pertinent information on a specific topic. In fact, research is an art of scientific investigation. The Advanced Learner's Dictionary of Current English lays down the meaning of research as "a careful investigation or inquiry specially through search for new facts in any branch of knowledge."[1] Redman and Mory define research as a "systematized effort to gain new knowledge."[2] Some people consider research as a movement, a movement from the known to the unknown. It is actually a voyage of discovery. We all possess the vital instinct of inquisitiveness for, when the unknown confronts us, we wonder and our inquisitiveness makes us probe and attain full and fuller understanding of the unknown. This inquisitiveness is the mother of all knowledge and the method, which man employs for obtaining the knowledge of whatever the unknown, can be termed as research.

Research is an academic activity and as such the term should be used in a technical sense. According to Clifford Woody research comprises defining and redefining problems, formulating hypothesis or suggested solutions; collecting, organising and evaluating data; making deductions and reaching conclusions; and at last carefully testing the conclusions to determine whether they fit the formulating hypothesis. D. Slesinger and M. Stephenson in the Encyclopaedia of Social Sciences define research as "the manipulation of things, concepts or symbols for the purpose of generalising to extend, correct or verify knowledge, whether that knowledge aids in construction of theory or in the practice of an art."[3] Research is, thus, an original contribution to the existing stock of knowledge making for its advancement. It is the persuit of truth with the help of study, observation, comparison and experiment. In short, the search for knowledge through objective and systematic method of finding solution to a problem is research. The systematic approach concerning generalisation and the formulation of a theory is also research. As such the term 'research' refers to the systematic method

[1] *The Advanced Learner's Dictionary of Current English*, Oxford, 1952, p. 1069.

[2] L.V. Redman and A.V.H. Mory, *The Romance of Research*, 1923, p.10.

[3] *The Encyclopaedia of Social Sciences*, Vol. IX, MacMillan, 1930.

consisting of enunciating the problem, formulating a hypothesis, collecting the facts or data, analysing the facts and reaching certain conclusions either in the form of solutions(s) towards the concerned problem or in certain generalisations for some theoretical formulation.

OBJECTIVES OF RESEARCH

The purpose of research is to discover answers to questions through the application of scientific procedures. The main aim of research is to find out the truth which is hidden and which has not been discovered as yet. Though each research study has its own specific purpose, we may think of research objectives as falling into a number of following broad groupings:

1. To gain familiarity with a phenomenon or to achieve new insights into it (studies with this object in view are termed as *exploratory* or *formulative* research studies);
2. To portray accurately the characteristics of a particular individual, situation or a group (studies with this object in view are known as *descriptive* research studies);
3. To determine the frequency with which something occurs or with which it is associated with something else (studies with this object in view are known as *diagnostic* research studies);
4. To test a hypothesis of a causal relationship between variables (such studies are known as *hypothesis-testing* research studies).

MOTIVATION IN RESEARCH

What makes people to undertake research? This is a question of fundamental importance. The possible motives for doing research may be either one or more of the following:

1. Desire to get a research degree along with its consequential benefits;
2. Desire to face the challenge in solving the unsolved problems, i.e., concern over practical problems initiates research;
3. Desire to get intellectual joy of doing some creative work;
4. Desire to be of service to society;
5. Desire to get respectability.

However, this is not an exhaustive list of factors motivating people to undertake research studies. Many more factors such as directives of government, employment conditions, curiosity about new things, desire to understand causal relationships, social thinking and awakening, and the like may as well motivate (or at times compel) people to perform research operations.

TYPES OF RESEARCH

The basic types of research are as follows:

(i) *Descriptive vs. Analytical: Descriptive research* includes surveys and fact-finding enquiries of different kinds. The major purpose of descriptive research is description of the state of affairs as it exists at present. In social science and business research we quite often use the term *Ex post facto research* for descriptive research studies. The main characteristic of this method is that the researcher has no control over the variables; he can only report what has happened or what is happening. Most *ex post facto research* projects are used for descriptive studies in which the researcher seeks to measure such items as, for example, frequency of shopping, preferences of people, or similar data. *Ex post facto studies* also include attempts by researchers to discover causes even when they cannot control the variables. The methods of research utilized in descriptive research are survey methods of all kinds, including comparative and correlational methods. In *analytical research*, on the other hand, the researcher has to use facts or information already available, and analyze these to make a critical evaluation of the material.

(ii) *Applied vs. Fundamental:* Research can either be applied (or action) research or fundamental (to basic or pure) research. *Applied research* aims at finding a solution for an immediate problem facing a society or an industrial/business organisation, whereas *fundamental research* is mainly concerned with generalisations and with the formulation of a theory. "Gathering knowledge for knowledge's sake is termed 'pure' or 'basic' research."[4] Research concerning some natural phenomenon or relating to pure mathematics are examples of fundamental research. Similarly, research studies, concerning human behaviour carried on with a view to make generalisations about human behaviour, are also examples of fundamental research, but research aimed at certain conclusions (say, a solution) facing a concrete social or business problem is an example of applied research. Research to identify social, economic or political trends that may affect a particular institution or the copy research (research to find out whether certain communications will be read and understood) or the marketing research or evaluation research are examples of applied research. Thus, the central aim of applied research is to discover a solution for some pressing practical problem, whereas basic research is directed towards finding information that has a broad base of applications and thus, adds to the already existing organized body of scientific knowledge.

(iii) *Quantitative vs. Qualitative:* Quantitative research is based on the measurement of quantity or amount. It is applicable to phenomena that can be expressed in terms of quantity. Qualitative research, on the other hand, is concerned with qualitative phenomenon, i.e., phenomena relating to or involving quality or kind. For instance, when we are interested in investigating the reasons for human behaviour (i.e., why people think or do certain things), we quite often talk of 'Motivation Research', an important type of qualitative research. This type of research aims at discovering the underlying motives and desires, using in depth interviews for the purpose. Other techniques of such research are word association tests, sentence completion tests, story completion tests and similar other projective techniques. Attitude or opinion research i.e., research designed to find out how people feel or what they think about a particular subject or institution is also qualitative research. Qualitative research is specially important in the behavioural sciences where the aim is to discover the underlying motives of human behaviour. Through such research we can analyse the various factors which motivate people to behave in a particular manner or which make people like or dislike a particular thing. It may be stated, however, that to apply qualitative research in

---

[4] Pauline V. Young, *Scientific Social Surveys and Research*, p. 30.

practice is relatively a difficult job and therefore, while doing such research, one should seek guidance from experimental psychologists.

(iv) *Conceptual vs. Empirical:* Conceptual research is that related to some abstract idea(s) or theory. It is generally used by philosophers and thinkers to develop new concepts or to reinterpret existing ones. On the other hand, empirical research relies on experience or observation alone, often without due regard for system and theory. It is data-based research, coming up with conclusions which are capable of being verified by observation or experiment. We can also call it as experimental type of research. In such a research it is necessary to get at facts firsthand, at their source, and actively to go about doing certain things to stimulate the production of desired information. In such a research, the researcher must first provide himself with a working hypothesis or guess as to the probable results. He then works to get enough facts (data) to prove or disprove his hypothesis. He then sets up experimental designs which he thinks will manipulate the persons or the materials concerned so as to bring forth the desired information. Such research is thus characterised by the experimenter's control over the variables under study and his deliberate manipulation of one of them to study its effects. Empirical research is appropriate when proof is sought that certain variables affect other variables in some way. Evidence gathered through experiments or empirical studies is today considered to be the most powerful support possible for a given hypothesis.

(v) *Some Other Types of Research:* All other types of research are variations of one or more of the above stated approaches, based on either the purpose of research, or the time required to accomplish research, on the environment in which research is done, or on the basis of some other similar factor. Form the point of view of time, we can think of research either as *one-time research or longitudinal research.* In the former case the research is confined to a single time-period, whereas in the latter case the research is carried on over several time-periods. Research can be *field-setting research or laboratory research or simulation research,* depending upon the environment in which it is to be carried out. Research can as well be understood as *clinical or diagnostic research.* Such research follow case-study methods or indepth approaches to reach the basic causal relations. Such studies usually go deep into the causes of things or events that interest us, using very small samples and very deep probing data gathering devices. The research may be *exploratory* or it may be formalized. The objective of exploratory research is the development of hypotheses rather than their testing, whereas formalized research studies are those with substantial structure and with specific hypotheses to be tested. *Historical research* is that which utilizes historical sources like documents, remains, etc. to study events or ideas of the past, including the philosophy of persons and groups at any remote point of time. Research can also be classified as *conclusion-oriented* and decision-oriented. While doing conclusion-oriented research, a researcher is free to pick up a problem, redesign the enquiry as he proceeds and is prepared to conceptualize as he wishes. Decision-oriented research is always for the need of a decision maker and the researcher in this case is not free to embark upon research according to his own inclination. Operations research is an example of decision oriented research since it is a scientific method of providing executive departments with a quantitative basis for decisions regarding operations under their control.

Research Approaches

The above description of the types of research brings to light the fact that there are two basic approaches to research, viz., *quantitative approach* and the *qualitative approach*. The former involves the generation of data in quantitative form which can be subjected to rigorous quantitative analysis in a formal and rigid fashion. This approach can be further sub-classified into *inferential*, *experimental* and *simulation approaches* to research. The purpose of *inferential approach* to research is to form a data base from which to infer characteristics or relationships of population. This usually means survey research where a sample of population is studied (questioned or observed) to determine its characteristics, and it is then inferred that the population has the same characteristics. *Experimental approach* is characterised by much greater control over the research environment and in this case some variables are manipulated to observe their effect on other variables. *Simulation approach* involves the construction of an artificial environment within which relevant information and data can be generated. This permits an observation of the dynamic behaviour of a system (or its sub-system) under controlled conditions. The term 'simulation' in the context of business and social sciences applications refers to "the operation of a numerical model that represents the structure of a dynamic process. Given the values of initial conditions, parameters and exogenous variables, a simulation is run to represent the behaviour of the process over time."[5] Simulation approach can also be useful in building models for understanding future conditions.

Qualitative approach to research is concerned with subjective assessment of attitudes, opinions and behaviour. Research in such a situation is a function of researcher's insights and impressions. Such an approach to research generates results either in non-quantitative form or in the form which are not subjected to rigorous quantitative analysis. Generally, the techniques of focus group interviews, projective techniques and depth interviews are used. All these are explained at length in chapters that follow.

Significance of Research

"All progress is born of inquiry. Doubt is often better than overconfidence, for it leads to inquiry, and inquiry leads to invention" is a famous Hudson Maxim in context of which the significance of research can well be understood. Increased amounts of research make progress possible. *Research inculcates scientific and inductive thinking and it promotes the development of logical habits of thinking and organisation.*

The role of research in several fields of applied economics, whether related to business or to the economy as a whole, has greatly increased in modern times. The increasingly complex nature of business and government has focused attention on the use of research in solving operational problems. Research, as an aid to economic policy, has gained added importance, both for government and business.

Research provides the basis for nearly all government policies in our economic system. For instance, government's budgets rest in part on an analysis of the needs and desires of the people and on the availability of revenues to meet these needs. The cost of needs has to be equated to probable revenues and this is a field where research is most needed. Through research we can devise alternative policies and can as well examine the consequences of each of these alternatives.

---

[5] Robert C. Meir, William T. Newell and Harold L. Dazier, *Simulation in Business and Economics,* p. 1.

Decision-making may not be a part of research, but research certainly facilitates the decisions of the policy maker. Government has also to chalk out programmes for dealing with all facets of the country's existence and most of these will be related directly or indirectly to economic conditions. The plight of cultivators, the problems of big and small business and industry, working conditions, trade union activities, the problems of distribution, even the size and nature of defence services are matters requiring research. Thus, research is considered necessary with regard to the allocation of nation's resources. Another area in government, where research is necessary, is collecting information on the economic and social structure of the nation. Such information indicates what is happening in the economy and what changes are taking place. Collecting such statistical information is by no means a routine task, but it involves a variety of research problems. These day nearly all governments maintain large staff of research technicians or experts to carry on this work. Thus, in the context of government, research as a tool to economic policy has three distinct phases of operation, viz., (i) investigation of economic structure through continual compilation of facts; (ii) diagnosis of events that are taking place and the analysis of the forces underlying them; and (iii) the prognosis, i.e., the prediction of future developments.

Research has its special significance in solving various operational and planning problems of business and industry. Operations research and market research, along with motivational research, are considered crucial and their results assist, in more than one way, in taking business decisions. Market research is the investigation of the structure and development of a market for the purpose of formulating efficient policies for purchasing, production and sales. Operations research refers to the application of mathematical, logical and analytical techniques to the solution of business problems of cost minimisation or of profit maximisation or what can be termed as optimisation problems. Motivational research of determining why people behave as they do is mainly concerned with market characteristics. In other words, it is concerned with the determination of motivations underlying the consumer (market) behaviour. All these are of great help to people in business and industry who are responsible for taking business decisions. Research with regard to demand and market factors has great utility in business. Given knowledge of future demand, it is generally not difficult for a firm, or for an industry to adjust its supply schedule within the limits of its projected capacity. Market analysis has become an integral tool of business policy these days. Business budgeting, which ultimately results in a projected profit and loss account, is based mainly on sales estimates which in turn depends on business research. Once sales forecasting is done, efficient production and investment programmes can be set up around which are grouped the purchasing and financing plans. Research, thus, replaces intuitive business decisions by more logical and scientific decisions.

Research is equally important for social scientists in studying social relationships and in seeking answers to various social problems. It provides the intellectual satisfaction of knowing a few things just for the sake of knowledge and also has practical utility for the social scientist to know for the sake of being able to do something better or in a more efficient manner. Research in social sciences is concerned both with knowledge for its own sake and with knowledge for what it can contribute to practical concerns. "This double emphasis is perhaps especially appropriate in the case of social science. On the one hand, its responsibility as a science is to develop a body of principles that make possible the understanding and prediction of the whole range of human interactions. On the other hand, because of its social orientation, it is increasingly being looked to for practical guidance in solving immediate problems of human relations."[6]

---

[6] Marie Jahoda, Morton Deutsch and Stuart W. Cook, *Research Methods in Social Relations,* p. 4.

In addition to what has been stated above, the significance of research can also be understood keeping in view the following points:

(a) To those students who are to write a master's or Ph.D. thesis, research may mean a careerism or a way to attain a high position in the social structure;

(b) To professionals in research methodology, research may mean a source of livelihood;

(c) To philosophers and thinkers, research may mean the outlet for new ideas and insights;

(d) To literary men and women, research may mean the development of new styles and creative work;

(e) To analysts and intellectuals, research may mean the generalisations of new theories.

Thus, research is the fountain of knowledge for the sake of knowledge and an important source of providing guidelines for solving different business, governmental and social problems. It is a sort of formal training which enables one to understand the new developments in one's field in a better way.

Research Methods versus Methodology

It seems appropriate at this juncture to explain the difference between research methods and research methodology. *Research methods* may be understood as all those methods/techniques that are used for conduction of research. *Research methods or techniques**, *thus, refer to the methods the researchers*

*At times, a distinction is also made between research techniques and research methods. *Research techniques* refer to the behaviour and instruments we use in performing research operations such as making observations, recording data, techniques of processing data and the like. *Research methods* refer to the behaviour and instruments used in selecting and constructing research technique. For instance, the difference between methods and techniques of data collection can better be understood from the details given in the following chart—

Type	Methods	Techniques
1. Library Research	(i) Analysis of historical records	Recording of notes, Content analysis, Tape and Film listening and analysis.
	(ii) Analysis of documents	Statistical compilations and manipulations, reference and abstract guides, contents analysis.
2. Field Research	(i) Non-participant direct observation	Observational behavioural scales, use of score cards, etc.
	(ii) Participant observation	Interactional recording, possible use of tape recorders, photo graphic techniques.
	(iii) Mass observation	Recording mass behaviour, interview using independent observers in public places.
	(iv) Mail questionnaire	Identification of social and economic background of respondents.
	(v) Opinionnaire	Use of attitude scales, projective techniques, use of sociometric scales.
	(vi) Personal interview	Interviewer uses a detailed schedule with open and closed questions.
	(vii) Focused interview	Interviewer focuses attention upon a given experience and its effects.
	(viii) Group interview	Small groups of respondents are interviewed simultaneously.
	(ix) Telephone survey	Used as a survey technique for information and for discerning opinion; may also be used as a follow up of questionnaire.
	(x) Case study and life history	Cross sectional collection of data for intensive analysis, longitudinal collection of data of intensive character.
3. Laboratory Research	Small group study of random behaviour, play and role analysis	Use of audio-visual recording devices, use of observers, etc.

From what has been stated above, we can say that methods are more general. It is the methods that generate techniques. However, in practice, the two terms are taken as interchangeable and when we talk of research methods we do, by implication, include research techniques within their compass.

use in performing research operations. In other words, all those methods which are used by the researcher during the course of studying his research problem are termed as research methods. Since the object of research, particularly the applied research, it to arrive at a solution for a given problem, the available data and the unknown aspects of the problem have to be related to each other to make a solution possible. Keeping this in view, research methods can be put into the following three groups:

1. In the first group we include those methods which are concerned with the collection of data. These methods will be used where the data already available are not sufficient to arrive at the required solution;

2. The second group consists of those statistical techniques which are used for establishing relationships between the data and the unknowns;

3. The third group consists of those methods which are used to evaluate the accuracy of the results obtained.

Research methods falling in the above stated last two groups are generally taken as the analytical tools of research.

Research methodology is a way to systematically solve the research problem. It may be understood as a science of studying how research is done scientifically. In it we study the various steps that are generally adopted by a researcher in studying his research problem along with the logic behind them. It is necessary for the researcher to know not only the research methods/techniques but also the methodology. Researchers not only need to know how to develop certain indices or tests, how to calculate the mean, the mode, the median or the standard deviation or chi-square, how to apply particular research techniques, but they also need to know which of these methods or techniques, are relevant and which are not, and what would they mean and indicate and why. Researchers also need to understand the assumptions underlying various techniques and they need to know the criteria by which they can decide that certain techniques and procedures will be applicable to certain problems and others will not. All this means that it is necessary for the researcher to design his methodology for his problem as the same may differ from problem to problem. For example, an architect, who designs a building, has to consciously evaluate the basis of his decisions, i.e., he has to evaluate why and on what basis he selects particular size, number and location of doors, windows and ventilators, uses particular materials and not others and the like. Similarly, in research the scientist has to expose the research decisions to evaluation before they are implemented. He has to specify very clearly and precisely what decisions he selects and why he selects them so that they can be evaluated by others also.

From what has been stated above, we can say that research methodology has many dimensions and research methods do constitute a part of the research methodology. The scope of research methodology is wider than that of research methods. *Thus, when we talk of research methodology we not only talk of the research methods but also consider the logic behind the methods we use in the context of our research study and explain why we are using a particular method or technique and why we are not using others so that research results are capable of being evaluated either by the researcher himself or by others.* Why a research study has been undertaken, how the research problem has been defined, in what way and why the hypothesis has been formulated, what data have been collected and what particular method has been adopted, why particular technique of analysing data has been used and a host of similar other questions are usually answered when we talk of research methodology concerning a research problem or study.

Research and Scientific Method

For a clear perception of the term research, one should know the meaning of scientific method. The two terms, research and scientific method, are closely related. Research, as we have already stated, can be termed as "an inquiry into the nature of, the reasons for, and the consequences of any particular set of circumstances, whether these circumstances are experimentally controlled or recorded just as they occur. Further, research implies the researcher is interested in more than particular results; he is interested in the repeatability of the results and in their extension to more complicated and general situations."[7] On the other hand, the philosophy common to all research methods and techniques, although they may vary considerably from one science to another, is usually given the name of scientific method. In this context, Karl Pearson writes, "The scientific method is one and same in the branches (of science) and that method is the method of all logically trained minds ... the unity of all sciences consists alone in its methods, not its material; the man who classifies facts of any kind whatever, who sees their mutual relation and describes their sequences, is applying the Scientific Method and is a man of science."[8] Scientific method is the pursuit of truth as determined by logical considerations. The ideal of science is to achieve a systematic interrelation of facts. Scientific method attempts to achieve "this ideal by experimentation, observation, logical arguments from accepted postulates and a combination of these three in varying proportions."[9] In scientific method, logic aids in formulating propositions explicitly and accurately so that their possible alternatives become clear. Further, logic develops the consequences of such alternatives, and when these are compared with observable phenomena, it becomes possible for the researcher or the scientist to state which alternative is most in harmony with the observed facts. All this is done through experimentation and survey investigations which constitute the integral parts of scientific method.

Experimentation is done to test hypotheses and to discover new relationships. If any, among variables. But the conclusions drawn on the basis of experimental data are generally criticized for either faulty assumptions, poorly designed experiments, badly executed experiments or faulty interpretations. As such the researcher must pay all possible attention while developing the experimental design and must state only probable inferences. The purpose of survey investigations may also be to provide scientifically gathered information to work as a basis for the researchers for their conclusions.

The scientific method is, thus, based on certain basic postulates which can be stated as under:

1. It relies on empirical evidence;
2. It utilizes relevant concepts;
3. It is committed to only objective considerations;
4. It presupposes ethical neutrality, i.e., it aims at nothing but making only adequate and correct statements about population objects;
5. It results into probabilistic predictions;
6. Its methodology is made known to all concerned for critical scrutiny are for use in testing the conclusions through replication;
7. It aims at formulating most general axioms or what can be termed as scientific theories.

[7] Bernard Ostle and Richard W. Mensing, *Statistics in Research*, p. 2

[8] Karl Pearson, *The Grammar of Science*, Part I, pp. 10–12.

[9] Ostle and Mensing: *op. cit.*, p. 2.

Thus, "the scientific method encourages a rigorous, impersonal mode of procedure dictated by the demands of logic and objective procedure."[10] Accordingly, scientific method implies an objective, logical and systematic method, i.e., a method free from personal bias or prejudice, a method to ascertain demonstrable qualities of a phenomenon capable of being verified, a method wherein the researcher is guided by the rules of logical reasoning, a method wherein the investigation proceeds in an orderly manner and a method that implies internal consistency.

Importance of Knowing How Research is Done

The study of research methodology gives the student the necessary training in gathering material and arranging or card-indexing them, participation in the field work when required, and also training in techniques for the collection of data appropriate to particular problems, in the use of statistics, questionnaires and controlled experimentation and in recording evidence, sorting it out and interpreting it. In fact, importance of knowing the methodology of research or how research is done stems from the following considerations:

(i) For one who is preparing himself for a career of carrying out research, the importance of knowing research methodology and research techniques is obvious since the same constitute the tools of his trade. The knowledge of methodology provides good training specially to the new research worker and enables him to do better research. It helps him to develop disciplined thinking or a 'bent of mind' to observe the field objectively. Hence, those aspiring for careerism in research must develop the skill of using research techniques and must thoroughly understand the logic behind them.

(ii) Knowledge of how to do research will inculcate the ability to evaluate and use research results with reasonable confidence. In other words, we can state that the knowledge of research methodology is helpful in various fields such as government or business administration, community development and social work where persons are increasingly called upon to evaluate and use research results for action.

(iii) When one knows how research is done, then one may have the satisfaction of acquiring a new intellectual tool which can become a way of looking at the world and of judging every day experience. Accordingly, it enables use to make intelligent decisions concerning problems facing us in practical life at different points of time. Thus, the knowledge of research methodology provides tools to took at things in life objectively.

(iv) In this scientific age, all of us are in many ways consumers of research results and we can use them intelligently provided we are able to judge the adequacy of the methods by which they have been obtained. The knowledge of methodology helps the consumer of research results to evaluate them and enables him to take rational decisions.

Research Process

Before embarking on the details of research methodology and techniques, it seems appropriate to present a brief overview of the research process. Research process consists of series of actions or steps necessary to effectively carry out research and the desired sequencing of these steps. The chart shown in Figure 1.1 well illustrates a research process.

---

[10] Carlos L. Lastrucci, *The Scientific Approach: Basic Principles of the Scientific Method*, p. 7.

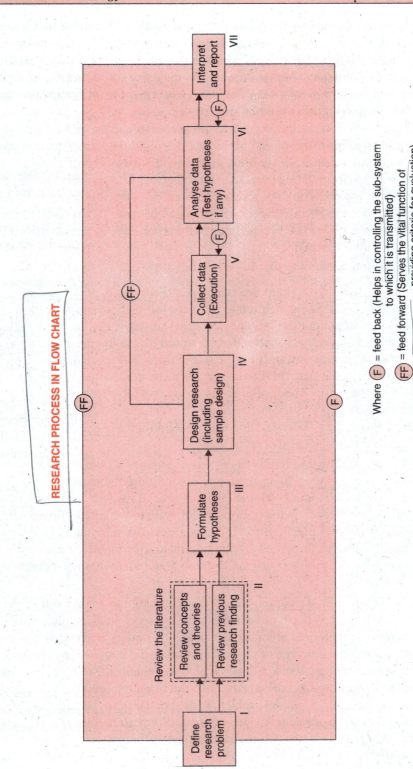

RESEARCH PROCESS IN FLOW CHART

Where F = feed back (Helps in controlling the sub-system to which it is transmitted)

FF = feed forward (Serves the vital function of providing criteria for evaluation)

Fig. 1.1

The chart indicates that the research process consists of a number of closely related activities, as shown through I to VII. But such activities overlap continuously rather than following a strictly prescribed sequence. At times, the first step determines the nature of the last step to be undertaken. If subsequent procedures have not been taken into account in the early stages, serious difficulties may arise which may even prevent the completion of the study. One should remember that the various steps involved in a research process are not mutually exclusive; nor they are separate and distinct. They do not necessarily follow each other in any specific order and the researcher has to be constantly anticipating at each step in the research process the requirements of the subsequent steps. However, the following order concerning various steps provides a useful procedural guideline regarding the research process: (1) formulating the research problem; (2) extensive literature survey; (3) developing the hypothesis; (4) preparing the research design; (5) determining sample design; (6) collecting the data; (7) execution of the project; (8) analysis of data; (9) hypothesis testing; (10) generalisations and interpretation, and (11) preparation of the report or presentation of the results, i.e., formal write-up of conclusions reached.

A brief description of the above stated steps will be helpful.

1. Formulating the research problem: There are two types of research problems, viz., those which relate to states of nature and those which relate to relationships between variables. At the very outset the researcher must single out the problem he wants to study, i.e., he must decide the general area of interest or aspect of a subject-matter that he would like to inquire into. Initially the problem may be stated in a broad general way and then the ambiguities, if any, relating to the problem be resolved. Then, the feasibility of a particular solution has to be considered before a working formulation of the problem can be set up. The formulation of a general topic into a specific research problem, thus, constitutes the first step in a scientific enquiry. Essentially two steps are involved in formulating the research problem, viz., understanding the problem thoroughly, and rephrasing the same into meaningful terms from an analytical point of view.

The best way of understanding the problem is to discuss it with one's own colleagues or with those having some expertise in the matter. In an academic institution the researcher can seek the help from a guide who is usually an experienced man and has several research problems in mind. Often, the guide puts forth the problem in general terms and it is up to the researcher to narrow it down and phrase the problem in operational terms. In private business units or in governmental organisations, the problem is usually earmarked by the administrative agencies with whom the researcher can discuss as to how the problem originally came about and what considerations are involved in its possible solutions.

The researcher must at the same time examine all available literature to get himself acquainted with the selected problem. He may review two types of literature—the conceptual literature concerning the concepts and theories, and the empirical literature consisting of studies made earlier which are similar to the one proposed. The basic outcome of this review will be the knowledge as to what data and other materials are available for operational purposes which will enable the researcher to specify his own research problem in a meaningful context. After this the researcher rephrases the problem into analytical or operational terms i.e., to put the problem in as specific terms as possible. This task of formulating, or defining, a research problem is a step of greatest importance in the entire research process. The problem to be investigated must be defined unambiguously for that will help discriminating relevant data from irrelevant ones. Care must, however, be taken to verify the objectivity and validity of the background facts concerning the problem. Professor W.A. Neiswanger correctly states that the statement of the objective is of basic importance because it determines the data which are to be collected, the characteristics of the data which are relevant, relations which are to be explored, the choice of techniques to be used in these explorations and the form of the final report. If there are certain pertinent terms, the same should be clearly defined along with the task of formulating the problem. In fact, formulation of the problem often follows a sequential pattern where a number of formulations are set up, each formulation more specific than the preceeding one, each one phrased in more analytical terms, and each more realistic in terms of the available data and resources.

2. Extensive literature survey: Once the problem is formulated, a brief summary of it should be written down. It is compulsory for a research worker writing a thesis for a Ph.D. degree to write a synopsis of the topic and submit it to the necessary Committee or the Research Board for approval. At this juncture the researcher should undertake extensive literature survey connected with the problem. For this purpose, the abstracting and indexing journals and published or unpublished bibliographies are the first place to go to. Academic journals, conference proceedings, government reports, books etc., must be tapped depending on the nature of the problem. In this process, it should be remembered that one source will lead to another. The earlier studies, if any, which are similar to the study in hand should be carefully studied. A good library will be a great help to the researcher at this stage.

3. Development of working hypotheses: After extensive literature survey, researcher should state in clear terms the working hypothesis or hypotheses. Working hypothesis is tentative assumption made in order to draw out and test its logical or empirical consequences. As such the manner in which research hypotheses are developed is particularly important since they provide the focal point for research. They also affect the manner in which tests must be conducted in the analysis of data and indirectly the quality of data which is required for the analysis. In most types of research, the development of working hypothesis plays an important role. Hypothesis should be very specific and limited to the piece of research in hand because it has to be tested. The role of the hypothesis is to guide the researcher by delimiting the area of research and to keep him on the right track. It sharpens his thinking and focuses attention on the more important facets of the problem. It also indicates the type of data required and the type of methods of data analysis to be used.

How does one go about developing working hypotheses? The answer is by using the following approach:

(a) Discussions with colleagues and experts about the problem, its origin and the objectives in seeking a solution;

(b) Examination of data and records, if available, concerning the problem for possible trends, peculiarities and other clues;

(c) Review of similar studies in the area or of the studies on similar problems; and

(d) Exploratory personal investigation which involves original field interviews on a limited scale with interested parties and individuals with a view to secure greater insight into the practical aspects of the problem.

Thus, working hypotheses arise as a result of a-priori thinking about the subject, examination of the available data and material including related studies and the counsel of experts and interested parties. Working hypotheses are more useful when stated in precise and clearly defined terms. It may as well be remembered that occasionally we may encounter a problem where we do not need working hypotheses, specially in the case of exploratory or formulative researches which do not aim at testing the hypothesis. But as a general rule, specification of working hypotheses in another basic step of the research process in most research problems.

4. Preparing the research design: The research problem having been formulated in clear cut terms, the researcher will be required to prepare a research design, i.e., he will have to state the conceptual structure within which research would be conducted. The preparation of such a design facilitates research to be as efficient as possible yielding maximal information. In other words, the function of research design is to provide for the collection of relevant evidence with minimal expenditure of effort, time and money. But how all these can be achieved depends mainly on the research purpose. Research purposes may be grouped into four categories, viz., (i) Exploration, (ii) Description, (iii) Diagnosis, and (iv) Experimentation. A flexible research design which provides opportunity for considering many different aspects of a problem is considered appropriate if the purpose of the research study is that of exploration. But when the purpose happens to be an accurate description of a situation or of an association between variables, the suitable design will be one that minimises bias and maximises the reliability of the data collected and analysed.

There are several research designs, such as, experimental and non-experimental hypothesis testing. Experimental designs can be either informal designs (such as before-and-after without control, after-only with control, before-and-after with control) or formal designs (such as completely randomized design, randomized block design, Latin square design, simple and complex factorial designs), out of which the researcher must select one for his own project.

The preparation of the research design, appropriate for a particular research problem, involves usually the consideration of the following:

  (i) the means of obtaining the information;
 (ii) the availability and skills of the researcher and his staff (if any);
(iii) explanation of the way in which selected means of obtaining information will be organised and the reasoning leading to the selection;
(iv) the time available for research; and
 (v) the cost factor relating to research, i.e., the finance available for the purpose.

5. Determining sample design: All the items under consideration in any field of inquiry constitute a 'universe' or 'population'. A complete enumeration of all the items in the 'population' is known as a census inquiry. It can be presumed that in such an inquiry when all the items are covered no element of chance is left and highest accuracy is obtained. But in practice this may not be true. Even the slightest element of bias in such an inquiry will get larger and larger as the number of observations increases. Moreover, there is no way of checking the element of bias or its extent except through a resurvey or use of sample checks. Besides, this type of inquiry involves a great deal of time, money and energy. Not only this, census inquiry is not possible in practice under many circumstances. For instance, blood testing is done only on sample basis. Hence, quite often we select only a few items from the universe for our study purposes. The items so selected constitute what is technically called a sample.

The researcher must decide the way of selecting a sample or what is popularly known as the sample design. In other words, a sample design is a definite plan determined before any data are actually collected for obtaining a sample from a given population. Thus, the plan to select 12 of a city's 200 drugstores in a certain way constitutes a sample design. Samples can be either probability samples or non-probability samples. With probability samples each element has a known probability of being included in the sample but the non-probability samples do not allow the researcher to determine this probability. Probability samples are those based on simple random sampling, systematic sampling, stratified sampling, cluster/area sampling whereas non-probability samples are those based on convenience sampling, judgement sampling and quota sampling techniques. A brief mention of the important sample designs is as follows:

(i) *Deliberate sampling:* Deliberate sampling is also known as purposive or non-probability sampling. This sampling method involves purposive or deliberate selection of particular units of the universe for constituting a sample which represents the universe. When population elements are selected for inclusion in the sample based on the ease of access, it can be called *convenience sampling*. If a researcher wishes to secure data from, say, gasoline buyers, he may select a fixed number of petrol stations and may conduct interviews at these stations. This would be an example of convenience sample of gasoline buyers. At times such a procedure may give very biased results particularly when the population is not homogeneous. On the other hand, in *judgement sampling* the researcher's judgement is used for selecting items which he considers as representative of the population. For example, a judgement sample of college students might be taken to secure reactions to a new method of teaching. Judgement sampling is used quite frequently in qualitative research where the desire happens to be to develop hypotheses rather than to generalise to larger populations.

(ii) *Simple random sampling:* This type of sampling is also known as chance sampling or probability sampling where each and every item in the population has an equal chance of inclusion in the sample and each one of the possible samples, in case of finite universe, has the same probability of being selected. For example, if we have to select a sample of 300 items from a universe of 15,000 items, then we can put the names or numbers of all the 15,000 items on slips of paper and conduct a lottery. Using the random number tables is another method of random sampling. To select the sample, each item is assigned a number from 1 to 15,000. Then, 300 five digit random numbers are selected from the table. To do this we select some random starting point and then a systematic pattern is used in proceeding through the table. We might start in the 4th row, second column and proceed down the column to the bottom of the table and then move to the top of the next column to the right. When a number exceeds the limit of the numbers in the frame, in our case over 15,000, it is simply passed over and the next number selected that does fall within the relevant range. Since the numbers were placed in the table in a completely random fashion, the resulting sample is random. This procedure gives each item an equal probability of being selected. In case of infinite population, the selection of each item in a random sample is controlled by the same probability and that successive selections are independent of one another.

(iii) *Systematic sampling:* In some instances the most practical way of sampling is to select every 15th name on a list, every 10th house on one side of a street and so on. Sampling of this type is known as systematic sampling. An element of randomness is usually introduced into this kind of sampling by using random numbers to pick up the unit with which to start. This procedure is useful when sampling frame is available in the form of a list. In such a design the selection process starts by picking some random point in the list and then every *n*th element is selected until the desired number is secured.

(iv) *Stratified sampling:* If the population from which a sample is to be drawn does not constitute a homogeneous group, then stratified sampling technique is applied so as to obtain a representative sample. In this technique, the population is stratified into a number of non-overlapping subpopulations or strata and sample items are selected from each stratum. If the items selected from each stratum is based on simple random sampling the entire procedure, first stratification and then simple random sampling, is known as *stratified random sampling*.

(v) *Quota sampling:* In stratified sampling the cost of taking random samples from individual strata is often so expensive that interviewers are simply given quota to be filled from different strata, the actual selection of items for sample being left to the interviewer's judgement. This is called quota sampling. The size of the quota for each stratum is generally proportionate to the size of that stratum in the population. Quota sampling is thus an important form of non-probability sampling. Quota samples generally happen to be judgement samples rather than random samples.

(vi) *Cluster sampling and area sampling:* Cluster sampling involves grouping the population and then selecting the groups or the clusters rather than individual elements for inclusion in the sample. Suppose some departmental store wishes to sample its credit card holders. It has issued its cards to 15,000 customers. The sample size is to be kept say 450. For cluster sampling this list of 15,000 card holders could be formed into 100 clusters of 150 card holders each. Three clusters might then be selected for the sample randomly. The sample size must often be larger than the simple random sample to ensure the same level of accuracy because is cluster sampling procedural potential for order bias and other sources of error is usually accentuated. The clustering approach can, however, make the sampling procedure relatively easier and increase the efficiency of field work, specially in the case of personal interviews.

Area sampling is quite close to cluster sampling and is often talked about when the total geographical area of interest happens to be big one. Under area sampling we first divide the total area into a number of smaller non-overlapping areas, generally called geographical clusters, then a number of these smaller areas are randomly selected, and all units in these small areas are included in the sample. Area sampling is specially helpful where we do not have the list of the population concerned. It also makes the field interviewing more efficient since interviewer can do many interviews at each location.

(vii) *Multi-stage sampling:* This is a further development of the idea of cluster sampling. This technique is meant for big inquiries extending to a considerably large geographical area like an entire country. Under multi-stage sampling the first stage may be to select large primary sampling units such as states, then districts, then towns and finally certain families within towns. If the technique of random-sampling is applied at all stages, the sampling procedure is described as multi-stage random sampling.

(viii) *Sequential sampling:* This is somewhat a complex sample design where the ultimate size of the sample is not fixed in advance but is determined according to mathematical decisions on the basis of information yielded as survey progresses. This design is usually adopted under acceptance sampling plan in the context of statistical quality control.

In practice, several of the methods of sampling described above may well be used in the same study in which case it can be called mixed sampling. It may be pointed out here that normally one should resort to random sampling so that bias can be eliminated and sampling error can be estimated. But purposive sampling is considered desirable when the universe happens to be small and a known characteristic of it is to be studied intensively. Also, there are conditions under which sample designs other than random sampling may be considered better for reasons like convenience and low costs. *The sample design to be used must be decided by the researcher taking into consideration the nature of the inquiry and other related factors.*

6. Collecting the data: In dealing with any real life problem it is often found that data at hand are inadequate, and hence, it becomes necessary to collect data that are appropriate. There are several ways of collecting the appropriate data which differ considerably in context of money costs, time and other resources at the disposal of the researcher.

Primary data can be collected either through experiment or through survey. If the researcher conducts an experiment, he observes some quantitative measurements, or the data, with the help of which he examines the truth contained in his hypothesis. But in the case of a survey, data can be collected by any one or more of the following ways:

(i) *By observation:* This method implies the collection of information by way of investigator's own observation, without interviewing the respondents. The information obtained relates to what is currently happening and is not complicated by either the past behaviour or future intentions or attitudes of respondents. This method is no doubt an expensive method and the information provided by this method is also very limited. As such this method is not suitable in inquiries where large samples are concerned.

(ii) *Through personal interview:* The investigator follows a rigid procedure and seeks answers to a set of pre-conceived questions through personal interviews. This method of collecting data is usually carried out in a structured way where output depends upon the ability of the interviewer to a large extent.

(iii) *Through telephone interviews:* This method of collecting information involves contacting the respondents on telephone itself. This is not a very widely used method but it plays an important role in industrial surveys in developed regions, particularly, when the survey has to be accomplished in a very limited time.

(iv) *By mailing of questionnaires:* The researcher and the respondents do come in contact with each other if this method of survey is adopted. Questionnaires are mailed to the respondents with a request to return after completing the same. It is the most extensively used method in various economic and business surveys. Before applying this method, usually a Pilot Study for testing the questionnaire is conduced which reveals the weaknesses, if any, of the questionnaire. Questionnaire to be used must be prepared very carefully so that it may prove to be effective in collecting the relevant information.

(v) *Through schedules:* Under this method the enumerators are appointed and given training. They are provided with schedules containing relevant questions. These enumerators go to respondents with these schedules. Data are collected by filling up the schedules by enumerators on the basis of replies given by respondents. Much depends upon the capability of enumerators so far as this method is concerned. Some occasional field checks on the work of the enumerators may ensure sincere work.

The researcher should select one of these methods of collecting the data taking into consideration the nature of investigation, objective and scope of the inquiry, finanical resources, available time and the desired degree of accuracy. Though he should pay attention to all these factors but much depends upon the ability and experience of the researcher. In this context *Dr A.L. Bowley* very aptly remarks that in collection of statistical data commonsense is the chief requisite and experience the chief teacher.

7. Execution of the project: Execution of the project is a very important step in the research process. If the execution of the project proceeds on correct lines, the data to be collected would be adequate and dependable. The researcher should see that the project is executed in a systematic manner and in time. If the survey is to be conducted by means of structured questionnaires, data can be readily machine-processed. In such a situation, questions as well as the possible answers may be coded. If the data are to be collected through interviewers, arrangements should be made for proper selection and training of the interviewers. The training may be given with the help of instruction manuals which explain clearly the job of the interviewers at each step. Occasional field checks should be made to ensure that the interviewers are doing their assigned job sincerely and efficiently. A careful watch should be kept for unanticipated factors in order to keep the survey as much realistic as possible. This, in other words, means that steps should be taken to ensure that the survey is under statistical control so that the collected information is in accordance with the pre-defined standard of accuracy. If some of the respondents do not cooperate, some suitable methods should be designed to tackle this problem. One method of dealing with the non-response problem is to make a list of the non-respondents and take a small sub-sample of them, and then with the help of experts vigorous efforts can be made for securing response.

8. Analysis of data: After the data have been collected, the researcher turns to the task of analysing them. The analysis of data requires a number of closely related operations such as establishment of categories, the application of these categories to raw data through coding, tabulation and then drawing statistical inferences. The unwieldy data should necessarily be condensed into a few manageable groups and tables for further analysis. Thus, researcher should classify the raw data into some purposeful and usable categories. *Coding* operation is usually done at this stage through which the categories of data are transformed into symbols that may be tabulated and counted. *Editing* is the procedure that improves the quality of the data for coding. With coding the stage is ready for tabulation. *Tabulation* is a part of the technical procedure wherein the classified data are put in the form of tables. The mechanical devices can be made use of at this juncture. A great deal of data, specially in large inquiries, is tabulated by computers. Computers not only save time but also make it possible to study large number of variables affecting a problem simultaneously.

Analysis work after tabulation is generally based on the computation of various percentages, coefficients, etc., by applying various well defined statistical formulae. In the process of analysis, relationships or differences supporting or conflicting with original or new hypotheses should be subjected to tests of significance to determine with what validity data can be said to indicate any conclusion(s). For instance, if there are two samples of weekly wages, each sample being drawn from factories in different parts of the same city, giving two different mean values, then our problem may be whether the two mean values are significantly different or the difference is just a matter of chance. Through the use of statistical tests we can establish whether such a difference is a real one or is the result of random fluctuations. If the difference happens to be real, the inference will be that the two samples come from different universes and if the difference is due to chance, the conclusion would be that the two samples belong to the same universe. Similarly, the technique of analysis of variance can help us in analysing whether three or more varieties of seeds grown on certain fields yield significantly different results or not. In brief, the researcher can analyse the collected data with the help of various statistical measures.

9. Hypothesis-testing: After analysing the data as stated above, the researcher is in a position to test the hypotheses, if any, he had formulated earlier. Do the facts support the hypotheses or they happen to be contrary? This is the usual question which should be answered while testing hypotheses. Various tests, such as Chi square test, *t*-test, *F*-test, have been developed by statisticians for the purpose. The hypotheses may be tested through the use of one or more of such tests, depending upon the nature and object of research inquiry. Hypothesis-testing will result in either accepting the hypothesis or in rejecting it. If the researcher had no hypotheses to start with, generalisations established on the basis of data may be stated as hypotheses to be tested by subsequent researches in times to come.

10. Generalisations and interpretation: If a hypothesis is tested and upheld several times, it may be possible for the researcher to arrive at generalisation, i.e., to build a theory. As a matter of fact, the real value of research lies in its ability to arrive at certain generalisations. If the researcher had no hypothesis to start with, he might seek to explain his findings on the basis of some theory. It is known as interpretation. The process of interpretation may quite often trigger off new questions which in turn may lead to further researches.

11. Preparation of the report or the thesis: Finally, the researcher has to prepare the report of what has been done by him. Writing of report must be done with great care keeping in view the following:

1. The layout of the report should be as follows: (*i*) the preliminary pages; (*ii*) the main text, and (*iii*) the end matter.

   In its preliminary pages the report should carry title and date followed by acknowledgements and foreword. Then there should be a table of contents followed by a list of tables and list of graphs and charts, if any, given in the report.

   The main text of the report should have the following parts:
   (a) *Introduction:* It should contain a clear statement of the objective of the research and an explanation of the methodology adopted in accomplishing the research. The scope of the study along with various limitations should as well be stated in this part.
   (b) *Summary of findings:* After introduction there would appear a statement of findings and recommendations in non-technical language. If the findings are extensive, they should be summarised.
   (c) *Main report:* The main body of the report should be presented in logical sequence and broken-down into readily identifiable sections.
   (d) *Conclusion:* Towards the end of the main text, researcher should again put down the results of his research clearly and precisely. In fact, it is the final summing up.

At the end of the report, appendices should be enlisted in respect of all technical data. Bibliography, i.e., list of books, journals, reports, etc., consulted, should also be given in the end. Index should also be given specially in a published research report.

2. Report should be written in a concise and objective style in simple language avoiding vague expressions such as 'it seems,' 'there may be', and the like.

3. Charts and illustrations in the main report should be used only if they present the information more clearly and forcibly.

4. Calculated 'confidence limits' must be mentioned and the various constraints experienced in conducting research operations may as well be stated.

Criteria of Good Research

Whatever may be the types of research works and studies, one thing that is important is that they all meet on the common ground of scientific method employed by them. One expects scientific research to satisfy the following criteria:[11]

1. The purpose of the research should be clearly defined and common concepts be used.

2. The research procedure used should be described in sufficient detail to permit another researcher to repeat the research for further advancement, keeping the continuity of what has already been attained.

3. The procedural design of the research should be carefully planned to yield results that are as objective as possible.

4. The researcher should report with complete frankness, flaws in procedural design and estimate their effects upon the findings.

5. The analysis of data should be sufficiently adequate to reveal its significance and the methods of analysis used should be appropriate. The validity and reliability of the data should be checked carefully.

6. Conclusions should be confined to those justified by the data of the research and limited to those for which the data provide an adequate basis.

7. Greater confidence in research is warranted if the researcher is experienced, has a good reputation in research and is a person of integrity.

In other words, we can state the qualities of a good research[12] as under:

1. *Good research is systematic:* It means that research is structured with specified steps to be taken in a specified sequence in accordance with the well defined set of rules. Systematic characteristic of the research does not rule out creative thinking but it certainly does reject the use of guessing and intuition in arriving at conclusions.

2. *Good research is logical:* This implies that research is guided by the rules of logical reasoning and the logical process of induction and deduction are of great value in carrying out research. Induction is the process of reasoning from a part to the whole whereas deduction is the process of reasoning from some premise to a conclusion which follows from that very premise. In fact, logical reasoning makes research more meaningful in the context of decision making.

[11] James Harold Fox, Criteria of Good Research, Phi Delta Kappan, Vol. 39 (March, 1958), pp. 285–86.

[12] See, Danny N. Bellenger and Barnett, A. Greenberg, "*Marketing Research—A Management Information Approach*", p. 107–108.

3. *Good research is empirical:* It implies that research is related basically to one or more aspects of a real situation and deals with concrete data that provides a basis for external validity to research results.

4. *Good research is replicable:* This characteristic allows research results to be verified by replicating the study and thereby building a sound basis for decisions.

Problems Encountered by Researchers in India

Researchers in India, particularly those engaged in empirical research, are facing several problems. Some of the important problems are as follows:

1. *The lack of a scientific training in the methodology of research* is a great impediment for researchers in our country. There is paucity of competent researchers. Many researchers take a leap in the dark without knowing research methods. Most of the work, which goes in the name of research is not methodologically sound. Research to many researchers and even to their guides, is mostly a scissor and paste job without any insight shed on the collated materials. The consequence is obvious, viz., the research results, quite often, do not reflect the reality or realities. Thus, a systematic study of research methodology is an urgent necessity. Before undertaking research projects, researchers should be well equipped with all the methodological aspects. As such, *efforts should be made to provide short-duration intensive courses for meeting this requirement.*

2. There is *insufficient interaction* between the university research departments on one side and business establishments, government departments and research institutions on the other side. A great deal of primary data of non-confidential nature remain untouched/untreated by the researchers for want of proper contacts. *Efforts should be made to develop satisfactory liaison among all concerned for better and realistic researches.* There is need for developing some mechanisms of a university—industry interaction programme so that academics can get ideas from practitioners on what needs to be researched and practitioners can apply the research done by the academics.

3. Most of the business units in our country do not have the confidence that the material supplied by them to researchers will not be misused and as such they are often reluctant in supplying the needed information to researchers. The concept of secrecy seems to be sacrosanct to business organisations in the country so much so that it proves an impermeable barrier to researchers. Thus, *there is the need for generating the confidence that the information/data obtained from a business unit will not be misused.*

4. *Research studies overlapping one another are undertaken quite often for want of adequate information.* This results in duplication and fritters away resources. This problem can be solved by proper compilation and revision, at regular intervals, of a list of subjects on which and the places where the research is going on. Due attention should be given toward identification of research problems in various disciplines of applied science which are of immediate concern to the industries.

5. *There does not exist a code of conduct for researchers* and inter-university and inter-departmental rivalries are also quite common. Hence, there is need for developing a code of conduct for researchers which, if adhered sincerely, can win over this problem.

6. Many researchers in our country also face *the difficulty of adequate and timely secretarial assistance,* including computerial assistance. This causes unnecessary delays in the completion of research studies. All possible efforts be made in this direction so that efficient secretarial assistance is made available to researchers and that too well in time. University Grants Commission must play a dynamic role in solving this difficulty.

7. *Library management and functioning is not satisfactory at many places* and much of the time and energy of researchers are spent in tracing out the books, journals, reports, etc., rather than in tracing out relevant material from them.

8. *There is also the problem that many of our libraries are not able to get copies of old and new Acts/Rules, reports and other government publications in time.* This problem is felt more in libraries which are away in places from Delhi and/or the state capitals. Thus, efforts should be made for the regular and speedy supply of all governmental publications to reach our libraries.

9. *There is also the difficulty of timely availability of published data* from various government and other agencies doing this job in our country. Researcher also faces the problem on account of the fact that the published data vary quite significantly because of differences in coverage by the concerning agencies.

10. There may, at times, take place *the problem of conceptualization* and also problems relating to the process of data collection and related things.

Questions

1. Briefly describe the different steps involved in a research process.
2. What do you mean by research? Explain its significance in modern times.
3. Distinguish between Research methods and Research methodology.
4. Describe the different types of research, clearly pointing out the difference between an experiment and a survey.
5. Write short notes on:
   (1) Design of the research project;
   (2) Ex post facto research;
   (3) Motivation in research;
   (4) Objectives of research;
   (5) Criteria of good research;
   (7) Research and scientific method.
6. "Empirical research in India in particular creates so many problems for the researchers". State the problems that are usually faced by such researchers.

                                                        (Raj. Univ. EAFM., M. Phil. Exam., 1979)

7. "A research scholar has to work as a judge and derive the truth and not as a pleader who is only eager to prove his case in favour of his plaintiff." Discuss the statement pointing out the objectives of research.

8. "Creative management, whether in public administration or private industry, depends on methods of inquiry that maintain objectivity, clarity, accuracy and consistency". Discuss this statement and examine the significance of research".

(Raj. Univ. EAFM., M. Phil. Exam., 1978)

9. "Research is much concerned with proper fact finding, analysis and evaluation." Do you agree with this statement? Give reasons in support of your answer.

10. It is often said that there is not a proper link between some of the activities under way in the world of academics and in most business in our country. Account for this state of affairs and give suggestions for improvement.

2

Defining the Research Problem

In research process, the first and foremost step happens to be that of selecting and properly defining a research problem.* A researcher must find the problem and formulate it so that it becomes susceptible to research. Like a medical doctor, a researcher must examine all the symptoms (presented to him or observed by him) concerning a problem before he can diagnose correctly. To define a problem correctly, a researcher must know: what a problem is?

WHAT IS A RESEARCH PROBLEM?

A research problem, in general, refers to some difficulty which a researcher experiences in the context of either a theoretical or practical situation and wants to obtain a solution for the same. Usually we say that a research problem does exist if the following conditions are met with:

(i) There must be an individual (or a group or an organisation), let us call it 'I,' to whom the problem can be attributed. The individual or the organisation, as the case may be, occupies an environment, say 'N', which is defined by values of the uncontrolled variables, Y_j.

(ii) There must be at least two courses of action, say C_1 and C_2, to be pursued. A course of action is defined by one or more values of the controlled variables. For example, the number of items purchased at a specified time is said to be one course of action.

(iii) There must be at least two possible outcomes, say O_1 and O_2, of the course of action, of which one should be preferable to the other. In other words, this means that there must be at least one outcome that the researcher wants, i.e., an objective.

(iv) The courses of action available must provides some chance of obtaining the objective, but they cannot provide the same chance, otherwise the choice would not matter. Thus, if $P(O_j | I, C_j, N)$ represents the probability that an outcome O_j will occur, if I select C_j in N, then $P(O_1 | I, C_1, N) \neq P(O_1 | I, C_2, N)$. In simple words, we can say that the choices must have unequal efficiencies for the desired outcomes.

---

* We talk of a research problem or hypothesis in case of descriptive or hypothesis testing research studies. Exploratory or formulative research studies do not start with a problem or hypothesis, their problem is to find a problem or the hypothesis to be tested. One should make a clear statement to this effect. This aspect has been dealt with in chapter entitled "Research Design".

Over and above these conditions, the individual or the organisation can be said to have the problem only if '*I*' does not know what course of action is best, i.e., '*I*', must be in doubt about the solution. Thus, an individual or a group of persons can be said to have a problem which can be technically described as a research problem, if they (individual or the group), having one or more desired outcomes, are confronted with two or more courses of action that have some but not equal efficiency for the desired objective(s) and are in doubt about which course of action is best.

We can, thus, state the components[1] of a research problem as under:

(i) There must be an individual or a group which has some difficulty or the problem.

(ii) There must be some objective(s) to be attained at. If one wants nothing, one cannot have a problem.

(iii) There must be alternative means (or the courses of action) for obtaining the objective(s) one wishes to attain. This means that there must be *at least two means* available to a researcher for if he has no choice of means, he cannot have a problem.

(iv) There must remain some doubt in the mind of a researcher with regard to the selection of alternatives. This means that research must answer the question concerning the relative efficiency of the possible alternatives.

(v) There must be some environment(s) to which the difficulty pertains.

Thus, a research problem is one which requires a researcher to find out the best solution for the given problem, i.e., to find out by which course of action the objective can be attained optimally in the context of a given environment. There are several factors which may result in making the problem complicated. For instance, the environment may change affecting the efficiencies of the courses of action or the values of the outcomes; the number of alternative courses of action may be very large; persons not involved in making the decision may be affected by it and react to it favourably or unfavourably, and similar other factors. All such elements (or at least the important ones) may be thought of in context of a research problem.

SELECTING THE PROBLEM

The research problem undertaken for study must be carefully selected. The task is a difficult one, although it may not appear to be so. Help may be taken from a research guide in this connection. Nevertheless, every researcher must find out his own salvation for research problems cannot be borrowed. A problem must spring from the researcher's mind like a plant springing from its own seed. If our eyes need glasses, it is not the optician alone who decides about the number of the lens we require. We have to see ourselves and enable him to prescribe for us the right number by cooperating with him. Thus, a research guide can at the most only help a researcher choose a subject. However, the following points may be observed by a researcher in selecting a research problem or a subject for research:

(i) Subject which is overdone should not be normally chosen, for it will be a difficult task to throw any new light in such a case.

(ii) Controversial subject should not become the choice of an average researcher.

[1] R.L. Ackoff, *The Design of Social Research*, Chicago University Press, Chicago, 1961.

(iii) Too narrow or too vague problems should be avoided.

(iv) The subject selected for research should be familiar and feasible so that the related research material or sources of research are within one's reach. Even then it is quite difficult to supply definitive ideas concerning how a researcher should obtain ideas for his research. For this purpose, a researcher should contact an expert or a professor in the University who is already engaged in research. He may as well read articles published in current literature available on the subject and may think how the techniques and ideas discussed therein might be applied to the solution of other problems. He may discuss with others what he has in mind concerning a problem. In this way he should make all possible efforts in selecting a problem.

(v) The importance of the subject, the qualifications and the training of a researcher, the costs involved, the time factor are few other criteria that must also be considered in selecting a problem. In other words, before the final selection of a problem is done, a researcher must ask himself the following questions:

    (a) Whether he is well equipped in terms of his background to carry out the research?

    (b) Whether the study falls within the budget he can afford?

    (c) Whether the necessary cooperation can be obtained from those who must participate in research as subjects?

If the answers to all these questions are in the affirmative, one may become sure so far as the practicability of the study is concerned.

(vi) The selection of a problem must be preceded by a preliminary study. This may not be necessary when the problem requires the conduct of a research closely similar to one that has already been done. But when the field of inquiry is relatively new and does not have available a set of well developed techniques, a brief feasibility study must always be undertaken.

If the subject for research is selected properly by observing the above mentioned points, the research will not be a boring drudgery, rather it will be love's labour. In fact, zest for work is a must. The subject or the problem selected must involve the researcher and must have an upper most place in his mind so that he may undertake all pains needed for the study.

NECESSITY OF DEFINING THE PROBLEM

Quite often we all hear that a problem clearly stated is a problem half solved. This statement signifies the need for defining a research problem. The problem to be investigated must be defined unambiguously for that will help to discriminate relevant data from the irrelevant ones. A proper definition of research problem will enable the researcher to be on the track whereas an ill-defined problem may create hurdles. Questions like: What data are to be collected? What characteristics of data are relevant and need to be studied? What relations are to be explored. What techniques are to be used for the purpose? and similar other questions crop up in the mind of the researcher who can well plan his strategy and find answers to all such questions only when the research problem has been well defined. Thus, defining a research problem properly is a prerequisite for any study and is a step of the highest importance. In fact, formulation of a problem is often more essential than its solution. It is only on careful detailing the research problem that we can work out the research design and can smoothly carry on all the consequential steps involved while doing research.

TECHNIQUE INVOLVED IN DEFINING A PROBLEM

Let us start with the question: What does one mean when he/she wants to define a research problem? The answer may be that one wants to state the problem along with the bounds within which it is to be studied. In other words, defining a problem involves the task of laying down boundaries within which a researcher shall study the problem with a pre-determined objective in view.

How to define a research problem is undoubtedly a herculean task. However, it is a task that must be tackled intelligently to avoid the perplexity encountered in a research operation. The usual approach is that the researcher should himself pose a question (or in case someone else wants the researcher to carry on research, the concerned individual, organisation or an authority should pose the question to the researcher) and set-up techniques and procedures for throwing light on the question concerned for formulating or defining the research problem. But such an approach generally does not produce definitive results because the question phrased in such a fashion is usually in broad general terms and as such may not be in a form suitable for testing.

Defining a research problem properly and clearly is a crucial part of a research study and must in no case be accomplished hurriedly. However, in practice this a frequently overlooked which causes a lot of problems later on. Hence, the research problem should be defined in a systematic manner, giving due weightage to all relating points. The technique for the purpose involves the undertaking of the following steps generally one after the other: (i) statement of the problem in a general way; (ii) understanding the nature of the problem; (iii) surveying the available literature (iv) developing the ideas through discussions; and (v) rephrasing the research problem into a working proposition.

A brief description of all these points will be helpful.

(i) Statement of the problem in a general way: First of all the problem should be stated in a broad general way, keeping in view either some practical concern or some scientific or intellectual interest. For this purpose, the researcher must immerse himself thoroughly in the subject matter concerning which he wishes to pose a problem. In case of social research, it is considered advisable to do some field observation and as such the researcher may undertake some sort of preliminary survey or what is often called *pilot survey*. Then the researcher can himself state the problem or he can seek the guidance of the guide or the subject expert in accomplishing this task. Often, the guide puts forth the problem in general terms, and it is then up to the researcher to narrow it down and phrase the problem in operational terms. In case there is some directive from an organisational authority, the problem then can be stated accordingly. The problem stated in a broad general way may contain various ambiguities which must be resolved by cool thinking and rethinking over the problem. At the same time the feasibility of a particular solution has to be considered and the same should be kept in view while stating the problem.

(ii) Understanding the nature of the problem: The next step in defining the problem is to understand its origin and nature clearly. The best way of understanding the problem is to discuss it with those who first raised it in order to find out how the problem originally came about and with what objectives in view. If the researcher has stated the problem himself, he should consider once again all those points that induced him to make a general statement concerning the problem. For a better understanding of the nature of the problem involved, he can enter into discussion with those who have a good knowledge of the problem concerned or similar other problems. The researcher should also keep in view the environment within which the problem is to be studied and understood.

(iii) Surveying the available literature: All available literature concerning the problem at hand must necessarily be surveyed and examined before a definition of the research problem is given. This means that the researcher must be well-conversant with relevant theories in the field, reports and records as also all other relevant literature. He must devote sufficient time in reviewing of research already undertaken on related problems. This is done to find out what data and other materials, if any, are available for operational purposes. "Knowing what data are available often serves to narrow the problem itself as well as the technique that might be used."[2]. This would also help a researcher to know if there are certain gaps in the theories, or whether the existing theories applicable to the problem under study are inconsistent with each other, or whether the findings of the different studies do not follow a pattern consistent with the theoretical expectations and so on. All this will enable a researcher to take new strides in the field for furtherance of knowledge i.e., he can move up starting from the existing premise. Studies on related problems are useful for indicating the type of difficulties that may be encountered in the present study as also the possible analytical shortcomings. At times such studies may also suggest useful and even new lines of approach to the present problem.

(iv) Developing the ideas through discussions: Discussion concerning a problem often produces useful information. Various new ideas can be developed through such an exercise. Hence, a researcher must discuss his problem with his colleagues and others who have enough experience in the same area or in working on similar problems. This is quite often known as an *experience survey*. People with rich experience are in a position to enlighten the researcher on different aspects of his proposed study and their advice and comments are usually invaluable to the researcher. They help him sharpen his focus of attention on specific aspects within the field. Discussions with such persons should not only be confined to the formulation of the specific problem at hand, but should also be concerned with the general approach to the given problem, techniques that might be used, possible solutions, etc.

(v) Rephrasing the research problem: Finally, the researcher must sit to rephrase the research problem into a working proposition. Once the nature of the problem has been clearly understood, the environment (within which the problem has got to be studied) has been defined, discussions over the problem have taken place and the available literature has been surveyed and examined, rephrasing the problem into analytical or operational terms is not a difficult task. Through rephrasing, the researcher puts the research problem in as specific terms as possible so that it may become operationally viable and may help in the development of working hypotheses.*

In addition to what has been stated above, the following points must also be observed while defining a research problem:

---

[2] Robert Ferber and P.J. Verdoorn, *Research Methods in Economics and Business*, p. 33–34.

* Working hypotheses are a set of suggested tentative solutions of explanations of a research problem which may or may not be the real solutions. The task of research is to test and establish such hypotheses. Hypotheses should be clearly and precisely stated in simple terms, they should be testable, limited in scope and should state relationship between variables. They should be amenable to testing within a reasonable time and should be consistent with most of the known facts (Testing of hypotheses has been dealt with later in the book).

(a) Technical terms and words or phrases, with special meanings used in the statement of the problem, should be clearly defined.

(b) Basic assumptions or postulates (if any) relating to the research problem should be clearly stated.

(c) A straight forward statement of the value of the investigation (i.e., the criteria for the selection of the problem) should be provided.

(d) The suitability of the time-period and the sources of data available must also be considered by the researcher in defining the problem.

(e) The scope of the investigation or the limits within which the problem is to be studied must be mentioned explicitly in defining a research problem.

AN ILLUSTRATION

The technique of defining a problem outlined above can be illustrated for better understanding by taking an example as under:

Let us suppose that a research problem in a broad general way is as follows:

"Why is productivity in Japan so much higher than in India"?

In this form the question has a number of ambiguities such as: What sort of productivity is being referred to? With what industries the same is related? With what period of time the productivity is being talked about? In view of all such ambiguities the given statement or the question is much too general to be amenable to analysis. Rethinking and discussions about the problem may result in narrowing down the question to:

"What factors were responsible for the higher labour productivity of Japan's manufacturing industries during the decade 1971 to 1980 relative to India's manufacturing industries?"

This latter version of the problem is definitely an improvement over its earlier version for the various ambiguities have been removed to the extent possible. Further rethinking and rephrasing might place the problem on a still better operational basis as shown below:

"To what extent did labour productivity in 1971 to 1980 in Japan exceed that of India in respect of 15 selected manufacturing industries? What factors were responsible for the productivity differentials between the two countries by industries?"

With this sort of formulation, the various terms involved such as 'labour productivity', 'productivity differentials', etc. must be explained clearly. The researcher must also see that the necessary data are available. In case the data for one or more industries selected are not available for the concerning time-period, then the said industry or industries will have to be substituted by other industry or industries. The suitability of the time-period must also be examined. Thus, all relevant factors must be considered by a researcher before finally defining a research problem.

CONCLUSION

We may conclude by saying that the task of defining a research problem, very often, follows a sequential pattern—the problem is stated in a general way, the ambiguities are resolved, thinking and rethinking process results in a more specific formulation of the problem so that it may be a realistic one in terms of the available data and resources and is also analytically meaningful. All this results in a well defined research problem that is not only meaningful from an operational point of view, but is equally capable of paving the way for the development of working hypotheses and for means of solving the problem itself.

Questions

1. Describe fully the techniques of defining a research problem.
2. What is research problem? Define the main issues which should receive the attention of the researcher in formulating the research problem. Give suitable examples to elucidate your points.

   (Raj. Uni. EAFM, M. Phil. Exam. 1979)

3. How do you define a research problem? Give three examples to illustrate your answer.

   (Raj. Uni. EAFM, M. Phil. Exam. 1978)

4. What is the necessity of defining a research problem? Explain.
5. Write short notes on:
   (a) Experience survey;
   (b) Pilot survey;
   (c) Components of a research problem;
   (d) Rephrasing the research problem.
6. "The task of defining the research problem often follows a sequential pattern". Explain.
7. "Knowing what data are available often serves to narrow down the problem itself as well as the technique that might be used." Explain the underlying idea in this statement in the context of defining a research problem.
8. Write a comprehensive note on the "Task of defining a research problem".

3

Research Design

MEANING OF RESEARCH DESIGN ✓

The formidable problem that follows the task of defining the research problem is the preparation of the design of the research project, popularly known as the "research design". Decisions regarding what, where, when, how much, by what means concerning an inquiry or a research study constitute a research design. "A research design is the arrangement of conditions for collection and analysis of data in a manner that aims to combine relevance to the research purpose with economy in procedure."[1] In fact, the research design is the conceptual structure within which research is conducted; it constitutes the blueprint for the collection, measurement and analysis of data. As such the design includes an outline of what the researcher will do from writing the hypothesis and its operational implications to the final analysis of data. More explicitly, the desing decisions happen to be in respect of:

   (i) What is the study about?

   (ii) Why is the study being made?

   (iii) Where will the study be carried out?

   (iv) What type of data is required?

   (v) Where can the required data be found?

   (vi) What periods of time will the study include?

   (vii) What will be the sample design?

   (viii) What techniques of data collection will be used?

   (ix) How will the data be analysed?

   (x) In what style will the report be prepared?

Keeping in view the above stated design decisions, one may split the overall research design into the following parts:

   (a) *the sampling design* which deals with the method of selecting items to be observed for the given study;

[1] Claire Selltiz and others, *Research Methods in Social Sciences*, 1962, p. 50.

(b) *the observational design* which relates to the conditions under which the observations are to be made;

(c) *the statistical design* which concerns with the question of how many items are to be observed and how the information and data gathered are to be analysed; and

(d) *the operational design* which deals with the techniques by which the procedures specified in the sampling, statistical and observational designs can be carried out.

From what has been stated above, we can state the important features of a research design as under:

(i) It is a plan that specifies the sources and types of information relevant to the research problem.

(ii) It is a strategy specifying which approach will be used for gathering and analysing the data.

(iii) It also includes the time and cost budgets since most studies are done under these two constraints.

In brief, research design must, at least, contain—(a) a clear statement of the research problem; (b) procedures and techniques to be used for gathering information; (c) the population to be studied; and (d) methods to be used in processing and analysing data.

NEED FOR RESEARCH DESIGN

Research design is needed because it facilitates the smooth sailing of the various research operations, thereby making research as efficient as possible yielding maximal information with minimal expenditure of effort, time and money. Just as for better, economical and attractive construction of a house, we need a blueprint (or what is commonly called the map of the house) well thought out and prepared by an expert architect, similarly we need a research design or a plan in advance of data collection and analysis for our research project. Research design stands for advance planning of the methods to be adopted for collecting the relevant data and the techniques to be used in their analysis, keeping in view the objective of the research and the availability of staff, time and money. Preparation of the research design should be done with great care as any error in it may upset the entire project. Research design, in fact, has a great bearing on the reliability of the results arrived at and as such constitutes the firm foundation of the entire edifice of the research work.

Even then the need for a well thought out research design is at times not realised by many. The importance which this problem deserves is not given to it. As a result many researches do not serve the purpose for which they are undertaken. In fact, they may even give misleading conclusions. Thoughtlessness in designing the research project may result in rendering the research exercise futile. It is, therefore, imperative that an efficient and appropriate design must be prepared before starting research operations. The design helps the researcher to organize his ideas in a form whereby it will be possible for him to look for flaws and inadequacies. Such a design can even be given to others for their comments and critical evaluation. In the absence of such a course of action, it will be difficult for the critic to provide a comprehensive review of the proposed study.

FEATURES OF A GOOD DESIGN

A good design is often characterised by adjectives like flexible, appropriate, efficient, economical and so on. Generally, the design which minimises bias and maximises the reliability of the data collected and analysed is considered a good design. The design which gives the smallest experimental error is supposed to be the best design in many investigations. Similarly, a design which yields maximal information and provides an opportunity for considering many different aspects of a problem is considered most appropriate and efficient design in respect of many research problems. Thus, the question of good design is related to the purpose or objective of the research problem and also with the nature of the problem to be studied. A design may be quite suitable in one case, but may be found wanting in one respect or the other in the context of some other research problem. One single design cannot serve the purpose of all types of research problems.

A research design appropriate for a particular research problem, usually involves the consideration of the following factors:

(i) the means of obtaining information;

(ii) the availability and skills of the researcher and his staff, if any;

(iii) the objective of the problem to be studied;

(iv) the nature of the problem to be studied; and

(v) the availability of time and money for the research work.

If the research study happens to be an exploratory or a formulative one, wherein the major emphasis is on discovery of ideas and insights, the research design most appropriate must be flexible enough to permit the consideration of many different aspects of a phenomenon. But when the purpose of a study is accurate description of a situation or of an association between variables (or in what are called the descriptive studies), accuracy becomes a major consideration and a research design which minimises bias and maximises the reliability of the evidence collected is considered a good design. Studies involving the testing of a hypothesis of a causal relationship between variables require a design which will permit inferences about causality in addition to the minimisation of bias and maximisation of reliability. But in practice it is the most difficult task to put a particular study in a particular group, for a given research may have in it elements of two or more of the functions of different studies. It is only on the basis of its primary function that a study can be categorised either as an exploratory or descriptive or hypothesis-testing study and accordingly the choice of a research design may be made in case of a particular study. Besides, the availability of time, money, skills of the research staff and the means of obtaining the information must be given due weightage while working out the relevant details of the research design such as experimental design, survey design, sample design and the like.

IMPORTANT CONCEPTS RELATING TO RESEARCH DESIGN

Before describing the different research designs, it will be appropriate to explain the various concepts relating to designs so that these may be better and easily understood.

1. Dependent and independent variables: A concept which can take on different quantitative values is called a variable. As such the concepts like weight, height, income are all examples of variables. Qualitative phenomena (or the attributes) are also quantified on the basis of the presence or absence of the concerning attribute(s). Phenomena which can take on quantitatively different values even in decimal points are called 'continuous variables'.* But all variables are not continuous. If they can only be expressed in integer values, they are non-continuous variables or in statistical language 'discrete variables'.** Age is an example of continuous variable, but the number of children is an example of non-continuous variable. If one variable depends upon or is a consequence of the other variable, it is termed as a dependent variable, and the variable that is antecedent to the dependent variable is termed as an independent variable. For instance, if we say that height depends upon age, then height is a dependent variable and age is an independent variable. Further, if in addition to being dependent upon age, height also depends upon the individual's sex, then height is a dependent variable and age and sex are independent variables. Similarly, readymade films and lectures are examples of independent variables, whereas behavioural changes, occurring as a result of the environmental manipulations, are examples of dependent variables.

2. Extraneous variable: Independent variables that are not related to the purpose of the study, but may affect the dependent variable are termed as extraneous variables. Suppose the researcher wants to test the hypothesis that there is a relationship between children's gains in social studies achievement and their self-concepts. In this case self-concept is an independent variable and social studies achievement is a dependent variable. Intelligence may as well affect the social studies achievement, but since it is not related to the purpose of the study undertaken by the researcher, it will be termed as an extraneous variable. Whatever effect is noticed on dependent variable as a result of extraneous variable(s) is technically described as an 'experimental error'. A study must always be so designed that *the effect upon the dependent variable is attributed entirely to the independent variable(s), and not to some extraneous variable or variables.*

3. Control: One important characteristic of a good research design is to minimise the influence or effect of extraneous variable(s). The technical term 'control' is used when we design the study minimising the effects of extraneous independent variables. In experimental researches, the term 'control' is used to refer to restrain experimental conditions.

4. Confounded relationship: When the dependent variable is not free from the influence of extraneous variable(s), the relationship between the dependent and independent variables is said to be confounded by an extraneous variable(s).

5. Research hypothesis: When a prediction or a hypothesised relationship is to be tested by scientific methods, it is termed as research hypothesis. The research hypothesis is a predictive statement that relates an independent variable to a dependent variable. Usually a research hypothesis must contain, at least, one independent and one dependent variable. Predictive statements which are not to be objectively verified or the relationships that are assumed but not to be tested, are not termed research hypotheses.

6. Experimental and non-experimental hypothesis-testing research: When the purpose of research is to test a research hypothesis, it is termed as hypothesis-testing research. It can be of the experimental design or of the non-experimental design. Research in which the independent variable is manipulated is termed 'experimental hypothesis-testing research' and a research in which an independent variable is not manipulated is called 'non-experimental hypothesis-testing research'. For instance, suppose a researcher wants to study whether intelligence affects reading ability for a group

---

* A continuous variable is that which can assume any numerical value within a specific range.
** A variable for which the individual values fall on the scale only with distinct gaps is called a discrete variable.

of students and for this purpose he randomly selects 50 students and tests their intelligence and reading ability by calculating the coefficient of correlation between the two sets of scores. This is an example of non-experimental hypothesis-testing research because herein the independent variable, intelligence, is not manipulated. But now suppose that our researcher randomly selects 50 students from a group of students who are to take a course in statistics and then divides them into two groups by randomly assigning 25 to Group A, the usual studies programme, and 25 to Group B, the special studies programme. At the end of the course, he administers a test to each group in order to judge the effectiveness of the training programme on the student's performance-level. This is an example of experimental hypothesis-testing research because in this case the independent variable, viz., the type of training programme, is manipulated.

7. Experimental and control groups: In an experimental hypothesis-testing research when a group is exposed to usual conditions, it is termed a 'control group', but when the group is exposed to some novel or special condition, it is termed an 'experimental group'. In the above illustration, the Group A can be called a control group and the Group B an experimental group. If both groups A and B are exposed to special studies programmes, then both groups would be termed 'experimental groups.' It is possible to design studies which include only experimental groups or studies which include both experimental and control groups.

8. Treatments: The different conditions under which experimental and control groups are put are usually referred to as 'treatments'. In the illustration taken above, the two treatments are the usual studies programme and the special studies programme. Similarly, if we want to determine through an experiment the comparative impact of three varieties of fertilizers on the yield of wheat, in that case the three varieties of fertilizers will be treated as three treatments.

9. Experiment: The process of examining the truth of a statistical hypothesis, relating to some research problem, is known as an experiment. For example, we can conduct an experiment to examine the usefulness of a certain newly developed drug. Experiments can be of two types viz., absolute experiment and comparative experiment. If we want to determine the impact of a fertilizer on the yield of a crop, it is a case of absolute experiment; but if we want to determine the impact of one fertilizer as compared to the impact of some other fertilizer, our experiment then will be termed as a comparative experiment. Often, we undertake comparative experiments when we talk of designs of experiments.

10. Experimental unit(s): The pre-determined plots or the blocks, where different treatments are used, are known as experimental units. Such experimental units must be selected (defined) very carefully.

DIFFERENT RESEARCH DESIGNS

Different research designs can be conveniently described if we categorize them as: (1) research design in case of exploratory research studies; (2) research design in case of descriptive and diagnostic research studies, and (3) research design in case of hypothesis-testing research studies.

We take up each category separately.

1. Research design in case of exploratory research studies: Exploratory research studies are also termed as formulative research studies. The main purpose of such studies is that of formulating a problem for more precise investigation or of developing the working hypotheses from an operational point of view. The major emphasis in such studies is on the discovery of ideas and insights. As such the research design appropriate for such studies must be flexible enough to provide opportunity for considering different aspects of a problem under study. Inbuilt flexibility in research design is needed because the research problem, broadly defined initially, is transformed into one with more precise meaning in exploratory studies, which fact may necessitate changes in the research procedure for gathering relevant data. Generally, the following three methods in the context of research design for such studies are talked about: (a) the survey of concerning literature; (b) the experience survey and (c) the analysis of 'insight-stimulating' examples.

The survey of concerning literature happens to be the most simple and fruitful method of formulating precisely the research problem or developing hypothesis. Hypotheses stated by earlier workers may be reviewed and their usefulness be evaluated as a basis for further research. It may also be considered whether the already stated hypotheses suggest new hypothesis. In this way the researcher should review and build upon the work already done by others, but in cases where hypotheses have not yet been formulated, his task is to review the available material for deriving the relevant hypotheses from it.

Besides, the bibliographical survey of studies, already made in one's area of interest may as well as made by the researcher for precisely formulating the problem. He should also make an attempt to apply concepts and theories developed in different research contexts to the area in which he is himself working. Sometimes the works of creative writers also provide a fertile ground for hypothesis-formulation and as such may be looked into by the researcher.

Experience survey means the survey of people who have had practical experience with the problem to be studied. The object of such a survey is to obtain insight into the relationships between variables and new ideas relating to the research problem. For such a survey people who are competent and can contribute new ideas may be carefully selected as respondents to ensure a representation of different types of experience. The respondents so selected may then be interviewed by the investigator. The researcher must prepare an interview schedule for the systematic questioning of informants. But the interview must ensure flexibility in the sense that the respondents should be allowed to raise issues and questions which the investigator has not previously considered. Generally, the experience-collecting interview is likely to be long and may last for few hours. Hence, it is often considered desirable to send a copy of the questions to be discussed to the respondents well in advance. This will also give an opportunity to the respondents for doing some advance thinking over the various issues involved so that, at the time of interview, they may be able to contribute effectively. Thus, an experience survey may enable the researcher to define the problem more concisely and help in the formulation of the research hypothesis. This survey may as well provide information about the practical possibilities for doing different types of research.

Analysis of 'insight-stimulating' examples is also a fruitful method for suggesting hypotheses for research. It is particularly suitable in areas where there is little experience to serve as a guide. This method consists of the intensive study of selected instances of the phenomenon in which one is interested. For this purpose the existing records, if any, may be examined, the unstructured interviewing may take place, or some other approach may be adopted. Attitude of the investigator, the intensity of the study and the ability of the researcher to draw together diverse information into a unified interpretation are the main features which make this method an appropriate procedure for evoking insights.

Now, what sort of examples are to be selected and studied? There is no clear cut answer to it. Experience indicates that for particular problems certain types of instances are more appropriate than others. One can mention few examples of 'insight-stimulating' cases such as the reactions of strangers, the reactions of marginal individuals, the study of individuals who are in transition from one stage to another, the reactions of individuals from different social strata and the like. In general, cases that provide sharp contrasts or have striking features are considered relatively more useful while adopting this method of hypotheses formulation.

Thus, in an exploratory of formulative research study which merely leads to insights or hypotheses, whatever method or research design outlined above is adopted, the only thing essential is that it must continue to remain flexible so that many different facets of a problem may be considered as and when they arise and come to the notice of the researcher.

2. Research design in case of descriptive and diagnostic research studies: Descriptive research studies are those studies which are concerned with describing the characteristics of a particular individual, or of a group, whereas diagnostic research studies determine the frequency with which something occurs or its association with something else. The studies concerning whether certain variables are associated are examples of diagnostic research studies. As against this, studies concerned with specific predictions, with narration of facts and characteristics concerning individual, group or situation are all examples of descriptive research studies. Most of the social research comes under this category. From the point of view of the research design, the descriptive as well as diagnostic studies share common requirements and as such we may group together these two types of research studies. In descriptive as well as in diagnostic studies, the researcher must be able to define clearly, what he wants to measure and must find adequate methods for measuring it along with a clear cut definition of 'population' he wants to study. Since the aim is to obtain complete and accurate information in the said studies, the procedure to be used must be carefully planned. The research design must make enough provision for protection against bias and must maximise reliability, with due concern for the economical completion of the research study. The design in such studies must be rigid and not flexible and must focus attention on the following:

(a) Formulating the objective of the study (what the study is about and why is it being made?)
(b) Designing the methods of data collection (what techniques of gathering data will be adopted?)
(c) Selecting the sample (how much material will be needed?)
(d) Collecting the data (where can the required data be found and with what time period should the data be related?)
(e) Processing and analysing the data.
(f) Reporting the findings.

In a descriptive/diagnostic study the first step is to specify the objectives with sufficient precision to ensure that the data collected are relevant. If this is not done carefully, the study may not provide the desired information.

Then comes the question of selecting the methods by which the data are to be obtained. In other words, techniques for collecting the information must be devised. Several methods (viz., observation, questionnaires, interviewing, examination of records, etc.), with their merits and limitations, are available for the purpose and the researcher may user one or more of these methods which have been discussed in detail in later chapters. While designing data-collection procedure, adequate safeguards against bias and unreliability must be ensured. Whichever method is selected, questions must be well examined and be made unambiguous; interviewers must be instructed not to express their own opinion; observers must be trained so that they uniformly record a given item of behaviour. It is always desirable to pre-test the data collection instruments before they are finally used for the study purposes. In other words, we can say that "*structured instruments*" are used in such studies.

In most of the descriptive/diagnostic studies the researcher takes out sample(s) and then wishes to make statements about the population on the basis of the sample analysis or analyses. More often than not, sample has to be designed. Different sample designs have been discussed in detail in a separate chapter in this book. Here we may only mention that the problem of designing samples should be tackled in such a fashion that the samples may yield accurate information with a minimum amount of research effort. Usually one or more forms of probability sampling, or what is often described as random sampling, are used.

To obtain data free from errors introduced by those responsible for collecting them, it is necessary to supervise closely the staff of field workers as they collect and record information. Checks may be set up to ensure that the data collecting staff perform their duty honestly and without prejudice. "As data are collected, they should be examined for completeness, comprehensibility, consistency and reliability."[2]

The data collected must be processed and analysed. This includes steps like coding the interview replies, observations, etc.; tabulating the data; and performing several statistical computations. To the extent possible, the processing and analysing procedure should be planned in detail before actual work is started. This will prove economical in the sense that the researcher may avoid unnecessary labour such as preparing tables for which he later finds he has no use or on the other hand, re-doing some tables because he failed to include relevant data. Coding should be done carefully to avoid error in coding and for this purpose the reliability of coders needs to be checked. Similarly, the accuracy of tabulation may be checked by having a sample of the tables re-done. In case of mechanical tabulation the material (i.e., the collected data or information) must be entered on appropriate cards which is usually done by punching holes corresponding to a given code. The accuracy of punching is to be checked and ensured. Finally, statistical computations are needed and as such averages, percentages and various coefficients must be worked out. Probability and sampling analysis may as well be used. The appropriate statistical operations, along with the use of appropriate tests of significance should be carried out to safeguard the drawing of conclusions concerning the study.

Last of all comes the question of reporting the findings. This is the task of communicating the findings to others and the researcher must do it in an efficient manner. The layout of the report needs to be well planned so that all things relating to the research study may be well presented in simple and effective style.

Thus, the research design in case of descriptive/diagnostic studies is a comparative design throwing light on all points narrated above and must be prepared keeping in view the objective(s) of the study and the resources available. However, it must ensure the minimisation of bias and maximisation of reliability of the evidence collected. The said design can be appropriately referred to as a *survey design* since it takes into account all the steps involved in a survey concerning a phenomenon to be studied.

[2] Claire Selltiz *et al., op. cit.,* p. 74.

The difference between research designs in respect of the above two types of research studies can be conveniently summarised in tabular form as under:

Table 3.1

	Type of study	
Research Design	*Exploratory of Formulative*	*Descriptive/Diagnostic*
Overall design	Flexible design (design must provide opportunity for considering different aspects of the problem)	Rigid design (design must make enough provision for protection against bias and must maximise reliability)
(i) Sampling design	Non-probability sampling design (purposive or judgement sampling)	Probability sampling design (random sampling)
(ii) Statistical design	No pre-planned design for analysis	Pre-planned design for analysis
(iii) Observational design	Unstructured instruments for collection of data	Structured or well thought out instruments for collection of data
(iv) Operational design	No fixed decisions about the operational procedures	Advanced decisions about operational procedures.

3. Research design in case of hypothesis-testing research studies: Hypothesis-testing research studies (generally known as experimental studies) are those where the researcher tests the hypotheses of causal relationships between variables. Such studies require procedures that will not only reduce bias and increase reliability, but will permit drawing inferences about causality. Usually experiments meet this requirement. Hence, when we talk of research design in such studies, we often mean the design of experiments.

Professor R.A. Fisher's name is associated with experimental designs. Beginning of such designs was made by him when he was working at Rothamsted Experimental Station (Centre for Agricultural Research in England). As such the study of experimental designs has its origin in agricultural research. Professor Fisher found that by dividing agricultural fields or plots into different blocks and then by conducting experiments in each of these blocks, whatever information is collected and inferences drawn from them, happens to be more reliable. This fact inspired him to develop certain experimental designs for testing hypotheses concerning scientific investigations. Today, the experimental designs are being used in researches relating to phenomena of several disciplines. Since experimental designs originated in the context of agricultural operations, we still use, though in a technical sense, several terms of agriculture (such as treatment, yield, plot, block etc.) in experimental designs.

BASIC PRINCIPLES OF EXPERIMENTAL DESIGNS

Professor Fisher has enumerated three principles of experimental designs: (1) the Principle of Replication; (2) the Principle of Randomization; and the (3) Principle of Local Control.

According to the *Principle of Replication*, the experiment should be repeated more than once. Thus, each treatment is applied in many experimental units instead of one. By doing so the statistical accuracy of the experiments is increased. For example, suppose we are to examine the effect of two varieties of rice. For this purpose we may divide the field into two parts and grow one variety in one part and the other variety in the other part. We can then compare the yield of the two parts and draw conclusion on that basis. But if we are to apply the principle of replication to this experiment, then we first divide the field into several parts, grow one variety in half of these parts and the other variety in the remaining parts. We can then collect the data of yield of the two varieties and draw conclusion by comparing the same. The result so obtained will be more reliable in comparison to the conclusion we draw without applying the principle of replication. The entire experiment can even be repeated several times for better results. Conceptually replication does not present any difficulty, but computationally it does. For example, if an experiment requiring a two-way analysis of variance is replicated, it will then require a three-way analysis of variance since replication itself may be a source of variation in the data. However, it should be remembered that replication is introduced in order to increase the precision of a study; that is to say, to increase the accuracy with which the main effects and interactions can be estimated.

The *Principle of Randomization* provides protection, when we conduct an experiment, against the effect of extraneous factors by randomization. In other words, this principle indicates that we should design or plan the experiment in such a way that the variations caused by extraneous factors can all be combined under the general heading of "chance." For instance, if we grow one variety of rice, say, in the first half of the parts of a field and the other variety is grown in the other half, then it is just possible that the soil fertility may be different in the first half in comparison to the other half. If this is so, our results would not be realistic. In such a situation, we may assign the variety of rice to be grown in different parts of the field on the basis of some random sampling technique i.e., we may apply randomization principle and protect ourselves against the effects of the extraneous factors (soil fertility differences in the given case). As such, through the application of the principle of randomization, we can have a better estimate of the experimental error.

The *Principle of Local Control* is another important principle of experimental designs. Under it the extraneous factor, the known source of variability, is made to vary deliberately over as wide a range as necessary and this needs to be done in such a way that the variability it causes can be measured and hence eliminated from the experimental error. This means that we should plan the experiment in a manner that we can perform a two-way analysis of variance, in which the total variability of the data is divided into three components attributed to treatments (varieties of rice in our case), the extraneous factor (soil fertility in our case) and experimental error.[*] In other words, according to the principle of local control, we first divide the field into several homogeneous parts, known as blocks, and then each such block is divided into parts equal to the number of treatments. Then the treatments are randomly assigned to these parts of a block. Dividing the field into several homogenous parts is known as 'blocking'. In general, blocks are the levels at which we hold an extraneous factor fixed, so that we can measure its contribution to the total variability of the data by means of a two-way analysis of variance. In brief, through the principle of local control we can eliminate the variability due to extraneous factor(s) from the experimental error.

[*] See Chapter Analysis of Variance for details.

Important Experimental Designs

Experimental design refers to the framework or structure of an experiment and as such there are several experimental designs. We can classify experimental designs into two broad categories, viz., informal experimental designs and formal experimental designs. Informal experimental designs are those designs that normally use a less sophisticated form of analysis based on differences in magnitudes, whereas formal experimental designs offer relatively more control and use precise statistical procedures for analysis. Important experiment designs are as follows:

(*a*) Informal experimental designs:
   (i) Before-and-after without control design.
   (ii) After-only with control design.
   (iii) Before-and-after with control design.

(*b*) Formal experimental designs:
   (i) Completely randomized design (C.R. Design).
   (ii) Randomized block design (R.B. Design).
   (iii) Latin square design (L.S. Design).
   (iv) Factorial designs.

We may briefly deal with each of the above stated informal as well as formal experimental designs.

1. Before-and-after without control design: In such a design a single test group or area is selected and the dependent variable is measured before the introduction of the treatment. The treatment is then introduced and the dependent variable is measured again after the treatment has been introduced. The effect of the treatment would be equal to the level of the phenomenon after the treatment minus the level of the phenomenon before the treatment. The design can be represented thus:

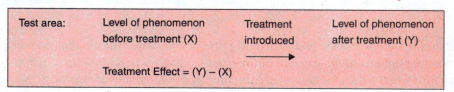

Fig. 3.1

The main difficulty of such a design is that with the passage of time considerable extraneous variations may be there in its treatment effect.

2. After-only with control design: In this design two groups or areas (test area and control area) are selected and the treatment is introduced into the test area only. The dependent variable is then measured in both the areas at the same time. Treatment impact is assessed by subtracting the value of the dependent variable in the control area from its value in the test area. This can be exhibited in the following form:

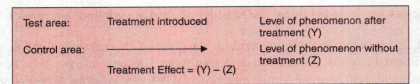

Fig. 3.2

The basic assumption in such a design is that the two areas are identical with respect to their behaviour towards the phenomenon considered. If this assumption is not true, there is the possibility of extraneous variation entering into the treatment effect. However, data can be collected in such a design without the introduction of problems with the passage of time. In this respect the design is superior to before-and-after without control design.

3. Before-and-after with control design: In this design two areas are selected and the dependent variable is measured in both the areas for an identical time-period before the treatment. The treatment is then introduced into the test area only, and the dependent variable is measured in both for an identical time-period after the introduction of the treatment. The treatment effect is determined by subtracting the change in the dependent variable in the control area from the change in the dependent variable in test area. This design can be shown in this way:

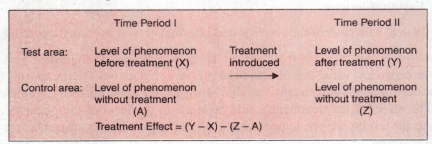

Fig. 3.3

This design is superior to the above two designs for the simple reason that it avoids extraneous variation resulting both from the passage of time and from non-comparability of the test and control areas. But at times, due to lack of historical data, time or a comparable control area, we should prefer to select one of the first two informal designs stated above.

4. Completely randomized design (C.R. design): Involves only two principles viz., the principle of replication and the principle of randomization of experimental designs. It is the simplest possible design and its procedure of analysis is also easier. The essential characteristic of the design is that subjects are randomly assigned to experimental treatments (or vice-versa). For instance, if we have 10 subjects and if we wish to test 5 under treatment A and 5 under treatment B, the randomization process gives every possible group of 5 subjects selected from a set of 10 an equal opportunity of being assigned to treatment A and treatment B. One-way analysis of variance (or one-way ANOVA)[*] is used to analyse such a design. Even unequal replications can also work in this design. It provides maximum number of degrees of freedom to the error. Such a design is generally used when experimental areas happen to be homogeneous. Technically, when all the variations due to uncontrolled

[*] See Chapter 11 for one-way ANOVA technique.

extraneous factors are included under the heading of chance variation, we refer to the design of experiment as C.R. design.

We can present a brief description of the two forms of such a design as given in Fig 3.4.

(i) **Two-group simple randomized design:** In a two-group simple randomized design, first of all the population is defined and then from the population a sample is selected randomly. Further, requirement of this design is that items, after being selected randomly from the population, be randomly assigned to the experimental and control groups (Such random assignment of items to two groups is technically described as principle of randomization). Thus, this design yields two groups as representatives of the population. In a diagram form this design can be shown in this way:

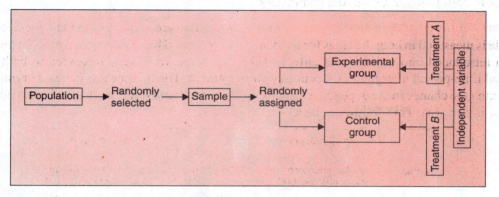

Fig. 3.4: Two-group simple randomized experimental design (in diagram form)

Since in the sample randomized design the elements constituting the sample are randomly drawn from the same population and randomly assigned to the experimental and control groups, it becomes possible to draw conclusions on the basis of samples applicable for the population. The two groups (experimental and control groups) of such a design are given different treatments of the independent variable. This design of experiment is quite common in research studies concerning behavioural sciences. The merit of such a design is that it is simple and randomizes the differences among the sample items. But the limitation of it is that the individual differences among those conducting the treatments are not eliminated, i.e., it does not control the extraneous variable and as such the result of the experiment may not depict a correct picture. This can be illustrated by taking an example. Suppose the researcher wants to compare two groups of students who have been randomly selected and randomly assigned. Two different treatments viz., the usual training and the specialised training are being given to the two groups. The researcher hypothesises greater gains for the group receiving specialised training. To determine this, he tests each group before and after the training, and then compares the amount of gain for the two groups to accept or reject his hypothesis. This is an illustration of the two-groups randomized design, wherein individual differences among students are being randomized. But this does not control the differential effects of the extraneous independent variables (in this case, the individual differences among those conducting the training programme).

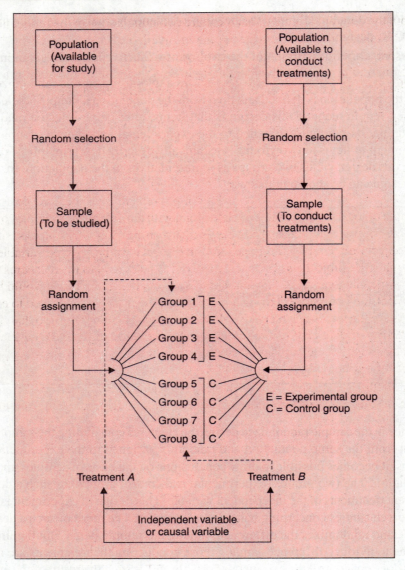

Fig. 3.5: Random replication design (in diagram form)

(ii) **Random replications design:** The limitation of the two-group randomized design is usually eliminated within the random replications design. In the illustration just cited above, the *teacher differences* on the dependent variable were ignored, i.e., the extraneous variable was not controlled. But in a random replications design, the effect of such differences are minimised (or reduced) by providing a number of repetitions for each treatment. Each repetition is technically called a 'replication'. Random replication design serves two purposes viz., it provides controls for the differential effects of the extraneous independent variables and secondly, it randomizes any individual differences among those conducting the treatments. Diagrammatically we can illustrate the random replications design thus: (Fig. 3.5)

From the diagram it is clear that there are two populations in the replication design. The sample is taken randomly from the population available for study and is randomly assigned to, say, four experimental and four control groups. Similarly, sample is taken randomly from the population available to conduct experiments (because of the eight groups eight such individuals be selected) and the eight individuals so selected should be randomly assigned to the eight groups. Generally, equal number of items are put in each group so that the size of the group is not likely to affect the result of the study. Variables relating to both population characteristics are assumed to be randomly distributed among the two groups. Thus, this random replication design is, in fact, an extension of the two-group simple randomized design.

5. Randomized block design (R.B. design) is an improvement over the C.R. design. In the R.B. design the principle of local control can be applied along with the other two principles of experimental designs. In the R.B. design, subjects are first divided into groups, known as blocks, such that within each group the subjects are relatively homogeneous in respect to some selected variable. The variable selected for grouping the subjects is one that is believed to be related to the measures to be obtained in respect of the dependent variable. The number of subjects in a given block would be equal to the number of treatments and one subject in each block would be randomly assigned to each treatment. In general, blocks are the levels at which we hold the extraneous factor fixed, so that its contribution to the total variability of data can be measured. The main feature of the R.B. design is that in this each treatment appears the same number of times in each block. The R.B. design is analysed by the two-way analysis of variance (two-way ANOVA)* technique.

Let us illustrate the R.B. design with the help of an example. Suppose four different forms of a standardised test in statistics were given to each of five students (selected one from each of the five I.Q. blocks) and following are the scores which they obtained.

	Very low I.Q. Student A	Low I.Q. Student B	Average I.Q. Student C	High I.Q. Student D	Very high I.Q. Student E
Form 1	82	67	57	71	73
Form 2	90	68	54	70	81
Form 3	86	73	51	69	84
Form 4	93	77	60	65	71

Fig. 3.6

If each student separately randomized the order in which he or she took the four tests (by using random numbers or some similar device), we refer to the design of this experiment as a R.B. design. The purpose of this randomization is to take care of such possible extraneous factors (say as fatigue) or perhaps the experience gained from repeatedly taking the test.

---

*See Chapter 11 for the two-way ANOVA technique.

6. Latin square design (L.S. design) is an experimental design very frequently used in agricultural research. The conditions under which agricultural investigations are carried out are different from those in other studies for nature plays an important role in agriculture. For instance, an experiment has to be made through which the effects of five different varieties of fertilizers on the yield of a certain crop, say wheat, it to be judged. In such a case the varying fertility of the soil in different blocks in which the experiment has to be performed must be taken into consideration; otherwise the results obtained may not be very dependable because the output happens to be the effect not only of fertilizers, but it may also be the effect of fertility of soil. Similarly, there may be impact of varying seeds on the yield. To overcome such difficulties, the L.S. design is used when there are two major extraneous factors such as the varying soil fertility and varying seeds.

The Latin-square design is one wherein each fertilizer, in our example, appears five times but is used only once in each row and in each column of the design. In other words, the treatments in a L.S. design are so allocated among the plots that no treatment occurs more than once in any one row or any one column. The two blocking factors may be represented through rows and columns (one through rows and the other through columns). The following is a diagrammatic form of such a design in respect of, say, five types of fertilizers, viz., A, B, C, D and E and the two blocking factor viz., the varying soil fertility and the varying seeds:

FERTILITY LEVEL

	I	II	III	IV	V
X_1	A	B	C	D	E
X_2	B	C	D	E	A
X_3	C	D	E	A	B
X_4	D	E	A	B	C
X_5	E	A	B	C	D

Seeds differences

Fig. 3.7

The above diagram clearly shows that in a L.S. design the field is divided into as many blocks as there are varieties of fertilizers and then each block is again divided into as many parts as there are varieties of fertilizers in such a way that each of the fertilizer variety is used in each of the block (whether column-wise or row-wise) only once. The analysis of the L.S. design is very similar to the two-way ANOVA technique.

The merit of this experimental design is that it enables differences in fertility gradients in the field to be eliminated in comparison to the effects of different varieties of fertilizers on the yield of the crop. But this design suffers from one limitation, and it is that although each row and each column represents equally all fertilizer varieties, there may be considerable difference in the row and column means both up and across the field. This, in other words, means that in L.S. design we must assume that there is no interaction between treatments and blocking factors. This defect can, however, be removed by taking the means of rows and columns equal to the field mean by adjusting the results. Another limitation of this design is that it requires number of rows, columns and treatments to be equal. This reduces the utility of this design. In case of (2×2) L.S. design, there are no degrees of freedom available for the mean square error and hence the design cannot be used. If treatments are 10 or more, than each row and each column will be larger in size so that rows and columns may not be homogeneous. This may make the application of the principle of local control ineffective. Therefore, L.S. design of orders (5×5) to (9×9) are generally used.

7. Factorial designs: Factorial designs are used in experiments where the effects of varying more than one factor are to be determined. They are specially important in several economic and social phenomena where usually a large number of factors affect a particular problem. Factorial designs can be of two types: (i) simple factorial designs and (ii) complex factorial designs. We take them separately

(i) *Simple factorial designs:* In case of simple factorial designs, we consider the effects of varying two factors on the dependent variable, but when an experiment is done with more than two factors, we use complex factorial designs. Simple factorial design is also termed as a 'two-factor-factorial design', whereas complex factorial design is known as 'multi-factor-factorial design.' Simple factorial design may either be a 2×2 simple factorial design, or it may be, say, 3×4 or 5×3 or the like type of simple factorial design. We illustrate some simple factorial designs as under:

Illustration 1: $(2 \times 2$ simple factorial design).

A 2×2 simple factorial design can graphically be depicted as follows:

2 × 2 SIMPLE FACTORIAL DESIGN

	Experimental Variable	
Control variables	Treatment A	Treatment B
Level I	Cell 1	Cell 3
Level II	Cell 2	Cell 4

Fig. 3.8

In this design the extraneous variable to be controlled by homogeneity is called the control variable and the independent variable, which is manipulated, is called the experimental variable. Then there are two treatments of the experimental variable and two levels of the control variable. As such there are four cells into which the sample is divided. Each of the four combinations would provide one treatment or experimental condition. Subjects are assigned at random to each treatment in the same manner as in a randomized group design. The means for different cells may be obtained along with the means for different rows and columns. Means of different cells represent the mean scores for the dependent variable and the column means in the given design are termed the main effect for treatments without taking into account any differential effect that is due to the level of the control variable. Similarly, the row means in the said design are termed the main effects for levels without regard to treatment. Thus, through this design we can study the main effects of treatments as well as the main effects of levels. An additional merit of this design is that one can examine the interaction between treatments and levels, through which one may say whether the treatment and levels are independent of each other or they are not so. The following examples make clear the interaction effect between treatments and levels. The data obtained in case of two (2 × 2) simple factorial studies may be as given in Fig. 3.9.

STUDY I DATA

		Training		Row Mean
		Treatment A	Treatment B	
Control (Intelligence)	Level I (Low)	15.5	23.3	19.4
	Level II (High)	35.8	30.2	33.0
	Column mean	25.6	26.7	

STUDY II DATA

		Training		Row Mean
		Treatment A	Treatment B	
Control (Intelligence)	Level I (Low)	10.4	20.6	15.5
	Level II (High)	30.6	40.4	35.5
	Column mean	20.5	30.5	

Fig. 3.9

All the above figures (the study I data and the study II data) represent the respective means. Graphically, these can be represented as shown in Fig. 3.10.

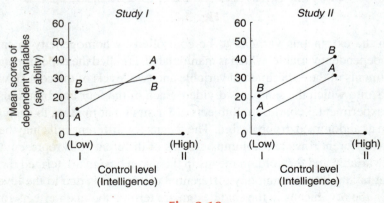

Fig. 3.10

The graph relating to Study I indicates that there is an interaction between the treatment and the level which, in other words, means that the treatment and the level are not independent of each other. The graph relating to Study II shows that there is no interaction effect which means that treatment and level in this study are relatively independent of each other.

The 2 × 2 design need not be restricted in the manner as explained above i.e., having one experimental variable and one control variable, but it may also be of the type having two experimental variables or two control variables. For example, a college teacher compared the effect of the class-size as well as the introduction of the new instruction technique on the learning of research methodology. For this purpose he conducted a study using a 2 × 2 simple factorial design. His design in the graphic form would be as follows:

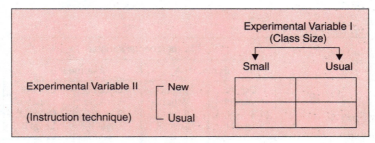

Fig. 3.11

But if the teacher uses a design for comparing males and females and the senior and junior students in the college as they relate to the knowledge of research methodology, in that case we will have a 2 × 2 simple factorial design wherein both the variables are control variables as no manipulation is involved in respect of both the variables.

Illustration 2: (4 × 3 simple factorial design).

The 4 × 3 simple factorial design will usually include four treatments of the experimental variable and three levels of the control variable. Graphically it may take the following form:

4 × 3 SIMPLE FACTORIAL DESIGN

Control Variable	Experimental Variable			
	Treatment A	Treatment B	Treatment C	Treatment D
Level I	Cell 1	Cell 4	Cell 7	Cell 10
Level II	Cell 2	Cell 5	Cell 8	Cell 11
Level III	Cell 3	Cell 6	Cell 9	Cell 12

Fig. 3.12

This model of a simple factorial design includes four treatments viz., A, B, C, and D of the experimental variable and three levels viz., I, II, and III of the control variable and has 12 different cells as shown above. This shows that a 2 × 2 simple factorial design can be generalised to any number of treatments and levels. Accordingly we can name it as such and such (–×–) design. In such a design the means for the columns provide the researcher with an estimate of the main effects for treatments and the means for rows provide an estimate of the main effects for the levels. Such a design also enables the researcher to determine the interaction between treatments and levels.

(ii) *Complex factorial designs:* Experiments with more than two factors at a time involve the use of complex factorial designs. A design which considers three or more independent variables simultaneously is called a complex factorial design. In case of three factors with one experimental variable having two treatments and two control variables, each one of which having two levels, the design used will be termed $2 \times 2 \times 2$ complex factorial design which will contain a total of eight cells as shown below in Fig. 3.13.

$2 \times 2 \times 2$ COMPLEX FACTORIAL DESIGN

		Experimental Variable			
		Treatment A		Treatment B	
		Control Variable 2 Level I	Control Variable 2 Level II	Control Variable 2 Level I	Control Variable 2 Level II
Control Variable 1 — Level I		Cell 1	Cell 3	Cell 5	Cell 7
— Level II		Cell 2	Cell 4	Cell 6	Cell 8

Fig. 3.13

In Fig. 3.14 a pictorial presentation is given of the design shown below.

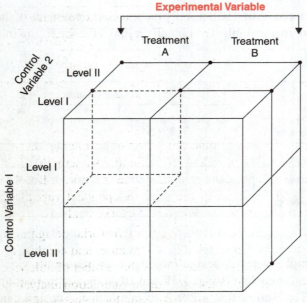

Fig. 3.14

The dotted line cell in the diagram corresponds to Cell 1 of the above stated 2 × 2 × 2 design and is for Treatment A, level I of the control variable 1, and level I of the control variable 2. From this design it is possible to determine the main effects for three variables i.e., one experimental and two control variables. The researcher can also determine the interactions between each possible pair of variables (such interactions are called 'First Order interactions') and interaction between variable taken in triplets (such interactions are called Second Order interactions). In case of a 2 × 2 × 2 design, the further given first order interactions are possible:

Experimental variable with control variable 1 (or EV × CV 1);

Experimental variable with control variable 2 (or EV × CV 2);

Control variable 1 with control variable 2   (or CV1 × CV2);

Three will be one second order interaction as well in the given design (it is between all the three variables i.e., EV × CV1 × CV2).

To determine the main effects for the experimental variable, the researcher must necessarily compare the combined mean of data in cells 1, 2, 3 and 4 for Treatment A with the combined mean of data in cells 5, 6, 7 and 8 for Treatment B. In this way the main effect for experimental variable, independent of control variable 1 and variable 2, is obtained. Similarly, the main effect for control variable 1, independent of experimental variable and control variable 2, is obtained if we compare the combined mean of data in cells 1, 3, 5 and 7 with the combined mean of data in cells 2, 4, 6 and 8 of our 2 × 2 × 2 factorial design. On similar lines, one can determine the main effect for the control variable 2 independent of experimental variable and control variable 1, if the combined mean of data in cells 1, 2, 5 and 6 are compared with the combined mean of data in cells 3, 4, 7 and 8.

To obtain the first order interaction, say, for EV × CV1 in the above stated design, the researcher must necessarily ignore control variable 2 for which purpose he may develop 2 × 2 design from the 2 × 2 × 2 design by combining the data of the relevant cells of the latter design as shown in Fig. 3.15.

		Experimental Variables	
		Treatment A	Treatment B
Control	Level I	Cells 1, 3	Cells 5, 7
Variable 1	Level II	Cells 2, 4	Cells 6, 8

Fig. 3.15

Similarly, the researcher can determine other first order interactions. The analysis of the first order interaction, in the manner described above, is essentially a sample factorial analysis as only two variables are considered at a time and the remaining one is ignored. But the analysis of the second order interaction would not ignore one of the three independent variables in case of a 2 × 2 × 2 design. The analysis would be termed as a complex factorial analysis.

It may, however, be remembered that the complex factorial design need not necessarily be of 2 × 2 × 2 type design, but can be generalised to any number and combination of experimental and control independent variables. Of course, the greater the number of independent variables included in a complex factorial design, the higher the order of the interaction analysis possible. But the overall task goes on becoming more and more complicated with the inclusion of more and more independent variables in our design.

Factorial designs are used mainly because of the two advantages. (i) They provide equivalent accuracy (as happens in the case of experiments with only one factor) with less labour and as such are a source of economy. Using factorial designs, we can determine the main effects of two (in simple factorial design) or more (in case of complex factorial design) factors (or variables) in one single experiment. (ii) They permit various other comparisons of interest. For example, they give information about such effects which cannot be obtained by treating one single factor at a time. The determination of interaction effects is possible in case of factorial designs.

CONCLUSION

There are several research designs and the researcher must decide in advance of collection and analysis of data as to which design would prove to be more appropriate for his research project. He must give due weight to various points such as the type of universe and its nature, the objective of his study, the resource list or the sampling frame, desired standard of accuracy and the like when taking a decision in respect of the design for his research project.

Questions

1. Explain the meaning and significance of a Research design.
2. Explain the meaning of the following in context of Research design.
   (a) Extraneous variables;
   (b) Confounded relationship;
   (c) Research hypothesis;
   (d) Experimental and Control groups;
   (e) Treatments.
3. Describe some of the important research designs used in experimental hypothesis-testing research study.
4. "Research design in exploratory studies must be flexible but in descriptive studies, it must minimise bias and maximise reliability." Discuss.
5. Give your understanding of a good research design. Is single research design suitable in all research studies? If not, why?
6. Explain and illustrate the following research designs:
   (a) Two group simple randomized design;
   (b) Latin square design;
   (c) Random replications design;
   (d) Simple factorial design;
   (e) Informal experimental designs.
7. Write a short note on 'Experience Survey' explaining fully its utility in exploratory research studies.
8. What is research design? Discuss the basis of stratification to be employed in sampling public opinion on inflation.

(Raj. Uni. EAFM M. Phil, Exam. 1978)

Appendix

Developing a Research Plan[*]

After identifying and defining the problem as also accomplishing the relating task, researcher must arrange his ideas in order and write them in the form of an experimental plan or what can be described as 'Research Plan'. This is essential specially for new researcher because of the following:

(a) It helps him to organize his ideas in a form whereby it will be possible for him to look for flaws and inadequacies, if any.

(b) It provides an inventory of what must be done and which materials have to be collected as a preliminary step.

(c) It is a document that can be given to others for comment.

Research plan must contain the following items.

1. Research objective should be clearly stated in a line or two which tells exactly what it is that the researcher expects to do.

2. The problem to be studied by researcher must be explicitly stated so that one may know what information is to be obtained for solving the problem.

3. Each major concept which researcher wants to measure should be defined in operational terms in context of the research project.

4. The plan should contain the method to be used in solving the problem. An overall description of the approach to be adopted is usually given and assumptions, if any, of the concerning method to be used are clearly mentioned in the research plan.

5. The plan must also state the details of the techniques to be adopted. For instance, if interview method is to be used, an account of the nature of the contemplated interview procedure should be given. Similarly, if tests are to be given, the conditions under which they are to be administered should be specified along with the nature of instruments to be used. If public records are to be consulted as sources of data, the fact should be recorded in the research plan. Procedure for quantifying data should also be written out in all details.

[*] Based on the matter given in the following two books:

(i) Robert M.W. Travers, *An Introduction to Educational Research,* p. 82–84.

(ii) C. William Emory, *Business Research Methods,* p. 415–416.

6. A clear mention of the population to be studied should be made. If the study happens to be sample based, the research plan should state the sampling plan i.e., how the sample is to be identified. The method of identifying the sample should be such that generalisation from the sample to the original population is feasible.

7. The plan must also contain the methods to be used in processing the data. Statistical and other methods to be used must be indicated in the plan. Such methods should not be left until the data have been collected. This part of the plan may be reviewed by experts in the field, for they can often suggest changes that result in substantial saving of time and effort.

8. Results of pilot test, if any, should be reported. Time and cost budgets for the research project should also be prepared and laid down in the plan itself.

4

Sampling Design

CENSUS AND SAMPLE SURVEY

All items in any field of inquiry constitute a 'Universe' or 'Population.' A complete enumeration of all items in the 'population' is known as a census inquiry. It can be presumed that in such an inquiry, when all items are covered, no element of chance is left and highest accuracy is obtained. But in practice this may not be true. Even the slightest element of bias in such an inquiry will get larger and larger as the number of observation increases. Moreover, there is no way of checking the element of bias or its extent except through a resurvey or use of sample checks. Besides, this type of inquiry involves a great deal of time, money and energy. Therefore, when the field of inquiry is large, this method becomes difficult to adopt because of the resources involved. At times, this method is practically beyond the reach of ordinary researchers. Perhaps, government is the only institution which can get the complete enumeration carried out. Even the government adopts this in very rare cases such as population census conducted once in a decade. Further, many a time it is not possible to examine every item in the population, and sometimes it is possible to obtain sufficiently accurate results by studying only a part of total population. In such cases there is no utility of census surveys.

However, it needs to be emphasised that when the universe is a small one, it is no use resorting to a sample survey. When field studies are undertaken in practical life, considerations of time and cost almost invariably lead to a selection of respondents i.e., selection of only a few items. The respondents selected should be as representative of the total population as possible in order to produce a miniature cross-section. The selected respondents constitute what is technically called a 'sample' and the selection process is called 'sampling technique.' The survey so conducted is known as 'sample survey'. Algebraically, let the population size be N and if a part of size n (which is $< N$) of this population is selected according to some rule for studying some characteristic of the population, the group consisting of these n units is known as 'sample'. Researcher must prepare a sample design for his study i.e., he must plan how a sample should be selected and of what size such a sample would be.

IMPLICATIONS OF A SAMPLE DESIGN

A sample design is a definite plan for obtaining a sample from a given population. It refers to the technique or the procedure the researcher would adopt in selecting items for the sample. Sample design may as well lay down the number of items to be included in the sample i.e., the size of the sample. Sample design is determined before data are collected. There are many sample designs from which a researcher can choose. Some designs are relatively more precise and easier to apply than others. Researcher must select/prepare a sample design which should be reliable and appropriate for his research study.

STEPS IN SAMPLE DESIGN

While developing a sampling design, the researcher must pay attention to the following points:

(i) **Type of universe:** The first step in developing any sample design is to clearly define the set of objects, technically called the Universe, to be studied. The universe can be finite or infinite. In finite universe the number of items is certain, but in case of an infinite universe the number of items is infinite, i.e., we cannot have any idea about the total number of items. The population of a city, the number of workers in a factory and the like are examples of finite universes, whereas the number of stars in the sky, listeners of a specific radio programme, throwing of a dice etc. are examples of infinite universes.

(ii) **Sampling unit:** A decision has to be taken concerning a sampling unit before selecting sample. Sampling unit may be a geographical one such as state, district, village, etc., or a construction unit such as house, flat, etc., or it may be a social unit such as family, club, school, etc., or it may be an individual. The researcher will have to decide one or more of such units that he has to select for his study.

(iii) **Source list:** It is also known as 'sampling frame' from which sample is to be drawn. It contains the names of all items of a universe (in case of finite universe only). If source list is not available, researcher has to prepare it. Such a list should be comprehensive, correct, reliable and appropriate. It is extremely important for the source list to be as representative of the population as possible.

(iv) **Size of sample:** This refers to the number of items to be selected from the universe to constitute a sample. This a major problem before a researcher. The size of sample should neither be excessively large, nor too small. It should be optimum. An optimum sample is one which fulfills the requirements of efficiency, representativeness, reliability and flexibility. While deciding the size of sample, researcher must determine the desired precision as also an acceptable confidence level for the estimate. The size of population variance needs to be considered as in case of larger variance usually a bigger sample is needed. The size of population must be kept in view for this also limits the sample size. The parameters of interest in a research study must be kept in view, while deciding the size of the sample. Costs too dictate the size of sample that we can draw. As such, budgetary constraint must invariably be taken into consideration when we decide the sample size.

(v) **Parameters of interest:** In determining the sample design, one must consider the question of the specific population parameters which are of interest. For instance, we may be interested in estimating the proportion of persons with some characteristic in the population, or we may be interested in knowing some average or the other measure concerning the population. There may also be important sub-groups in the population about whom we would like to make estimates. All this has a strong impact upon the sample design we would accept.

(vi) **Budgetary constraint:** Cost considerations, from practical point of view, have a major impact upon decisions relating to not only the size of the sample but also to the type of sample. This fact can even lead to the use of a non-probability sample.

(vii) **Sampling procedure:** Finally, the researcher must decide the type of sample he will use i.e., he must decide about the technique to be used in selecting the items for the sample. In fact, this technique or procedure stands for the sample design itself. There are several sample designs (explained in the pages that follow) out of which the researcher must choose one for his study. Obviously, he must select that design which, for a given sample size and for a given cost, has a smaller sampling error.

CRITERIA OF SELECTING A SAMPLING PROCEDURE

In this context one must remember that two costs are involved in a sampling analysis viz., the cost of collecting the data and the cost of an incorrect inference resulting from the data. Researcher must keep in view the two causes of incorrect inferences viz., systematic bias and sampling error. A *systematic bias* results from errors in the sampling procedures, and it cannot be reduced or eliminated by increasing the sample size. At best the causes responsible for these errors can be detected and corrected. Usually a systematic bias is the result of one or more of the following factors:

1. Inappropriate sampling frame: If the sampling frame is inappropriate i.e., a biased representation of the universe, it will result in a systematic bias.

2. Defective measuring device: If the measuring device is constantly in error, it will result in systematic bias. In survey work, systematic bias can result if the questionnaire or the interviewer is biased. Similarly, if the physical measuring device is defective there will be systematic bias in the data collected through such a measuring device.

3. Non-respondents: If we are unable to sample all the individuals initially included in the sample, there may arise a systematic bias. The reason is that in such a situation the likelihood of establishing contact or receiving a response from an individual is often correlated with the measure of what is to be estimated.

4. Indeterminancy principle: Sometimes we find that individuals act differently when kept under observation than what they do when kept in non-observed situations. For instance, if workers are aware that somebody is observing them in course of a work study on the basis of which the average length of time to complete a task will be determined and accordingly the quota will be set for piece work, they generally tend to work slowly in comparison to the speed with which they work if kept unobserved. Thus, the indeterminancy principle may also be a cause of a systematic bias.

5. Natural bias in the reporting of data: Natural bias of respondents in the reporting of data is often the cause of a systematic bias in many inquiries. There is usually a downward bias in the income data collected by government taxation department, whereas we find an upward bias in the income data collected by some social organisation. People in general understate their incomes if asked about it for tax purposes, but they overstate the same if asked for social status or their affluence. Generally in psychological surveys, people tend to give what they think is the 'correct' answer rather than revealing their true feelings.

Sampling errors are the random variations in the sample estimates around the true population parameters. Since they occur randomly and are equally likely to be in either direction, their nature happens to be of compensatory type and the expected value of such errors happens to be equal to zero. Sampling error decreases with the increase in the size of the sample, and it happens to be of a smaller magnitude in case of homogeneous population.

Sampling error can be measured for a given sample design and size. The measurement of sampling error is usually called the 'precision of the sampling plan'. If we increase the sample size, the precision can be improved. But increasing the size of the sample has its own limitations viz., a large sized sample increases the cost of collecting data and also enhances the systematic bias. Thus the effective way to increase precision is usually to select a better sampling design which has a smaller sampling error for a given sample size at a given cost. In practice, however, people prefer a less precise design because it is easier to adopt the same and also because of the fact that systematic bias can be controlled in a better way in such a design.

In brief, *while selecting a sampling procedure, researcher must ensure that the procedure causes a relatively small sampling error and helps to control the systematic bias in a better way.*

CHARACTERISTICS OF A GOOD SAMPLE DESIGN

From what has been stated above, we can list down the characteristics of a good sample design as under:

(a) Sample design must result in a truly representative sample.

(b) Sample design must be such which results in a small sampling error.

(c) Sample design must be viable in the context of funds available for the research study.

(d) Sample design must be such so that systematic bias can be controlled in a better way.

(e) Sample should be such that the results of the sample study can be applied, in general, for the universe with a reasonable level of confidence.

DIFFERENT TYPES OF SAMPLE DESIGNS

There are different types of sample designs based on two factors viz., the representation basis and the element selection technique. On the representation basis, the sample may be probability sampling or it may be non-probability sampling. Probability sampling is based on the concept of random selection, whereas non-probability sampling is 'non-random' sampling. On element selection basis, the sample may be either unrestricted or restricted. When each sample element is drawn individually from the population at large, then the sample so drawn is known as 'unrestricted sample', whereas all other forms of sampling are covered under the term 'restricted sampling'. The following chart exhibits the sample designs as explained above.

Thus, sample designs are basically of two types viz., non-probability sampling and probability sampling. We take up these two designs separately.

CHART SHOWING BASIC SAMPLING DESIGNS

Element selection technique ↓	Representation basis	
	Probability sampling	Non-probability sampling
Unrestricted sampling	Simple random sampling	Haphazard sampling or convenience sampling
Restricted sampling	Complex random sampling (such as cluster sampling, systematic sampling, stratified sampling etc.)	Purposive sampling (such as quota sampling, judgement sampling)

Fig. 4.1

Non-probability sampling: Non-probability sampling is that sampling procedure which does not afford any basis for estimating the probability that each item in the population has of being included in the sample. Non-probability sampling is also known by different names such as deliberate sampling, purposive sampling and judgement sampling. In this type of sampling, items for the sample are selected deliberately by the researcher; his choice concerning the items remains supreme. In other words, under non-probability sampling the organisers of the inquiry purposively choose the particular units of the universe for constituting a sample on the basis that the small mass that they so select out of a huge one will be typical or representative of the whole. For instance, if economic conditions of people living in a state are to be studied, a few towns and villages may be purposively selected for intensive study on the principle that they can be representative of the entire state. Thus, the judgement of the organisers of the study plays an important part in this sampling design.

In such a design, personal element has a great chance of entering into the selection of the sample. The investigator may select a sample which shall yield results favourable to his point of view and if that happens, the entire inquiry may get vitiated. Thus, there is always the danger of bias entering into this type of sampling technique. But in the investigators are impartial, work without bias and have the necessary experience so as to take sound judgement, the results obtained from an analysis of deliberately selected sample may be tolerably reliable. However, in such a sampling, there is no assurance that every element has some specifiable chance of being included. Sampling error in this type of sampling cannot be estimated and the element of bias, great or small, is always there. As such this sampling design in rarely adopted in large inquires of importance. However, in small inquiries and researches by individuals, this design may be adopted because of the relative advantage of time and money inherent in this method of sampling. *Quota sampling* is also an example of non-probability sampling. Under quota sampling the interviewers are simply given quotas to be filled from the different strata, with some restrictions on how they are to be filled. In other words, the actual selection of the items for the sample is left to the interviewer's discretion. This type of sampling is very convenient and is relatively inexpensive. But the samples so selected certainly do not possess the characteristic of random samples. Quota samples are essentially judgement samples and inferences drawn on their basis are not amenable to statistical treatment in a formal way.

Probability sampling: Probability sampling is also known as 'random sampling' or 'chance sampling'. Under this sampling design, every item of the universe has an equal chance of inclusion in the sample. It is, so to say, a lottery method in which individual units are picked up from the whole group not deliberately but by some mechanical process. Here it is blind chance alone that determines whether one item or the other is selected. The results obtained from probability or random sampling can be assured in terms of probability i.e., we can measure the errors of estimation or the significance of results obtained from a random sample, and this fact brings out the superiority of random sampling design over the deliberate sampling design. Random sampling ensures the law of Statistical Regularity which states that if on an average the sample chosen is a random one, the sample will have the same composition and characteristics as the universe. This is the reason why random sampling is considered as the best technique of selecting a representative sample.

Random sampling from a finite population refers to that method of sample selection which gives each possible sample combination an equal probability of being picked up and each item in the entire population to have an equal chance of being included in the sample. This applies to sampling without replacement i.e., once an item is selected for the sample, it cannot appear in the sample again (Sampling with replacement is used less frequently in which procedure the element selected for the sample is returned to the population before the next element is selected. In such a situation the same element could appear twice in the same sample before the second element is chosen). In brief, the implications of random sampling (or simple random sampling) are:

(a) It gives each element in the population an equal probability of getting into the sample; and all choices are independent of one another.

(b) It gives each possible sample combination an equal probability of being chosen.

Keeping this in view we can define a simple random sample (or simply a random sample) from a finite population as a sample which is chosen in such a way that each of the $^{N}C_{n}$ possible samples has the same probability, $1/^{N}C_{n}$, of being selected. To make it more clear we take a certain finite population consisting of six elements (say a, b, c, d, e, f) i.e., $N = 6$. Suppose that we want to take a sample of size $n = 3$ from it. Then there are $^{6}C_{3} = 20$ possible distinct samples of the required size, and they consist of the elements *abc, abd, abe, abf, acd, ace, acf, ade, adf, aef, bcd, bce, bcf, bde, bdf, bef, cde, cdf, cef,* and *def.* If we choose one of these samples in such a way that each has the probability 1/20 of being chosen, we will then call this a random sample.

HOW TO SELECT A RANDOM SAMPLE?

With regard to the question of how to take a random sample in actual practice, we could, in simple cases like the one above, write each of the possible samples on a slip of paper, mix these slips thoroughly in a container and then draw as a lottery either blindfolded or by rotating a drum or by any other similar device. Such a procedure is obviously impractical, if not altogether impossible in complex problems of sampling. In fact, the practical utility of such a method is very much limited.

Fortunately, we can take a random sample in a relatively easier way without taking the trouble of enlisting all possible samples on paper-slips as explained above. Instead of this, we can write the name of each element of a finite population on a slip of paper, put the slips of paper so prepared into a box or a bag and mix them thoroughly and then draw (without looking) the required number of slips for the sample one after the other without replacement. In doing so we must make sure that in successive drawings each of the remaining elements of the population has the same chance of being selected. This procedure will also result in the same probability for each possible sample. We can verify this by taking the above example. Since we have a finite population of 6 elements and we want to select a sample of size 3, the probability of drawing any one element for our sample in the first draw is 3/6, the probability of drawing one more element in the second draw is 2/5, (the first element drawn is not replaced) and similarly the probability of drawing one more element in the third draw is 1/4. Since these draws are independent, the joint probability of the three elements which constitute our sample is the product of their individual probabilities and this works out to $3/6 \times 2/5 \times 1/4 = 1/20$. This verifies our earlier calculation.

Even this relatively easy method of obtaining a random sample can be simplified in actual practice by the use of random number tables. Various statisticians like Tippett, Yates, Fisher have prepared tables of random numbers which can be used for selecting a random sample. Generally, Tippett's random number tables are used for the purpose. Tippett gave10400 four figure numbers. He selected 41600 digits from the census reports and combined them into fours to give his random numbers which may be used to obtain a random sample.

We can illustrate the procedure by an example. First of all we reproduce the first thirty sets of Tippett's numbers

2952	6641	3992	9792	7979	5911
3170	5624	4167	9525	1545	1396
7203	5356	1300	2693	2370	7483
3408	2769	3563	6107	6913	7691
0560	5246	1112	9025	6008	8126

Suppose we are interested in taking a sample of 10 units from a population of 5000 units, bearing numbers from 3001 to 8000. We shall select 10 such figures from the above random numbers which are not less than 3001 and not greater than 8000. If we randomly decide to read the table numbers from left to right, starting from the first row itself, we obtain the following numbers: 6641, 3992, 7979, 5911, 3170, 5624, 4167, 7203, 5356, and 7483.

The units bearing the above serial numbers would then constitute our required random sample.

One may note that it is easy to draw random samples from finite populations with the aid of random number tables only when lists are available and items are readily numbered. But in some situations it is often impossible to proceed in the way we have narrated above. For example, if we want to estimate the mean height of trees in a forest, it would not be possible to number the trees, and choose random numbers to select a random sample. In such situations what we should do is to select some trees for the sample haphazardly without aim or purpose, and should treat the sample as a random sample for study purposes.

RANDOM SAMPLE FROM AN INFINITE UNIVERSE

So far we have talked about random sampling, keeping in view only the finite populations. But what about random sampling in context of infinite populations? It is relatively difficult to explain the concept of random sample from an infinite population. However, a few examples will show the basic characteristic of such a sample. Suppose we consider the 20 throws of a fair dice as a sample from the hypothetically infinite population which consists of the results of all possible throws of the dice. If the probability of getting a particular number, say 1, is the same for each throw and the 20 throws are all independent, then we say that the sample is random. Similarly, it would be said to be sampling from an infinite population if we sample with replacement from a finite population and our sample would be considered as a random sample if in each draw all elements of the population have the same probability of being selected and successive draws happen to be independent. In brief, one can say that the selection of each item in a random sample from an infinite population is controlled by the same probabilities and that successive selections are independent of one another.

COMPLEX RANDOM SAMPLING DESIGNS

Probability sampling under restricted sampling techniques, as stated above, may result in complex random sampling designs. Such designs may as well be called 'mixed sampling designs' for many of such designs may represent a combination of probability and non-probability sampling procedures in selecting a sample. Some of the popular complex random sampling designs are as follows:

(i) Systematic sampling: In some instances, the most practical way of sampling is to select every *i*th item on a list. Sampling of this type is known as systematic sampling. An element of randomness is introduced into this kind of sampling by using random numbers to pick up the unit with which to start. For instance, if a 4 per cent sample is desired, the first item would be selected randomly from the first twenty-five and thereafter every 25th item would automatically be included in the sample. Thus, in systematic sampling only the first unit is selected randomly and the remaining units of the sample are selected at fixed intervals. Although a systematic sample is not a random sample in the strict sense of the term, but it is often considered reasonable to treat systematic sample as if it were a random sample.

Systematic sampling has certain plus points. It can be taken as an improvement over a simple random sample in as much as the systematic sample is spread more evenly over the entire population. It is an easier and less costlier method of sampling and can be conveniently used even in case of large populations. But there are certain dangers too in using this type of sampling. If there is a hidden periodicity in the population, systematic sampling will prove to be an inefficient method of sampling. For instance, every 25th item produced by a certain production process is defective. If we are to select a 4% sample of the items of this process in a systematic manner, we would either get all defective items or all good items in our sample depending upon the random starting position. If all elements of the universe are ordered in a manner representative of the total population, i.e., the population list is in random order, systematic sampling is considered equivalent to random sampling. But if this is not so, then the results of such sampling may, at times, not be very reliable. In practice, systematic sampling is used when lists of population are available and they are of considerable length.

(ii) Stratified sampling: If a population from which a sample is to be drawn does not constitute a homogeneous group, stratified sampling technique is generally applied in order to obtain a representative sample. Under stratified sampling the population is divided into several sub-populations that are individually more homogeneous than the total population (the different sub-populations are called 'strata') and then we select items from each stratum to constitute a sample. Since each stratum is more homogeneous than the total population, we are able to get more precise estimates for each stratum and by estimating more accurately each of the component parts, we get a better estimate of the whole. In brief, stratified sampling results in more reliable and detailed information.

The following three questions are highly relevant in the context of stratified sampling:

(a) How to form strata?

(b) How should items be selected from each stratum?

(c) How many items be selected from each stratum or how to allocate the sample size of each stratum?

Regarding the first question, we can say that the strata be formed on the basis of common characteristic(s) of the items to be put in each stratum. This means that various strata be formed in such a way as to ensure elements being most homogeneous within each stratum and most heterogeneous between the different strata. Thus, strata are purposively formed and are usually based on past experience and personal judgement of the researcher. One should always remember that careful consideration of the relationship between the characteristics of the population and the characteristics to be estimated are normally used to define the strata. At times, pilot study may be conducted for determining a more appropriate and efficient stratification plan. We can do so by taking small samples of equal size from each of the proposed strata and then examining the variances within and among the possible stratifications, we can decide an appropriate stratification plan for our inquiry.

In respect of the second question, we can say that the usual method, for selection of items for the sample from each stratum, resorted to is that of simple random sampling. Systematic sampling can be used if it is considered more appropriate in certain situations.

Regarding the third question, we usually follow the method of proportional allocation under which the sizes of the samples from the different strata are kept proportional to the sizes of the strata. That is, if P_i represents the proportion of population included in stratum i, and n represents the total sample size, the number of elements selected from stratum i is $n \cdot P_i$. To illustrate it, let us suppose that we want a sample of size $n = 30$ to be drawn from a population of size $N = 8000$ which is divided into three strata of size $N_1 = 4000$, $N_2 = 2400$ and $N_3 = 1600$. Adopting proportional allocation, we shall get the sample sizes as under for the different strata:

For strata with $N_1 = 4000$, we have $P_1 = 4000/8000$

and hence $n_1 = n \cdot P_1 = 30 \ (4000/8000) = 15$

Similarly, for strata with $N_2 = 2400$, we have

$n_2 = n \cdot P_2 = 30 \ (2400/8000) = 9$, and

for strata with $N_3 = 1600$, we have

$n_3 = n \cdot P_3 = 30 \ (1600/8000) = 6$.

Thus, using proportional allocation, the sample sizes for different strata are 15, 9 and 6 respectively which is in proportion to the sizes of the strata viz., 4000 : 2400 : 1600. Proportional allocation is considered most efficient and an optimal design when the cost of selecting an item is equal for each stratum, there is no difference in within-stratum variances, and the purpose of sampling happens to be to estimate the population value of some characteristic. But in case the purpose happens to be to compare the differences among the strata, then equal sample selection from each stratum would be more efficient even if the strata differ in sizes. In cases where strata differ not only in size but also in variability and it is considered reasonable to take larger samples from the more variable strata and smaller samples from the less variable strata, we can then account for both (differences in stratum size and differences in stratum variability) by using disproportionate sampling design by requiring:

$$n_1/N_1\sigma_1 = n_2/N_2\sigma_2 = \ldots\ldots = n_k/N_k\sigma_k$$

where $\sigma_1, \sigma_2, \ldots$ and σ_k denote the standard deviations of the k strata, $N_1, N_2, \ldots, N_k$ denote the sizes of the k strata and $n_1, n_2, \ldots, n_k$ denote the sample sizes of k strata. This is called '*optimum allocation*' in the context of disproportionate sampling. The allocation in such a situation results in the following formula for determining the sample sizes different strata:

$$n_i = \frac{n \cdot N_i \sigma_i}{N_1 \sigma_1 + N_2 \sigma_2 + \ldots + N_k \sigma_k} \qquad \text{for } i = 1, 2, \ldots \text{ and } k.$$

We may illustrate the use of this by an example.

Illustration 1

A population is divided into three strata so that $N_1 = 5000$, $N_2 = 2000$ and $N_3 = 3000$. Respective standard deviations are:

$$\sigma_1 = 15, \sigma_2 = 18 \text{ and } \sigma_3 = 5.$$

How should a sample of size $n = 84$ be allocated to the three strata, if we want optimum allocation using disproportionate sampling design?

Solution: Using the disproportionate sampling design for optimum allocation, the sample sizes for different strata will be determined as under:

Sample size for strata with $N_1 = 5000$

$$n_1 = \frac{84\,(5000)\,(15)}{(5000)\,(15) + (2000)\,(18) + (3000)\,(5)}$$

$$= 6300000/126000 = 50$$

Sample size for strata with $N_2 = 2000$

$$n_2 = \frac{84\,(2000)\,(18)}{(5000)\,(15) + (2000)\,(18) + (3000)\,(5)}$$

$$= 3024000/126000 = 24$$

Sample size for strata with $N_3 = 3000$

$$n_3 = \frac{84\,(3000)\,(5)}{(5000)\,(15) + (2000)\,(18) + (3000)\,(5)}$$

$$= 1260000/126000 = 10$$

In addition to differences in stratum size and differences in stratum variability, we may have differences in stratum sampling cost, then we can have cost optimal disproportionate sampling design by requiring

$$\frac{n_1}{N_1 \sigma_1 \sqrt{C_1}} = \frac{n_2}{N_2 \sigma_2 \sqrt{C_2}} = \ldots = \frac{n_k}{N_k \sigma_k \sqrt{C_k}}$$

where

C_1 = Cost of sampling in stratum 1

C_2 = Cost of sampling in stratum 2

C_k = Cost of sampling in stratum k

and all other terms remain the same as explained earlier. The allocation in such a situation results in the following formula for determining the sample sizes for different strata:

$$n_i = \frac{n \cdot N_i \sigma_i / \sqrt{C_i}}{N_1 \sigma_1 / \sqrt{C_1} + N_2 \sigma_2 / \sqrt{C_2} + ... + N_k \sigma_k / \sqrt{C_k}} \text{ for } i = 1, 2, ..., k$$

It is not necessary that stratification be done keeping in view a single characteristic. Populations are often stratified according to several characteristics. For example, a system-wide survey designed to determine the attitude of students toward a new teaching plan, a state college system with 20 colleges might stratify the students with respect to class, sec and college. Stratification of this type is known as *cross-stratification*, and up to a point such stratification increases the reliability of estimates and is much used in opinion surveys.

From what has been stated above in respect of stratified sampling, we can say that the sample so constituted is the result of successive application of purposive (involved in stratification of items) and random sampling methods. As such it is an example of mixed sampling. The procedure wherein we first have stratification and then simple random sampling is known as stratified random sampling.

(iii) Cluster sampling: If the total area of interest happens to be a big one, a convenient way in which a sample can be taken is to divide the area into a number of smaller non-overlapping areas and then to randomly select a number of these smaller areas (usually called clusters), with the ultimate sample consisting of all (or samples of) units in these small areas or clusters.

Thus in cluster sampling the total population is divided into a number of relatively small subdivisions which are themselves clusters of still smaller units and then some of these clusters are randomly selected for inclusion in the overall sample. Suppose we want to estimate the proportion of machine-parts in an inventory which are defective. Also assume that there are 20000 machine parts in the inventory at a given point of time, stored in 400 cases of 50 each. Now using a cluster sampling, we would consider the 400 cases as clusters and randomly select 'n' cases and examine all the machine-parts in each randomly selected case.

Cluster sampling, no doubt, reduces cost by concentrating surveys in selected clusters. But certainly it is less precise than random sampling. There is also not as much information in 'n' observations within a cluster as there happens to be in 'n' randomly drawn observations. Cluster sampling is used only because of the economic advantage it possesses; estimates based on cluster samples are usually more reliable per unit cost.

(iv) Area sampling: If clusters happen to be some geographic subdivisions, in that case cluster sampling is better known as area sampling. In other words, cluster designs, where the primary sampling unit represents a cluster of units based on geographic area, are distinguished as area sampling. The plus and minus points of cluster sampling are also applicable to area sampling.

(v) Multi-stage sampling: Multi-stage sampling is a further development of the principle of cluster sampling. Suppose we want to investigate the working efficiency of nationalised banks in India and we want to take a sample of few banks for this purpose. The first stage is to select large primary sampling unit such as states in a country. Then we may select certain districts and interview all banks in the chosen districts. This would represent a two-stage sampling design with the ultimate sampling units being clusters of districts.

If instead of taking a census of all banks within the selected districts, we select certain towns and interview all banks in the chosen towns. This would represent a three-stage sampling design. If instead of taking a census of all banks within the selected towns, we randomly sample banks from each selected town, then it is a case of using a four-stage sampling plan. If we select randomly at all stages, we will have what is known as 'multi-stage random sampling design'.

Ordinarily multi-stage sampling is applied in big inquires extending to a considerable large geographical area, say, the entire country. There are two advantages of this sampling design viz., (a) It is easier to administer than most single stage designs mainly because of the fact that sampling frame under multi-stage sampling is developed in partial units. (b) A large number of units can be sampled for a given cost under multistage sampling because of sequential clustering, whereas this is not possible in most of the simple designs.

(vi) Sampling with probability proportional to size: In case the cluster sampling units do not have the same number or approximately the same number of elements, it is considered appropriate to use a random selection process where the probability of each cluster being included in the sample is proportional to the size of the cluster. For this purpose, we have to list the number of elements in each cluster irrespective of the method of ordering the cluster. Then we must sample systematically the appropriate number of elements from the cumulative totals. The actual numbers selected in this way do not refer to individual elements, but indicate which clusters and how many from the cluster are to be selected by simple random sampling or by systematic sampling. The results of this type of sampling are equivalent to those of a simple random sample and the method is less cumbersome and is also relatively less expensive. We can illustrate this with the help of an example.

Illustration 2

The following are the number of departmental stores in 15 cities: 35, 17, 10, 32, 70, 28, 26, 19, 26, 66, 37, 44, 33, 29 and 28. If we want to select a sample of 10 stores, using cities as clusters and selecting within clusters proportional to size, how many stores from each city should be chosen? (Use a starting point of 10).

Solution: Let us put the information as under (Table 4.1):

Since in the given problem, we have 500 departmental stores from which we have to select a sample of 10 stores, the appropriate sampling interval is 50. As we have to use the starting point of 10*, so we add successively increments of 50 till 10 numbers have been selected. The numbers, thus, obtained are: 10, 60, 110, 160, 210, 260, 310, 360, 410 and 460 which have been shown in the last column of the table (Table 4.1) against the concerning cumulative totals. From this we can say that two stores should be selected randomly from city number five and one each from city number 1, 3, 7, 9, 10, 11, 12, and 14. This sample of 10 stores is the sample with probability proportional to size.

---

*If the starting point is not mentioned, then the same can randomly be selected.

Table 4.1

City number	No. of departmental stores	Cumulative total	Sample	
1	35	35	10	
2	17	52		
3	10	62	60	
4	32	94		
5	70	164	110	160
6	28	192		
7	26	218	210	
8	19	237		
9	26	263	260	
10	66	329	310	
11	37	366	360	
12	44	410	410	
13	33	443		
14	29	472	460	
15	28	500		

(vii) Sequential sampling: This sampling design is some what complex sample design. The ultimate size of the sample under this technique is not fixed in advance, but is determined according to mathematical decision rules on the basis of information yielded as survey progresses. This is usually adopted in case of acceptance sampling plan in context of statistical quality control. When a particular lot is to be accepted or rejected on the basis of a single sample, it is known as single sampling; when the decision is to be taken on the basis of two samples, it is known as double sampling and in case the decision rests on the basis of more than two samples but the number of samples is certain and decided in advance, the sampling is known as multiple sampling. But when the number of samples is more than two but it is neither certain nor decided in advance, this type of system is often referred to as sequential sampling. Thus, in brief, we can say that in sequential sampling, one can go on taking samples one after another as long as one desires to do so.

CONCLUSION

From a brief description of the various sample designs presented above, we can say that normally one should resort to simple random sampling because under it bias is generally eliminated and the sampling error can be estimated. But purposive sampling is considered more appropriate when the universe happens to be small and a known characteristic of it is to be studied intensively. There are situations in real life under which sample designs other than simple random samples may be considered better (say easier to obtain, cheaper or more informative) and as such the same may be used. In a situation when random sampling is not possible, then we have to use necessarily a sampling design other than random sampling. At times, several methods of sampling may well be used in the same study.

Questions

1. What do you mean by 'Sample Design'? What points should be taken into consideration by a researcher in developing a sample design for this research project.

2. How would you differentiate between simple random sampling and complex random sampling designs? Explain clearly giving examples.

3. Why probability sampling is generally preferred in comparison to non-probability sampling? Explain the procedure of selecting a simple random sample.

4. Under what circumstances stratified random sampling design is considered appropriate? How would you select such sample? Explain by means of an example.

5. Distinguish between:
   (a) Restricted and unrestricted sampling;
   (b) Convenience and purposive sampling;
   (c) Systematic and stratified sampling;
   (d) Cluster and area sampling.

6. Under what circumstances would you recommend:
   (a) A probability sample?
   (b) A non-probability sample?
   (c) A stratified sample?
   (d) A cluster sample?

7. Explain and illustrate the procedure of selecting a random sample.

8. "A systematic bias results from errors in the sampling procedures". What do you mean by such a systematic bias? Describe the important causes responsible for such a bias.

9. (a) The following are the number of departmental stores in 10 cities: 35, 27, 24, 32, 42, 30, 34, 40, 29 and 38. If we want to select a sample of 15 stores using cities as clusters and selecting within clusters proportional to size, how many stores from each city should be chosen? (Use a starting point of 4).

   (b) What sampling design might be used to estimate the weight of a group of men and women?

10. A certain population is divided into five strata so that $N_1 = 2000$, $N_2 = 2000$, $N_3 = 1800$, $N_4 = 1700$, and $N_5 = 2500$. Respective standard deviations are: $\sigma_1 = 1.6$, $\sigma_2 = 2.0$, $\sigma_3 = 4.4$, $\sigma_4 = 4.8$, $\sigma_5 = 6.0$ and further the expected sampling cost in the first two strata is Rs 4 per interview and in the remaining three strata the sampling cost is Rs 6 per interview. How should a sample of size $n = 226$ be allocated to five strata if we adopt proportionate sampling design; if we adopt disproportionate sampling design considering (i) only the differences in stratum variability (ii) differences in stratum variability as well as the differences in stratum sampling costs.

5

Measurement and Scaling Techniques

MEASUREMENT IN RESEARCH

In our daily life we are said to measure when we use some yardstick to determine weight, height, or some other feature of a physical object. We also measure when we judge how well we like a song, a painting or the personalities of our friends. We, thus, measure physical objects as well as abstract concepts. Measurement is a relatively complex and demanding task, specially so when it concerns qualitative or abstract phenomena. By measurement we mean the process of assigning numbers to objects or observations, the level of measurement being a function of the rules under which the numbers are assigned.

It is easy to assign numbers in respect of properties of some objects, but it is relatively difficult in respect of others. For instance, measuring such things as social conformity, intelligence, or marital adjustment is much less obvious and requires much closer attention than measuring physical weight, biological age or a person's financial assets. In other words, properties like weight, height, etc., can be measured directly with some standard unit of measurement, but it is not that easy to measure properties like motivation to succeed, ability to stand stress and the like. We can expect high accuracy in measuring the length of pipe with a yard stick, but if the concept is abstract and the measurement tools are not standardized, we are less confident about the accuracy of the results of measurement.

Technically speaking, measurement is a process of mapping aspects of a domain onto other aspects of a range according to some rule of correspondence. In measuring, we devise some form of scale in the range (in terms of set theory, range may refer to some set) and then transform or map the properties of objects from the domain (in terms of set theory, domain may refer to some other set) onto this scale. For example, in case we are to find the male to female attendance ratio while conducting a study of persons who attend some show, then we may tabulate those who come to the show according to sex. In terms of set theory, this process is one of mapping the observed physical properties of those coming to the show (the domain) on to a sex classification (the range). The rule of correspondence is: If the object in the domain appears to be male, assign to "0" and if female assign to "1". Similarly, we can record a person's marital status as 1, 2, 3 or 4, depending on whether the person is single, married, widowed or divorced. We can as well record "Yes or No" answers to a question as "0" and "1" (or as 1 and 2 or perhaps as 59 and 60). In this artificial or nominal way, categorical data (qualitative or descriptive) can be made into numerical data and if we thus code the various categories, we refer to the numbers we record as nominal data. *Nominal data* are numerical in name only, because they do not share any of the properties of the numbers we deal in ordinary arithmetic. For instance if we record marital status as 1, 2, 3, or 4 as stated above, we cannot write $4 > 2$ or $3 < 4$ and we cannot write $3 - 1 = 4 - 2$, $1 + 3 = 4$ or $4 \div 2 = 2$.

In those situations when we cannot do anything except set up inequalities, we refer to the data as *ordinal data.* For instance, if one mineral can scratch another, it receives a higher hardness number and on Mohs' scale the numbers from 1 to 10 are assigned respectively to talc, gypsum, calcite, fluorite, apatite, feldspar, quartz, topaz, sapphire and diamond. With these numbers we can write $5 > 2$ or $6 < 9$ as apatite is harder than gypsum and feldspar is softer than sapphire, but we cannot write for example $10 - 9 = 5 - 4$, because the difference in hardness between diamond and sapphire is actually much greater than that between apatite and fluorite. It would also be meaningless to say that topaz is twice as hard as fluorite simply because their respective hardness numbers on Mohs' scale are 8 and 4. The greater than symbol (i.e., >) in connection with ordinal data may be used to designate "happier than" "preferred to" and so on.

When in addition to setting up inequalities we can also form differences, we refer to the data as *interval data.* Suppose we are given the following temperature readings (in degrees Fahrenheit): $58°$, $63°$, $70°$, $95°$, $110°$, $126°$ and $135°$. In this case, we can write $100° > 70°$ or $95° < 135°$ which simply means that $110°$ is warmer than $70°$ and that $95°$ is cooler than $135°$. We can also write for example $95° - 70° = 135° - 110°$, since equal temperature differences are equal in the sense that the same amount of heat is required to raise the temperature of an object from $70°$ to $95°$ or from $110°$ to $135°$. On the other hand, it would not mean much if we said that $126°$ is twice as hot as $63°$, even though $126° \div 63° = 2$. To show the reason, we have only to change to the centigrade scale, where the first temperature becomes $5/9 (126 - 32) = 52°$, the second temperature becomes $5/9 (63 - 32) = 17°$ and the first figure is now more than three times the second. This difficulty arises from the fact that Fahrenheit and Centigrade scales both have artificial origins (zeros) i.e., the number 0 of neither scale is indicative of the absence of whatever quantity we are trying to measure.

When in addition to setting up inequalities and forming differences we can also form quotients (i.e., when we can perform all the customary operations of mathematics), we refer to such data as *ratio data.* In this sense, ratio data includes all the usual measurement (or determinations) of length, height, money amounts, weight, volume, area, pressures etc.

The above stated distinction between nominal, ordinal, interval and ratio data is important for the nature of a set of data may suggest the use of particular statistical techniques[*]. A researcher has to be quite alert about this aspect while measuring properties of objects or of abstract concepts.

---

[*]When data can be measured in units which are interchangeable e.g., weights (by ratio scales), temperatures (by interval scales), that data is said to be parametric and can be subjected to most kinds of statistical and mathematical processes. But when data is measured in units which are not interchangeable, e.g., product preferences (by ordinal scales), the data is said to be non-parametric and is susceptible only to a limited extent to mathematical and statistical treatment.

MEASUREMENT SCALES

From what has been stated above, we can write that scales of measurement can be considered in terms of their mathematical properties. The most widely used classification of measurement scales are: (a) nominal scale; (b) ordinal scale; (c) interval scale; and (d) ratio scale.

(a) Nominal scale: Nominal scale is simply a system of assigning number symbols to events in order to label them. The usual example of this is the assignment of numbers of basketball players in order to identify them. Such numbers cannot be considered to be associated with an ordered scale for their order is of no consequence; the numbers are just convenient labels for the particular class of events and as such have no quantitative value. Nominal scales provide convenient ways of keeping track of people, objects and events. One cannot do much with the numbers involved. For example, one cannot usefully average the numbers on the back of a group of football players and come up with a meaningful value. Neither can one usefully compare the numbers assigned to one group with the numbers assigned to another. The counting of members in each group is the only possible arithmetic operation when a nominal scale is employed. Accordingly, we are restricted to use mode as the measure of central tendency. There is no generally used measure of dispersion for nominal scales. Chi-square test is the most common test of statistical significance that can be utilized, and for the measures of correlation, the contingency coefficient can be worked out.

Nominal scale is the least powerful level of measurement. It indicates no order or distance relationship and has no arithmetic origin. A nominal scale simply describes differences between things by assigning them to categories. Nominal data are, thus, counted data. The scale wastes any information that we may have about varying degrees of attitude, skills, understandings, etc. In spite of all this, nominal scales are still very useful and are widely used in surveys and other *ex-post-facto* research when data are being classified by major sub-groups of the population.

(b) Ordinal scale: The lowest level of the ordered scale that is commonly used is the ordinal scale. The ordinal scale places events in order, but there is no attempt to make the intervals of the scale equal in terms of some rule. Rank orders represent ordinal scales and are frequently used in research relating to qualitative phenomena. A student's rank in his graduation class involves the use of an ordinal scale. One has to be very careful in making statement about scores based on ordinal scales. For instance, if Ram's position in his class is 10 and Mohan's position is 40, it cannot be said that Ram's position is four times as good as that of Mohan. The statement would make no sense at all. Ordinal scales only permit the ranking of items from highest to lowest. Ordinal measures have no absolute values, and the real differences between adjacent ranks may not be equal. All that can be said is that one person is higher or lower on the scale than another, but more precise comparisons cannot be made.

Thus, the use of an ordinal scale implies a statement of 'greater than' or 'less than' (an equality statement is also acceptable) without our being able to state how much greater or less. The real difference between ranks 1 and 2 may be more or less than the difference between ranks 5 and 6. Since the numbers of this scale have only a rank meaning, the appropriate measure of central tendency is the median. A percentile or quartile measure is used for measuring dispersion. Correlations are restricted to various rank order methods. Measures of statistical significance are restricted to the non-parametric methods.

(c) Interval scale: In the case of interval scale, the intervals are adjusted in terms of some rule that has been established as a basis for making the units equal. The units are equal only in so far as one accepts the assumptions on which the rule is based. Interval scales can have an arbitrary zero, but it is not possible to determine for them what may be called an absolute zero or the unique origin. The primary limitation of the interval scale is the lack of a true zero; it does not have the capacity to measure the complete absence of a trait or characteristic. The Fahrenheit scale is an example of an interval scale and shows similarities in what one can and cannot do with it. One can say that an increase in temperature from 30° to 40° involves the same increase in temperature as an increase from 60° to 70°, but one cannot say that the temperature of 60° is twice as warm as the temperature of 30° because both numbers are dependent on the fact that the zero on the scale is set arbitrarily at the temperature of the freezing point of water. The ratio of the two temperatures, 30° and 60°, means nothing because zero is an arbitrary point.

Interval scales provide more powerful measurement than ordinal scales for interval scale also incorporates the concept of equality of interval. As such more powerful statistical measures can be used with interval scales. Mean is the appropriate measure of central tendency, while standard deviation is the most widely used measure of dispersion. Product moment correlation techniques are appropriate and the generally used tests for statistical significance are the 't' test and 'F' test.

(d) **Ratio scale:** Ratio scales have an absolute or true zero of measurement. The term 'absolute zero' is not as precise as it was once believed to be. We can conceive of an absolute zero of length and similarly we can conceive of an absolute zero of time. For example, the zero point on a centimeter scale indicates the complete absence of length or height. But an absolute zero of temperature is theoretically unobtainable and it remains a concept existing only in the scientist's mind. The number of minor traffic-rule violations and the number of incorrect letters in a page of type script represent scores on ratio scales. Both these scales have absolute zeros and as such all minor traffic violations and all typing errors can be assumed to be equal in significance. With ratio scales involved one can make statements like "Jyoti's" typing performance was twice as good as that of "Reetu." The ratio involved does have significance and facilitates a kind of comparison which is not possible in case of an interval scale.

Ratio scale represents the actual amounts of variables. Measures of physical dimensions such as weight, height, distance, etc. are examples. Generally, all statistical techniques are usable with ratio scales and all manipulations that one can carry out with real numbers can also be carried out with ratio scale values. Multiplication and division can be used with this scale but not with other scales mentioned above. Geometric and harmonic means can be used as measures of central tendency and coefficients of variation may also be calculated.

Thus, proceeding from the nominal scale (the least precise type of scale) to ratio scale (the most precise), relevant information is obtained increasingly. If the nature of the variables permits, the researcher should use the scale that provides the most precise description. Researchers in physical sciences have the advantage to describe variables in ratio scale form but the behavioural sciences are generally limited to describe variables in interval scale form, a less precise type of measurement.

Sources of Error in Measurement

Measurement should be precise and unambiguous in an ideal research study. This objective, however, is often not met with in entirety. As such the researcher must be aware about the sources of error in measurement. The following are the possible sources of error in measurement.

(a) Respondent: At times the respondent may be reluctant to express strong negative feelings or it is just possible that he may have very little knowledge but may not admit his ignorance. All this reluctance is likely to result in an interview of 'guesses.' Transient factors like fatigue, boredom, anxiety, etc. may limit the ability of the respondent to respond accurately and fully.

(b) Situation: Situational factors may also come in the way of correct measurement. Any condition which places a strain on interview can have serious effects on the interviewer-respondent rapport. For instance, if someone else is present, he can distort responses by joining in or merely by being present. If the respondent feels that anonymity is not assured, he may be reluctant to express certain feelings.

(c) Measurer: The interviewer can distort responses by rewording or reordering questions. His behaviour, style and looks may encourage or discourage certain replies from respondents. Careless mechanical processing may distort the findings. Errors may also creep in because of incorrect coding, faulty tabulation and/or statistical calculations, particularly in the data-analysis stage.

(d) Instrument: Error may arise because of the defective measuring instrument. The use of complex words, beyond the comprehension of the respondent, ambiguous meanings, poor printing, inadequate space for replies, response choice omissions, etc. are a few things that make the measuring instrument defective and may result in measurement errors. Another type of instrument deficiency is the poor sampling of the universe of items of concern.

Researcher must know that correct measurement depends on successfully meeting all of the problems listed above. He must, to the extent possible, try to eliminate, neutralize or otherwise deal with all the possible sources of error so that the final results may not be contaminated.

Tests of Sound Measurement

Sound measurement must meet the tests of validity, reliability and practicality. In fact, these are the three major considerations one should use in evaluating a measurement tool. "Validity refers to the extent to which a test measures what we actually wish to measure. Reliability has to do with the accuracy and precision of a measurement procedure ... Practicality is concerned with a wide range of factors of economy, convenience, and interpretability ..."[1] We briefly take up the relevant details concerning these tests of sound measurement.

1. Test of Validity*

Validity is the most critical criterion and indicates the degree to which an instrument measures what it is supposed to measure. Validity can also be thought of as utility. In other words, validity is the extent to which differences found with a measuring instrument reflect true differences among those being tested. But the question arises: how can one determine validity without direct confirming knowledge? The answer may be that we seek other relevant evidence that confirms the answers we have found with our measuring tool. What is relevant, evidence often depends upon the nature of the

---

[1] Robert L. Thorndike and Elizabeth Hagen: *Measurement and Evaluation in Psychology and Education,* 3rd Ed., p. 162.

*Two forms of validity are usually mentioned in research literature viz., the external validity and the internal validity. External validity of research findings is their generalizability to populations, settings, treatment variables and measurement variables. We shall talk about it in the context of significance tests later on. The internal validity of a research design is its ability to measure what it aims to measure. We shall deal with this validity only in the present chapter.

research problem and the judgement of the researcher. But one can certainly consider three types of validity in this connection: (i) Content validity; (ii) Criterion-related validity and (iii) Construct validity.

(i) *Content validity* is the extent to which a measuring instrument provides adequate coverage of the topic under study. If the instrument contains a representative sample of the universe, the content validity is good. Its determination is primarily judgemental and intuitive. It can also be determined by using a panel of persons who shall judge how well the measuring instrument meets the standards, but there is no numerical way to express it.

(ii) *Criterion-related validity* relates to our ability to predict some outcome or estimate the existence of some current condition. This form of validity reflects the success of measures used for some empirical estimating purpose. The concerned criterion must possess the following qualities:

Relevance: (A criterion is relevant if it is defined in terms we judge to be the proper measure.)

Freedom from bias: (Freedom from bias is attained when the criterion gives each subject an equal opportunity to score well.)

Reliability: (A reliable criterion is stable or reproducible.)

Availability: (The information specified by the criterion must be available.)

In fact, a Criterion-related validity is a broad term that actually refers to (i) *Predictive validity* and *(ii) Concurrent validity.* The former refers to the usefulness of a test in predicting some future performance whereas the latter refers to the usefulness of a test in closely relating to other measures of known validity. Criterion-related validity is expressed as the coefficient of correlation between test scores and some measure of future performance or between test scores and scores on another measure of known validity.

(iii) *Construct validity* is the most complex and abstract. A measure is said to possess construct validity to the degree that it confirms to predicted correlations with other theoretical propositions. Construct validity is the degree to which scores on a test can be accounted for by the explanatory constructs of a sound theory. For determining construct validity, we associate a set of other propositions with the results received from using our measurement instrument. If measurements on our devised scale correlate in a predicted way with these other propositions, we can conclude that there is some construct validity.

If the above stated criteria and tests are met with, we may state that our measuring instrument is valid and will result in correct measurement; otherwise we shall have to look for more information and/or resort to exercise of judgement.

2. Test of Reliability

The test of reliability is another important test of sound measurement. A measuring instrument is reliable if it provides consistent results. Reliable measuring instrument does contribute to validity, but a reliable instrument need not be a valid instrument. For instance, a scale that consistently overweighs objects by five kgs., is a reliable scale, but it does not give a valid measure of weight. But the other way is not true i.e., a valid instrument is always reliable. Accordingly reliability is not as valuable as validity, but it is easier to assess reliability in comparison to validity. If the quality of reliability is satisfied by an instrument, then while using it we can be confident that the transient and situational factors are not interfering.

Two aspects of reliability viz., stability and equivalence deserve special mention. The *stability aspect* is concerned with securing consistent results with repeated measurements of the same person and with the same instrument. We usually determine the degree of stability by comparing the results of repeated measurements. The *equivalence aspect* considers how much error may get introduced by different investigators or different samples of the items being studied. A good way to test for the equivalence of measurements by two investigators is to compare their observations of the same events. Reliability can be improved in the following two ways:

(i) By standardising the conditions under which the measurement takes place i.e., we must ensure that external sources of variation such as boredom, fatigue, etc., are minimised to the extent possible. That will improve stability aspect.

(ii) By carefully designed directions for measurement with no variation from group to group, by using trained and motivated persons to conduct the research and also by broadening the sample of items used. This will improve equivalence aspect.

3. Test of Practicality

The practicality characteristic of a measuring instrument can be judged in terms of economy, convenience and interpretability. From the operational point of view, the measuring instrument ought to be practical i.e., it should be economical, convenient and interpretable. *Economy* consideration suggests that some trade-off is needed between the ideal research project and that which the budget can afford. The length of measuring instrument is an important area where economic pressures are quickly felt. Although more items give greater reliability as stated earlier, but in the interest of limiting the interview or observation time, we have to take only few items for our study purpose. Similarly, data-collection methods to be used are also dependent at times upon economic factors. *Convenience* test suggests that the measuring instrument should be easy to administer. For this purpose one should give due attention to the proper layout of the measuring instrument. For instance, a questionnaire, with clear instructions (illustrated by examples), is certainly more effective and easier to complete than one which lacks these features. *Interpretability* consideration is specially important when persons other than the designers of the test are to interpret the results. The measuring instrument, in order to be interpretable, must be supplemented by (a) detailed instructions for administering the test; (b) scoring keys; (c) evidence about the reliability and (d) guides for using the test and for interpreting results.

TECHNIQUE OF DEVELOPING MEASUREMENT TOOLS

The technique of developing measurement tools involves a four-stage process, consisting of the following:

(a) Concept development;

(b) Specification of concept dimensions;

(c) Selection of indicators; and

(d) Formation of index.

The first and foremost step is that of *concept development* which means that the researcher should arrive at an understanding of the major concepts pertaining to his study. This step of concept development is more apparent in theoretical studies than in the more pragmatic research, where the fundamental concepts are often already established.

The second step requires the researcher to specify the *dimensions of the concepts* that he developed in the first stage. This task may either be accomplished by deduction i.e., by adopting a more or less intuitive approach or by empirical correlation of the individual dimensions with the total concept and/or the other concepts. For instance, one may think of several dimensions such as product reputation, customer treatment, corporate leadership, concern for individuals, sense of social responsibility and so forth when one is thinking about the image of a certain company.

Once the dimensions of a concept have been specified, the researcher must *develop indicators* for measuring each concept element. Indicators are specific questions, scales, or other devices by which respondent's knowledge, opinion, expectation, etc., are measured. As there is seldom a perfect measure of a concept, the researcher should consider several alternatives for the purpose. The use of more than one indicator gives stability to the scores and it also improves their validity.

The last step is that of combining the various indicators into an index, i.e., *formation of an index*. When we have several dimensions of a concept or different measurements of a dimension, we may need to combine them into a single index. One simple way for getting an overall index is to provide scale values to the responses and then sum up the corresponding scores. Such an overall index would provide a better measurement tool than a single indicator because of the fact that an "individual indicator has only a probability relation to what we really want to know."[2] This way we must obtain an overall index for the various concepts concerning the research study.

Scaling ✓

In research we quite often face measurement problem (since we want a valid measurement but may not obtain it), specially when the concepts to be measured are complex and abstract and we do not possess the standardised measurement tools. Alternatively, we can say that while measuring attitudes and opinions, we face the problem of their valid measurement. Similar problem may be faced by a researcher, of course in a lesser degree, while measuring physical or institutional concepts. As such we should study some procedures which may enable us to measure abstract concepts more accurately. This brings us to the study of scaling techniques.

Meaning of Scaling

Scaling describes the procedures of assigning numbers to various degrees of opinion, attitude and other concepts. This can be done in two ways viz., (i) making a judgement about some characteristic of an individual and then placing him directly on a scale that has been defined in terms of that characteristic and (ii) constructing questionnaires in such a way that the score of individual's responses assigns him a place on a scale. It may be stated here that a scale is a continuum, consisting of the highest point (in terms of some characteristic e.g., preference, favourableness, etc.) and the lowest point along with several intermediate points between these two extreme points. These scale-point positions are so related to each other that when the first point happens to be the highest point, the second point indicates a higher degree in terms of a given characteristic as compared to the third

[2] Lazersfeld, *Evidence and Inference*, p. 112.

point and the third point indicates a higher degree as compared to the fourth and so on. Numbers for measuring the distinctions of degree in the attitudes/opinions are, thus, assigned to individuals corresponding to their scale-positions. All this is better understood when we talk about scaling technique(s). Hence the term 'scaling' is applied to the procedures for attempting to determine quantitative measures of subjective abstract concepts. Scaling has been defined as a "procedure for the assignment of numbers (or other symbols) to a property of objects in order to impart some of the characteristics of numbers to the properties in question."[3]

Scale Classification Bases

The number assigning procedures or the scaling procedures may be broadly classified on one or more of the following bases: (a) subject orientation; (b) response form; (c) degree of subjectivity; (d) scale properties; (e) number of dimensions and (f) scale construction techniques. We take up each of these separately.

(a) Subject orientation: Under it a scale may be designed to measure characteristics of the respondent who completes it or to judge the stimulus object which is presented to the respondent. In respect of the former, we presume that the stimuli presented are sufficiently homogeneous so that the between-stimuli variation is small as compared to the variation among respondents. In the latter approach, we ask the respondent to judge some specific object in terms of one or more dimensions and we presume that the between-respondent variation will be small as compared to the variation among the different stimuli presented to respondents for judging.

(b) Response form: Under this we may classify the scales as categorical and comparative. Categorical scales are also known as rating scales. These scales are used when a respondent scores some object without direct reference to other objects. Under comparative scales, which are also known as ranking scales, the respondent is asked to compare two or more objects. In this sense the respondent may state that one object is superior to the other or that three models of pen rank in order 1, 2 and 3. The essence of ranking is, in fact, a relative comparison of a certain property of two or more objects.

(c) Degree of subjectivity: With this basis the scale data may be based on whether we measure subjective personal preferences or simply make non-preference judgements. In the former case, the respondent is asked to choose which person he favours or which solution he would like to see employed, whereas in the latter case he is simply asked to judge which person is more effective in some aspect or which solution will take fewer resources without reflecting any personal preference.

(d) Scale properties: Considering scale properties, one may classify the scales as nominal, ordinal, interval and ratio scales. Nominal scales merely classify without indicating order, distance or unique origin. Ordinal scales indicate magnitude relationships of 'more than' or 'less than', but indicate no distance or unique origin. Interval scales have both order and distance values, but no unique origin. Ratio scales possess all these features.

(e) Number of dimensions: In respect of this basis, scales can be classified as 'unidimensional' and 'multidimensional' scales. Under the former we measure only one attribute of the respondent or object, whereas multidimensional scaling recognizes that an object might be described better by using the concept of an attribute space of 'n' dimensions, rather than a single-dimension continuum.

[3] Bernard S. Phillips, *Social Research Strategy and Tactics,* 2nd ed., p. 205.

(f) Scale construction techniques: Following are the five main techniques by which scales can be developed.

(i) *Arbitrary approach:* It is an approach where scale is developed on *ad hoc* basis. This is the most widely used approach. It is presumed that such scales measure the concepts for which they have been designed, although there is little evidence to support such an assumption.

(ii) *Consensus approach:* Here a panel of judges evaluate the items chosen for inclusion in the instrument in terms of whether they are relevant to the topic area and unambiguous in implication.

(iii) *Item analysis approach:* Under it a number of individual items are developed into a test which is given to a group of respondents. After administering the test, the total scores are calculated for every one. Individual items are then analysed to determine which items discriminate between persons or objects with high total scores and those with low scores.

(iv) *Cumulative scales* are chosen on the basis of their conforming to some ranking of items with ascending and descending discriminating power. For instance, in such a scale the endorsement of an item representing an extreme position should also result in the endorsement of all items indicating a less extreme position.

(v) *Factor scales* may be constructed on the basis of intercorrelations of items which indicate that a common factor accounts for the relationship between items. This relationship is typically measured through factor analysis method.

Important Scaling Techniques

We now take up some of the important scaling techniques often used in the context of research specially in context of social or business research.

Rating scales: The rating scale involves qualitative description of a limited number of aspects of a thing or of traits of a person. When we use rating scales (or categorical scales), we judge an object in absolute terms against some specified criteria i.e., we judge properties of objects without reference to other similar objects. These ratings may be in such forms as "like-dislike", "above average, average, below average", or other classifications with more categories such as "like very much—like some what—neutral—dislike somewhat—dislike very much"; "excellent—good—average—below average—poor", "always—often—occasionally—rarely—never", and so on. There is no specific rule whether to use a two-points scale, three-points scale or scale with still more points. In practice, three to seven points scales are generally used for the simple reason that more points on a scale provide an opportunity for greater sensitivity of measurement.

Rating scale may be either a graphic rating scale or an itemized rating scale.

(i) *The graphic rating scale* is quite simple and is commonly used in practice. Under it the various points are usually put along the line to form a continuum and the rater indicates his rating by simply making a mark (such as ✓) at the appropriate point on a line that runs from one extreme to the other. Scale-points with brief descriptions may be indicated along the line, their function being to assist the rater in performing his job. The following is an example of five-points graphic rating scale when we wish to ascertain people's liking or disliking any product:

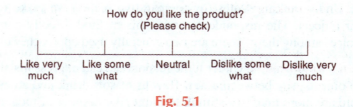

Fig. 5.1

This type of scale has several limitations. The respondents may check at almost any position along the line which fact may increase the difficulty of analysis. The meanings of the terms like "very much" and "some what" may depend upon respondent's frame of reference so much so that the statement might be challenged in terms of its equivalency. Several other rating scale variants (e.g., boxes replacing line) may also be used.

(ii) The *itemized rating scale* (also known as numerical scale) presents a series of statements from which a respondent selects one as best reflecting his evaluation. These statements are ordered progressively in terms of more or less of some property. An example of itemized scale can be given to illustrate it.

Suppose we wish to inquire as to how well does a worker get along with his fellow workers? In such a situation we may ask the respondent to select one, to express his opinion, from the following:

- He is almost always involved in some friction with a fellow worker.
- He is often at odds with one or more of his fellow workers.
- He sometimes gets involved in friction.
- He infrequently becomes involved in friction with others.
- He almost never gets involved in friction with fellow workers.

The chief merit of this type of scale is that it provides more information and meaning to the rater, and thereby increases reliability. This form is relatively difficult to develop and the statements may not say exactly what the respondent would like to express.

Rating scales have certain good points. The results obtained from their use compare favourably with alternative methods. They require less time, are interesting to use and have a wide range of applications. Besides, they may also be used with a large number of properties or variables. But their value for measurement purposes depends upon the assumption that the respondents can and do make good judgements. If the respondents are not very careful while rating, errors may occur. Three types of errors are common viz., the error of leniency, the error of central tendency and the error of hallo effect. The error of leniency occurs when certain respondents are either easy raters or hard raters. When raters are reluctant to give extreme judgements, the result is the error of central tendency. The error of hallo effect or the systematic bias occurs when the rater carries over a generalised impression of the subject from one rating to another. This sort of error takes place when we conclude for example, that a particular report is good because we like its form or that someone is intelligent because he agrees with us or has a pleasing personality. In other words, hallo effect is likely to appear when the rater is asked to rate many factors, on a number of which he has no evidence for judgement.

Ranking scales: Under ranking scales (or comparative scales) we make relative judgements against other similar objects. The respondents under this method directly compare two or more objects and make choices among them. There are two generally used approaches of ranking scales viz.

(a) Method of paired comparisons: Under it the respondent can express his attitude by making a choice between two objects, say between a new flavour of soft drink and an established brand of drink. But when there are more than two stimuli to judge, the number of judgements required in a paired comparison is given by the formula:

$$N = \frac{n(n-1)}{2}$$

where N = number of judgements

      n = number of stimuli or objects to be judged.

For instance, if there are ten suggestions for bargaining proposals available to a workers union, there are 45 paired comparisons that can be made with them. When N happens to be a big figure, there is the risk of respondents giving ill considered answers or they may even refuse to answer. We can reduce the number of comparisons per respondent either by presenting to each one of them only a sample of stimuli or by choosing a few objects which cover the range of attractiveness at about equal intervals and then comparing all other stimuli to these few standard objects. Thus, paired-comparison data may be treated in several ways. If there is substantial consistency, we will find that if X is preferred to Y, and Y to Z, then X will consistently be preferred to Z. If this is true, we may take the total number of preferences among the comparisons as the score for that stimulus.

It should be remembered that paired comparison provides ordinal data, but the same may be converted into an interval scale by the method of the *Law of Comparative Judgement* developed by L.L. Thurstone. This technique involves the conversion of frequencies of preferences into a table of proportions which are then transformed into Z matrix by referring to the table of area under the normal curve. J.P. Guilford in his book "Psychometric Methods" has given a procedure which is relatively easier. The method is known as the *Composite Standard Method* and can be illustrated as under:

Suppose there are four proposals which some union bargaining committee is considering. The committee wants to know how the union membership ranks these proposals. For this purpose a sample of 100 members might express the views as shown in the following table:

Table 5.1: Response Patterns of 100 Members' Paired Comparisons of 4 Suggestions for Union Bargaining Proposal Priorities

		Suggestion			
		A	B	C	D
A		–	65*	32	20
B		40	–	38	42
C		45	50	–	70
D		80	20	98	–
	TOTAL:	165	135	168	132

*Read as 65 members preferred suggestion B to suggestion A.

Contd.

Rank order	2	3	1	4
M_p	0.5375	0.4625	0.5450	0.4550
Z_j	0.09	(–).09	0.11	(–).11
R_j	0.20	0.02	0.22	0.00

Comparing the total number of preferences for each of the four proposals, we find that C is the most popular, followed by A, B and D respectively in popularity. The rank order shown in the above table explains all this.

By following the composite standard method, we can develop an interval scale from the paired-comparison ordinal data given in the above table for which purpose we have to adopt the following steps in order:

(i) Using the data in the above table, we work out the column mean with the help of the formula given below:

$$M_p = \frac{C + .5(N)}{nN} = \frac{165 + .5(100)}{4(100)} = .5375$$

where

M_p = the mean proportion of the columns

C = the total number of choices for a given suggestion

n = number of stimuli (proposals in the given problem)

N = number of items in the sample.

The column means have been shown in the M_p row in the above table.

(ii) The Z values for the M_p are secured from the table giving the area under the normal curve. When the M_p value is less than .5, the Z value is negative and for all M_p values higher than .5, the Z values are positive.[*] These Z values are shown in Z_j row in the above table.

(iii) As the Z_j values represent an interval scale, zero is an arbitrary value. Hence we can eliminate negative scale values by giving the value of zero to the lowest scale value (this being (–).11 in our example which we shall take equal to zero) and then adding the absolute value of this lowest scale value to all other scale items. This scale has been shown in R_j row in the above table.

Graphically we can show this interval scale that we have derived from the paired-comparison data using the composite standard method as follows:

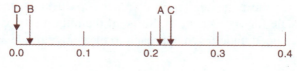

Fig. 5.2

[*]To use Normal curve area table for this sort of transformation, we must subtract 0.5 from all M_p values which exceed .5 to secure the values with which to enter the normal curve area table for which Z values can be obtained. For all M_p values of less than .5 we must subtract all such values from 0.5 to secure the values with which to enter the normal curve area table for which Z values can be obtained but the Z values in this situation will be with negative sign.

(b) Method of rank order: Under this method of comparative scaling, the respondents are asked to rank their choices. This method is easier and faster than the method of paired comparisons stated above. For example, with 10 items it takes 45 pair comparisons to complete the task, whereas the method of rank order simply requires ranking of 10 items only. The problem of transitivity (such as *A* prefers to *B, B* to *C,* but *C* prefers to *A*) is also not there in case we adopt method of rank order. Moreover, a complete ranking at times is not needed in which case the respondents may be asked to rank only their first, say, four choices while the number of overall items involved may be more than four, say, it may be 15 or 20 or more. To secure a simple ranking of all items involved we simply total rank values received by each item. There are methods through which we can as well develop an interval scale of these data. But then there are limitations of this method. The first one is that data obtained through this method are ordinal data and hence rank ordering is an ordinal scale with all its limitations. Then there may be the problem of respondents becoming careless in assigning ranks particularly when there are many (usually more than 10) items.

Scale Construction Techniques

In social science studies, while measuring attitudes of the people we generally follow the technique of preparing the opinionnaire* (or attitude scale) in such a way that the score of the individual responses assigns him a place on a scale. Under this approach, the respondent expresses his agreement or disagreement with a number of statements relevant to the issue. While developing such statements, the researcher must note the following two points:

   (i) That the statements must elicit responses which are psychologically related to the attitude being measured;

   (ii) That the statements need be such that they discriminate not merely between extremes of attitude but also among individuals who differ slightly.

Researchers must as well be aware that inferring attitude from what has been recorded in opinionnaires has several limitations. People may conceal their attitudes and express socially acceptable opinions. They may not really know how they feel about a social issue. People may be unaware of their attitude about an abstract situation; until confronted with a real situation, they may be unable to predict their reaction. Even behaviour itself is at times not a true indication of attitude. For instance, when politicians kiss babies, their behaviour may not be a true expression of affection toward infants. Thus, there is no sure method of measuring attitude; we only try to measure the expressed opinion and then draw inferences from it about people's real feelings or attitudes.

With all these limitations in mind, psychologists and sociologists have developed several scale construction techniques for the purpose. The researcher should know these techniques so as to develop an appropriate scale for his own study. Some of the important approaches, along with the corresponding scales developed under each approach to measure attitude are as follows:

---

*An information form that attempts to measure the attitude or belief of an individual is known as opinionnaire.

Table 5.2: Different Scales for Measuring Attitudes of People

Name of the scale construction approach	*Name of the scale developed*
1. Arbitrary approach	Arbitrary scales
2. Consensus scale approach	Differential scales (such as Thurstone Differential scale)
3. Item analysis approach	Summated scales (such as Likert Scale)
4. Cumulative scale approach	Cumulative scales (such as Guttman's Scalogram)
5. Factor analysis approach	Factor scales (such as Osgood's Semantic Differential, Multi-dimensional Scaling, etc.)

A brief description of each of the above listed scales will be helpful.

Arbitrary Scales

Arbitrary scales are developed on *ad hoc* basis and are designed largely through the researcher's own subjective selection of items. The researcher first collects few statements or items which he believes are unambiguous and appropriate to a given topic. Some of these are selected for inclusion in the measuring instrument and then people are asked to check in a list the statements with which they agree.

The chief merit of such scales is that they can be developed very easily, quickly and with relatively less expense. They can also be designed to be highly specific and adequate. Because of these benefits, such scales are widely used in practice.

At the same time there are some limitations of these scales. The most important one is that we do not have objective evidence that such scales measure the concepts for which they have been developed. We have simply to rely on researcher's insight and competence.

Differential Scales (or Thurstone-type Scales)

The name of L.L. Thurstone is associated with differential scales which have been developed using consensus scale approach. Under such an approach the selection of items is made by a panel of judges who evaluate the items in terms of whether they are relevant to the topic area and unambiguous in implication. The detailed procedure is as under:

(a) The researcher gathers a large number of statements, usually twenty or more, that express various points of view toward a group, institution, idea, or practice (i.e., statements belonging to the topic area).

(b) These statements are then submitted to a panel of judges, each of whom arranges them in eleven groups or piles ranging from one extreme to another in position. Each of the judges is requested to place generally in the first pile the statements which he thinks are most unfavourable to the issue, in the second pile to place those statements which he thinks are next most unfavourable and he goes on doing so in this manner till in the eleventh pile he puts the statements which he considers to be the most favourable.

(c) This sorting by each judge yields a composite position for each of the items. In case of marked disagreement between the judges in assigning a position to an item, that item is discarded.

(d) For items that are retained, each is given its median scale value between one and eleven as established by the panel. In other words, the scale value of any one statement is computed as the 'median' position to which it is assigned by the group of judges.

(e) A final selection of statements is then made. For this purpose a sample of statements, whose median scores are spread evenly from one extreme to the other is taken. The statements so selected, constitute the final scale to be administered to respondents. The position of each statement on the scale is the same as determined by the judges.

After developing the scale as stated above, the respondents are asked during the administration of the scale to check the statements with which they agree. The median value of the statements that they check is worked out and this establishes their score or quantifies their opinion. It may be noted that in the actual instrument the statements are arranged in random order of scale value. If the values are valid and if the opinionnaire deals with only one attitude dimension, the typical respondent will choose one or several contiguous items (in terms of scale values) to reflect his views. However, at times divergence may occur when a statement appears to tap a different attitude dimension.

The Thurstone method has been widely used for developing differential scales which are utilised to measure attitudes towards varied issues like war, religion, etc. Such scales are considered most appropriate and reliable when used for measuring a single attitude. But an important deterrent to their use is the cost and effort required to develop them. Another weakness of such scales is that the values assigned to various statements by the judges may reflect their own attitudes. The method is not completely objective; it involves ultimately subjective decision process. Critics of this method also opine that some other scale designs give more information about the respondent's attitude in comparison to differential scales.

Summated Scales (or Likert-type Scales)

Summated scales (or Likert-type scales) are developed by utilizing the item analysis approach wherein a particular item is evaluated on the basis of how well it discriminates between those persons whose total score is high and those whose score is low. Those items or statements that best meet this sort of discrimination test are included in the final instrument.

Thus, summated scales consist of a number of statements which express either a favourable or unfavourable attitude towards the given object to which the respondent is asked to react. The respondent indicates his agreement or disagreement with each statement in the instrument. Each response is given a numerical score, indicating its favourableness or unfavourableness, and the scores are totalled to measure the respondent's attitude. In other words, the overall score represents the respondent's position on the continuum of favourable-unfavourableness towards an issue.

Most frequently used summated scales in the study of social attitudes follow the pattern devised by Likert. For this reason they are often referred to as Likert-type scales. In a Likert scale, the respondent is asked to respond to each of the statements in terms of several degrees, usually five degrees (but at times 3 or 7 may also be used) of agreement or disagreement. For example, when asked to express opinion whether one considers his job quite pleasant, the respondent may respond in any one of the following ways: (i) strongly agree, (ii) agree, (iii) undecided, (iv) disagree, (v) strongly disagree.

We find that these five points constitute the scale. At one extreme of the scale there is strong agreement with the given statement and at the other, strong disagreement, and between them lie intermediate points. We may illustrate this as under:

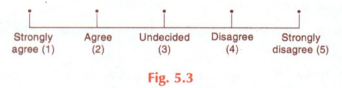

Strongly agree (1)   Agree (2)   Undecided (3)   Disagree (4)   Strongly disagree (5)

Fig. 5.3

Each point on the scale carries a score. Response indicating the least favourable degree of job satisfaction is given the least score (say 1) and the most favourable is given the highest score (say 5). These score—values are normally not printed on the instrument but are shown here just to indicate the scoring pattern. The Likert scaling technique, thus, assigns a scale value to each of the five responses. The same thing is done in respect of each and every statement in the instrument. This way the instrument yields a total score for each respondent, which would then measure the respondent's favourableness toward the given point of view. If the instrument consists of, say 30 statements, the following score values would be revealing.

$30 \times 5 = 150$ Most favourable response possible

$30 \times 3 = 90$ A neutral attitude

$30 \times 1 = 30$ Most unfavourable attitude.

The scores for any individual would fall between 30 and 150. If the score happens to be above 90, it shows favourable opinion to the given point of view, a score of below 90 would mean unfavourable opinion and a score of exactly 90 would be suggestive of a neutral attitude.

Procedure: The procedure for developing a Likert-type scale is as follows:

(i) As a first step, the researcher collects a large number of statements which are relevant to the attitude being studied and each of the statements expresses definite favourableness or unfavourableness to a particular point of view or the attitude and that the number of favourable and unfavourable statements is approximately equal.

(ii) After the statements have been gathered, a trial test should be administered to a number of subjects. In other words, a small group of people, from those who are going to be studied finally, are asked to indicate their response to each statement by checking one of the categories of agreement or disagreement using a five point scale as stated above.

(iii) The response to various statements are scored in such a way that a response indicative of the most favourable attitude is given the highest score of 5 and that with the most unfavourable attitude is given the lowest score, say, of 1.

(iv) Then the total score of each respondent is obtained by adding his scores that he received for separate statements.

(v) The next step is to array these total scores and find out those statements which have a high discriminatory power. For this purpose, the researcher may select some part of the highest and the lowest total scores, say the top 25 per cent and the bottom 25 per cent. These two extreme groups are interpreted to represent the most favourable and the least favourable attitudes and are used as criterion groups by which to evaluate individual statements. This way we determine which statements consistently correlate with low favourability and which with high favourability.

(vi) Only those statements that correlate with the total test should be retained in the final instrument and all others must be discarded from it.

Advantages: The Likert-type scale has several advantages. Mention may be made of the important ones.

(a) It is relatively easy to construct the Likert-type scale in comparison to Thurstone-type scale because Likert-type scale can be performed without a panel of judges.

(b) Likert-type scale is considered more reliable because under it respondents answer each statement included in the instrument. As such it also provides more information and data than does the Thurstone-type scale.

(c) Each statement, included in the Likert-type scale, is given an empirical test for discriminating ability and as such, unlike Thurstone-type scale, the Likert-type scale permits the use of statements that are not manifestly related (to have a direct relationship) to the attitude being studied.

(d) Likert-type scale can easily be used in respondent-centred and stimulus-centred studies i.e., through it we can study how responses differ between people and how responses differ between stimuli.

(e) Likert-type scale takes much less time to construct, it is frequently used by the students of opinion research. Moreover, it has been reported in various research studies* that there is high degree of correlation between Likert-type scale and Thurstone-type scale.

Limitations: There are several limitations of the Likert-type scale as well. One important limitation is that, with this scale, we can simply examine whether respondents are more or less favourable to a topic, but we cannot tell how much more or less they are. There is no basis for belief that the five positions indicated on the scale are equally spaced. The interval between 'strongly agree' and 'agree', may not be equal to the interval between "agree" and "undecided". This means that Likert scale does not rise to a stature more than that of an ordinal scale, whereas the designers of Thurstone scale claim the Thurstone scale to be an interval scale. One further disadvantage is that often the total score of an individual respondent has little clear meaning since a given total score can be secured by a variety of answer patterns. It is unlikely that the respondent can validly react to a short statement on a printed form in the absence of real-life qualifying situations. Moreover, there "remains a possibility that people may answer according to what they think they should feel rather than how they do feel."[4] This particular weakness of the Likert-type scale is met by using a cumulative scale which we shall take up later in this chapter.

In spite of all the limitations, the Likert-type summated scales are regarded as the most useful in a situation wherein it is possible to compare the respondent's score with a distribution of scores from some well defined group. They are equally useful when we are concerned with a programme of

*A.L. Edwards and K.C. Kenney, "A comparison of the Thurstone and Likert techniques of attitude scale construction", *Journal of Applied Psychology*, 30, 72–83, 1946.

[4] John W. Best and James V. Kahn, "Research in Education", 5 ed., Prentice-Hall of India Pvt. Ltd., New Delhi, 1986, p. 183.

change or improvement in which case we can use the scales to measure attitudes before and after the programme of change or improvement in order to assess whether our efforts have had the desired effects. We can as well correlate scores on the scale to other measures without any concern for the absolute value of what is favourable and what is unfavourable. All this accounts for the popularity of Likert-type scales in social studies relating to measuring of attitudes.

Cumulative scales: Cumulative scales or Louis Guttman's scalogram analysis, like other scales, consist of series of statements to which a respondent expresses his agreement or disagreement. The special feature of this type of scale is that statements in it form a cumulative series. This, in other words, means that the statements are related to one another in such a way that an individual, who replies favourably to say item No. 3, also replies favourably to items No. 2 and 1, and one who replies favourably to item No. 4 also replies favourably to items No. 3, 2 and 1, and so on. This being so an individual whose attitude is at a certain point in a cumulative scale will answer favourably all the items on one side of this point, and answer unfavourably all the items on the other side of this point. The individual's score is worked out by counting the number of points concerning the number of statements he answers favourably. If one knows this total score, one can estimate as to how a respondent has answered individual statements constituting cumulative scales. The major scale of this type of cumulative scales is the Guttman's scalogram. We attempt a brief description of the same below.

The technique developed by Louis Guttman is known as scalogram analysis, or at times simply 'scale analysis'. Scalogram analysis refers to the procedure for determining whether a set of items forms a unidimensional scale. A scale is said to be unidimensional if the responses fall into a pattern in which endorsement of the item reflecting the extreme position results also in endorsing all items which are less extreme. Under this technique, the respondents are asked to indicate in respect of each item whether they agree or disagree with it, and if these items form a unidimensional scale, the response pattern will be as under:

Table 5.3: Response Pattern in Scalogram Analysis

Item Number				Respondent Score
4	*3*	*2*	*1*	
X	X	X	X	4
–	X	X	X	3
–	–	X	X	2
–	–	–	X	1
–	–	–	–	0

X = Agree

– = Disagree

A score of 4 means that the respondent is in agreement with all the statements which is indicative of the most favourable attitude. But a score of 3 would mean that the respondent is not agreeable to item 4, but he agrees with all others. In the same way one can interpret other values of the respondents' scores. This pattern reveals that the universe of content is scalable.

Procedure: The procedure for developing a scalogram can be outlined as under:

(a) The universe of content must be defined first of all. In other words, we must lay down in clear terms the issue we want to deal within our study.

(b) The next step is to develop a number of items relating the issue and to eliminate by inspection the items that are ambiguous, irrelevant or those that happen to be too extreme items.

(c) The third step consists in pre-testing the items to determine whether the issue at hand is scalable (The pretest, as suggested by Guttman, should include 12 or more items, while the final scale may have only 4 to 6 items. Similarly, the number of respondents in a pretest may be small, say 20 or 25 but final scale should involve relatively more respondents, say 100 or more).

In a pretest the respondents are asked to record their opinions on all selected items using a Likert-type 5-point scale, ranging from 'strongly agree' to 'strongly disagree'. The strongest favourable response is scored as 5, whereas the strongest unfavourable response as 1. The total score can thus range, if there are 15 items in all, from 75 for most favourable to 15 for the least favourable.

Respondent opinionnaires are then arrayed according to total score for analysis and evaluation. If the responses of an item form a cumulative scale, its response category scores should decrease in an orderly fashion as indicated in the above table. Failure to show the said decreasing pattern means that there is overlapping which shows that the item concerned is not a good cumulative scale item i.e., the item has more than one meaning. Sometimes the overlapping in category responses can be reduced by combining categories. After analysing the pretest results, a few items, say 5 items, may be chosen.

(d) The next step is again to total the scores for the various opinionnaires, and to rearray them to reflect any shift in order, resulting from reducing the items, say, from 15 in pretest to, say, 5 for the final scale. The final pretest results may be tabulated in the form of a table given in Table 5.4.

Table 5.4: The Final Pretest Results in a Scalogram Analysis[*]

Scale type	Item					Errors per case	Number of cases	Number of errors
	5	12	3	10	7			
5 (perfect)	X	X	X	X	X	0	7	0
4 (perfect)	–	X	X	X	X	0	3	0
(nonscale)	–	X	–	X	X	1	1	1
(nonscale)	–	X	X	–	X	1	2	2
3 (perfect)	–	–	X	X	X	0	5	0
2 (perfect)	–	–	–	X	X	0	2	0
1 (perfect)	–	–	–	–	X	0	1	0
(nonscale)	–	–	X	–	–	2	1	2
(nonscale)	–	–	X	–	–	2	1	2
0 (perfect)	–	–	–	–	–	0	2	0
			$n = 5$				$N = 25$	$e = 7$

[*] (Figures in the table are arbitrary and have been used to explain the tabulation process only.)

The table shows that five items (numbering 5, 12, 3, 10 and 7) have been selected for the final scale. The number of respondents is 25 whose responses to various items have been tabulated along with the number of errors. Perfect scale types are those in which the respondent's answers fit the pattern that would be reproduced by using the person's total score as a guide. *Non-scale types* are those in which the category pattern differs from that expected from the respondent's total score i.e., non-scale cases have deviations from unidimensionality or errors. Whether the items (or series of statements) selected for final scale may be regarded a perfect cumulative (or a unidimensional scale), we have to examine on the basis of the coefficient of reproducibility. Guttman has set 0.9 as the level of minimum reproducibility in order to say that the scale meets the test of unidimensionality. He has given the following formula for measuring the level of reproducibility:

Guttman's Coefficient of Reproducibility = $1 - e/n(N)$

where e = number of errors

   n = number of items

   N = number of cases

For the above table figures,

Coefficient of Reproducibility = $1 - 7/5(25) = .94$

This shows that items number 5, 12, 3, 10 and 7 in this order constitute the cumulative or unidimensional scale, and with this we can reproduce the responses to each item, knowing only the total score of the respondent concerned.

Scalogram, analysis, like any other scaling technique, has several advantages as well as limitations. One advantage is that it assures that only a single dimension of attitude is being measured. Researcher's subjective judgement is not allowed to creep in the development of scale since the scale is determined by the replies of respondents. Then, we require only a small number of items that make such a scale easy to administer. Scalogram analysis can appropriately be used for personal, telephone or mail surveys. The main difficulty in using this scaling technique is that in practice perfect cumulative or unidimensional scales are very rarely found and we have only to use its approximation testing it through coefficient of reproducibility or examining it on the basis of some other criteria. This method is not a frequently used method for the simple reason that its development procedure is tedious and complex. Such scales hardly constitute a reliable basis for assessing attitudes of persons towards complex objects for predicting the behavioural responses of individuals towards such objects. Conceptually, this analysis is a bit more difficult in comparison to other scaling methods.

Factor Scales[*]

Factor scales are developed through factor analysis or on the basis of intercorrelations of items which indicate that a common factor accounts for the relationships between items. Factor scales are particularly "useful in uncovering latent attitude dimensions and approach scaling through the concept of multiple-dimension attribute space."[5] More specifically the two problems viz., how to deal

---

[*] A detailed study of the factor scales and particularly the statistical procedures involved in developing factor scales is beyond the scope of this book. As such only an introductory idea of factor scales is presented here.

[5] C. William Emory, *Business Research Methods*, p. 264–65.

appropriately with the universe of content which is multi-dimensional and how to uncover underlying (latent) dimensions which have not been identified, are dealt with through factor scales. An important factor scale based on factor analysis is *Semantic Differential (S.D.)* and the other one is *Multidimensional Scaling.* We give below a brief account of these factor scales.

Semantic differential scale: Semantic differential scale or the S.D. scale developed by Charles E. Osgood, G.J. Suci and P.H. Tannenbaum (1957), is an attempt to measure the psychological meanings of an object to an individual. This scale is based on the presumption that an object can have different dimensions of connotative meanings which can be located in multidimensional property space, or what can be called the semantic space in the context of S.D. scale. This scaling consists of a set of bipolar rating scales, usually of 7 points, by which one or more respondents rate one or more concepts on each scale item. For instance, the S.D. scale items for analysing candidates for leadership position may be shown as under:

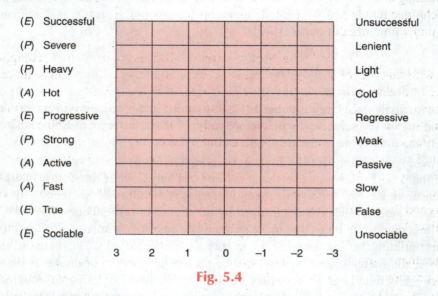

Fig. 5.4

Candidates for leadership position (along with the concept—the 'ideal' candidate) may be compared and we may score them from +3 to –3 on the basis of the above stated scales. (The letters, *E, P, A* showing the relevant factor viz., evaluation, potency and activity respectively, written along the left side are not written in actual scale. Similarly the numeric values shown are also not written in actual scale.)

Osgood and others did produce a list of some adjective pairs for attitude research purposes and concluded that semantic space is multidimensional rather than unidimensional. They made sincere efforts and ultimately found that three factors, viz., evaluation, potency and activity, contributed most to meaningful judgements by respondents. The evaluation dimension generally accounts for 1/2 and 3/4 of the extractable variance and the other two factors account for the balance.

Procedure: Various steps involved in developing S.D. scale are as follows:

    (a) First of all the concepts to be studied are selected. The concepts are usually chosen by personal judgement, keeping in view the nature of the problem.

(b) The next step is to select the scales bearing in mind the criterion of factor composition and the criterion of scale's relevance to the concepts being judged (it is common practice to use at least three scales for each factor with the help of which an average factor score has to be worked out). One more criterion to be kept in view is that scales should be stable across subjects and concepts.

(c) Then a panel of judges are used to rate the various stimuli (or objects) on the various selected scales and the responses of all judges would then be combined to determine the composite scaling.

To conclude, "the S.D. has a number of specific advantages. It is an efficient and easy way to secure attitudes from a large sample. These attitudes may be measured in both direction and intensity. The total set of responses provides a comprehensive picture of the meaning of an object, as well as a measure of the subject doing the rating. It is a standardised technique that is easily repeated, but escapes many of the problems of response distortion found with more direct methods."[6]

Multidimensional scaling: Multidimensional scaling (MDS) is relatively more complicated scaling device, but with this sort of scaling one can scale objects, individuals or both with a minimum of information. Multidimensional scaling (or MDS) can be characterized as a set of procedures for portraying perceptual or affective dimensions of substantive interest. It "provides useful methodology for portraying subjective judgements of diverse kinds."[7] MDS is used when all the variables (whether metric or non-metric) in a study are to be analyzed simultaneously and all such variables happen to be independent. The underlying assumption in MDS is that people (respondents) "perceive a set of objects as being more or less similar to one another on a number of dimensions (usually uncorrelated with one another) instead of only one."[8] Through MDS techniques one can represent geometrically the locations and interrelationships among a set of points. In fact, these techniques attempt to locate the points, given the information about a set of interpoint distances, in space of one or more dimensions such as to best summarise the information contained in the interpoint distances. The distances in the solution space then optimally reflect the distances contained in the input data. For instance, if objects, say X and Y, are thought of by the respondent as being most similar as compared to all other possible pairs of objects, MDS techniques will position objects X and Y in such a way that the distance between them in multidimensional space is shorter than that between any two other objects.

Two approaches, viz., the metric approach and the non-metric approach, are usually talked about in the context of MDS, while attempting to construct a space containing m points such that $m(m-1)/2$ interpoint distances reflect the input data. The *metric approach to MDS* treats the input data as interval scale data and solves applying statistical methods for the additive constant[*] which

---

[6] *Ibid.,* p. 260.

[7] Paul E. Green, *"Analyzing Multivariate Data"*, p. 421.

[8] Jagdish N. Sheth, "The Multivariate Revolution in Marketing Research", quoted in *"Marketing Research"* by Danny N. Bellenger and Barnett A. Greenberg, p. 255.

[*] Additive constant refers to that constant with which one can, either by subtracting or adding, convert interval scale to a ratio scale. For instance, suppose we know that distances, say *a—b, b—c, c—d* among stimuli on a ratio scale are 7, 6 and 3 respectively. If one were to subtract 3 from each of these distances, they would be 4, 3 and 0 respectively. The converted distances would be on an interval scale of measurement, but not on a ratio scale. Obviously, one can add 3 to all the converted distances and reachieve the ratio scale of distances. Thus 3 will be taken as the additive constant in this case. Well defined iterative approach is employed in practice for estimating appropriate additive constant.

minimises the dimensionality of the solution space. This approach utilises all the information in the data in obtaining a solution. The data (i.e., the metric similarities of the objects) are often obtained on a bipolar similarity scale on which pairs of objects are rated one at a time. If the data reflect exact distances between real objects in an *r*-dimensional space, their solution will reproduce the set of interpoint distances. But as the true and real data are rarely available, we require random and systematic procedures for obtaining a solution. Generally, the judged similarities among a set of objects are statistically transformed into distances by placing those objects in a multidimensional space of some dimensionality.

The *non-metric approach* first gathers the non-metric similarities by asking respondents to rank order all possible pairs that can be obtained from a set of objects. Such non-metric data is then transformed into some arbitrary metric space and then the solution is obtained by reducing the dimensionality. In other words, this non-metric approach seeks "a representation of points in a space of minimum dimensionality such that the rank order of the interpoint distances in the solution space maximally corresponds to that of the data. This is achieved by requiring only that the distances in the solution be monotone with the input data."[9] The non-metric approach has come into prominence during the sixties with the coming into existence of high speed computers to generate metric solutions for ordinal input data.

The significance of MDS lies in the fact that it enables the researcher to study "the perceptual structure of a set of stimuli and the cognitive processes underlying the development of this structure. Psychologists, for example, employ multidimensional scaling techniques in an effort to scale psychophysical stimuli and to determine appropriate labels for the dimensions along which these stimuli vary."[10] The MDS techniques, infact, do away with the need in the data collection process to specify the attribute(s) along which the several brands, say of a particular product, may be compared as ultimately the MDS analysis itself reveals such attribute(s) that presumably underlie the expressed relative similarities among objects. Thus, MDS is an important tool in attitude measurement and the techniques falling under MDS promise "a great advance from a series of unidimensional measurements (e.g., a distribution of intensities of feeling towards single attribute such as colour, taste or a preference ranking with indeterminate intervals), to a perceptual mapping in multidimensional space of objects ... company images, advertisement brands, etc."[11]

In spite of all the merits stated above, the MDS is not widely used because of the computation complications involved under it. Many of its methods are quite laborious in terms of both the collection of data and the subsequent analyses. However, some progress has been achieved (due to the pioneering efforts of Paul Green and his associates) during the last few years in the use of non-metric MDS in the context of market research problems. The techniques have been specifically applied in "finding out the perceptual dimensions, and the spacing of stimuli along these dimensions, that people, use in making judgements about the relative similarity of pairs of Stimuli."[12] But, "in the long run, the worth of MDS will be determined by the extent to which it advances the behavioral sciences."[13]

[9] Robert Ferber (ed.), *Handbook of Marketing Research*, p. 3–51.

[10] *Ibid.*, p. 3–52.

[11] G.B. Giles, *Marketing*, p. 43.

[12] Paul E. Green, *Analyzing Multivariate Data*, p. 421.

[13] Jum C. Nunnally, *Psychometric Theory*, p. 496:

Questions

1. What is the meaning of measurement in research? What difference does it make whether we measure in terms of a nominal, ordinal, interval or ratio scale? Explain giving examples.

2. Are you in agreement with the following statements? If so, give reasons:
   (1) Validity is more critical to measurement than reliability.
   (2) Stability and equivalence aspects of reliability essentially mean the same thing.
   (3) Content validity is the most difficult type of validity to determine.
   (4) There is no difference between concept development and concept specification.
   (5) Reliable measurement is necessarily a valid measurement.

3. Point out the possible sources of error in measurement. Describe the tests of sound measurement.

4. Are the following nominal, ordinal, interval or ratio data? Explain your answers.
   (a) Temperatures measured on the Kelvin scale.
   (b) Military ranks.
   (c) Social security numbers.
   (d) Number of passengers on buses from Delhi to Mumbai.
   (e) Code numbers given to the religion of persons attempting suicide.

5. Discuss the relative merits and demerits of:
   (a) Rating vs. Ranking scales.
   (b) Summated vs. Cumulative scales.
   (c) Scalogram analysis *vs.* Factor analysis.

6. The following table shows the results of a paired-comparison preference test of four cold drinks from a sample of 200 persons:

Name	Coca Cola	Limca	Goldspot	Thumps up
Coca Cola	–	60*	105	45
Limca	160	–	150	70
Goldspot	75	40	–	65
Thumps up	165	120	145	–

* To be read as 60 persons preferred Limca over Coca Cola.

   (a) How do these brands rank in overall preference in the given sample.
   (b) Develop an interval scale for the four varieties of cold drinks.

7. (1) Narrate the procedure for developing a scalogram and illustrate the same by an example.
   (2) Workout Guttman's coefficient of reproducibility from the following information:

   Number of cases (N) = 30

   Number of items (n) = 6

   Number of errors (e) = 10

   Interpret the meaning of coefficient you work out in this example.

8. Write short notes on:
   (a) Semantic differential scale;
   (b) Scalogram analysis;

    (c) Likert-type scale;

    (d) Arbitrary scales;

    (e) Multidimensional scaling (MDS).

9. Describe the different methods of scale construction, pointing out the merits and demerits of each.

10. "Scaling describes the procedures by which numbers are assigned to various degrees of opinion, attitude and other concepts." Discuss. Also point out the bases for scale classification.

6

Methods of Data Collection

The task of data collection begins after a research problem has been defined and research design/plan chalked out. While deciding about the method of data collection to be used for the study, the researcher should keep in mind two types of data viz., primary and secondary. The *primary data* are those which are collected afresh and for the first time, and thus happen to be original in character. The *secondary data,* on the other hand, are those which have already been collected by someone else and which have already been passed through the statistical process. The researcher would have to decide which sort of data he would be using (thus collecting) for his study and accordingly he will have to select one or the other method of data collection. The methods of collecting primary and secondary data differ since primary data are to be originally collected, while in case of secondary data the nature of data collection work is merely that of compilation. We describe the different methods of data collection, with the pros and cons of each method.

COLLECTION OF PRIMARY DATA

We collect primary data during the course of doing experiments in an experimental research but in case we do research of the descriptive type and perform surveys, whether sample surveys or census surveys, then we can obtain primary data either through observation or through direct communication with respondents in one form or another or through personal interviews.[*] This, in other words, means

---

[*] An experiment refers to an investigation in which a factor or variable under test is isolated and its effect(s) measured. In an experiment the investigator measures the effects of an experiment which he conducts intentionally. Survey refers to the method of securing information concerning a phenomena under study from all or a selected number of respondents of the concerned universe. In a survey, the investigator examines those phenomena which exist in the universe independent of his action. The difference between an experiment and a survey can be depicted as under:

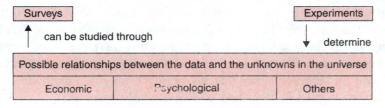

that there are several methods of collecting primary data, particularly in surveys and descriptive researches. Important ones are: (i) observation method, (ii) interview method, (iii) through questionnaires, (iv) through schedules, and (v) other methods which include (a) warranty cards; (b) distributor audits; (c) pantry audits; (d) consumer panels; (e) using mechanical devices; (f) through projective techniques; (g) depth interviews, and (h) content analysis. We briefly take up each method separately.

Observation Method

The observation method is the most commonly used method specially in studies relating to behavioural sciences. In a way we all observe things around us, but this sort of observation is not scientific observation. Observation becomes a scientific tool and the method of data collection for the researcher, when it serves a formulated research purpose, is systematically planned and recorded and is subjected to checks and controls on validity and reliability. Under the observation method, the information is sought by way of investigator's own direct observation without asking from the respondent. For instance, in a study relating to consumer behaviour, the investigator instead of asking the brand of wrist watch used by the respondent, may himself look at the watch. The main advantage of this method is that subjective bias is eliminated, if observation is done accurately. Secondly, the information obtained under this method relates to what is currently happening; it is not complicated by either the past behaviour or future intentions or attitudes. Thirdly, this method is independent of respondents' willingness to respond and as such is relatively less demanding of active cooperation on the part of respondents as happens to be the case in the interview or the questionnaire method. This method is particularly suitable in studies which deal with subjects (i.e., respondents) who are not capable of giving verbal reports of their feelings for one reason or the other

However, observation method has various limitations. Firstly, it is an expensive method. Secondly, the information provided by this method is very limited. Thirdly, sometimes unforeseen factors may interfere with the observational task. At times, the fact that some people are rarely accessible to direct observation creates obstacle for this method to collect data effectively.

While using this method, the researcher should keep in mind things like: What should be observed? How the observations should be recorded? Or how the accuracy of observation can be ensured? In case the observation is characterised by a careful definition of the units to be observed, the style of recording the observed information, standardised conditions of observation and the selection of pertinent data of observation, then the observation is called as *structured observation*. But when observation is to take place without these characteristics to be thought of in advance, the same is termed *as unstructured observation*. Structured observation is considered appropriate in descriptive studies, whereas in an exploratory study the observational procedure is most likely to be relatively unstructured.

We often talk about participant and non-participant types of observation in the context of studies, particularly of social sciences. This distinction depends upon the observer's sharing or not sharing the life of the group he is observing. If the observer observes by making himself, more or less, a member of the group he is observing so that he can experience what the members of the group experience, the observation is called as the *participant observation*. But when the observer observes as a detached emissary without any attempt on his part to experience through participation what others feel, the observation of this type is often termed as *non-participant observation*. (When the observer is observing in such a manner that his presence may be unknown to the people he is observing, such an observation is described as *disguised observation*.)

There are several merits of the participant type of observation: (i) The researcher is enabled to record the natural behaviour of the group. (ii) The researcher can even gather information which could not easily be obtained if he observes in a disinterested fashion. (iii) The researcher can even verify the truth of statements made by informants in the context of a questionnaire or a schedule. But there are also certain demerits of this type of observation viz., the observer may lose the objectivity to the extent he participates emotionally; the problem of observation-control is not solved; and it may narrow-down the researcher's range of experience.

Sometimes we talk of *controlled* and *uncontrolled observation*. If the observation takes place in the natural setting, it may be termed as uncontrolled observation, but when observation takes place according to definite pre-arranged plans, involving experimental procedure, the same is then termed controlled observation. In non-controlled observation, no attempt is made to use precision instruments. The major aim of this type of observation is to get a spontaneous picture of life and persons. It has a tendency to supply naturalness and completeness of behaviour, allowing sufficient time for observing it. But in controlled observation, we use mechanical (or precision) instruments as aids to accuracy and standardisation. Such observation has a tendency to supply formalised data upon which generalisations can be built with some degree of assurance. The main pitfall of non-controlled observation is that of subjective interpretation. There is also the danger of having the feeling that we know more about the observed phenomena than we actually do. Generally, controlled observation takes place in various experiments that are carried out in a laboratory or under controlled conditions, whereas uncontrolled observation is resorted to in case of exploratory researches.

Interview Method

The interview method of collecting data involves presentation of oral-verbal stimuli and reply in terms of oral-verbal responses. This method can be used through personal interviews and, if possible, through telephone interviews.

(a) *Personal interviews:* Personal interview method requires a person known as the interviewer asking questions generally in a face-to-face contact to the other person or persons. (At times the interviewee may also ask certain questions and the interviewer responds to these, but usually the interviewer initiates the interview and collects the information.) This sort of interview may be in the form of direct personal investigation or it may be indirect oral investigation. In the case of direct personal investigation the interviewer has to collect the information personally from the sources concerned. He has to be on the spot and has to meet people from whom data have to be collected. This method is particularly suitable for intensive investigations. But in certain cases it may not be possible or worthwhile to contact directly the persons concerned or on account of the extensive scope of enquiry, the direct personal investigation technique may not be used. In such cases an indirect oral examination can be conducted under which the interviewer has to cross-examine other persons who are supposed to have knowledge about the problem under investigation and the information, obtained is recorded. Most of the commissions and committees appointed by government to carry on investigations make use of this method.

The method of collecting information through personal interviews is usually carried out in a structured way. As such we call the interviews as *structured interviews*. Such interviews involve the use of a set of predetermined questions and of highly standardised techniques of recording. Thus, the interviewer in a structured interview follows a rigid procedure laid down, asking questions in a form and order prescribed. As against it, the *unstructured interviews* are characterised by a flexibility of approach to questioning. Unstructured interviews do not follow a system of pre-determined questions and standardised techniques of recording information. In a non-structured interview, the interviewer is allowed much greater freedom to ask, in case of need, supplementary questions or at times he may omit certain questions if the situation so requires. He may even change the sequence of questions. He has relatively greater freedom while recording the responses to include some aspects and exclude others. But this sort of flexibility results in lack of comparability of one interview with another and the analysis of unstructured responses becomes much more difficult and time-consuming than that of the structured responses obtained in case of structured interviews. Unstructured interviews also demand deep knowledge and greater skill on the part of the interviewer. Unstructured interview, however, happens to be the central technique of collecting information in case of exploratory or formulative research studies. But in case of descriptive studies, we quite often use the technique of structured interview because of its being more economical, providing a safe basis for generalisation and requiring relatively lesser skill on the part of the interviewer.

We may as well talk about focussed interview, clinical interview and the non-directive interview. *Focussed interview* is meant to focus attention on the given experience of the respondent and its effects. Under it the interviewer has the freedom to decide the manner and sequence in which the questions would be asked and has also the freedom to explore reasons and motives. The main task of the interviewer in case of a focussed interview is to confine the respondent to a discussion of issues with which he seeks conversance. Such interviews are used generally in the development of hypotheses and constitute a major type of unstructured interviews. The *clinical interview* is concerned with broad underlying feelings or motivations or with the course of individual's life experience. The method of eliciting information under it is generally left to the interviewer's discretion. In case of *non-directive interview*, the interviewer's function is simply to encourage the respondent to talk about the given topic with a bare minimum of direct questioning. The interviewer often acts as a catalyst to a comprehensive expression of the respondents' feelings and beliefs and of the frame of reference within which such feelings and beliefs take on personal significance.

Despite the variations in interview-techniques, the major advantages and weaknesses of personal interviews can be enumerated in a general way. The chief merits of the interview method are as follows:

(i)   More information and that too in greater depth can be obtained.

(ii) Interviewer by his own skill can overcome the resistance, if any, of the respondents; the interview method can be made to yield an almost perfect sample of the general population.

(iii) There is greater flexibility under this method as the opportunity to restructure questions is always there, specially in case of unstructured interviews.

(iv) Observation method can as well be applied to recording verbal answers to various questions.

(v)   Personal information can as well be obtained easily under this method.

(vi) Samples can be controlled more effectively as there arises no difficulty of the missing returns; non-response generally remains very low.

(vii) The interviewer can usually control which person(s) will answer the questions. This is not possible in mailed questionnaire approach. If so desired, group discussions may also be held.

(viii) The interviewer may catch the informant off-guard and thus may secure the most spontaneous reactions than would be the case if mailed questionnaire is used.

(ix) The language of the interview can be adopted to the ability or educational level of the person interviewed and as such misinterpretations concerning questions can be avoided.

(x) The interviewer can collect supplementary information about the respondent's personal characteristics and environment which is often of great value in interpreting results.

But there are also certain weaknesses of the interview method. Among the important weaknesses, mention may be made of the following:

(i) It is a very expensive method, specially when large and widely spread geographical sample is taken.

(ii) There remains the possibility of the bias of interviewer as well as that of the respondent; there also remains the headache of supervision and control of interviewers.

(iii) Certain types of respondents such as important officials or executives or people in high income groups may not be easily approachable under this method and to that extent the data may prove inadequate.

(iv) This method is relatively more-time-consuming, specially when the sample is large and re-calls upon the respondents are necessary.

(v) The presence of the interviewer on the spot may over-stimulate the respondent, sometimes even to the extent that he may give imaginary information just to make the interview interesting.

(vi) Under the interview method the organisation required for selecting, training and supervising the field-staff is more complex with formidable problems.

(vii) Interviewing at times may also introduce systematic errors.

(viii) Effective interview presupposes proper rapport with respondents that would facilitate free and frank responses. This is often a very difficult requirement.

Pre-requisites and basic tenets of interviewing: For successful implementation of the interview method, interviewers should be carefully selected, trained and briefed. They should be honest, sincere, hardworking, impartial and must possess the technical competence and necessary practical experience. Occasional field checks should be made to ensure that interviewers are neither cheating, nor deviating from instructions given to them for performing their job efficiently. In addition, some provision should also be made in advance so that appropriate action may be taken if some of the selected respondents refuse to cooperate or are not available when an interviewer calls upon them.

In fact, interviewing is an art governed by certain scientific principles. Every effort should be made to create friendly atmosphere of trust and confidence, so that respondents may feel at ease while talking to and discussing with the interviewer. The interviewer must ask questions properly and intelligently and must record the responses accurately and completely. At the same time, the interviewer must answer legitimate question(s), if any, asked by the respondent and must clear any doubt that the latter has. The interviewers approach must be friendly, courteous, conversational and unbiased. The interviewer should not show surprise or disapproval of a respondent's answer but he must keep the direction of interview in his own hand, discouraging irrelevant conversation and must make all possible effort to keep the respondent on the track.

(b) *Telephone interviews:* This method of collecting information consists in contacting respondents on telephone itself. It is not a very widely used method, but plays important part in industrial surveys, particularly in developed regions. The chief merits of such a system are:

1. It is more flexible in comparison to mailing method.
2. It is faster than other methods i.e., a quick way of obtaining information.
3. It is cheaper than personal interviewing method; here the cost per response is relatively low.
4. Recall is easy; callbacks are simple and economical.
5. There is a higher rate of response than what we have in mailing method; the non-response is generally very low.
6. Replies can be recorded without causing embarrassment to respondents.
7. Interviewer can explain requirements more easily.
8. At times, access can be gained to respondents who otherwise cannot be contacted for one reason or the other.
9. No field staff is required.
10. Representative and wider distribution of sample is possible.

But this system of collecting information is not free from demerits. Some of these may be highlighted.

1. Little time is given to respondents for considered answers; interview period is not likely to exceed five minutes in most cases.
2. Surveys are restricted to respondents who have telephone facilities.
3. Extensive geographical coverage may get restricted by cost considerations.
4. It is not suitable for intensive surveys where comprehensive answers are required to various questions.
5. Possibility of the bias of the interviewer is relatively more.
6. Questions have to be short and to the point; probes are difficult to handle.

COLLECTION OF DATA THROUGH QUESTIONNAIRES

This method of data collection is quite popular, particularly in case of big enquiries. It is being adopted by private individuals, research workers, private and public organisations and even by governments. In this method a questionnaire is sent (usually by post) to the persons concerned with a request to answer the questions and return the questionnaire. A questionnaire consists of a number of questions printed or typed in a definite order on a form or set of forms. The questionnaire is mailed to respondents who are expected to read and understand the questions and write down the reply in the space meant for the purpose in the questionnaire itself. The respondents have to answer the questions on their own.

The method of collecting data by mailing the questionnaires to respondents is most extensively employed in various economic and business surveys. The merits claimed on behalf of this method are as follows:

1. There is low cost even when the universe is large and is widely spread geographically.

2. It is free from the bias of the interviewer; answers are in respondents' own words.
3. Respondents have adequate time to give well thought out answers.
4. Respondents, who are not easily approachable, can also be reached conveniently.
5 Large samples can be made use of and thus the results can be made more dependable and reliable.

The main demerits of this system can also be listed here:

1. Low rate of return of the duly filled in questionnaires; bias due to no-response is often indeterminate.
2. It can be used only when respondents are educated and cooperating.
3. The control over questionnaire may be lost once it is sent.
4. There is inbuilt inflexibility because of the difficulty of amending the approach once questionnaires have been despatched.
5. There is also the possibility of ambiguous replies or omission of replies altogether to certain questions; interpretation of omissions is difficult.
6. It is difficult to know whether willing respondents are truly representative.
7. This method is likely to be the slowest of all.

Before using this method, it is always advisable to conduct 'pilot study' (Pilot Survey) for testing the questionnaires. In a big enquiry the significance of pilot survey is felt very much. Pilot survey is infact the replica and rehearsal of the main survey. Such a survey, being conducted by experts, brings to the light the weaknesses (if any) of the questionnaires and also of the survey techniques. From the experience gained in this way, improvement can be effected.

Main aspects of a questionnaire: Quite often questionnaire is considered as the heart of a survey operation. Hence it should be very carefully constructed. If it is not properly set up, then the survey is bound to fail. This fact requires us to study the main aspects of a questionnaire viz., the general form, question sequence and question formulation and wording. Researcher should note the following with regard to these three main aspects of a questionnaire:

1. *General form:* So far as the general form of a questionnaire is concerned, it can either be structured or unstructured questionnaire. Structured questionnaires are those questionnaires in which there are definite, concrete and pre-determined questions. The questions are presented with exactly the same wording and in the same order to all respondents. Resort is taken to this sort of standardisation to ensure that all respondents reply to the same set of questions. The form of the question may be either closed (i.e., of the type 'yes' or 'no') or open (i.e., inviting free response) but should be stated in advance and not constructed during questioning. Structured questionnaires may also have fixed alternative questions in which responses of the informants are limited to the stated alternatives. Thus a highly structured questionnaire is one in which all questions and answers are specified and comments in the respondent's own words are held to the minimum. When these characteristics are not present in a questionnaire, it can be termed as unstructured or non-structured questionnaire. More specifically, we can say that in an unstructured questionnaire, the interviewer is provided with a general guide on the type of information to be obtained, but the exact question formulation is largely his own responsibility and the replies are to be taken down in the respondent's own words to the extent possible; in some situations tape recorders may be used to achieve this goal.

Structured questionnaires are simple to administer and relatively inexpensive to analyse. The provision of alternative replies, at times, helps to understand the meaning of the question clearly. But such questionnaires have limitations too. For instance, wide range of data and that too in respondent's own words cannot be obtained with structured questionnaires. They are usually considered inappropriate in investigations where the aim happens to be to probe for attitudes and reasons for certain actions or feelings. They are equally not suitable when a problem is being first explored and working hypotheses sought. In such situations, unstructured questionnaires may be used effectively. Then on the basis of the results obtained in pretest (testing before final use) operations from the use of unstructured questionnaires, one can construct a structured questionnaire for use in the main study.

2. *Question sequence:* In order to make the questionnaire effective and to ensure quality to the replies received, a researcher should pay attention to the question-sequence in preparing the questionnaire. A proper sequence of questions reduces considerably the chances of individual questions being misunderstood. The question-sequence must be clear and smoothly-moving, meaning thereby that the relation of one question to another should be readily apparent to the respondent, with questions that are easiest to answer being put in the beginning. The first few questions are particularly important because they are likely to influence the attitude of the respondent and in seeking his desired cooperation. The opening questions should be such as to arouse human interest. The following type of questions should generally be avoided as opening questions in a questionnaire:

1. questions that put too great a strain on the memory or intellect of the respondent;
2. questions of a personal character;
3. questions related to personal wealth, etc.

Following the opening questions, we should have questions that are really vital to the research problem and a connecting thread should run through successive questions. Ideally, the question-sequence should conform to the respondent's way of thinking. Knowing what information is desired, the researcher can rearrange the order of the questions (this is possible in case of unstructured questionnaire) to fit the discussion in each particular case. But in a structured questionnaire the best that can be done is to determine the question-sequence with the help of a Pilot Survey which is likely to produce good rapport with most respondents. Relatively difficult questions must be relegated towards the end so that even if the respondent decides not to answer such questions, considerable information would have already been obtained. Thus, question-sequence should usually go from the general to the more specific and the researcher must always remember that the answer to a given question is a function not only of the question itself, but of all previous questions as well. For instance, if one question deals with the price usually paid for coffee and the next with reason for preferring that particular brand, the answer to this latter question may be couched largely in terms of price-differences.

3. *Question formulation and wording:* With regard to this aspect of questionnaire, the researcher should note that each question must be very clear for any sort of misunderstanding can do irreparable harm to a survey. Question should also be impartial in order not to give a biased picture of the true state of affairs. Questions should be constructed with a view to their forming a logical part of a well thought out tabulation plan. In general, all questions should meet the following standards—(a) should be easily understood; (b) should be simple i.e., should convey only one thought at a time; (c) should be concrete and should conform as much as possible to the respondent's way of thinking. (For

instance, instead of asking. "How many razor blades do you use annually?" The more realistic question would be to ask, "How many razor blades did you use last week?"

Concerning the form of questions, we can talk about two principal forms, viz., multiple choice question and the open-end question. In the former the respondent selects one of the alternative possible answers put to him, whereas in the latter he has to supply the answer in his own words. The question with only two possible answers (usually 'Yes' or 'No') can be taken as a special case of the multiple choice question, or can be named as a 'closed question.' There are some advantages and disadvantages of each possible form of question. Multiple choice or closed questions have the advantages of easy handling, simple to answer, quick and relatively inexpensive to analyse. They are most amenable to statistical analysis. Sometimes, the provision of alternative replies helps to make clear the meaning of the question. But the main drawback of fixed alternative questions is that of "putting answers in people's mouths" i.e., they may force a statement of opinion on an issue about which the respondent does not infact have any opinion. They are not appropriate when the issue under consideration happens to be a complex one and also when the interest of the researcher is in the exploration of a process. In such situations, open-ended questions which are designed to permit a free response from the respondent rather than one limited to certain stated alternatives are considered appropriate. Such questions give the respondent considerable latitude in phrasing a reply. Getting the replies in respondent's own words is, thus, the major advantage of open-ended questions. But one should not forget that, from an analytical point of view, open-ended questions are more difficult to handle, raising problems of interpretation, comparability and interviewer bias.[*]

In practice, one rarely comes across a case when one questionnaire relies on one form of questions alone. The various forms complement each other. As such questions of different forms are included in one single questionnaire. For instance, multiple-choice questions constitute the basis of a structured questionnaire, particularly in a mail survey. But even there, various open-ended questions are generally inserted to provide a more complete picture of the respondent's feelings and attitudes.

Researcher must pay proper attention to the wordings of questions since reliable and meaningful returns depend on it to a large extent. Since words are likely to affect responses, they should be properly chosen. Simple words, which are familiar to all respondents should be employed. Words with ambiguous meanings must be avoided. Similarly, danger words, catch-words or words with emotional connotations should be avoided. Caution must also be exercised in the use of phrases which reflect upon the prestige of the respondent. Question wording, in no case, should bias the answer. In fact, question wording and formulation is an art and can only be learnt by practice.

Essentials of a good questionnaire: To be successful, questionnaire should be comparatively short and simple i.e., the size of the questionnaire should be kept to the minimum. Questions should proceed in logical sequence moving from easy to more difficult questions. Personal and intimate questions should be left to the end. Technical terms and vague expressions capable of different interpretations should be avoided in a questionnaire. Questions may be dichotomous (yes or no answers), multiple choice (alternative answers listed) or open-ended. The latter type of questions are often difficult to analyse and hence should be avoided in a questionnaire to the extent possible. There should be some control questions in the questionnaire which indicate the reliability of the respondent. For instance, a question designed to determine the consumption of particular material may be asked

---

[*] Interviewer bias refers to the extent to which an answer is altered in meaning by some action or attitude on the part of the interviewer.

first in terms of financial expenditure and later in terms of weight. The control questions, thus, introduce a cross-check to see whether the information collected is correct or not. Questions affecting the sentiments of respondents should be avoided. Adequate space for answers should be provided in the questionnaire to help editing and tabulation. There should always be provision for indications of uncertainty, e.g., "do not know," "no preference" and so on. Brief directions with regard to filling up the questionnaire should invariably be given in the questionnaire itself. Finally, the physical appearance of the questionnaire affects the cooperation the researcher receives from the recipients and as such an attractive looking questionnaire, particularly in mail surveys, is a plus point for enlisting cooperation. The quality of the paper, along with its colour, must be good so that it may attract the attention of recipients.

COLLECTION OF DATA THROUGH SCHEDULES

This method of data collection is very much like the collection of data through questionnaire, with little difference which lies in the fact that schedules (proforma containing a set of questions) are being filled in by the enumerators who are specially appointed for the purpose. These enumerators along with schedules, go to respondents, put to them the questions from the proforma in the order the questions are listed and record the replies in the space meant for the same in the proforma. In certain situations, schedules may be handed over to respondents and enumerators may help them in recording their answers to various questions in the said schedules. Enumerators explain the aims and objects of the investigation and also remove the difficulties which any respondent may feel in understanding the implications of a particular question or the definition or concept of difficult terms:

This method requires the selection of enumerators for filling up schedules or assisting respondents to fill up schedules and as such enumerators should be very carefully selected. The enumerators should be trained to perform their job well and the nature and scope of the investigation should be explained to them thoroughly so that they may well understand the implications of different questions put in the schedule. Enumerators should be intelligent and must possess the capacity of cross-examination in order to find out the truth. Above all, they should be honest, sincere, hardworking and should have patience and perseverance.

This method of data collection is very useful in extensive enquiries and can lead to fairly reliable results. It is, however, very expensive and is usually adopted in investigations conducted by governmental agencies or by some big organisations. Population census all over the world is conducted through this method.

DIFFERENCE BETWEEN QUESTIONNAIRES AND SCHEDULES

Both questionnaire and schedule are popularly used methods of collecting data in research surveys. There is much resemblance in the nature of these two methods and this fact has made many people to remark that from a practical point of view, the two methods can be taken to be the same. But from the technical point of view there is difference between the two. The important points of difference are as under:

1. The questionnaire is generally sent through mail to informants to be answered as specified in a covering letter, but otherwise without further assistance from the sender. The schedule

is generally filled out by the research worker or the enumerator, who can interpret questions when necessary.

2. To collect data through questionnaire is relatively cheap and economical since we have to spend money only in preparing the questionnaire and in mailing the same to respondents. Here no field staff required. To collect data through schedules is relatively more expensive since considerable amount of money has to be spent in appointing enumerators and in importing training to them. Money is also spent in preparing schedules.

3. Non-response is usually high in case of questionnaire as many people do not respond and many return the questionnaire without answering all questions. Bias due to non-response often remains indeterminate. As against this, non-response is generally very low in case of schedules because these are filled by enumerators who are able to get answers to all questions. But there remains the danger of interviewer bias and cheating.

4. In case of questionnaire, it is not always clear as to who replies, but in case of schedule the identity of respondent is known.

5. The questionnaire method is likely to be very slow since many respondents do not return the questionnaire in time despite several reminders, but in case of schedules the information is collected well in time as they are filled in by enumerators.

6. Personal contact is generally not possible in case of the questionnaire method as questionnaires are sent to respondents by post who also in turn return the same by post. But in case of schedules direct personal contact is established with respondents.

7. Questionnaire method can be used only when respondents are literate and cooperative, but in case of schedules the information can be gathered even when the respondents happen to be illiterate.

8. Wider and more representative distribution of sample is possible under the questionnaire method, but in respect of schedules there usually remains the difficulty in sending enumerators over a relatively wider area.

9. Risk of collecting incomplete and wrong information is relatively more under the questionnaire method, particularly when people are unable to understand questions properly. But in case of schedules, the information collected is generally complete and accurate as enumerators can remove the difficulties, if any, faced by respondents in correctly understanding the questions. As a result, the information collected through schedules is relatively more accurate than that obtained through questionnaires.

10. The success of questionnaire method lies more on the quality of the questionnaire itself, but in the case of schedules much depends upon the honesty and competence of enumerators.

11. In order to attract the attention of respondents, the physical appearance of questionnaire must be quite attractive, but this may not be so in case of schedules as they are to be filled in by enumerators and not by respondents.

12. Along with schedules, observation method can also be used but such a thing is not possible while collecting data through questionnaires.

SOME OTHER METHODS OF DATA COLLECTION

Let us consider some other methods of data collection, particularly used by big business houses in modern times.

1. Warranty cards: Warranty cards are usually postal sized cards which are used by dealers of consumer durables to collect information regarding their products. The information sought is printed in the form of questions on the 'warranty cards' which is placed inside the package along with the product with a request to the consumer to fill in the card and post it back to the dealer.

2. Distributor or store audits: Distributor or store audits are performed by distributors as well as manufactures through their salesmen at regular intervals. Distributors get the retail stores audited through salesmen and use such information to estimate market size, market share, seasonal purchasing pattern and so on. The data are obtained in such audits not by questioning but by observation. For instance, in case of a grocery store audit, a sample of stores is visited periodically and data are recorded on inventories on hand either by observation or copying from store records. Store audits are invariably panel operations, for the derivation of sales estimates and compilation of sales trends by stores are their principal '*raison detre*'. The principal advantage of this method is that it offers the most efficient way of evaluating the effect on sales of variations of different techniques of in-store promotion.

3. Pantry audits: Pantry audit technique is used to estimate consumption of the basket of goods at the consumer level. In this type of audit, the investigator collects an inventory of types, quantities and prices of commodities consumed. Thus in pantry audit data are recorded from the examination of consumer's pantry. The usual objective in a pantry audit is to find out what types of consumers buy certain products and certain brands, the assumption being that the contents of the pantry accurately portray consumer's preferences. Quite often, pantry audits are supplemented by direct questioning relating to reasons and circumstances under which particular products were purchased in an attempt to relate these factors to purchasing habits. A pantry audit may or may not be set up as a panel operation, since a single visit is often considered sufficient to yield an accurate picture of consumers' preferences. An important limitation of pantry audit approach is that, at times, it may not be possible to identify consumers' preferences from the audit data alone, particularly when promotion devices produce a marked rise in sales.

4. Consumer panels: An extension of the pantry audit approach on a regular basis is known as 'consumer panel', where a set of consumers are arranged to come to an understanding to maintain detailed daily records of their consumption and the same is made available to investigator on demands. In other words, a consumer panel is essentially a sample of consumers who are interviewed repeatedly over a period of time. Mostly consume panels are of two types viz., the transitory consumer panel and the continuing consumer panel. *A transitory consumer panel* is set up to measure the effect of a particular phenomenon. Usually such a panel is conducted on a before-and-after-basis. Initial interviews are conducted before the phenomenon takes place to record the attitude of the consumer. A second set of interviews is carried out after the phenomenon has taken place to find out the consequent changes that might have occurred in the consumer's attitude. It is a favourite tool of advertising and of social research. A *continuing consumer panel* is often set up for an indefinite period with a view to collect data on a particular aspect of consumer behaviour over time, generally at periodic intervals or may be meant to serve as a general purpose panel for researchers on a variety of subjects. Such panels have been used in the area of consumer expenditure, public opinion and radio and TV listenership among others. Most of these panels operate by mail. The representativeness of the panel relative to the population and the effect of panel membership on the information obtained after the two major problems associated with the use of this method of data collection.

5. Use of mechanical devices: The use of mechanical devices has been widely made to collect information by way of indirect means. Eye camera, Pupilometric camera, Psychogalvanometer, Motion picture camera and Audiometer are the principal devices so far developed and commonly used by modern big business houses, mostly in the developed world for the purpose of collecting the required information.

Eye cameras are designed to record the focus of eyes of a respondent on a specific portion of a sketch or diagram or written material. Such an information is useful in designing advertising material. Pupilometric cameras record dilation of the pupil as a result of a visual stimulus. The extent of dilation shows the degree of interest aroused by the stimulus. Psychogalvanometer is used for measuring the extent of body excitement as a result of the visual stimulus. Motion picture cameras can be used to record movement of body of a buyer while deciding to buy a consumer good from a shop or big store. Influence of packaging or the information given on the label would stimulate a buyer to perform certain physical movements which can easily be recorded by a hidden motion picture camera in the shop's four walls. Audiometers are used by some TV concerns to find out the type of programmes as well as stations preferred by people. A device is fitted in the television instrument itself to record these changes. Such data may be used to find out the market share of competing television stations.

6. Projective techniques: Projective techniques (or what are sometimes called as indirect interviewing techniques) for the collection of data have been developed by psychologists to use projections of respondents for inferring about underlying motives, urges, or intentions which are such that the respondent either resists to reveal them or is unable to figure out himself. In projective techniques the respondent in supplying information tends unconsciously to project his own attitudes or feelings on the subject under study. Projective techniques play an important role in motivational researches or in attitude surveys.

The use of these techniques requires intensive specialised training. In such techniques, the individual's responses to the stimulus-situation are not taken at their face value. The stimuli may arouse many different kinds of reactions. The nature of the stimuli and the way in which they are presented under these techniques do not clearly indicate the way in which the response is to be interpreted. The stimulus may be a photograph, a picture, an inkblot and so on. Responses to these stimuli are interpreted as indicating the individual's own view, his personality structure, his needs, tensions, etc. in the context of some pre-established psychological conceptualisation of what the individual's responses to the stimulus mean.

We may now briefly deal with the important projective techniques.

(i) *Word association tests:* These tests are used to extract information regarding such words which have maximum association. In this sort of test the respondent is asked to mention the first word that comes to mind, ostensibly without thinking, as the interviewer reads out each word from a list. If the interviewer says *cold*, the respondent may say *hot* and the like ones. The general technique is to use a list of as many as 50 to 100 words. Analysis of the matching words supplied by the respondents indicates whether the given word should be used for the contemplated purpose. The same idea is exploited in marketing research to find out the quality that is mostly associated to a brand of a product. A number of qualities of a product may be listed and informants may be asked to write brand names possessing one or more of these. This technique is quick and easy to use, but yields reliable results when applied to words that are widely known and which possess essentially one type of meaning. This technique is frequently used in advertising research.

(ii) *Sentence completion tests:* These tests happen to be an extension of the technique of word association tests. Under this, informant may be asked to complete a sentence (such as: persons who wear Khadi are...) to find association of Khadi clothes with certain personality characteristics. Several sentences of this type might be put to the informant on the same subject. Analysis of replies from the same informant reveals his attitude toward that subject, and the combination of these attitudes of all the sample members is then taken to reflect the views of the population. This technique permits the testing not only of words (as in case of word association tests), but of ideas as well and thus, helps in developing hypotheses and in the construction of questionnaires. This technique is also quick and easy to use, but it often leads to analytical problems, particularly when the response happens to be multidimensional.

(iii) *Story completion tests:* Such tests are a step further wherein the researcher may contrive stories instead of sentences and ask the informants to complete them. The respondent is given just enough of story to focus his attention on a given subject and he is asked to supply a conclusion to the story.

(iv) *Verbal projection tests:* These are the tests wherein the respondent is asked to comment on or to explain what other people do. For example, why do people smoke? Answers may reveal the respondent's own motivations.

(v) *Pictorial techniques:* There are several pictorial techniques. The important ones are as follows:

(a) *Thematic apperception test (T.A.T.):* The TAT consists of a set of pictures (some of the pictures deal with the ordinary day-to-day events while others may be ambiguous pictures of unusual situations) that are shown to respondents who are asked to describe what they think the pictures represent. The replies of respondents constitute the basis for the investigator to draw inferences about their personality structure, attitudes, etc.

(b) *Rosenzweig test:* This test uses a cartoon format wherein we have a series of cartoons with words inserted in 'balloons' above. The respondent is asked to put his own words in an empty balloon space provided for the purpose in the picture. From what the respondents write in this fashion, the study of their attitudes can be made.

(c) *Rorschach test:* This test consists of ten cards having prints of inkblots. The design happens to be symmetrical but meaningless. The respondents are asked to describe what they perceive in such symmetrical inkblots and the responses are interpreted on the basis of some pre-determined psychological framework. This test is frequently used but the problem of validity still remains a major problem of this test.

(d) *Holtzman Inkblot Test (HIT):* This test from W.H. Holtzman is a modification of the Rorschach Test explained above. This test consists of 45 inkblot cards (and not 10 inkblots as we find in case of Rorschach Test) which are based on colour, movement, shading and other factors involved in inkblot perception. Only one response per card is obtained from the subject (or the respondent) and the responses of a subject are interpreted at three levels of form appropriateness. Form responses are interpreted for knowing the accuracy (F) or inaccuracy (F–) of respondent's percepts; shading and colour for ascertaining his affectional and emotional needs; and movement responses for assessing the dynamic aspects of his life.

Holtzman Inkblot Test or H.I.T. has several special features or advantages. For example, it elicits relatively constant number of responses per respondent. Secondly, it facilitates studying the responses of a respondent to different cards in the light of norms of each card instead of lumping them together. Thirdly, it elicits much more information from the respondent then is possible with merely 10 cards in Rorschach test; the 45 cards used in this test provide a variety of stimuli to the respondent and as such the range of responses elicited by the test is comparatively wider.

There are some limitations of this test as well. One difficulty that remains in using this test is that most of the respondents do not know the determinants of their perceptions, but for the researcher, who has to interpret the protocols of a subject and understand his personality (or attitude) through them, knowing the determinant of each of his response is a must. This fact emphasises that the test must be administered individually and a post-test inquiry must as well be conducted for knowing the nature and sources of responses and this limits the scope of HIT as a group test of personality. Not only this, "the usefulness of HIT for purposes of personal selection, vocational guidance, etc. is still to be established."[1]

In view of these limitations, some people have made certain changes in applying this test. For instance, Fisher and Cleveland in their approach for obtaining Barrier score of an individual's personality have developed a series of multiple choice items for 40 of HIT cards. Each of these cards is presented to the subject along with three acceptable choices [such as 'Knight in armour' (Barrier response), 'X-Ray' (Penetrating response) and 'Flower' (Neutral response)]. Subject taking the test is to check the choice he likes most, make a different mark against the one he likes least and leave the third choice blank. The number of barrier responses checked by him determines his barrier score on the test.

   (e) *Tomkins-Horn picture arrangement test:* This test is designed for group administration. It consists of twenty-five plates, each containing three sketches that may be arranged in different ways to portray sequence of events. The respondent is asked to arrange them in a sequence which he considers as reasonable. The responses are interpreted as providing evidence confirming certain norms, respondent's attitudes, etc.

(vi) *Play techniques:* Under play techniques subjects are asked to improvise or act out a situation in which they have been assigned various roles. The researcher may observe such traits as hostility, dominance, sympathy, prejudice or the absence of such traits. These techniques have been used for knowing the attitudes of younger ones through manipulation of dolls. Dolls representing different racial groups are usually given to children who are allowed to play with them freely. The manner in which children organise dolls would indicate their attitude towards the class of persons represented by dolls. This is also known as *doll-play test*, and is used frequently in studies pertaining to sociology. The choice of colour, form, words, the sense of orderliness and other reactions may provide opportunities to infer deep-seated feelings.

(vii) *Quizzes, tests and examinations:* This is also a technique of extracting information regarding specific ability of candidates indirectly. In this procedure both long and short questions are framed to test through them the memorising and analytical ability of candidates.

(viii) *Sociometry:* Sociometry is a technique for describing the social relationships among individuals in a group. In an indirect way, sociometry attempts to describe attractions or repulsions between

[1] S.L. Dass, "*Personality Assessment Through Projective Movie Pictures*", p. 17.

individuals by asking them to indicate whom they would choose or reject in various situations. Thus, sociometry is a new technique of studying the underlying motives of respondents. "Under this an attempt is made to trace the flow of information amongst groups and then examine the ways in which new ideas are diffused. Sociograms are constructed to identify leaders and followers."[2] Sociograms are charts that depict the sociometric choices. There are many versions of the sociogram pattern and the reader is suggested to consult specialised references on sociometry for the purpose. This approach has been applied to the diffusion of ideas on drugs amongst medical practitioners.

7. Depth interviews: Depth interviews are those interviews that are designed to discover underlying motives and desires and are often used in motivational research. Such interviews are held to explore needs, desires and feelings of respondents. In other words, they aim to elicit unconscious as also other types of material relating especially to personality dynamics and motivations. As such, depth interviews require great skill on the part of the interviewer and at the same time involve considerable time. Unless the researcher has specialised training, depth interviewing should not be attempted.

Depth interview may be projective in nature or it may be a non-projective interview. The difference lies in the nature of the questions asked. Indirect questions on seemingly irrelevant subjects provide information that can be related to the informant's behaviour or attitude towards the subject under study. Thus, for instance, the informant may be asked on his frequency of air travel and he might again be asked at a later stage to narrate his opinion concerning the feelings of relatives of some other man who gets killed in an airplane accident. Reluctance to fly can then be related to replies to questions of the latter nature. If the depth interview involves questions of such type, the same may be treated as projective depth interview. But in order to be useful, depth interviews do not necessarily have to be projective in nature; even non-projective depth interviews can reveal important aspects of psycho-social situation for understanding the attitudes of people.

8. Content-analysis: Content-analysis consists of analysing the contents of documentary materials such as books, magazines, newspapers and the contents of all other verbal materials which can be either spoken or printed. Content-analysis prior to 1940's was mostly quantitative analysis of documentary materials concerning certain characteristics that can be identified and counted. But since 1950's content-analysis is mostly qualitative analysis concerning the general import or message of the existing documents. "The difference is somewhat like that between a casual interview and depth interviewing."[3] Bernard Berelson's name is often associated with. the latter type of content-analysis. "Content-analysis is measurement through proportion.... Content analysis measures pervasiveness and that is sometimes an index of the intensity of the force."[4]

The analysis of content is a central activity whenever one is concerned with the study of the nature of the verbal materials. A review of research in any area, for instance, involves the analysis of the contents of research articles that have been published. The analysis may be at a relatively simple level or may be a subtle one. It is at a simple level when we pursue it on the basis of certain characteristics of the document or verbal materials that can be identified and counted (such as on the basis of major scientific concepts in a book). It is at a subtle level when researcher makes a study of the attitude, say of the press towards education by feature writers.

[2] G.B. Giles, *Marketing*, p. 40–41.

[3] Carter V. Good and Douglas E. Scates, *Methods of Research*, p. 670.

[4] *Ibid.*, p. 670.

COLLECTION OF SECONDARY DATA

Secondary data means data that are already available i.e., they refer to the data which have already been collected and analysed by someone else. When the researcher utilises secondary data, then he has to look into various sources from where he can obtain them. In this case he is certainly not confronted with the problems that are usually associated with the collection of original data. Secondary data may either be published data or unpublished data. Usually published data are available in: (a) various publications of the central, state are local governments; (b) various publications of foreign governments or of international bodies and their subsidiary organisations; (c) technical and trade journals; (d) books, magazines and newspapers; (e) reports and publications of various associations connected with business and industry, banks, stock exchanges, etc.; (f) reports prepared by research scholars, universities, economists, etc. in different fields; and (g) public records and statistics, historical documents, and other sources of published information. The sources of unpublished data are many; they may be found in diaries, letters, unpublished biographies and autobiographies and also may be available with scholars and research workers, trade associations, labour bureaus and other public/ private individuals and organisations.

Researcher must be very careful in using secondary data. He must make a minute scrutiny because it is just possible that the secondary data may be unsuitable or may be inadequate in the context of the problem which the researcher wants to study. In this connection Dr. A.L. Bowley very aptly observes that it is never safe to take published statistics at their face value without knowing their meaning and limitations and it is always necessary to criticise arguments that can be based on them.

By way of caution, the researcher, before using secondary data, must see that they possess following characteristics:

1. Reliability of data: The reliability can be tested by finding out such things about the said data: (a) Who collected the data? (b) What were the sources of data? (c) Were they collected by using proper methods (d) At what time were they collected?(e) Was there any bias of the compiler? (t) What level of accuracy was desired? Was it achieved ?

2. Suitability of data: The data that are suitable for one enquiry may not necessarily be found suitable in another enquiry. Hence, if the available data are found to be unsuitable, they should not be used by the researcher. In this context, the researcher must very carefully scrutinise the definition of various terms and units of collection used at the time of collecting the data from the primary source originally. Similarly, the object, scope and nature of the original enquiry must also be studied. If the researcher finds differences in these, the data will remain unsuitable for the present enquiry and should not be used.

3. Adequacy of data: If the level of accuracy achieved in data is found inadequate for the purpose of the present enquiry, they will be considered as inadequate and should not be used by the researcher. The data will also be considered inadequate, if they are related to an area which may be either narrower or wider than the area of the present enquiry.

From all this we can say that it is very risky to use the already available data. The already available data should be used by the researcher only when he finds them reliable, suitable and adequate. But he should not blindly discard the use of such data if they are readily available from authentic sources and are also suitable and adequate for in that case it will not be economical to spend time and energy in field surveys for collecting information. At times, there may be wealth of usable information in the already available data which must be used by an intelligent researcher but with due precaution.

SELECTION OF APPROPRIATE METHOD FOR DATA COLLECTION

Thus, there are various methods of data collection. As such the researcher must judiciously select the method/methods for his own study, keeping in view the following factors:

1. Nature, scope and object of enquiry: This constitutes the most important factor affecting the choice of a particular method. The method selected should be such that it suits the type of enquiry that is to be conducted by the researcher. This factor is also important in deciding whether the data already available (secondary data) are to be used or the data not yet available (primary data) are to be collected.

2. Availability of funds: Availability of funds for the research project determines to a large extent the method to be used for the collection of data. When funds at the disposal of the researcher are very limited, he will have to select a comparatively cheaper method which may not be as efficient and effective as some other costly method. Finance, in fact, is a big constraint in practice and the researcher has to act within this limitation.

3. Time factor: Availability of time has also to be taken into account in deciding a particular method of data collection. Some methods take relatively more time, whereas with others the data can be collected in a comparatively shorter duration. The time at the disposal of the researcher, thus, affects the selection of the method by which the data are to be collected.

4. Precision required: Precision required is yet another important factor to be considered at the time of selecting the method of collection of data.

But one must always remember that each method of data collection has its uses and none is superior in all situations. For instance, telephone interview method may be considered appropriate (assuming telephone population) if funds are restricted, time is also restricted and the data is to be collected in respect of few items with or without a certain degree of precision. In case funds permit and more information is desired, personal interview method may be said to be relatively better. In case time is ample, funds are limited and much information is to be gathered with no precision, then mail-questionnaire method can be regarded more reasonable. When funds are ample, time is also ample and much information with no precision is to be collected, then either personal interview or the mail-questionnaire or the joint use of these two methods may be taken as an appropriate method of collecting data. Where a wide geographic area is to be covered, the use of mail-questionnaires supplemented by personal interviews will yield more reliable results per rupee spent than either method alone. The secondary data may be used in case the researcher finds them reliable, adequate and appropriate for his research. While studying motivating influences in market researches or studying people's attitudes in psychological/social surveys, we can resort to the use of one or more of the projective techniques stated earlier. Such techniques are of immense value in case the reason is obtainable from the respondent who knows the reason but does not want to admit it or the reason relates to some underlying psychological attitude and the respondent is not aware of it. But when the respondent knows the reason and can tell the same if asked, than a non-projective questionnaire, using direct questions, may yield satisfactory results even in case of attitude surveys. Since projective techniques are as yet in an early stage of development and with the validity of many of them remaining an open question, it is usually considered better to rely on the straight forward statistical methods with only supplementary use of projective techniques. Nevertheless, in pre-testing and in searching for hypotheses they can be highly valuable.

Thus, the most desirable approach with regard to the selection of the method depends on the nature of the particular problem and on the time and resources (money and personnel) available along with the desired degree of accuracy. But, over and above all this, much depends upon the ability and experience of the researcher. Dr. A.L. Bowley's remark in this context is very appropriate when he says that "in collection of statistical data common sense is the chief requisite and experience the chief teacher."

CASE STUDY METHOD

Meaning: The case study method is a very popular form of qualitative analysis and involves a careful and complete observation of a social unit, be that unit a person, a family, an institution, a cultural group or even the entire community. It is a method of study in depth rather than breadth. The case study places more emphasis on the full analysis of a limited number of events or conditions and their interrelations. The case study deals with the processes that take place and their interrelationship. Thus, case study is essentially an intensive investigation of the particular unit under consideration. The object of the case study method is to locate the factors that account for the behaviour-patterns of the given unit as an integrated totality.

According to H. Odum, "The case study method is a technique by which individual factor whether it be an institution or just an episode in the life of an individual or a group is analysed in its relationship to any other in the group."[5] Thus, a fairly exhaustive study of a person (as to what he does and has done, what he thinks he does and had done and what he expects to do and says he ought to do) or group is called a life or case history. Burgess has used the words "the social microscope" for the case study method."[6] Pauline V. Young describes case study as "a comprehensive study of a social unit be that unit a person, a group, a social institution, a district or a community."[7] In brief, we can say that case study method is a form of qualitative analysis where in careful and complete observation of an individual or a situation or an institution is done; efforts are made to study each and every aspect of the concerning unit in minute details and then from case data generalisations and inferences are drawn.

Characteristics: The important characteristics of the case study method are as under:

1. Under this method the researcher can take one single social unit or more of such units for his study purpose; he may even take a situation to study the same comprehensively.

2. Here the selected unit is studied intensively i.e., it is studied in minute details. Generally, the study extends over a long period of time to ascertain the natural history of the unit so as to obtain enough information for drawing correct inferences.

[5] H. Odum, *An Introduction to Social Research,* p. 229.

[6] Burgess, *Research Methods in Sociology,* p. 26 in Georges Gurvitch and W.E. Moore (Eds.) *Twentieth Century Sociology.*

[7] Pauline V. Young, *Scientific Social Surveys and Research,* p. 247.

3. In the context of this method we make complete study of the social unit covering all facets. Through this method we try to understand the complex of factors that are operative within a social unit as an integrated totality.

4 Under this method the approach happens to be qualitative and not quantitative. Mere quantitative information is not collected. Every possible effort is made to collect information concerning all aspects of life. As such, case study deepens our perception and gives us a clear insight into life. For instance, under this method we not only study how many crimes a man has done but shall peep into the factors that forced him to commit crimes when we are making a case study of a man as a criminal. The objective of the study may be to suggest ways to reform the criminal.

5. In respect of the case study method an effort is made to know the mutual inter-relationship of causal factors.

6. Under case study method the behaviour pattern of the concerning unit is studied directly and not by an indirect and abstract approach.

7. Case study method results in fruitful hypotheses along with the data which may be helpful in testing them, and thus it enables the generalised knowledge to get richer and richer. In its absence, generalised social science may get handicapped.

Evolution and scope: The case study method is a widely used systematic field research technique in sociology these days. The credit for introducing this method to the field of social investigation goes to Frederic Le Play who used it as a hand-maiden to statistics in his studies of family budgets. Herbert Spencer was the first to use case material in his comparative study of different cultures. Dr. William Healy resorted to this method in his study of juvenile delinquency, and considered it as a better method over and above the mere use of statistical data. Similarly, anthropologists, historians, novelists and dramatists have used this method concerning problems pertaining to their areas of interests. Even management experts use case study methods for getting clues to several management problems. In brief, case study method is being used in several disciplines. Not only this, its use is increasing day by day.

Assumptions: The case study method is based on several assumptions. The important assumptions may be listed as follows:

(i) The assumption of uniformity in the basic human nature in spite of the fact that human behaviour may vary according to situations.

(ii) The assumption of studying the natural history of the unit concerned.

(iii) The assumption of comprehensive study of the unit concerned.

Major phases involved: Major phases involved in case study are as follows:

(i) Recognition and determination of the status of the phenomenon to be investigated or the unit of attention.

(ii) Collection of data, examination and history of the given phenomenon.

(iii) Diagnosis and identification of causal factors as a basis for remedial or developmental treatment.

(iv) Application of remedial measures i.e., treatment and therapy (this phase is often characterised as case work).

(v) Follow-up programme to determine effectiveness of the treatment applied.

Advantages: There are several advantages of the case study method that follow from the various characteristics outlined above. Mention may be made here of the important advantages.

(i) Being an exhaustive study of a social unit, the case study method enables us to understand fully the behaviour pattern of the concerned unit. In the words of Charles Horton Cooley, "case study deepens our perception and gives us a clearer insight into life…. It gets at behaviour directly and not by an indirect and abstract approach."

(ii) Through case study a researcher can obtain a real and enlightened record of personal experiences which would reveal man's inner strivings, tensions and motivations that drive him to action along with the forces that direct him to adopt a certain pattern of behaviour.

(iii) This method enables the researcher to trace out the natural history of the social unit and its relationship with the social factors and the forces involved in its surrounding environment.

(iv) It helps in formulating relevant hypotheses along with the data which may be helpful in testing them. Case studies, thus, enable the generalised knowledge to get richer and richer.

(v) The method facilitates intensive study of social units which is generally not possible if we use either the observation method or the method of collecting information through schedules. This is the reason why case study method is being frequently used, particularly in social researches.

(vi) Information collected under the case study method helps a lot to the researcher in the task of constructing the appropriate questionnaire or schedule for the said task requires thorough knowledge of the concerning universe.

(vii) The researcher can use one or more of the several research methods under the case study method depending upon the prevalent circumstances. In other words, the use of different methods such as depth interviews, questionnaires, documents, study reports of individuals, letters, and the like is possible under case study method.

(viii) Case study method has proved beneficial in determining the nature of units to be studied along with the nature of the universe. This is the reason why at times the case study method is alternatively known as "mode of organising data".

(ix) This method is a means to well understand the past of a social unit because of its emphasis of historical analysis. Besides, it is also a technique to suggest measures for improvement in the context of the present environment of the concerned social units.

(x) Case studies constitute the perfect type of sociological material as they represent a real record of personal experiences which very often escape the attention of most of the skilled researchers using other techniques.

(xi) Case study method enhances the experience of the researcher and this in turn increases his analysing ability and skill.

(xii) This method makes possible the study of social changes. On account of the minute study of the different facets of a social unit, the researcher can well understand the social change then and now. This also facilitates the drawing of inferences and helps in maintaining the continuity of the research process. In fact, it may be considered the gateway to and at the same time the final destination of abstract knowledge.

(xiii) Case study techniques are indispensable for therapeutic and administrative purposes. They are also of immense value in taking decisions regarding several management problems. Case data are quite useful for diagnosis, therapy and other practical case problems.

Limitations: Important limitations of the case study method may as well be highlighted.

(i) Case situations are seldom comparable and as such the information gathered in case studies is often not comparable. Since the subject under case study tells history in his own words, logical concepts and units of scientific classification have to be read into it or out of it by the investigator.

(ii) Read Bain does not consider the case data as significant scientific data since they do not provide knowledge of the "impersonal, universal, non-ethical, non-practical, repetitive aspects of phenomena."[8] Real information is often not collected because the subjectivity of the researcher does enter in the collection of information in a case study.

(iii) The danger of false generalisation is always there in view of the fact that no set rules are followed in collection of the information and only few units are studied.

(iv) It consumes more time and requires lot of expenditure. More time is needed under case study method since one studies the natural history cycles of social units and that too minutely.

(v) The case data are often vitiated because the subject, according to Read Bain, may write what he thinks the investigator wants; and the greater the rapport, the more subjective the whole process is.

(vi) Case study method is based on several assumptions which may not be very realistic at times, and as such the usefulness of case data is always subject to doubt.

(vii) Case study method can be used only in a limited sphere., it is not possible to use it in case of a big society. Sampling is also not possible under a case study method.

(viii) Response of the investigator is an important limitation of the case study method. He often thinks that he has full knowledge of the unit and can himself answer about it. In case the same is not true, then consequences follow. In fact, this is more the fault of the researcher rather than that of the case method.

Conclusion: Despite the above stated limitations, we find that case studies are being undertaken in several disciplines, particularly in sociology, as a tool of scientific research in view of the several advantages indicated earlier. Most of the limitations can be removed if researchers are always conscious of these and are well trained in the modern methods of collecting case data and in the scientific techniques of assembling, classifying and processing the same. Besides, case studies, in modern times, can be conducted in such a manner that the data are amenable to quantification and statistical treatment. Possibly, this is also the reason why case studies are becoming popular day by day.

Question

1. Enumerate the different methods of collecting data. Which one is the most suitable for conducting enquiry regarding family welfare programme in India? Explain its merits and demerits.

[8] Pauline V. Young, *Scientific social surveys and research,* p. 262.

2. "It is never safe to take published statistics at their face value without knowing their meaning and limitations." Elucidate this statement by enumerating and explaining the various points which you would consider before using any published data. Illustrate your answer by examples wherever possible.

3. Examine the merits and limitations of the observation method in collecting material. Illustrate your answer with suitable examples.

4. Describe some of the major projective techniques and evaluate their significance as tools of scientific social research.

5. How does the case study method differ from the survey method? Analyse the merits and limitations of case study method in sociological research.

6. Clearly explain the difference between collection of data through questionnaires and schedules.

7. Discuss interview as a technique of data collection.

8. Write short notes on:
   (a) Depth interviews;
   (b) Important aspects of a questionnaire;
   (c) Pantry and store audits;
   (d) Thematic Apperception Test;
   (e) Holtzman Inkbolt Test.

9. What are the guiding considerations in the construction of questionnaire? Explain.

10. Critically examine the following:
    (i) Interviews introduce more bias than does the use of questionnaire.
    (ii) Data collection through projective techniques is considered relatively more reliable.
    (iii) In collection of statistical data commonsense is the chief requisite and experience the chief teacher.

11. Distinguish between an experiment and survey. Explain fully the survey method of research.

[M. Phi. (EAFM) Exam. 1987 Raj. Uni.]

12. "Experimental method of research is not suitable in management field." Discuss, what are the problems in the introduction of this research design in business organisation?

[M.B.A. (Part I) Exam. 1985 Raj. Uni.]

✓ Guidelines for Constructing Questionnaire/Schedule

The researcher must pay attention to the following points in constructing an appropriate and effective questionnaire or a schedule:

1. The researcher must keep in view the problem he is to study for it provides the starting point for developing the Questionnaire/Schedule. He must be clear about the various aspects of his research problem to be dealt with in the course of his research project.

2. Appropriate form of questions depends on the nature of information sought, the sampled respondents and the kind of analysis intended. The researcher must decide whether to use closed or open-ended question. Questions should be simple and must be constructed with a view to their forming a logical part of a well thought out tabulation plan. The units of enumeration should also be defined precisely so that they can ensure accurate and full information.

3. Rough draft of the Questionnaire/Schedule be prepared, giving due thought to the appropriate sequence of putting questions. Questionnaires or schedules previously drafted (if available) may as well be looked into at this stage.

4. Researcher must invariably re-examine, and in case of need may revise the rough draft for a better one. Technical defects must be minutely scrutinised and removed.

5. Pilot study should be undertaken for pre-testing the questionnaire. The questionnaire may be edited in the light of the results of the pilot study.

6. Questionnaire must contain simple but straight forward directions for the respondents so that they may not feel any difficulty in answering the questions.

Guidelines for Successful Interviewing

Interviewing is an art and one learns it by experience. However, the following points may be kept in view by an interviewer for eliciting the desired information:

1. Interviewer must plan in advance and should fully know the problem under consideration. He must choose a suitable time and place so that the interviewee may be at ease during the interview period. For this purpose some knowledge of the daily routine of the interviewee is essential.

2. Interviewer's approach must be friendly and informal. Initially friendly greetings in accordance with the cultural pattern of the interviewee should be exchanged and then the purpose of the interview should be explained.

3. All possible effort should be made to establish proper rapport with the interviewee; people are motivated to communicate when the atmosphere is favourable.

4. Interviewer must know that ability to listen with understanding, respect and curiosity is the gateway to communication, and hence must act accordingly during the interview. For all this, the interviewer must be intelligent and must be a man with self-restraint and self-discipline.

5. To the extent possible there should be a free-flowing interview and the questions must be well phrased in order to have full cooperation of the interviewee. But the interviewer must control the course of the interview in accordance with the objective of the study.

6. In case of big enquiries, where the task of collecting information is to be accomplished by several interviewers, there should be an interview guide to be observed by all so as to ensure reasonable uniformity in respect of all salient points in the study.

Difference Between Survey and Experiment

The following points are noteworthy so far as difference between survey and experiment is concerned:

(i) Surveys are conducted in case of descriptive research studies where as experiments are a part of experimental research studies.

(ii) Survey-type research studies usually have larger samples because the percentage of responses generally happens to be low, as low as 20 to 30%, especially in mailed questionnaire studies. Thus, the survey method gathers data from a relatively large number of cases at a particular time; it is essentially cross-sectional. As against this, experimental studies generally need small samples.

(iii) Surveys are concerned with describing, recording, analysing and interpreting conditions that either exist or existed. The researcher does not manipulate the variable or arrange for events to happen. Surveys are only concerned with conditions or relationships that exist, opinions that are held, processes that are going on, effects that are evident or trends that are developing. They are primarily concerned with the present but at times do consider past events and influences as they relate to current conditions. Thus, in surveys, variables that exist or have already occurred are selected and observed.

Experimental research provides a systematic and logical method for answering the question, "What will happen if this is done when certain variables are carefully controlled or manipulated?" In fact, deliberate manipulation is a part of the experimental method. In an experiment, the researcher measures the effects of an experiment which he conducts intentionally.

(iv) Surveys are usually appropriate in case of social and behavioural sciences (because many types of behaviour that interest the researcher cannot be arranged in a realistic setting) where as experiments are mostly an essential feature of physical and natural sciences.

(v) Surveys are an example of field research where as experiments generally constitute an example of laboratory research.

(vi) Surveys are concerned with hypothesis formulation and testing the analysis of the relationship between non-manipulated variables. Experimentation provides a method of hypothesis testing. After experimenters define a problem, they propose a hypothesis. They then test the hypothesis and confirm or disconfirm it in the light of the controlled variable relationship that they have observed. The confirmation or rejection is always stated in terms of probability rather than certainty. Experimentation, thus, is the most sophisticated, exacting and powerful method for discovering and developing an organised body of knowledge. The ultimate purpose of experimentation is to generalise the variable relationships so that they may be applied outside the laboratory to a wider population of interest.[*]

(vii) Surveys may either be census or sample surveys. They may also be classified as social surveys, economic surveys or public opinion surveys. Whatever be their type, the method of data collection happens to be either observation, or interview or questionnaire/opinionnaire or some projective technique(s). Case study method can as well be used. But in case of experiments, data are collected from several readings of experiments.

(viii) In case of surveys, research design must be rigid, must make enough provision for protection against bias and must maximise reliability as the aim happens to be to obtain complete and accurate information. Research design in case of experimental studies, apart reducing bias and ensuring reliability, must permit drawing inferences about causality.

(ix) Possible relationships between the data and the unknowns in the universe can be studied through surveys where as experiments are meant to determine such relationships.

(x) Causal analysis is considered relatively more important in experiments where as in most social and business surveys our interest lies in understanding and controlling relationships between variables and as such correlation analysis is relatively more important in surveys.

[*] John W. Best and James V. Kahn, "*Research in Education*", 5th ed., Prentice-Hall of India Pvt. Ltd., New Delhi, 1986, p.111.

7

Processing and Analysis of Data

The data, after collection, has to be processed and analysed in accordance with the outline laid down for the purpose at the time of developing the research plan. This is essential for a scientific study and for ensuring that we have all relevant data for making contemplated comparisons and analysis. Technically speaking, processing implies editing, coding, classification and tabulation of collected data so that they are amenable to analysis. The term analysis refers to the computation of certain measures along with searching for patterns of relationship that exist among data-groups. Thus, "in the process of analysis, relationships or differences supporting or conflicting with original or new hypotheses should be subjected to statistical tests of significance to determine with what validity data can be said to indicate any conclusions".[1] But there are persons (Selltiz, Jahoda and others) who do not like to make difference between processing and analysis. They opine that analysis of data in a general way involves a number of closely related operations which are performed with the purpose of summarising the collected data and organising these in such a manner that they answer the research question(s). We, however, shall prefer to observe the difference between the two terms as stated here in order to understand their implications more clearly.

PROCESSING OPERATIONS

With this brief introduction concerning the concepts of processing and analysis, we can now proceed with the explanation of all the processing operations.

1. Editing: Editing of data is a process of examining the collected raw data (specially in surveys) to detect errors and omissions and to correct these when possible. As a matter of fact, editing involves a careful scrutiny of the completed questionnaires and/or schedules. Editing is done to assure that the data are accurate, consistent with other facts gathered, uniformly entered, as completed as possible and have been well arranged to facilitate coding and tabulation.

With regard to points or stages at which editing should be done, one can talk of field editing and central editing. *Field editing* consists in the review of the reporting forms by the investigator for completing (translating or rewriting) what the latter has written in abbreviated and/or in illegible form

---

[1] G.B. Giles, *Marketing*, p. 44.

at the time of recording the respondents' responses. This type of editing is necessary in view of the fact that individual writing styles often can be difficult for others to decipher. This sort of editing should be done as soon as possible after the interview, preferably on the very day or on the next day. While doing field editing, the investigator must restrain himself and must not correct errors of omission by simply guessing what the informant would have said if the question had been asked.

Central editing should take place when all forms or schedules have been completed and returned to the office. This type of editing implies that all forms should get a thorough editing by a single editor in a small study and by a team of editors in case of a large inquiry. Editor(s) may correct the obvious errors such as an entry in the wrong place, entry recorded in months when it should have been recorded in weeks, and the like. In case of inappropriate on missing replies, the editor can sometimes determine the proper answer by reviewing the other information in the schedule. At times, the respondent can be contacted for clarification. The editor must strike out the answer if the same is inappropriate and he has no basis for determining the correct answer or the response. In such a case an editing entry of 'no answer' is called for. All the wrong replies, which are quite obvious, must be dropped from the final results, especially in the context of mail surveys.

Editors must keep in view several points while performing their work: (a) They should be familiar with instructions given to the interviewers and coders as well as with the editing instructions supplied to them for the purpose. (b) While crossing out an original entry for one reason or another, they should just draw a single line on it so that the same may remain legible. (c) They must make entries (if any) on the form in some distinctive colur and that too in a standardised form. (d) They should initial all answers which they change or supply. (e) Editor's initials and the date of editing should be placed on each completed form or schedule.

2. Coding: Coding refers to the process of assigning numerals or other symbols to answers so that responses can be put into a limited number of categories or classes. Such classes should be appropriate to the research problem under consideration. They must also possess the characteristic of exhaustiveness (i.e., there must be a class for every data item) and also that of mutual exclusively which means that a specific answer can be placed in one and only one cell in a given category set. Another rule to be observed is that of unidimensionality by which is meant that every class is defined in terms of only one concept.

Coding is necessary for efficient analysis and through it the several replies may be reduced to a small number of classes which contain the critical information required for analysis. Coding decisions should usually be taken at the designing stage of the questionnaire. This makes it possible to precode the questionnaire choices and which in turn is helpful for computer tabulation as one can straight forward key punch from the original questionnaires. But in case of hand coding some standard method may be used. One such standard method is to code in the margin with a coloured pencil. The other method can be to transcribe the data from the questionnaire to a coding sheet. Whatever method is adopted, one should see that coding errors are altogether eliminated or reduced to the minimum level.

3. Classification: Most research studies result in a large volume of raw data which must be reduced into homogeneous groups if we are to get meaningful relationships. This fact necessitates classification of data which happens to be the process of arranging data in groups or classes on the basis of common characteristics. Data having a common characteristic are placed in one class and in this way the entire data get divided into a number of groups or classes. Classification can be one of the following two types, depending upon the nature of the phenomenon involved:

(a) *Classification according to attributes:* As stated above, data are classified on the basis of common characteristics which can either be descriptive (such as literacy, sex, honesty, etc.) or numerical (such as weight, height, income, etc.). Descriptive characteristics refer to qualitative phenomenon which cannot be measured quantitatively; only their presence or absence in an individual item can be noticed. Data obtained this way on the basis of certain attributes are known as *statistics of attributes* and their classification is said to be classification according to attributes.

Such classification can be simple classification or manifold classification. In simple classification we consider only one attribute and divide the universe into two classes—one class consisting of items possessing the given attribute and the other class consisting of items which do not possess the given attribute. But in manifold classification we consider two or more attributes simultaneously, and divide that data into a number of classes (total number of classes of final order is given by 2^n, where n = number of attributes considered).[*] Whenever data are classified according to attributes, the researcher must see that the attributes are defined in such a manner that there is least possibility of any doubt/ambiguity concerning the said attributes.

(b) *Classification according to class-intervals:* Unlike descriptive characteristics, the numerical characteristics refer to quantitative phenomenon which can be measured through some statistical units. Data relating to income, production, age, weight, etc. come under this category. Such data are known as *statistics of variables* and are classified on the basis of class intervals. For instance, persons whose incomes, say, are within Rs 201 to Rs 400 can form one group, those whose incomes are within Rs 401 to Rs 600 can form another group and so on. In this way the entire data may be divided into a number of groups or classes or what are usually called, 'class-intervals.' Each group of class-interval, thus, has an upper limit as well as a lower limit which are known as class limits. The difference between the two class limits is known as class magnitude. We may have classes with equal class magnitudes or with unequal class magnitudes. The number of items which fall in a given class is known as the frequency of the given class. All the classes or groups, with their respective frequencies taken together and put in the form of a table, are described as group frequency distribution or simply frequency distribution. Classification according to class intervals usually involves the following three main problems:

(i) How may classes should be there? What should be their magnitudes?

There can be no specific answer with regard to the number of classes. The decision about this calls for skill and experience of the researcher. However, the objective should be to display the data in such a way as to make it meaningful for the analyst. Typically, we may have 5 to 15 classes. With regard to the second part of the question, we can say that, to the extent possible, class-intervals should be of equal magnitudes, but in some cases unequal magnitudes may result in better classification. Hence the

---

Classes of the final order are those classes developed on the basis of 'n' attributes considered. For example, if attributes A and B are studied and their presence is denoted by A and B respectively and absence by a and b respectively, then we have four classes of final order viz., class AB, class Ab, class aB, and class ab.

researcher's objective judgement plays an important part in this connection. Multiples of 2, 5 and 10 are generally preferred while determining class magnitudes. Some statisticians adopt the following formula, suggested by H.A. Sturges, determining the size of class interval:

$$i = R/(1 + 3.3 \log N)$$

where

i = size of class interval;

R = Range (i.e., difference between the values of the largest item and smallest item among the given items);

N = Number of items to be grouped.

It should also be kept in mind that in case one or two or very few items have very high or very low values, one may use what are known as open-ended intervals in the overall frequency distribution. Such intervals may be expressed like under Rs 500 or Rs 10001 and over. Such intervals are generally not desirable, but often cannot be avoided. The researcher must always remain conscious of this fact while deciding the issue of the total number of class intervals in which the data are to be classified.

(ii) How to choose class limits?

While choosing class limits, the researcher must take into consideration the criterion that the mid-point (generally worked out first by taking the sum of the upper limit and lower limit of a class and then divide this sum by 2) of a class-interval and the actual average of items of that class interval should remain as close to each other as possible. Consistent with this, the class limits should be located at multiples of 2, 5, 10, 20, 100 and such other figures. Class limits may generally be stated in any of the following forms:

Exclusive type class intervals: They are usually stated as follows:

10–20

20–30

30–40

40–50

The above intervals should be read as under:

10 and under 20

20 and under 30

30 and under 40

40 and under 50

Thus, under the exclusive type class intervals, the items whose values are equal to the upper limit of a class are grouped in the next higher class. For example, an item whose value is exactly 30 would be put in 30–40 class interval and not in 20–30 class interval. In simple words, we can say that under exclusive type class intervals, the upper limit of a class interval is excluded and items with values less than the upper limit (but not less than the lower limit) are put in the given class interval.

Inclusive type class intervals: They are usually stated as follows:

11–20

21–30

31–40

41–50

In inclusive type class intervals the upper limit of a class interval is also included in the concerning class interval. Thus, an item whose value is 20 will be put in 11–20 class interval. The stated upper limit of the class interval 11–20 is 20 but the real limit is 20.99999 and as such 11–20 class interval really means 11 and under 21.

When the phenomenon under consideration happens to be a discrete one (i.e., can be measured and stated only in integers), then we should adopt inclusive type classification. But when the phenomenon happens to be a continuous one capable of being measured in fractions as well, we can use exclusive type class intervals.*

(iii) How to determine the frequency of each class?

This can be done either by tally sheets or by mechanical aids. Under the technique of tally sheet, the class-groups are written on a sheet of paper (commonly known as the tally sheet) and for each item a stroke (usually a small vertical line) is marked against the class group in which it falls. The general practice is that after every four small vertical lines in a class group, the fifth line for the item falling in the same group, is indicated as horizontal line through the said four lines and the resulting flower (IIII) represents five items. All this facilitates the counting of items in each one of the class groups. An illustrative tally sheet can be shown as under:

Table 7.1: An Illustrative Tally Sheet for Determining the Number of 70 Families in Different Income Groups

Income groups (Rupees)	Tally mark	Number of families or (Class frequency)
Below 400	IHI IHI III	13
401–800	IHI IHI IHI IHI	20
801–1200	IHI IHI II	12
1201–1600	IHI IHI IHI III	18
1601 and above	IHI II	7
Total		70

Alternatively, class frequencies can be determined, specially in case of large inquires and surveys, by mechanical aids i.e., with the help of machines viz., sorting machines that are available for the purpose. Some machines are hand operated, whereas other work with electricity. There are machines

* The stated limits of class intervals are different than true limits. We should use true or real limits keeping in view the nature of the given phenomenon.

which can sort out cards at a speed of something like 25000 cards per hour. This method is fast but expensive.

4. Tabulation: When a mass of data has been assembled, it becomes necessary for the researcher to arrange the same in some kind of concise and logical order. This procedure is referred to as tabulation. Thus, tabulation is the process of summarising raw data and displaying the same in compact form (i.e., in the form of statistical tables) for further analysis. In a broader sense, tabulation is an orderly arrangement of data in columns and rows.

Tabulation is essential because of the following reasons.

1. It conserves space and reduces explanatory and descriptive statement to a minimum.
2. It facilitates the process of comparison.
3. It facilitates the summation of items and the detection of errors and omissions.
4. It provides a basis for various statistical computations.

Tabulation can be done by hand or by mechanical or electronic devices. The choice depends on the size and type of study, cost considerations, time pressures and the availaibility of tabulating machines or computers. In relatively large inquiries, we may use mechanical or computer tabulation if other factors are favourable and necessary facilities are available. Hand tabulation is usually preferred in case of small inquiries where the number of questionnaires is small and they are of relatively short length. Hand tabulation may be done using the direct tally, the list and tally or the card sort and count methods. When there are simple codes, it is feasible to tally directly from the questionnaire. Under this method, the codes are written on a sheet of paper, called tally sheet, and for each response a stroke is marked against the code in which it falls. Usually after every four strokes against a particular code, the fifth response is indicated by drawing a diagonal or horizontal line through the strokes. These groups of five are easy to count and the data are sorted against each code conveniently. In the listing method, the code responses may be transcribed onto a large work-sheet, allowing a line for each questionnaire. This way a large number of questionnaires can be listed on one work sheet. Tallies are then made for each question. The card sorting method is the most flexible hand tabulation. In this method the data are recorded on special cards of convenient size and shape with a series of holes. Each hole stands for a code and when cards are stacked, a needle passes through particular hole representing a particular code. These cards are then separated and counted. In this way frequencies of various codes can be found out by the repetition of this technique. We can as well use the mechanical devices or the computer facility for tabulation purpose in case we want quick results, our budget permits their use and we have a large volume of straight forward tabulation involving a number of cross-breaks.

Tabulation may also be classified as simple and complex tabulation. The former type of tabulation gives information about one or more groups of independent questions, whereas the latter type of tabulation shows the division of data in two or more categories and as such is deigned to give information concerning one or more sets of inter-related questions. Simple tabulation generally results in one-way tables which supply answers to questions about one characteristic of data only. As against this, complex tabulation usually results in two-way tables (which give information about two inter-related characteristics of data), three-way tables (giving information about three interrelated characteristics of data) or still higher order tables, also known as manifold tables, which supply information about several interrelated characteristics of data. Two-way tables, three-way tables or manifold tables are all examples of what is sometimes described as cross tabulation.

Generally accepted principles of tabulation: Such principles of tabulation, particularly of constructing statistical tables, can be briefly states as follows:[*]

1. Every table should have a clear, concise and adequate title so as to make the table intelligible without reference to the text and this title should always be placed just above the body of the table.

2. Every table should be given a distinct number to facilitate easy reference.

3. The column headings (captions) and the row headings (stubs) of the table should be clear and brief.

4. The units of measurement under each heading or sub-heading must always be indicated.

5. Explanatory footnotes, if any, concerning the table should be placed directly beneath the table, along with the reference symbols used in the table.

6. Source or sources from where the data in the table have been obtained must be indicated just below the table.

7. Usually the columns are separated from one another by lines which make the table more readable and attractive. Lines are always drawn at the top and bottom of the table and below the captions.

8. There should be thick lines to separate the data under one class from the data under another class and the lines separating the sub-divisions of the classes should be comparatively thin lines.

9. The columns may be numbered to facilitate reference.

10. Those columns whose data are to be compared should be kept side by side. Similarly, percentages and/or averages must also be kept close to the data.

11. It is generally considered better to approximate figures before tabulation as the same would reduce unnecessary details in the table itself.

12. In order to emphasise the relative significance of certain categories, different kinds of type, spacing and indentations may be used.

13. It is important that all column figures be properly aligned. Decimal points and (+) or (−) signs should be in perfect alignment.

14. Abbreviations should be avoided to the extent possible and ditto marks should not be used in the table.

15. Miscellaneous and exceptional items, if any, should be usually placed in the last row of the table.

16. Table should be made as logical, clear, accurate and simple as possible. If the data happen to be very large, they should not be crowded in a single table for that would make the table unwieldy and inconvenient.

17. Total of rows should normally be placed in the extreme right column and that of columns should be placed at the bottom.

---

[*] All these points constitute the characteristics of a good table.

18. The arrangement of the categories in a table may be chronological, geographical, alphabetical or according to magnitude to facilitate comparison. Above all, the table must suit the needs and requirements of an investigation.

SOME PROBLEMS IN PROCESSING

We can take up the following two problems of processing the data for analytical purposes:

(a) *The problem concerning "Don't know" (or DK) responses:* While processing the data, the researcher often comes across some responses that are difficult to handle. One category of such responses may be 'Don't Know Response' or simply DK response. When the DK response group is small, it is of little significance. But when it is relatively big, it becomes a matter of major concern in which case the question arises: Is the question which elicited DK response useless? The answer depends on two points viz., the respondent actually may not know the answer or the researcher may fail in obtaining the appropriate information. In the first case the concerned question is said to be alright and DK response is taken as legitimate DK response. But in the second case, DK response is more likely to be a failure of the questioning process.

How DK responses are to be dealt with by researchers? The best way is to design better type of questions. Good rapport of interviewers with respondents will result in minimising DK responses. But what about the DK responses that have already taken place? One way to tackle this issue is to estimate the allocation of DK answers from other data in the questionnaire. The other way is to keep DK responses as a separate category in tabulation where we can consider it as a separate reply category if DK responses happen to be legitimate, otherwise we should let the reader make his own decision. Yet another way is to assume that DK responses occur more or less randomly and as such we may distribute them among the other answers in the ratio in which the latter have occurred. Similar results will be achieved if all DK replies are excluded from tabulation and that too without inflating the actual number of other responses.

(b) *Use or percentages:* Percentages are often used in data presentation for they simplify numbers, reducing all of them to a 0 to 100 range. Through the use of percentages, the data are reduced in the standard form with base equal to 100 which fact facilitates relative comparisons. While using percentages, the following rules should be kept in view by researchers:

1. Two or more percentages must not be averaged unless each is weighted by the group size from which it has been derived.

2. Use of too large percentages should be avoided, since a large percentage is difficult to understand and tends to confuse, defeating the very purpose for which percentages are used.

3. Percentages hide the base from which they have been computed. If this is not kept in view, the real differences may not be correctly read.

4. Percentage decreases can never exceed 100 per cent and as such for calculating the percentage of decrease, the higher figure should invariably be taken as the base.

5. Percentages should generally be worked out in the direction of the causal-factor in case of two-dimension tables and for this purpose we must select the more significant factor out of the two given factors as the causal factor.

ELEMENTS/TYPES OF ANALYSIS

As stated earlier, by analysis we mean the computation of certain indices or measures along with searching for patterns of relationship that exist among the data groups. Analysis, particularly in case of survey or experimental data, involves estimating the values of unknown parameters of the population and testing of hypotheses for drawing inferences. Analysis may, therefore, be categorised as descriptive analysis and inferential analysis (Inferential analysis is often known as statistical analysis). *"Descriptive analysis* is largely the study of distributions of one variable. This study provides us with profiles of companies, work groups, persons and other subjects on any of a multiple of characteristics such as size. Composition, efficiency, preferences, etc."[2]. this sort of analysis may be in respect of one variable (described as unidimensional analysis), or in respect of two variables (described as bivariate analysis) or in respect of more than two variables (described as multivariate analysis). In this context we work out various measures that show the size and shape of a distribution(s) along with the study of measuring relationships between two or more variables.

We may as well talk of correlation analysis and causal analysis. *Correlation analysis* studies the joint variation of two or more variables for determining the amount of correlation between two or more variables. *Causal analysis* is concerned with the study of how one or more variables affect changes in another variable. It is thus a study of functional relationships existing between two or more variables. This analysis can be termed as regression analysis. Causal analysis is considered relatively more important in experimental researches, whereas in most social and business researches our interest lies in understanding and controlling relationships between variables then with determining causes *per se* and as such we consider correlation analysis as relatively more important.

In modern times, with the availability of computer facilities, there has been a rapid development of *multivariate analysis* which may be defined as "all statistical methods which simultaneously analyse more than two variables on a sample of observations"[3]. Usually the following analyses[*] are involved when we make a reference of multivariate analysis:

(a) *Multiple regression analysis:* This analysis is adopted when the researcher has one dependent variable which is presumed to be a function of two or more independent variables. The objective of this analysis is to make a prediction about the dependent variable based on its covariance with all the concerned independent variables.

(b) *Multiple discriminant analysis:* This analysis is appropriate when the researcher has a single dependent variable that cannot be measured, but can be classified into two or more groups on the basis of some attribute. The object of this analysis happens to be to predict an entity's possibility of belonging to a particular group based on several predictor variables.

(c) *Multivariate analysis of variance (or multi-ANOVA)*: This analysis is an extension of two-way ANOVA, wherein the ratio of among group variance to within group variance is worked out on a set of variables.

(d) *Canonical analysis:* This analysis can be used in case of both measurable and non-measurable variables for the purpose of simultaneously predicting a set of dependent variables from their joint covariance with a set of independent variables.

[2] C. William Emory, *Business Research Methods,* p. 356.

[3] Jagdish N. Sheth, "The Multivariate Revolution in Marketing Research", *Journal of Marketing,* Vol. 35, No. 1 (Jan. 1971), pp. 13–19.

[*] Readers are referred to standard texts for more details about these analyses.

Inferential analysis is concerned with the various tests of significance for testing hypotheses in order to determine with what validity data can be said to indicate some conclusion or conclusions. It is also concerned with the estimation of population values. It is mainly on the basis of inferential analysis that the task of interpretation (i.e., the task of drawing inferences and conclusions) is performed.

STATISTICS IN RESEARCH

The role of statistics in research is to function as a tool in designing research, analysing its data and drawing conclusions therefrom. Most research studies result in a large volume of raw data which must be suitably reduced so that the same can be read easily and can be used for further analysis. Clearly the science of statistics cannot be ignored by any research worker, even though he may not have occasion to use statistical methods in all their details and ramifications. Classification and tabulation, as stated earlier, achieve this objective to some extent, but we have to go a step further and develop certain indices or measures to summarise the collected/classified data. Only after this we can adopt the process of generalisation from small groups (i.e., samples) to population. If fact, there are two major areas of statistics viz., descriptive statistics and inferential statistics. *Descriptive statistics* concern the development of certain indices from the raw data, whereas inferential statistics concern with the process of generalisation. *Inferential statistics* are also known as sampling statistics and are mainly concerned with two major type of problems: (i) the estimation of population parameters, and (ii) the testing of statistical hypotheses.

The important statistical measures[*] that are used to summarise the survey/research data are:

(1) measures of central tendency or statistical averages; (2) measures of dispersion; (3) measures of asymmetry (skewness); (4) measures of relationship; and (5) other measures.

Amongst the measures of central tendency, the three most important ones are the arithmetic average or mean, median and mode. Geometric mean and harmonic mean are also sometimes used.

From among the measures of dispersion, variance, and its square root—the standard deviation are the most often used measures. Other measures such as mean deviation, range, etc. are also used. For comparison purpose, we use mostly the coefficient of standard deviation or the coefficient of variation.

In respect of the measures of skewness and kurtosis, we mostly use the first measure of skewness based on mean and mode or on mean and median. Other measures of skewness, based on quartiles or on the methods of moments, are also used sometimes. Kurtosis is also used to measure the peakedness of the curve of the frequency distribution.

Amongst the measures of relationship, Karl Pearson's coefficient of correlation is the frequently used measure in case of statistics of variables, whereas Yule's coefficient of association is used in case of statistics of attributes. Multiple correlation coefficient, partial correlation coefficient, regression analysis, etc., are other important measures often used by a researcher.

Index numbers, analysis of time series, coefficient of contingency, etc., are other measures that may as well be used by a researcher, depending upon the nature of the problem under study.

We give below a brief outline of some important measures (our of the above listed measures) often used in the context of research studies.

---

[*] One may read any standard text book on statistical methods for details about these measures.

MEASURES OF CENTRAL TENDENCY

Measures of central tendency (or statistical averages) tell us the point about which items have a tendency to cluster. Such a measure is considered as the most representative figure for the entire mass of data. Measure of central tendency is also known as statistical average. Mean, median and mode are the most popular averages. *Mean,* also known as arithmetic average, is the most common measure of central tendency and may be defined as the value which we get by dividing the total of the values of various given items in a series by the total number of items. we can work it out as under:

$$\text{Mean (or } \overline{X})^* = \frac{\sum X_i}{n} = \frac{X_1 + X_2 + \ldots + X_n}{n}$$

where $\overline{X}$ = The symbol we use for mean (pronounced as X bar)

$\sum$ = Symbol for summation

X_i = Value of the ith item X, $i = 1, 2, \ldots, n$

n = total number of items

In case of a frequency distribution, we can work out mean in this way:

$$\overline{X} = \frac{\sum f_i X_i}{\sum f_i} = \frac{f_1 X_1 + f_2 X_2 + \ldots + f_n X_n}{f_1 + f_2 + \ldots + f_n = n}$$

Sometimes, instead of calculating the simple mean, as stated above, we may workout the weighted mean for a realistic average. The weighted mean can be worked out as follows:

$$\overline{X}_w = \frac{\sum w_i X_i}{\sum w_i}$$

where $\overline{X}_w$ = Weighted item

w_i = weight of ith item X

X_i = value of the ith item X

Mean is the simplest measurement of central tendency and is a widely used measure. Its chief use consists in summarising the essential features of a series and in enabling data to be compared. It is amenable to algebraic treatment and is used in further statistical calculations. It is a relatively stable measure of central tendency. But it suffers from some limitations viz., it is unduly affected by extreme items; it may not coincide with the actual value of an item in a series, and it may lead to wrong impressions, particularly when the item values are not given with the average. However, mean is better than other averages, specially in economic and social studies where direct quantitative measurements are possible.

Median is the value of the middle item of series when it is arranged in ascending or descending order of magnitude. It divides the series into two halves; in one half all items are less than median, whereas in the other half all items have values higher than median. If the values of the items arranged in the ascending order are: 60, 74, 80, 90, 95, 100, then the value of the 4th item viz., 88 is the value of median. We can also write thus:

---

* If we use assumed average A, then mean would be worked out as under:

$$\overline{X} = A + \frac{\sum (X_i - A)}{n} \quad \text{or} \quad \overline{X} = A + \frac{\sum f_i (X_i - A)}{\sum f_i}$$, in case of frequency distribution. This is also known as short cut

method of finding $\overline{X}$.

$$\text{Median } (M) = \text{Value of } \left(\frac{n+1}{2}\right)\text{th item}$$

Median is a positional average and is used only in the context of qualitative phenomena, for example, in estimating intelligence, etc., which are often encountered in sociological fields. Median is not useful where items need to be assigned relative importance and weights. It is not frequently used in sampling statistics.

Mode is the most commonly or frequently occurring value in a series. The mode in a distribution is that item around which there is maximum concentration. In general, mode is the size of the item which has the maximum frequency, but at items such an item may not be mode on account of the effect of the frequencies of the neighbouring items. Like median, mode is a positional average and is not affected by the values of extreme items. it is, therefore, useful in all situations where we want to eliminate the effect of extreme variations. Mode is particularly useful in the study of popular sizes. For example, a manufacturer of shoes is usually interested in finding out the size most in demand so that he may manufacture a larger quantity of that size. In other words, he wants a modal size to be determined for median or mean size would not serve his purpose. but there are certain limitations of mode as well. For example, it is not amenable to algebraic treatment and sometimes remains indeterminate when we have two or more model values in a series. It is considered unsuitable in cases where we want to give relative importance to items under consideration.

Geometric mean is also useful under certain conditions. It is defined as the nth root of the product of the values of n times in a given series. Symbolically, we can put it thus:

$$\text{Geometric mean (or G.M.)} = \sqrt[n]{\pi X_i}$$

$$= \sqrt[n]{X_1 \cdot X_2 \cdot X_3 \dots X_n}$$

where

      G.M. = geometric mean,

        n = number of items.

        X_i = ith value of the variable X

        π = conventional product notation

For instance, the geometric mean of the numbers, 4, 6, and 9 is worked out as

$$\text{G.M.} = \sqrt[3]{4.6.9}$$

$$= 6$$

The most frequently used application of this average is in the determination of average per cent of change i.e., it is often used in the preparation of index numbers or when we deal in ratios.

Harmonic mean is defined as the reciprocal of the average of reciprocals of the values of items of a series. Symbolically, we can express it as under:

$$\text{Harmonic mean (H. M.)} = \text{Rec.}\frac{\sum \text{Rec} X_i}{n}$$

$$= \text{Rec.}\frac{\text{Rec.} X_1 + \text{Rec.} X_2 + \dots + \text{Rec.} X_n}{n}$$

where

        H.M. = Harmonic mean

       Rec. = Reciprocal

        X_i = ith value of the variable X

        n = number of items

For instance, the harmonic mean of the numbers 4, 5, and 10 is worked out as

$$\text{H. M.} = \text{Rec} \frac{1/4 + 1/5 + 1/10}{3} = \text{Rec} \frac{\frac{15 + 12 + 6}{60}}{3}$$

$$= \text{Rec}\left(\frac{33}{60} \times \frac{1}{3}\right) = \frac{60}{11} = 5.45$$

Harmonic mean is of limited application, particularly in cases where time and rate are involved. The harmonic mean gives largest weight to the smallest item and smallest weight to the largest item. As such it is used in cases like time and motion study where time is variable and distance constant.

From what has been stated above, we can say that there are several types of statistical averages. Researcher has to make a choice for some average. There are no hard and fast rules for the selection of a particular average in statistical analysis for the selection of an average mostly depends on the nature, type of objectives of the research study. One particular type of average cannot be taken as appropriate for all types of studies. The chief characteristics and the limitations of the various averages must be kept in view; discriminate use of average is very essential for sound statistical analysis.

MEASURES OF DISPERSION

An averages can represent a series only as best as a single figure can, but it certainly cannot reveal the entire story of any phenomenon under study. Specially it fails to give any idea about the scatter of the values of items of a variable in the series around the true value of average. In order to measure this scatter, statistical devices called measures of dispersion are calculated. Important measures of dispersion are (a) range, (b) mean deviation, and (c) standard deviation.

(a) *Range* is the simplest possible measure of dispersion and is defined as the difference between the values of the extreme items of a series. Thus,

$$\text{Range} = \left(\begin{array}{c}\text{Highest value of an}\\\text{item in a series}\end{array}\right) - \left(\begin{array}{c}\text{Lowest value of an}\\\text{item in a series}\end{array}\right)$$

The utility of range is that it gives an idea of the variability very quickly, but the drawback is that range is affected very greatly by fluctuations of sampling. Its value is never stable, being based on only two values of the variable. As such, range is mostly used as a rough measure of variability and is not considered as an appropriate measure in serious research studies.

(b) *Mean deviation* is the average of difference of the values of items from some average of the series. Such a difference is technically described as deviation. In calculating mean deviation we ignore the minus sign of deviations while taking their total for obtaining the mean deviation. Mean deviation is, thus, obtained as under:

Mean deviation from mean $\left(\delta_{\overline{x}}\right) = \dfrac{\Sigma \left| X_i - \overline{X} \right|}{n}$, if deviations, $\left| X_i - \overline{X} \right|$, are obtained from

or   arithmetic average.

Mean deviation from median $\left(\delta_m\right) = \dfrac{\Sigma \left| X_i - M \right|}{n}$, if deviations, $\left| X_i - M \right|$, are obtained

or   from median

Mean deviation from mode $\left(\delta_z\right) = \dfrac{\Sigma \left| X_i - Z \right|}{n}$, if deviations, $\left| X_i - Z \right|$, are obtained from

mode.

where δ = Symbol for mean deviation (pronounced as delta);

       X_i = ith values of the variable X;

       n = number of items;

       $\overline{X}$ = Arithmetic average;

       M = Median;

       Z = Mode.

When mean deviation is divided by the average used in finding out the mean deviation itself, the resulting quantity is described as the *coefficient of mean deviation*. Coefficient of mean deviation is a relative measure of dispersion and is comparable to similar measure of other series. Mean deviation and its coefficient are used in statistical studies for judging the variability, and thereby render the study of central tendency of a series more precise by throwing light on the typicalness of an average. It is a better measure of variability than range as it takes into consideration the values of all items of a series. Even then it is not a frequently used measure as it is not amenable to algebraic process.

(c) *Standard deviation* is most widely used measure of dispersion of a series and is commonly denoted by the symbol ' σ ' (pronounced as sigma). Standard deviation is defined as the square-root of the average of squares of deviations, when such deviations for the values of individual items in a series are obtained from the arithmetic average. It is worked out as under:

$$\text{Standard deviation}^* (\sigma) = \sqrt{\dfrac{\Sigma \left(X_i - \overline{X} \right)^2}{n}}$$

---

*If we use assumed average, A, in place of $\overline{X}$ while finding deviations, then standard deviation would be worked out as under:

$$\sigma = \sqrt{\dfrac{\Sigma (X_i - A)^2}{n} - \left(\dfrac{\Sigma (X_i - A)}{n} \right)^2}$$

Or

$$\sigma = \sqrt{\dfrac{\Sigma f_i (X_i - A)^2}{\Sigma f_i} - \left(\dfrac{\Sigma f_i (X_i - A)}{\Sigma f_i} \right)^2}, \text{ in case of frequency distribution.}$$

This is also known as the short-cut method of finding σ.

Or

$$\text{Standard deviation}(\sigma) = \sqrt{\frac{\sum f_i\left(X_i - \overline{X}\right)^2}{\sum f_i}} \text{ , in case of frequency distribution}$$

where f_i means the frequency of the ith item.

When we divide the standard deviation by the arithmetic average of the series, the resulting quantity is known as *coefficient of standard deviation which* happens to be a relative measure and is often used for comparing with similar measure of other series. When this coefficient of standard deviation is multiplied by 100, the resulting figure is known as *coefficient of variation*. Sometimes, we work out the square of standard deviation, known as *variance*, which is frequently used in the context of analysis of variation.

The standard deviation (along with several related measures like variance, coefficient of variation, etc.) is used mostly in research studies and is regarded as a very satisfactory measure of dispersion in a series. It is amenable to mathematical manipulation because the algebraic signs are not ignored in its calculation (as we ignore in case of mean deviation). It is less affected by fluctuations of sampling. These advantages make standard deviation and its coefficient a very popular measure of the scatteredness of a series. It is popularly used in the context of estimation and testing of hypotheses.

MEASURES OF ASYMMETRY (SKEWNESS)

When the distribution of item in a series happens to be perfectly symmetrical, we then have the following type of curve for the distribution:

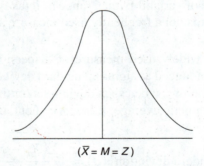

$(\overline{X} = M = Z)$

Curve showing no skewness in which case we have $\overline{X} = M = Z$

Fig. 7.1

Such a curve is technically described as a *normal curve* and the relating distribution as normal distribution. Such a curve is perfectly bell shaped curve in which case the value of $\overline{X}$ or M or Z is just the same and skewness is altogether absent. But if the curve is distorted (whether on the right side or on the left side), we have asymmetrical distribution which indicates that there is skewness. If the curve is distorted on the right side, we have positive skewness but when the curve is distorted towards left, we have negative skewness as shown here under:

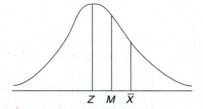

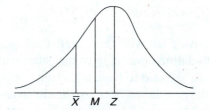

Curve showing positive skewness
In case of positive skewness we have:
$Z < M < \overline{X}$

Curve showing negative skewness
In case of negative skewness we have:
$\overline{X} < M < Z$

Fig. 7.2

Skewness is, thus, a measure of asymmetry and shows the manner in which the items are clustered around the average. In a symmetrical distribution, the items show a perfect balance on either side of the mode, but in a skew distribution the balance is thrown to one side. The amount by which the balance exceeds on one side measures the skewness of the series. The difference between the mean, median or the mode provides an easy way of expressing skewness in a series. In case of positive skewness, we have $Z < M < \overline{X}$ and in case of negative skewness we have $\overline{X} < M < Z$. Usually we measure skewness in this way:

Skewness = $\overline{X} - Z$ and its coefficient (j) is worked

out as $j = \dfrac{\overline{X} - Z}{\sigma}$

In case Z is not well defined, then we work out skewness as under:

Skewness = $3(\overline{X} - M)$ and its coefficient (j) is worked

out as $j = \dfrac{3(\overline{X} - M)}{\sigma}$

The significance of skewness lies in the fact that through it one can study the formation of series and can have the idea about the shape of the curve, whether normal or otherwise, when the items of a given series are plotted on a graph.

Kurtosis is the measure of flat-toppedness of a curve. A bell shaped curve or the normal curve is Mesokurtic because it is kurtic in the centre; but if the curve is relatively more peaked than the normal curve, it is called Leptokurtic whereas a curve is more flat than the normal curve, it is called Platykurtic. In brief, Kurtosis is the humpedness of the curve and points to the nature of distribution of items in the middle of a series.

It may be pointed out here that knowing the shape of the distribution curve is crucial to the use of statistical methods in research analysis since most methods make specific assumptions about the nature of the distribution curve.

MEASURES OF RELATIONSHIP

So far we have dealt with those statistical measures that we use in context of univariate population i.e., the population consisting of measurement of only one variable. But if we have the data on two variables, we are said to have a bivariate population and if the data happen to be on more than two variables, the population is known as multivariate population. If for every measurement of a variable, X, we have corresponding value of a second variable, Y, the resulting pairs of values are called a bivariate population. In addition, we may also have a corresponding value of the third variable, Z, or the forth variable, W, and so on, the resulting pairs of values are called a multivariate population. In case of bivariate or multivariate populations, we often wish to know the relation of the two and/or more variables in the data to one another. We may like to know, for example, whether the number of hours students devote for studies is somehow related to their family income, to age, to sex or to similar other factor. There are several methods of determining the relationship between variables, but no method can tell us for certain that a correlation is indicative of causal relationship. Thus we have to answer two types of questions in bivariate or multivariate populations viz.,

(i) Does there exist association or correlation between the two (or more) variables? If yes, of what degree?

(ii) Is there any cause and effect relationship between the two variables in case of the bivariate population or between one variable on one side and two or more variables on the other side in case of multivariate population? If yes, of what degree and in which direction?

The first question is answered by the use of correlation technique and the second question by the technique of regression. There are several methods of applying the two techniques, but the important ones are as under:

In case of bivariate population: Correlation can be studied through (a) cross tabulation; (b) Charles Spearman's coefficient of correlation; (c) Karl Pearson's coefficient of correlation; whereas cause and effect relationship can be studied through simple regression equations.

In case of multivariate population: Correlation can be studied through (a) coefficient of multiple correlation; (b) coefficient of partial correlation; whereas cause and effect relationship can be studied through multiple regression equations.

We can now briefly take up the above methods one by one.

Cross tabulation approach is specially useful when the data are in nominal form. Under it we classify each variable into two or more categories and then cross classify the variables in these sub-categories. Then we look for interactions between them which may be symmetrical, reciprocal or asymmetrical. A symmetrical relationship is one in which the two variables vary together, but we assume that neither variable is due to the other. A reciprocal relationship exists when the two variables mutually influence or reinforce each other. Asymmetrical relationship is said to exist if one variable (the independent variable) is responsible for another variable (the dependent variable). The cross classification procedure begins with a two-way table which indicates whether there is or there is not an interrelationship between the variables. This sort of analysis can be further elaborated in which case a third factor is introduced into the association through cross-classifying the three variables. By doing so we find conditional relationship in which factor X appears to affect factor Y only when factor Z is held constant. The correlation, if any, found through this approach is not considered a very powerful form of statistical correlation and accordingly we use some other methods when data happen to be either ordinal or interval or ratio data.

Charles Spearman's coefficient of correlation (*or rank correlation*) is the technique of determining the degree of correlation between two variables in case of ordinal data where ranks are given to the different values of the variables. The main objective of this coefficient is to determine the extent to which the two sets of ranking are similar or dissimilar. This coefficient is determined as under:

$$\text{Spearman's coefficient of correlation (or } r_s) = 1 - \left[\frac{6\sum d_i^2}{n(n^2 - 1)} \right]$$

where d_i = difference between ranks of ith pair of the two variables;

n = number of pairs of observations.

As rank correlation is a non-parametric technique for measuring relationship between paired observations of two variables when data are in the ranked form, we have dealt with this technique in greater details later on in the book in chapter entitled 'Hypotheses Testing II (Non-parametric tests)'.

Karl Pearson's coefficient of correlation (or simple correlation) is the most widely used method of measuring the degree of relationship between two variables. This coefficient assumes the following:

   (i)   that there is linear relationship between the two variables;

   (ii)   that the two variables are casually related which means that one of the variables is independent and the other one is dependent; and

   (iii)   a large number of independent causes are operating in both variables so as to produce a normal distribution.

Karl Pearson's coefficient of correlation can be worked out thus.

$$\text{Karl Pearson's coefficient of correlation (or } r)^* = \frac{\sum \left(X_i - \bar{X}\right)\left(Y_i - \bar{Y}\right)}{n \cdot \sigma_X \cdot \sigma_Y}$$

---

*Alternatively, the formula can be written as:

$$r = \frac{\sum \left(X_i - \bar{X}\right)\left(Y_i - \bar{Y}\right)}{\sqrt{\sum \left(X_i - \bar{X}\right)^2 \cdot \sum \left(Y_i - \bar{Y}\right)^2}}$$

Or

$$r = \frac{\text{Covariance between } X \text{ and } Y}{\sigma_x \cdot \sigma_y} = \frac{\sum \left(X_i - \bar{X}\right)\left(Y_i - \bar{Y}\right)/n}{\sigma_x \cdot \sigma_y}$$

Or

$$r = \frac{\sum X_i Y_i - n \cdot \bar{X} \cdot \bar{Y}}{\sqrt{\sum X_i^2 - n\bar{X}^2} \sqrt{\sum Y_i^2 - n\bar{Y}^2}}$$

(This applies when we take zero as the assumed mean for both variables, X and Y.)

where X_i = ith value of X variable

$\overline{X}$ = mean of X

Y_i = ith value of Y variable

$\overline{Y}$ = Mean of Y

n = number of pairs of observations of X and Y

σ_X = Standard deviation of X

σ_Y = Standard deviation of Y

In case we use assumed means (A_x and A_y for variables X and Y respectively) in place of true means, then Karl Person's formula is reduced to:

$$\frac{\dfrac{\sum dx_i \cdot dy_i}{n} - \left(\dfrac{\sum dx_i \cdot \sum dy_i}{n}\right)}{\sqrt{\dfrac{\sum dx_i^2}{n} - \left(\dfrac{\sum dx_i}{n}\right)^2} \sqrt{\dfrac{\sum dy_i^2}{n} - \left(\dfrac{\sum dy_i}{n}\right)^2}}$$

$$\frac{\dfrac{\sum dx_i \cdot dy_i}{n} - \left(\dfrac{\sum dx_i \cdot \sum dy_i}{n}\right)}{\sqrt{\dfrac{\sum dx_i^2}{n} - \left(\dfrac{\sum dx_i}{n}\right)^2} \sqrt{\dfrac{\sum dy_i^2}{n} - \left(\dfrac{\sum dy_i}{n}\right)^2}}$$

where $\sum dx_i = \sum(X_i - A_x)$

$\sum dy_i = \sum(Y_i - A_y)$

$\sum dx_i^2 = \sum(X_i - A_x)^2$

$\sum dy_i^2 = \sum(Y_i - A_y)^2$

$\sum dx_i \cdot dy_i = \sum(X_i - A_x)(Y_i - A_y)$

n = number of pairs of observations of X and Y.

This is the short cut approach for finding 'r' in case of ungrouped data. If the data happen to be grouped data (i.e., the case of bivariate frequency distribution), we shall have to write Karl Pearson's coefficient of correlation as under:

$$\frac{\dfrac{\sum f_{ij} \cdot dx_i \cdot dy_j}{n} - \left(\dfrac{\sum f_i dx_i}{n} \cdot \dfrac{\sum f_j dy_j}{n}\right)}{\sqrt{\dfrac{\sum f_i dx_i^2}{n} - \left(\dfrac{\sum f_i dx_i}{n}\right)} \sqrt{\dfrac{\sum f_i dy_j^2}{n} - \left(\dfrac{\sum f_j dy_j}{n}\right)^2}}$$

where f_{ij} is the frequency of a particular cell in the correlation table and all other values are defined as earlier.

Karl Pearson's coefficient of correlation is also known as the product moment correlation coefficient. The value of 'r' lies between ± 1. Positive values of r indicate positive correlation between the two variables (i.e., changes in both variables take place in the statement direction), whereas negative values of 'r' indicate negative correlation i.e., changes in the two variables taking place in the opposite directions. A zero value of 'r' indicates that there is no association between the two variables. When $r = (+)\,1$, it indicates perfect positive correlation and when it is $(-)1$, it indicates perfect negative correlation, meaning thereby that variations in independent variable (X) explain 100% of the variations in the dependent variable (Y). We can also say that for a unit change in independent variable, if there happens to be a constant change in the dependent variable in the same direction, then correlation will be termed as perfect positive. But if such change occurs in the opposite direction, the correlation will be termed as perfect negative. The value of 'r' nearer to +1 or –1 indicates high degree of correlation between the two variables.

SIMPLE REGRESSION ANALYSIS

Regression is the determination of a statistical relationship between two or more variables. In simple regression, we have only two variables, one variable (defined as independent) is the cause of the behaviour of another one (defined as dependent variable). Regression can only interpret what exists physically i.e., there must be a physical way in which independent variable X can affect dependent variable Y. The basic relationship between X and Y is given by

$$\hat{Y} = a + bX$$

where the symbol $\hat{Y}$ denotes the estimated value of Y for a given value of X. This equation is known as the regression equation of Y on X (also represents the regression line of Y on X when drawn on a graph) which means that each unit change in X produces a change of b in Y, which is positive for direct and negative for inverse relationships.

Then generally used method to find the 'best' fit that a straight line of this kind can give is the least-square method. To use it efficiently, we first determine

$$\sum x_i^2 = \sum X_i^2 - n\overline{X}^2$$

$$\sum y_i^2 = \sum Y_i^2 - n\overline{Y}^2$$

$$\sum x_i y_i = \sum X_i Y_i - n\overline{X} \cdot \overline{Y}$$

Then
$$b = \frac{\sum x_i y_i}{\sum x_i^2}, \; a = \overline{Y} - b\overline{X}$$

These measures define a and b which will give the best possible fit through the original X and Y points and the value of r can then be worked out as under:

$$r = \frac{b\sqrt{\sum x_i^2}}{\sqrt{\sum y_i^2}}$$

Thus, the regression analysis is a statistical method to deal with the formulation of mathematical model depicting relationship amongst variables which can be used for the purpose of prediction of the values of dependent variable, given the values of the independent variable.

[Alternatively, for fitting a regression equation of the type $\hat{Y} = a + bX$ to the given values of X and Y variables, we can find the values of the two constants viz., a and b by using the following two normal equations:

$$\sum Y_i = na + b \sum X_i$$

$$\sum X_i Y_i = a \sum X_i + b \sum X_i^2$$

and then solving these equations for finding a and b values. Once these values are obtained and have been put in the equation $\hat{Y} = a + bX$, we say that we have fitted the regression equation of Y on X to the given data. In a similar fashion, we can develop the regression equation of X and Y viz., $\hat{X} = a + bX$, presuming Y as an independent variable and X as dependent variable].

MULTIPLE CORRELATION AND REGRESSION

When there are two or more than two independent variables, the analysis concerning relationship is known as multiple correlation and the equation describing such relationship as the multiple regression equation. We here explain multiple correlation and regression taking only two independent variables and one dependent variable (Convenient computer programs exist for dealing with a great number of variables). In this situation the results are interpreted as shown below:

Multiple regression equation assumes the form

$$\hat{Y} = a + b_1 X_1 + b_2 X_2$$

where X_1 and X_2 are two independent variables and Y being the dependent variable, and the constants a, b_1 and b_2 can be solved by solving the following three normal equations:

$$\sum Y_i = na + b_1 \sum X_{1i} + b_2 \sum X_{2i}$$

$$\sum X_{1i} Y_i = a \sum X_{1i} + b_1 \sum X_{1i}^2 + b_2 \sum X_{1i} X_{2i}$$

$$\sum X_{2i} Y_i = a \sum X_{2i} + b_1 \sum X_{1i} X_{2i} + b_2 \sum X_{2i}^2$$

(It may be noted that the number of normal equations would depend upon the number of independent variables. If there are 2 independent variables, then 3 equations, if there are 3 independent variables then 4 equations and so on, are used.)

In multiple regression analysis, the regression coefficients (viz., b_1 b_2) become less reliable as the degree of correlation between the independent variables (viz., X_1, X_2) increases. If there is a high degree of correlation between independent variables, we have a problem of what is commonly described as the *problem of multicollinearity*. In such a situation we should use only one set of the independent variable to make our estimate. In fact, adding a second variable, say X_2, that is correlated with the first variable, say X_1, distorts the values of the regression coefficients. Nevertheless, the prediction for the dependent variable can be made even when multicollinearity is present, but in such a situation enough care should be taken in selecting the independent variables to estimate a dependent variable so as to ensure that multi-collinearity is reduced to the minimum.

With more than one independent variable, we may make a difference between the collective effect of the two independent variables and the individual effect of each of them taken separately. The collective effect is given by the coefficient of multiple correlation,

$R_{y \cdot x_1 x_2}$ defined as under:

$$R_{y \cdot x_1 x_2} = \sqrt{\frac{b_1 \sum Y_i X_{1i} - n\bar{Y}\bar{X}_1 + b_2 \sum Y_i X_{2i} - n\bar{Y}\bar{X}_2}{\sum Y_i^2 - n\bar{Y}^2}}$$

Alternatively, we can write

$$R_{y \cdot x_1 x_2} = \sqrt{\frac{b_1 \sum x_{1i} y_i + b_2 \sum x_{2i} y_i}{\sum Y_i^2}}$$

where

$$x_{1i} = (X_{1i} - \bar{X}_1)$$

$$x_{2i} = (X_{2i} - \bar{X}_2)$$

$$y_i = (Y_i - \bar{Y})$$

and b_1 and b_2 are the regression coefficients.

PARTIAL CORRELATION

Partial correlation measures separately the relationship between two variables in such a way that the effects of other related variables are eliminated. In other words, in partial correlation analysis, we aim at measuring the relation between a dependent variable and a particular independent variable by holding all other variables constant. Thus, each partial coefficient of correlation measures the effect of its independent variable on the dependent variable. To obtain it, it is first necessary to compute the simple coefficients of correlation between each set of pairs of variables as stated earlier. In the case of two independent variables, we shall have two partial correlation coefficients denoted $r_{yx_1 \cdot x_2}$ and $r_{yx_2 \cdot x_1}$ which are worked out as under:

$$r_{yx_1 \cdot x_2} = \frac{R^2_{y \cdot x_1 x_2} - r^2_{yx_2}}{1 - r^2_{yx_2}}$$

This measures the effort of X_1 on Y, more precisely, that proportion of the variation of Y not explained by X_2 which is explained by X_1. Also,

$$r_{yx_2 \cdot x_1} = \frac{R^2_{y \cdot x_1 x_2} - r^2_{yx_1}}{1 - r^2_{yx_1}} .$$

in which X_1 and X_2 are simply interchanged, given the added effect of X_2 on Y.

Alternatively, we can work out the partial correlation coefficients thus:

$$r_{yx_1 \cdot x_2} = \frac{r_{yx_1} - r_{yx_2} \cdot r_{x_1 x_2}}{\sqrt{1 - r_{yx_2}^2} \; \sqrt{1 - r_{x_1 x_2}^2}}$$

and

$$r_{yx_2 \cdot x_1} = \frac{r_{yx_2} - r_{yx_1} \cdot r_{x_1 x_2}}{\sqrt{1 - r_{yx_1}^2} \; \sqrt{1 - r_{x_1 x_2}^2}}$$

These formulae of the alternative approach are based on simple coefficients of correlation (also known as zero order coefficients since no variable is held constant when simple correlation coefficients are worked out). The partial correlation coefficients are called first order coefficients when one variable is held constant as shown above; they are known as second order coefficients when two variables are held constant and so on.

ASSOCIATION IN CASE OF ATTRIBUTES

When data is collected on the basis of some attribute or attributes, we have statistics commonly termed as statistics of attributes. It is not necessary that the objects may process only one attribute; rather it would be found that the objects possess more than one attribute. In such a situation our interest may remain in knowing whether the attributes are associated with each other or not. For example, among a group of people we may find that some of them are inoculated against small-pox and among the inoculated we may observe that some of them suffered from small-pox after inoculation. The important question which may arise for the observation is regarding the efficiency of inoculation for its popularity will depend upon the immunity which it provides against small-pox. In other words, we may be interested in knowing whether inoculation and immunity from small-pox are associated. Technically, we say that the two attributes are associated if they appear together in a greater number of cases than is to be expected if they are independent and not simply on the basis that they are appearing together in a number of cases as is done in ordinary life.

The association may be positive or negative (negative association is also known as disassociation). If class frequency of AB, symbolically written as (AB), is greater than the expectation of AB being together if they are independent, then we say the two attributes are positively associated; but if the class frequency of AB is less than this expectation, the two attributes are said to be negatively associated. In case the class frequency of AB is equal to expectation, the two attributes are considered as independent i.e., are said to have no association. It can be put symbolically as shown hereunder:

If $(AB) > \dfrac{(A)}{N} \times \dfrac{(B)}{N} \times N$, then AB are positively related/associated.

If $(AB) < \dfrac{(A)}{N} \times \dfrac{(B)}{N} \times N$, then AB are negatively related/associated.

If $(AB) = \dfrac{(A)}{N} \times \dfrac{(B)}{N} \times N$, then AB are independent i.e., have no association.

Where (AB) = frequency of class AB and

$$\frac{(A)}{N} \times \frac{(B)}{N} \times N = \text{Expectation of } AB, \text{ if } A \text{ and } B \text{ are independent, and } N \text{ being the number of}$$

items

In order to find out the degree or intensity of association between two or more sets of attributes, we should work out the coefficient of association. Professor Yule's coefficient of association is most popular and is often used for the purpose. It can be mentioned as under:

$$Q_{AB} = \frac{(AB)(ab) - (Ab)(aB)}{(AB)(ab) + (Ab)(aB)}$$

where,

Q_{AB} = Yule's coefficient of association between attributes A and B.

(AB) = Frequency of class AB in which A and B are present.

(Ab) = Frequency of class Ab in which A is present but B is absent.

(aB) = Frequency of class aB in which A is absent but B is present.

(ab) = Frequency of class ab in which both A and B are absent.

The value of this coefficient will be somewhere between +1 and –1. If the attributes are completely associated (perfect positive association) with each other, the coefficient will be +1, and if they are completely disassociated (perfect negative association), the coefficient will be –1. If the attributes are completely independent of each other, the coefficient of association will be 0. The varying degrees of the coefficients of association are to be read and understood according to their positive and negative nature between +1 and –1.

Sometimes the association between two attributes, A and B, may be regarded as unwarranted when we find that the observed association between A and B is due to the association of both A and B with another attribute C. For example, we may observe positive association between inoculation and exemption for small-pox, but such association may be the result of the fact that there is positive association between inoculation and richer section of society and also that there is positive association between exemption from small-pox and richer section of society. The sort of association between A and B in the population of C is described as *partial association* as distinguished from *total association* between A and B in the overall universe. We can workout the coefficient of partial association between A and B in the population of C by just modifying the above stated formula for finding association between A and B as shown below:

$$Q_{AB.C} = \frac{(ABC)(abC) - (AbC)(aBC)}{(ABC)(abC) + (AbC)(aBC)}$$

where,

$Q_{AB.C}$ = Coefficient of partial association between A and B in the population of C; and all other values are the class frequencies of the respective classes (A, B, C denotes the presence of concerning attributes and a, b, c denotes the absence of concerning attributes).

At times, we may come across cases of *illusory association*, wherein association between two attributes does not correspond to any real relationship. This sort of association may be the result of some attribute, say *C* with which attributes *A* and *B* are associated (but in reality there is no association between *A* and *B*). Such association may also be the result of the fact that the attributes *A* and *B* might not have been properly defined or might not have been correctly recorded. Researcher must remain alert and must not conclude association between *A* and *B* when in fact there is no such association in reality.

In order to judge the significance of association between two attributes, we make use of *Chi-square test** by finding the value of Chi-square (χ_2) and using Chi-square distribution the value of χ_2 can be worked out as under:

$$\chi^2 = \Sigma \frac{\left(O_{ij} - E_{ij}\right)^2}{E_{ij}} \qquad i = 1, 2, 3 \dots$$

where $\qquad\qquad j = 1, 2, 3 \dots$

O_{ij} = observed frequencies

E_{ij} = expected frequencies.

Association between two attributes in case of manifold classification and the resulting contingency table can be studied as explained below:

We can have manifold classification of the two attributes in which case each of the two attributes are first observed and then each one is classified into two or more subclasses, resulting into what is called as contingency table. The following is an example of 4×4 contingency table with two attributes *A* and *B*, each one of which has been further classified into four sub-categories.

Table 7.2: 4 × 4 Contingency Table

		Attribute A				
		A_1	A_2	A_3	A_4	Total
	B_1	$(A_1 B_1)$	$(A_2 B_1)$	$(A_3 B_1)$	$(A_4 B_1)$	(B_1)
Attribute B	B_2	$(A_1 B_2)$	$(A_2 B_2)$	$(A_3 B_2)$	$(A_4 B_2)$	(B_2)
	B_3	$(A_1 B_3)$	$(A_2 B_3)$	$(A_3 B_3)$	$(A_4 B_3)$	(B_3)
	B_4	$(A_1 B_4)$	$(A_2 B_4)$	$(A_3 B_4)$	$(A_4 B_4)$	(B_4)
	Total	(A_1)	(A_2)	(A_3)	(A_4)	N

Association can be studied in a contingency table through Yule's coefficient of association as stated above, but for this purpose we have to reduce the contingency table into 2×2 table by combining some classes. For instance, if we combine $(A_1) + (A_2)$ to form (A) and $(A_3) + (A_4)$ to form (a) and similarly if we combine $(B_1) + (B_2)$ to form (B) and $(B_3) + (B_4)$ to form (b) in the above contingency table, then we can write the table in the form of a 2×2 table as shown in Table 4.3

*See Chapter "Chi-square test" for all details.

Table 7.3

		Attribute		
		A	a	Total
Attribute	B	(AB)	(aB)	(B)
	b	(Ab)	(ab)	(b)
	Total	(A)	(a)	N

After reducing a contingency table in a two-by-two table through the process of combining some classes, we can work out the association as explained above. But the practice of combining classes is not considered very correct and at times it is inconvenient also, Karl Pearson has suggested a measure known as *Coefficient of mean square contingency* for studying association in contingency tables. This can be obtained as under:

$$C = \sqrt{\frac{\chi^2}{\chi^2 + N}}$$

where

C = Coefficient of contingency

χ^2 = Chi-square value which is $= \sum \frac{\left(O_{ij} - E_{ij}\right)^2}{E_{ij}}$

N = number of items.

This is considered a satisfactory measure of studying association in contingency tables.

OTHER MEASURES

1. Index numbers: When series are expressed in same units, we can use averages for the purpose of comparison, but when the units in which two or more series are expressed happen to be different, statistical averages cannot be used to compare them. In such situations we have to rely upon some relative measurement which consists in reducing the figures to a common base. Once such method is to convert the series into a series of index numbers. This is done when we express the given figures as percentages of some specific figure on a certain data. We can, thus, define an index number as a number which is used to measure the level of a given phenomenon as compared to the level of the same phenomenon at some standard date. The use of index number weights more as a special type of average, meant to study the changes in the effect of such factors which are incapable of being measured directly. But one must always remember that index numbers measure only the relative changes.

Changes in various economic and social phenomena can be measured and compared through index numbers. Different indices serve different purposes. Specific commodity indices are to serve as a measure of changes in the phenomenon of that commodity only. Index numbers may measure cost of living of different classes of people. In economic sphere, index numbers are often termed as 'economic barometers measuring the economic phenomenon in all its aspects either directly by measuring the same phenomenon or indirectly by measuring something else which reflects upon the main phenomenon.

But index numbers have their own limitations with which researcher must always keep himself aware. For instance, index numbers are only approximate indicators and as such give only a fair idea of changes but cannot give an accurate idea. Chances of error also remain at one point or the other while constructing an index number but this does not diminish the utility of index numbers for they still can indicate the trend of the phenomenon being measured. However, to avoid fallacious conclusions, index numbers prepared for one purpose should not be used for other purposes or for the same purpose at other places.

2. Time series analysis: In the context of economic and business researches, we may obtain quite often data relating to some time period concerning a given phenomenon. Such data is labelled as 'Time Series'. More clearly it can be stated that series of successive observations of the given phenomenon over a period of time are referred to as time series. Such series are usually the result of the effects of one or more of the following factors:

(i) *Secular trend* or long term trend that shows the direction of the series in a long period of time. The effect of trend (whether it happens to be a growth factor or a decline factor) is gradual, but extends more or less consistently throughout the entire period of time under consideration. Sometimes, secular trend is simply stated as trend (or T).

(ii) *Short time oscillations* i.e., changes taking place in the short period of time only and such changes can be the effect of the following factors:

(a) *Cyclical fluctuations* (*or C*) are the fluctuations as a result of business cycles and are generally referred to as long term movements that represent consistently recurring rises and declines in an activity.

(b) *Seasonal fluctuations* (*or S*) are of short duration occurring in a regular sequence at specific intervals of time. Such fluctuations are the result of changing seasons. Usually these fluctuations involve patterns of change within a year that tend to be repeated from year to year. Cyclical fluctuations and seasonal fluctuations taken together constitute short-period regular fluctuations.

(c) *Irregular fluctuations* (*or I*), also known as Random fluctuations, are variations which take place in a completely unpredictable fashion.

All these factors stated above are termed as components of time series and when we try to analyse time series, we try to isolate and measure the effects of various types of these factors on a series. To study the effect of one type of factor, the other type of factor is eliminated from the series. The given series is, thus, left with the effects of one type of factor only.

For analysing time series, we usually have two models; (1) multiplicative model; and (2) additive model. Multiplicative model assumes that the various components interact in a multiplicative manner to produce the given values of the overall time series and can be stated as under:

$$Y = T \times C \times S \times I$$

where

Y = observed values of time series, T = Trend, C = Cyclical fluctuations, S = Seasonal fluctuations, I = Irregular fluctuations.

Additive model considers the total of various components resulting in the given values of the overall time series and can be stated as:

$$Y = T + C + S + I$$

There are various methods of isolating trend from the given series viz., the free hand method, semi-average method, method of moving averages, method of least squares and similarly there are methods of measuring cyclical and seasonal variations and whatever variations are left over are considered as random or irregular fluctuations.

The analysis of time series is done to understand the dynamic conditions for achieving the short-term and long-term goals of business firm(s). The past trends can be used to evaluate the success or failure of management policy or policies practiced hitherto. On the basis of past trends, the future patterns can be predicted and policy or policies may accordingly be formulated. We can as well study properly the effects of factors causing changes in the short period of time only, once we have eliminated the effects of trend. By studying cyclical variations, we can keep in view the impact of cyclical changes while formulating various policies to make them as realistic as possible. The knowledge of seasonal variations will be of great help to us in taking decisions regarding inventory, production, purchases and sales policies so as to optimize working results. Thus, analysis of time series is important in context of long term as well as short term forecasting and is considered a very powerful tool in the hands of business analysts and researchers.

Questions

1. "Processing of data implies editing, coding, classification and tabulation". Describe in brief these four operations pointing out the significance of each in context of research study.

2. Classification according to class intervals involves three main problems viz., how many classes should be there? How to choose class limits? How to determine class frequency? State how these problems should be tackled by a researcher.

3. Why tabulation is considered essential in a research study? Narrate the characteristics of a good table.

4. (a) How the problem of DK responses should be dealt with by a researcher? Explain.

   (b) What points one should observe while using percentages in research studies?

5. Write a brief note on different types of analysis of data pointing out the significance of each.

6. What do you mean by multivariate analysis? Explain how it differs from bivariate analysis.

7. How will you differentiate between descriptive statistics and inferential statistics? Describe the important statistical measures often used to summarise the survey/research data.

8. What does a measure of central tendency indicate? Describe the important measures of central tendency pointing out the situation when one measure is considered relatively appropriate in comparison to other measures.

9. Describe the various measures of relationships often used in context of research studies. Explain the meaning of the following correlation coefficients:

   (i) r_{yx}, (ii) $r_{yx_1 \cdot x_2}$, (iii) $R_{y \cdot x_1 x_2}$

10. Write short notes on the following:

    (i) Cross tabulation;

    (ii) Discriminant analysis;

   (iii) Coefficient of contingency;

   (iv) Multicollinearity;

   (v) Partial association between two attributes.

11. "The analysis of time series is done to understand the dynamic conditions for achieving the short-term and long-term goals of business firms." Discuss.

12. "Changes in various economic and social phenomena can be measured and compared through index numbers". Explain this statement pointing out the utility of index numbers.

13. Distinguish between:

   (i) Field editing and central editing;

   (ii) Statistics of attributes and statistics of variables;

   (iii) Exclusive type and inclusive type class intervals;

   (iv) Simple and complex tabulation;

   (v) Mechanical tabulation and cross tabulation.

14. "Discriminate use of average is very essential for sound statistical analysis". Why? Answer giving examples.

15. Explain how would you work out the following statistical measures often used by researchers?

   (i) Coefficient of variation;

   (ii) Arithmetic average;

   (iii) Coefficient of skewness;

   (iv) Regression equation of X on Y;

   (v) Coefficient of $r_{yx_2 \cdot x_1}$.

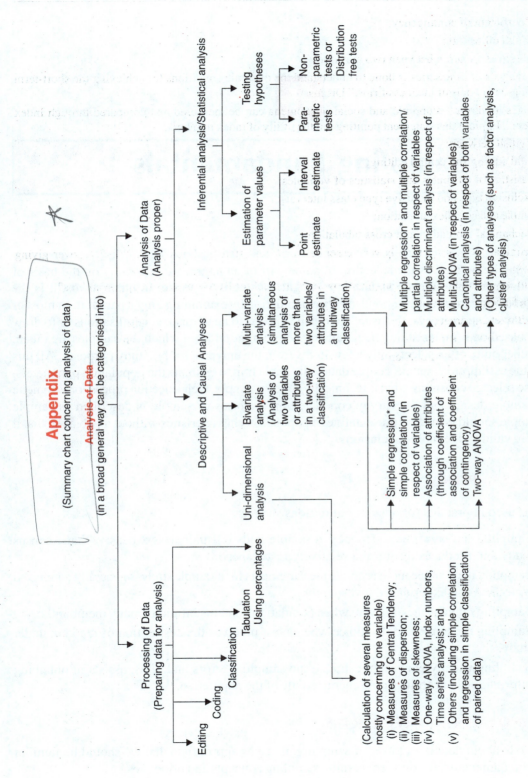

Appendix
(Summary chart concerning analysis of data)

Analysis of Data
(in a broad general way can be categorised into)

* Regression analysis (whether simple or multiple) is termed as Causal analysis whereas correlation analysis indicates simply co-variation between two or more variables.

8

Sampling Fundamentals

Sampling may be defined as the selection of some part of an aggregate or totality on the basis of which a judgement or inference about the aggregate or totality is made. In other words, it is the process of obtaining information about an entire population by examining only a part of it. In most of the research work and surveys, the usual approach happens to be to make generalisations or to draw inferences based on samples about the parameters of population from which the samples are taken. The researcher quite often selects only a few items from the universe for his study purposes. All this is done on the assumption that the sample data will enable him to estimate the population parameters. The items so selected constitute what is technically called a sample, their selection process or technique is called sample design and the survey conducted on the basis of sample is described as sample survey. Sample should be truly representative of population characteristics without any bias so that it may result in valid and reliable conclusions.

NEED FOR SAMPLING

Sampling is used in practice for a variety of reasons such as:

1. Sampling can save time and money. A sample study is usually less expensive than a census study and produces results at a relatively faster speed.
2. Sampling may enable more accurate measurements for a sample study is generally conducted by trained and experienced investigators.
3. Sampling remains the only way when population contains infinitely many members.
4. Sampling remains the only choice when a test involves the destruction of the item under study.
5. Sampling usually enables to estimate the sampling errors and, thus, assists in obtaining information concerning some characteristic of the population.

SOME FUNDAMENTAL DEFINITIONS

Before we talk about details and uses of sampling, it seems appropriate that we should be familiar with some fundamental definitions concerning sampling concepts and principles.

1. *Universe/Population:* From a statistical point of view, the term 'Universe'refers to the total of the items or units in any field of inquiry, whereas the term 'population' refers to the total of items about which information is desired. The attributes that are the object of study are referred to as characteristics and the units possessing them are called as elementary units. The aggregate of such units is generally described as population. Thus, all units in any field of inquiry constitute universe and all elementary units (on the basis of one characteristic or more) constitute population. Quit often, we do not find any difference between population and universe, and as such the two terms are taken as interchangeable. However, a researcher must necessarily define these terms precisely.

The population or universe can be *finite* or *infinite*. The population is said to be finite if it consists of a fixed number of elements so that it is possible to enumerate it in its totality. For instance, the population of a city, the number of workers in a factory are examples of finite populations. The symbol 'N' is generally used to indicate how many elements (or items) are there in case of a finite population. An infinite population is that population in which it is theoretically impossible to observe all the elements. Thus, in an infinite population the number of items is infinite i.e., we cannot have any idea about the total number of items. The number of stars in a sky, possible rolls of a pair of dice are examples of infinite population. One should remember that no truly infinite population of physical objects does actually exist in spite of the fact that many such populations appear to be very very large. From a practical consideration, we then use the term infinite population for a population that cannot be enumerated in a reasonable period of time. This way we use the theoretical concept of infinite population as an approximation of a very large finite population.

2. *Sampling frame:* The elementary units or the group or cluster of such units may form the basis of sampling process in which case they are called as sampling units. A list containing all such sampling units is known as sampling frame. Thus sampling frame consists of a list of items from which the sample is to be drawn. If the population is finite and the time frame is in the present or past, then it is possibe for the frame to be identical with the population. In most cases they are not identical because it is often impossible to draw a sample directly from population. As such this frame is either constructed by a researcher for the purpose of his study or may consist of some existing list of the population. For instance, one can use telephone directory as a frame for conducting opinion survey in a city. Whatever the frame may be, it should be a good representative of the population.

3. *Sampling design:* A sample design is a definite plan for obtaining a sample from the sampling frame. It refers to the technique or the procedure the researcher would adopt in selecting some sampling units from which inferences about the population is drawn. Sampling design is determined before any data are collected. Various sampling designs have already been explained earlier in the book.

4. *Statisitc(s) and parameter(s):* A statistic is a characteristic of a sample, whereas a parameter is a characteristic of a population. Thus, when we work out certain measures such as mean, median, mode or the like ones from samples, then they are called statistic(s) for they describe the characteristics of a sample. But when such measures describe the characteristics of a population, they are known as parameter(s). For instance, the population mean (μ) is a parameter,whereas the sample mean $(\overline{X})$ is a statistic. To obtain the estimate of a parameter from a statistic constitutes the prime objective of sampling analysis.

5. *Sampling error:* Sample surveys do imply the study of a small portion of the population and as such there would naturally be a certain amount of inaccuracy in the information collected. This inaccuracy may be termed as sampling error or error variance. In other words, sampling errors are

those errors which arise on account of sampling and they generally happen to be random variations (in case of random sampling) in the sample estimates around the true population values. The meaning of sampling error can be easily understood from the following diagram:

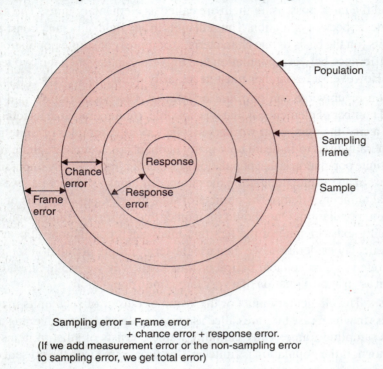

Sampling error = Frame error
              + chance error + response error.
(If we add measurement error or the non-sampling error
to sampling error, we get total error)

Fig. 8.1

Sampling error = Frame error + Chance error + Response error

(If we add measurement error or the non-sampling error to sampling error, we get total error).

Sampling errors occur randomly and are equally likely to be in either direction. The magnitude of the sampling error depends upon the nature of the universe; the more homogeneous the universe, the smaller the sampling error. Sampling error is inversely related to the size of the sample i.e., sampling error decreases as the sample size increases and vice-versa. A measure of the random sampling error can be calculated for a given sample design and size and this measure is often called the precision of the sampling plan. Sampling error is usually worked out as the product of the critical value at a certain level of significance and the standard error.

As opposed to sampling errors, we may have non-sampling errors which may creep in during the process of collecting actual information and such errors occur in all surveys whether census or sample. We have no way to measure non-sampling errors.

6. *Precision:* Precision is the range within which the population average (or other parameter) will lie in accordance with the reliability specified in the confidence level as a percentage of the estimate $\pm$ or as a numerical quantity. For instance, if the estimate is Rs 4000 and the precision desired is $\pm$ 4%, then the true value will be no less than Rs 3840 and no more than Rs 4160. This is the range (Rs 3840 to Rs 4160) within which the true answer should lie. But if we desire that the estimate

should not deviate from the actual value by more than Rs 200 in either direction, in that case the range would be Rs 3800 to Rs 4200.

7. *Confidence level and significance level:* The confidence level or reliability is the expected percentage of times that the actual value will fall within the stated precision limits. Thus, if we take a confidence level of 95%, then we mean that there are 95 chances in 100 (or .95 in 1) that the sample results represent the true condition of the population within a specified precision range against 5 chances in 100 (or .05 in 1) that it does not. Precision is the range within which the answer may vary and still be acceptable; confidence level indicates the likelihood that the answer will fall within that range, and the significance level indicates the likelihood that the answer will fall outside that range. We can always remember that if the confidence level is 95%, then the significance level will be (100 – 95) i.e., 5%; if the confidence level is 99%, the significance level is (100 – 99) i.e., 1%, and so on. We should also remember that the area of normal curve within precision limits for the specified confidence level constitute the acceptance region and the area of the curve outside these limits in either direction constitutes the rejection regions.[*]

8. *Sampling distribution:* We are often concerned with sampling distribution in sampling analysis. If we take certain number of samples and for each sample compute various statistical measures such as mean, standard deviation, etc., then we can find that each sample may give its own value for the statistic under consideration. All such values of a particular statistic, say mean, together with their relative frequencies will constitute the sampling distribution of the particular statistic, say mean. Accordingly, we can have sampling distribution of mean, or the sampling distribution of standard deviation or the sampling distribution of any other statistical measure. It may be noted that each item in a sampling distribution is a particular statistic of a sample. The sampling distribution tends quite closer to the normal distribution if the number of samples is large. The significance of sampling distribution follows from the fact that the mean of a sampling distribution is the same as the mean of the universe. Thus, the mean of the sampling distribution can be taken as the mean of the universe.

IMPORTANT SAMPLING DISTRIBUTIONS

Some important sampling distributions, which are commonly used, are: (1) sampling distribution of mean; (2) sampling distribution of proportion; (3) student's '*t*' distribution; (4) *F* distribution; and (5) Chi-square distribution. A brief mention of each one of these sampling distribution will be helpful.

1. *Sampling distribution of mean:* Sampling distribution of mean refers to the probability distribution of all the possible means of random samples of a given size that we take from a population. If samples are taken from a normal population, $N\left(\mu, \sigma_p\right)$, the sampling distribution of mean would also be normal with mean $\mu_{\bar{x}} = \mu$ and standard deviation $= \sigma_p \sqrt{n}$, where μ is the mean of the population, σ_p is the standard deviation of the population and n means the number of items in a sample. But when sampling is from a population which is not normal (may be positively or negatively skewed), even then, as per the central limit theorem, the sampling distribution of mean tends quite closer to the normal distribution, provided the number of sample items is large i.e., more than 30. In case we want to reduce the sampling distribution of mean to unit normal distribution i.e., $N(0,1)$, we can write the

---

[*]See Chapter 9 Testing of Hypotheses I for details.

normal variate $z = \dfrac{\overline{x} - \mu}{\sigma_p / \sqrt{n}}$ for the sampling distribution of mean. This characteristic of the sampling distribution of mean is very useful in several decision situations for accepting or rejection of hypotheses.

2. *Sampling distribution of proportion:* Like sampling distribution of mean, we can as well have a sampling distribution of proportion. This happens in case of statistics of attributes. Assume that we have worked out the proportion of defective parts in large number of samples, each with say 100 items, that have been taken from an infinite population and plot a probability distribution of the said proportions, we obtain what is known as the sampling distribution of the said proportions, we obtain what is known as the sampling distribution of proportion. Usually the statistics of attributes correspond to the conditions of a binomial distribution that tends to become normal distribution as n becomes larger and larger. If p represents the proportion of defectives i.e., of successes and q the proportion of non-defectives i.e., of failures (or $q = 1 - p$) and if p is treated as a random variable, then the sampling

distribution of proportion of successes has a mean $= p$ with standard deviation $= \sqrt{\dfrac{p \cdot q}{n}}$, where n

is the sample size. Presuming the binomial distribution approximating the normal distribution for large

n, the normal variate of the sampling distribution of proportion $z = \dfrac{\hat{p} - p}{\sqrt{(p \cdot q)/n}}$, where $\hat{p}$ (pronounced

as p-hat) is the sample proportion of successes, can be used for testing of hypotheses.

3. *Student's t-distribution:* When population standard deviation $\left(\sigma_p \right)$ is not known and the sample is of a small size $\left(\text{i.e., } n \overline{<} 30 \right)$, we use t distribution for the sampling distribution of mean and workout t variable as:

$$t = \left(\overline{X} - \mu \right) \big/ \left(\sigma_s / \sqrt{n} \right)$$

where $\sigma_s = \sqrt{\dfrac{\Sigma \left(X_i - \overline{X} \right)^2}{n} - 1}$

i.e., the sample standard deviation . t-distribution is also symmetrical and is very close to the distribution of standard normal variate, z, except for small values of n. The variable t differs from z in the sense that we use sample standard deviation $\left(\sigma_s \right)$ in the calculation of t, whereas we use standard deviation of population $\left(\sigma_p \right)$ in the calculation of z. There is a different t distribution for every possible sample size i.e., for different degrees of freedom. The degrees of freedom for a sample of size n is $n - 1$. As the sample size gets larger, the shape of the t distribution becomes apporximately equal to the normal distribution. In fact for sample sizes of more than 30, the t distribution is so close to the normal distribution that we can use the normal to approximate the t-distribution. But when n is small, the t-distribution is far from normal but when $n \rightarrow \alpha$, t-distribution is identical with normal distribution. The t-distribution tables are available which give the critical values of t for different degrees of freedom at various levels of significance. The table value of t for given degrees of freedom at a certain level of significance is compared with the calculated value of t from the sample data, and if the latter is either equal to or exceeds, we infer that the null hypothesis cannot be accepted.[*]

4. *F distribution:* If $(\sigma_{s1})^2$ and $(\sigma_{s2})^2$ are the variances of two independent samples of size n_1 and n_2 respectively taken from two independent normal populations, having the same variance, $(\sigma_{p1})^2 = (\sigma_{p2})^2$, the ratio $F = (\sigma_{s1})^2 / (\sigma_{s2})^2$, where $(\sigma_{s1})^2 = \Sigma \left(\overline{X}_{1i} - \overline{X}_1 \right)^2 / n_1 - 1$ and $(\sigma_{s2})^2 = \Sigma \left(\overline{X}_{2i} - \overline{X}_2 \right)^2 / n_2 - 1$ has an F distribution with $n_1 - 1$ and $n_2 - 1$ degrees of freedom.

F ratio is computed in a way that the larger variance is always in the numerator. Tables have been prepared for F distribution that give critical values of F for various values of degrees of freedom for larger as well as smaller variances. The calculated value of F from the sample data is compared with the corresponding table value of F and if the former is equal to or exceeds the latter, then we infer that the null hypothesis of the variances being equal cannot be accepted. We shall make use of the F ratio in the context of hypothesis testing and also in the context of ANOVA technique.

5. *Chi-square* $\left(\chi^2 \right)$ *distribution:* Chi-square distribution is encountered when we deal with collections of values that involve adding up squares. Variances of samples require us to add a collection of squared quantities and thus have distributions that are related to chi-square distribution. If we take each one of a collection of sample variances, divide them by the known population variance and multiply these quotients by $(n-1)$, where n means the number of items in the sample, we shall obtain a chi-square distribution. Thus, $\left(\sigma_s^2 / \sigma_p^2 \right) (n-1)$ would have the same distribution as chi-square distribution with $(n-1)$ degrees of freedom. Chi-square distribution is not symmetrical and all the values are positive. One must know the degrees of freedom for using chi-square distribution. This distribution may also be used for judging the significance of difference between observed and expected frequencies and also as a test of goodness of fit. The generalised shape of χ^2 distribution depends upon the d.f. and the χ^2 value is worked out as under:

$$\chi^2 = \sum_{i=1}^{k} \frac{(O_i - E_i)^2}{E_i}$$

Tables are there that give the value of χ^2 for given d.f. which may be used with calculated value of χ^2 for relevant d.f. at a desired level of significance for testing hypotheses. We will take it up in detail in the chapter 'Chi-square Test'.

CENTRAL LIMIT THEOREM

When sampling is from a normal population, the means of samples drawn from such a population are themselves normally distributed. But when sampling is not from a normal population, the size of the

---

[*] This aspect has been dealt with in details in the context of testing of hypotheses later in this book.

sample plays a critical role. When *n* is small, the shape of the distribution will depend largely on the shape of the parent population, but as *n* gets large ($n > 30$), the thape of the sampling distribution will become more and more like a normal distribution, irrespective of the shape of the parent population. The theorem which explains this sort of relationship between the shape of the population distribution and the sampling distribution of the mean is known as the central limit theorem. This theorem is by far the most important theorem in statistical inference. It assures that the sampling distribution of the mean approaches normal distribtion as the sample size increases. In formal terms, we may say that the central limit theorem states that "the distribution of means of random samples taken from a population having mean μ and finite variance σ^2 approaches the normal distribution with mean μ and variance σ^2/n as *n* goes to infinity."[1]

"The significance of the central limit theorem lies in the fact that it permits us to use sample statistics to make inferences about population parameters without knowing anything about the shape of the frequency distribution of that population other than what we can get from the sample."[2]

SAMPLING THEORY

Sampling theory is a study of relationships existing between a population and samples drawn from the population. Sampling theory is applicable only to random samples. For this purpose the population or a universe may be defined as an aggregate of items possessing a common trait or traits. In other words, a universe is the complete group of items about which knowledge is sought. The universe may be finite or infinite. finite universe is one which has a definite and certain number of items, but when the number of items is uncertain and infinite, the universe is said to be an infinite universe. Similarly, the universe may be hypothetical or existent. In the former case the universe in fact does not exist and we can only imagin the items constituting it. Tossing of a coin or throwing a dice are examples of hypothetical universe. Existent universe is a universe of concrete objects i.e., the universe where the items constituting it really exist. On the other hand, the term sample refers to that part of the universe which is selected for the purpose of investigation. The theory of sampling studies the relationships that exist between the universe and the sample or samples drawn from it.

The main problem of sampling theory is the problem of relationship between a parameter and a statistic. The theory of sampling is concerned with estimating the properties of the population from those of the sample and also with gauging the precision of the estimate. This sort of movement from particular (sample) towards general (universe) is what is known as statistical induction or statistical inference. In more clear terms "from the sample we attempt to draw inference concerning the universe. In order to be able to follow this inductive method, we first follow a deductive argument which is that we imagine a population or universe (finite or infinite) and investigate the behaviour of the samples drawn from this universe applying the laws of probability."[3] The methodology dealing with all this is known as sampling theory.

Sampling theory is designed to attain one or more of the following objectives:

[1] Donald L. Harnett and James L. Murphy, *Introductory Statistical Analysis,* p.223.

[2] Richard I. Levin, *Statistics for Management,* p. 199.

[3] J.C. Chaturvedi: *Mathematical Statistics,* p. 136.

(*i*) *Statistical estimation:* Sampling theory helps in estimating unknown population parameters from a knowledge of statistical measures based on sample studies. In other words, to obtain an estimate of parameter from statistic is the main objective of the sampling theory. The estimate can either be a point estimate or it may be an interval estimate. Point estimate is a single estimate expressed in the form of a single figure, but interval estimate has two limits viz., the upper limit and the lower limit within which the parameter value may lie. Interval estimates are often used in statistical induction.

(*ii*) *Testing of hypotheses:* The second objective of sampling theory is to enable us to decide whether to accept or reject hypothesis; the sampling theory helps in determining whether observed differences are actually due to chance or whether they are really significant.

(*iii*) *Statistical inference:* Sampling theory helps in making generalisation about the population/universe from the studies based on samples drawn from it. It also helps in determining the accuracy of such generalisations.

The theory of sampling can be studied under two heads viz., the sampling of attributes and the sampling of variables and that too in the context of large and small samples (By small sample is commonly understood any sample that includes 30 or fewer items, whereas a large sample is one in which the number of items is more than 30). When we study some qualitative characteristic of the items in a population, we obtain statistics of attributes in the form of two classes; one class consisting of items wherein the attribute is present and the other class consisting of items wherein the attribute is absent. The presence of an attribute may be termed as a 'success' and its absence a 'failure'. Thus, if out of 600 people selected randomly for the sample, 120 are found to possess a certain attribute and 480 are such people where the attribute is absent. In such a situation we would say that sample consists of 600 items (i.e., $n = 600$) out of which 120 are successes and 480 failures. The probability of success would be taken as $120/600 = 0.2$ (i.e., $p = 0.2$) and the probability of failure or $q = 480/600 = 0.8$. With such data the sampling distribution generally takes the form of binomial probability distribution whose mean (μ) would be equal to $n \cdot p$ and standard deviation (σ_p) would be equal to $\sqrt{n \cdot p \cdot q}$. If n is large, the binomial distribution tends to become normal distribution which may be used for sampling analysis. We generally consider the following three types of problems in case of sampling of attributes:

(*i*) The parameter value may be given and it is only to be tested if an observed 'statistic' is its estimate.

(*ii*) The parameter value is not known and we have to estimate it from the sample.

(*iii*) Examination of the reliability of the estimate i.e., the problem of finding out how far the estimate is expected to deviate from the true value for the population.

All the above stated problems are studied using the appropriate standard errors and the tests of significance which have been explained and illustrated in the pages that follow.

The theory of sampling can be applied in the context of statistics of variables (i.e., data relating to some characteristic concerning population which can be measured or enumerated with the help of some well defined statistical unit) in which case the objective happens to be : (*i*) to compare the observed and expected values and to find if the difference can be ascribed to the fluctuations of sampling; (*ii*) to estimate population parameters from the sample, and (*iii*) to find out the degree of reliability of the estimate.

The tests of significance used for dealing with problems relating to large samples are different from those used for small samples. This is so because the assumptions we make in case of large samples do not hold good for small samples. In case of large samples, we assume that the sampling distribution tends to be normal and the sample values are approximately close to the population values. As such we use the characteristics of normal distribution and apply what is known as z-test[*]. When *n* is large, the probability of a sample value of the statistic deviating from the parameter by more than 3 times its standard error is very small (it is 0.0027 as per the table giving area under normal curve) and as such the z-test is applied to find out the degree of reliability of a statistic in case of large samples. Appropriate standard errors have to be worked out which will enable us to give the limits within which the parameter values would lie or would enable us to judge whether the difference happens to be significant or not at certain confidence levels. For instance, $\overline{X} \pm 3\sigma_{\overline{X}}$ would give us the range within which the parameter mean value is expected to vary with 99.73% confidence. Important standard errors generally used in case of large samples have been stated and applied in the context of real life problems in the pages that follow.

The sampling theory for large samples is not applicable in small samples because when samples are small, we cannot assume that the sampling distribution is approximately normal. As such we require a new technique for handling small samples, particularly when population parameters are unknown. Sir William S. Gosset (pen name Student) developed a significance test, known as Student's *t*-test, based on *t* distribution and through it made significant contribution in the theory of sampling applicable in case of small samples. Student's *t*-test is used when two conditions are fulfilled viz., the sample size is 30 or less and the population variance is not known. While using *t*-test we assume that the population from which sample has been taken is normal or approximately normal, sample is a random sample, observations are independent, there is no measurement error and that in the case of two samples when equality of the two population means is to be tested, we assume that the population variances are equal. For applying *t*-test, we work out the value of test statistic (i.e., '*t*') and then compare with the table value of *t* (based on '*t*' distribution) at certain level of significance for given degrees of freedom. If the calculated value of '*t*' is either equal to or exceeds the table value, we infer that the difference is significant, but if calculated value of *t* is less than the concerning table value of *t*, the difference is not treated as significant. The following formulae are commonly used to calculate the *t* value:

(i) To test the significance of the mean of a random sample

$$t = \frac{\left(\overline{X} - \mu\right)}{\sigma_{\overline{X}}}$$

where $\overline{X}$ = Mean of the sample

μ = Mean of the universe/population

$\sigma_{\overline{X}}$ = Standard error of mean worked out as under

$$\sigma_{\overline{X}} = \frac{\sigma_s}{\sqrt{n}} = \sqrt{\frac{\Sigma\left(Xi - \overline{X}\right)^2}{n-1}} \Big/ \sqrt{n}$$

and the degrees of freedom = $(n - 1)$.

[*]The z-test may as well be applied in case of small sample provided we are given the variance of the population.

(ii) To test the difference between the means of two samples

$$t = \frac{\overline{X}_1 - \overline{X}_2}{\sigma_{\overline{X}_1 - \overline{X}_2}}$$

where $\overline{X}_1$ = Mean of sample one

$\overline{X}_2$ = Mean of sample two

$\sigma_{\overline{X}_1 - \overline{X}_2}$ = Standard error of difference between two sample means worked out as

$$\sigma_{\overline{X}_1 - \overline{X}_2} = \sqrt{\frac{\Sigma\left(X_{1i} - \overline{X}_1\right)^2 + \Sigma\left(X_{2i} - \overline{X}_2\right)^2}{n_1 + n_2 - 2}} \times \sqrt{\frac{1}{n_1} + \frac{1}{n_2}}$$

and the d.f. = $(n_1 + n_2 - 2)$.

(iii) To test the significance of the coefficient of simple correlation

$$t = \frac{r}{\sqrt{1 - r^2}} \times \sqrt{n - 2} \text{ or } t = r\sqrt{\frac{n - 2}{1 - r^2}}$$

where

r = the coefficient of simple correlation

and the d.f. = $(n - 2)$.

(iv) To test the significance of the coefficient of partial correlation

$$t = \frac{r_p}{\sqrt{1 - r_p^2}} \times \sqrt{n - k} \quad \text{or} \quad t = r_p\sqrt{\frac{(n - k)}{1 - r_p^2}}$$

where r_p is any partial coeficient of correlation

and the d.f. = $(n - k)$, n being the number of pairs of observations and k being the number of variables involved.

(v) To test the difference in case of paired or correlated samples data (in which case t test is ofter described as difference test)

$$t = \frac{\overline{D} - \mu_D}{\sigma_D}\sqrt{n} \quad \text{i.e.,} \quad t = \frac{\overline{D} - 0}{\sigma_D}\sqrt{n}$$

where

Hypothesised mean difference (μ_D) is taken as zero (0),

$\overline{D}$ = Mean of the differences of correlated sample items

σ_D = Standard deviation of differences worked out as under

$$\sigma_D = \sqrt{\frac{\Sigma D_i^2 - \overline{D}/n}{n - 1}}$$

D_i = Differences {i.e., $D_i = (X_i - Y_i)$}

n = number of pairs in two samples and the d.f. = $(n - 1)$.

SANDLER'S A-TEST

Joseph Sandler has developed an alternate approach based on a simplification of t-test. His approach is described as Sandler's A-test that serves the same purpose as is accomplished by t-test relating to paired data. Researchers can as well use A-test when correlated samples are employed and hypothesised mean difference is taken as zero i.e., $H_0 : \mu_D = 0$. Psychologists generally use this test in case of two groups that are matched with respect to some extraneous variable(s). While using A-test, we work out A-statistic that yields exactly the same results as Student's t-test[*]. A-statistic is found as follows:

$$A = \frac{\text{the sum of squares of the differences}}{\text{the squares of the sum of the differences}} = \frac{\Sigma D_i^2}{(\Sigma D_i)^2}$$

The number of degrees of freedom (d.f.) in A-test is the same as with Student's t-test i.e., d.f. $= n - 1$, n being equal to the number of pairs. The critical value of A, at a given level of significance for given d.f., can be obtained from the table of A-statistic (given in appendix at the end of the book). One has to compare the computed value of A with its corresponding table value for drawing inference concerning acceptance or rejection of null hypothesis.[**] If the calculated value of A is equal to or less than the table value, in that case A-statistic is considered significant where upon we reject H_0 and accept H_a. But if the calculated value of A is more than its table value, then A-statistic is taken as insignificant and accordingly we accept H_0. This is so because the two test statistics viz., t and A are inversely related. We can write these two statistics in terms of one another in this way:

(i) 'A' in terms of 't' can be expressed as

$$A = \frac{n-1}{n \cdot t^2} + \frac{1}{n}$$

(ii) 't' in terms of 'A' can be expressed as

$$t = \sqrt{\frac{n-1}{A \cdot n - 1}}$$

Computational work concerning A-statistic is relatively simple. As such the use of A-statistic result in considerable saving of time and labour, specially when matched groups are to be compared with respect to a large number of variables. Accordingly researchers may replace Student's t-test by Sandler's A-test whenever correlated sets of scores are employed.

Sandler's A-statistic can as well be used "in the one sample case as a direct substitute for the Student t-ratio."[4] This is so because Sandler's A is an algebraically equivalent to the Student's t. When we use A-test in one sample case, the following steps are involved:

(i) Subtract the hypothesised mean of the population (μ_H) from each individual score (X_i) to obtain D_i and then work out ΣD_i.

---

[*] For proof, see the article, "*A test of the significance of the difference between the means of correlated measures based on a simplification of Student's*" by Joseph Sandler, published in the *Brit. J Psych.*, 1955, pp. 225–226.

[**] See illustrations 11 and 12 of Chapter 9 of this book for the purpose.

[4] Richard P. Runyon, *Inferential Statistics: A Contemporary Approach*, p.28

(*ii*) Square each D_i and then obtain the sum of such squares i.e., ΣD_i^2.

(*iii*) Find *A*-statistic as under:

$$A = \Sigma D_i^2 \Big/ \left(\Sigma D_i\right)^2$$

(*iv*) Read the table of *A*-statistic for $(n-1)$ degrees of freedom at a given level of significance (using one-tailed or two-tailed values depending upon H_a) to find the critical value of *A*.

(*v*) Finally, draw the inference as under:

When calculated value of *A* is equal to or less than the table value, then reject H_0 (or accept H_a) but when computed *A* is greater than its table value, then accept H_0.

The practical application/use of *A*-statistic in one sample case can be seen from Illustration No. 5 of Chapter IX of this book itself.

CONCEPT OF STANDARD ERROR

The standard deviation of sampling distribution of a statistic is known as its standard error (S.E) and is considered the key to sampling theory. The utility of the concept of standard error in statistical induction arises on account of the following reasons:

1. The standard error helps in testing whether the difference between observed and expected frequencies could arise due to chance. The criterion usually adopted is that if a difference is less than 3 times the S.E., the difference is supposed to exist as a matter of chance and if the difference is equal to or more than 3 times the S.E., chance fails to account for it, and we conclude the difference as significant difference. This criterion is based on the fact that at $\overline{X} \pm 3$ (S.E.) the normal curve covers an area of 99.73 per cent. Sometimes the criterion of 2 S.E. is also used in place of 3 S.E. Thus the standard error is an important measure in significance tests or in examining hypotheses. If the estimated parameter differs from the calculated statistic by more than 1.96 times the S.E., the difference is taken as significant at 5 per cent level of significance. This, in other words, means that the difference is outside the limits i.e., it lies in the 5 per cent area (2.5 per cent on both sides) outside the 95 per cent area of the sampling distribution. Hence we can say with 95 per cent confidence that the said difference is not due to fluctuations of sampling. In such a situation our hypothesis that there is no difference is rejected at 5 per cent level of significance. But if the difference is less than 1.96 times the S.E., then it is considered not significant at 5 per cent level and we can say with 95 per cent confidence that it is because of the fluctuations of sampling. In such a situation our null hypothesis stands true. 1.96 is the critical value at 5 per cent level. The product of the critical value at a certain level of significance and the S.E. is often described as 'Sampling Error' at that particular level of significance. We can test the difference at certain other levels of significance as well depending upon our requirement. The following table gives some idea about the criteria at various levels for judging the significance of the difference between observed and expected values:

Table 8.1: Criteria for Judging Significance at Various Important Levels

Significance level	Confidence level	Critical value	Sampling error	Confidence limits	Difference Significant if	Difference Insignificant if
5.0%	95.0%	1.96	1.96σ	±1.96σ	$>$ 1.96σ	$<$ 1.96σ
1.0%	99.0%	2.5758	2.5758 σ	± 2.5758 σ	$>$ 2.5758 σ	$<$ 2.5758 σ
$=$ 0.27%.	99.73%	3	3 σ	± 3 σ	$>$ 3 σ	$<$ 3 σ
4.55%	95.45%	2	2 σ	± 2 σ	$>$ 2 σ	$<$ 2 σ

σ = Standard Error.

2. The standard error gives an idea about the reliability and precision of a sample. The smaller the S.E., the greater the uniformity of sampling distribution and hence, greater is the reliability of sample. Conversely, the greater the S.E., the greater the difference between observed and expected frequencies. In such a situation the unreliability of the sample is greater. The size of S.E., depends upon the sample size to a great extent and it varies inversely with the size of the sample. If double reliability is required i.e., reducing S.E. to 1/2 of its existing magnitude, the sample size should be increased four-fold.

3. The standard error enables us to specify the limits within which the parameters of the population are expected to lie with a specified degree of confidence. Such an interval is usually known as confidence interval. The following table gives the percentage of samples having their mean values within a range of population mean (μ) ± S.E.

Table 8.2

Range	Per cent Values
μ ± 1 S.E.	68.27%
μ ± 2 S.E.	95.45%
μ ± 3 S.E.	99.73%
μ ± 1.96 S.E.	95.00%
μ ± 2.5758 S.E.	99.00%

Important formulae for computing the standard errors concerning various measures based on samples are as under:

(a) *In case of sampling of attributes*:

(i) Standard error of number of successes = $\sqrt{n \cdot p \cdot q}$

where n = number of events in each sample,

p = probability of success in each event,

q = probability of failure in each event.

(ii) Standard error of proportion of successes $\sqrt{\dfrac{(p \cdot q)}{n}}$

(iii) Standard error of the difference between proportions of two samples:

$$\sigma_{p_1 - p_2} = \sqrt{p \cdot q \left(\frac{1}{n_1} + \frac{1}{n_2} \right)}$$

where p = best estimate of proportion in the population and is worked out as under:

$$p = \frac{n_1\, p_1 + n_2\, p_2}{n_1 + n_2}$$

$q = 1 - p$

n_1 = number of events in sample one

n_2 = number of events in sample two

Note: Instead of the above formula, we use the following formula:

$$\sigma_{p_1 - p_2} = \sqrt{\frac{p_1\, q_1}{n_1} + \frac{p_2\, q_2}{n_2}}$$

when samples are drawn from two heterogeneous populations where we cannot have the best estimate of proportion in the universe on the basis of given sample data. Such a situation often arises in study of association of attributes.

(b) *In case of sampling of variables (large samples):*

(i) Standard error of mean when population standard deviation is known:

$$\sigma_{\bar{X}} = \frac{\sigma_p}{\sqrt{n}}$$

where

σ_p = standard deviation of population

n = number of items in the sample

Note: This formula is used even when n is 30 or less.

(ii) Standard error of mean when population standard deviation is unknown:

$$\sigma_{\bar{X}} = \frac{\sigma_s}{\sqrt{n}}$$

where

σ_s = standard deviation of the sample and is worked out as under

$$\sigma_s = \sqrt{\frac{\Sigma \left(X_i - \bar{X} \right)^2}{n - 1}}$$

n = number of items in the sample.

(iii) Standard error of standard deviation when population standard deviation is known:

$$\sigma_{\sigma_s} = \frac{\sigma_p}{\sqrt{2n}}$$

(iv) Standard error of standard deviation when population standard deviation is unknown:

$$\sigma_{\sigma_s} = \frac{\sigma_s}{\sqrt{2n}}$$

where $\qquad \sigma_s = \sqrt{\dfrac{\Sigma\left(X_i - \overline{X}\right)^2}{n-1}}$

n = number of items in the sample.

(v) Standard error of the coeficient of simple correlation:

$$\sigma_r = \frac{1 - r^2}{\sqrt{n}}$$

where

r = coefficient of simple correlation

n = number of items in the sample.

(vi) Standard error of difference between means of two samples:

(a) When two samples are drawn from the same population:

$$\sigma_{\overline{X}_i - \overline{X}_2} = \sqrt{\sigma_p^2\left(\frac{1}{n_1} + \frac{1}{n_2}\right)}$$

(If σ_p is not known, sample standard deviation for combined samples $\left(\sigma_{s_{1\cdot2}}\right)^*$

may be substituted.)

(b) When two samples are drawn from different populations:

$$\sigma_{\overline{X}_1 - \overline{X}_2} = \sqrt{\frac{\left(\sigma_{p_1}\right)^2}{n_1} + \frac{\left(\sigma_{p_2}\right)^2}{n_2}}$$

(If σ_{p_1} and σ_{p_2} are not known, then in their places σ_{s_1} and σ_{s_2} respectively may be substituted.)

(c) *In case of sampling of variables* (*small samples*):

(i) Standard error of mean when σ_p is unknown:

$$\sigma_{s_{1 \cdot 2}} = \sqrt{\frac{n_1 \left(\sigma_{s_1}\right)^2 + n_2 \left(\sigma_{s_2}\right)^2 + n_1 \left(\overline{X}_1 - \overline{X}_{1 \cdot 2}\right)^2 + n_2 \left(\overline{X}_2 - \overline{X}_{1 \cdot 2}\right)^2}{n_1 + n_2}}$$

where $\overline{X}_{1 \cdot 2} = \dfrac{n_1 \left(\overline{X}_1\right) + n_2 \left(\overline{X}_2\right)}{n_1 + n_2}$

Note: (1) All these formulae apply in case of infinite population. But in case of finite population where sampling is done without replacement and the sample is more than 5% of the population, we must as well use the finite population multiplier in our standard error formulae. For instance, S.E.$_{\overline{X}}$ in case of finite population will be as under:

$$SE_{\overline{X}} = \frac{\sigma_p}{\sqrt{n}} \cdot \sqrt{\frac{(N - n)}{(N - 1)}}$$

It may be remembered that in cases in which the population is very large in relation to the size of the sample, the finite population multiplier is close to one and has little effect on the calculation of S.E. As such when sampling fraction is less than 0.5, the finite population multiplier is generally not used.

(2) The use of all the above stated formulae has been explained and illustrated in context of testing of hypotheses in chapters that follow.

$$\sigma_{\overline{X}} = \frac{\sigma_s}{\sqrt{n}} = \frac{\sqrt{\dfrac{\Sigma \left(X_i - \overline{X}\right)^2}{n - 1}}}{\sqrt{n}}$$

(ii) Standard error of difference between two sample means when σ_p is unknown

$$\sigma_{\overline{X}_1 - \overline{X}_2} = \sqrt{\frac{\Sigma \left(X_{1i} - \overline{X}_1\right)^2 + \Sigma \left(X_{2i} - \overline{X}_2\right)^2}{n_1 + n_2 - 2}} \cdot \sqrt{\frac{1}{n_1} + \frac{1}{n_2}}$$

ESTIMATION

In most statistical research studies, population parameters are usually unknown and have to be estimated from a sample. As such the methods for estimating the population parameters assume an important role in statistical anlysis.

The random variables (such as $\overline{X}$ and σ_s^2) used to estimate population parameters, such as μ and σ_p^2 are conventionally called as '*estimators*', while specific values of these (such as $\overline{X} = 105$ or $\sigma_s^2 = 21.44$) are referred to as '*estimates*' of the population parameters. The estimate of a population parameter may be one single value or it could be a range of values. In the former case it is referred as *point estimate*, whereas in the latter case it is termed as *interval estimate*. The researcher usually makes these two types of estimates through sampling analysis. While making estimates of population parameters, the researcher can give only the best point estimate or else he shall have to speak in terms of intervals and probabilities for he can never estimate with certainty the exact values of population parameters. Accordingly he must know the various properties of a good estimator so that he can select appropriate estimators for his study. He must know that a good estimator possesses the following properties:

(i) An estimator should on the average be equal to the value of the parameter being estimated. This is popularly known as the *property* of *unbiasedness*. An estimator is said to be unbiased if the expected value of the estimator is equal to the parameter being estimated. The sample mean $\left(\overline{X} \right)$ is he most widely used estimator because of the fact that it provides an unbiased estimate of the population mean (μ).

(ii) An estimator should have a relatively small variance. This means that the most efficient estimator, among a group of unbiased estimators, is one which has the smallest variance. This property is technically described as the *property of efficiency*.

(iii) An estimator should use as much as possible the information available from the sample. This property is known as the *property of sufficiency*.

(iv) An estimator should approach the value of population parameter as the sample size becomes larger and larger. This property is referred to as the *property of consistency*.

Keeping in view the above stated properties, the researcher must select appropriate estimator(s) for his study. We may now explain the methods which will enable us to estimate with reasonable accuracy the population mean and the population proportion, the two widely used concepts.

ESTIMATING THE POPULATION MEAN (μ)

So far as the point estimate is concerned, the sample mean $\overline{X}$ is the best estimator of the population mean, μ, and its sampling distribution, so long as the sample is sufficiently large, approximates the normal distribution. If we know the sampling distribution of $\overline{X}$, we can make statements about any estimate that we may make from the sampling information. Assume that we take a sample of 36 students and find that the sample yields an arithmetic mean of 6.2 i.e., $\overline{X} = 6.2$. Replace these student names on the population list and draw another sample of 36 randomly and let us assume that we get a mean of 7.5 this time. Similarly a third sample may yield a mean of 6.9; fourth a mean of 6.7, and so on. We go on drawing such samples till we accumulate a large number of means of samples of 36. Each such sample mean is a separate point estimate of the population mean. When such means are presented in the form of a distribution, the distribution happens to be quite close to normal. This is a characteristic of a distribution of sample means (and also of other sample statistics). Even if the population is not normal, the sample means drawn from that population are dispersed around the parameter in a distribution that is generally close to normal; the mean of the distribution of sample means is equal to the population mean.[5] This is true in case of large samples as per the dictates of the central limit theorem. This relationship between a population distribution and a distribution of sample

---

[5] C. William Emory, *Business Research Methods*, p.145

mean is critical for drawing inferences about parameters. The relationship between the dispersion of a population distribution and that of the sample mean can be stated as under:

$$\sigma_{\overline{X}} = \frac{\sigma_p}{\sqrt{n}}$$

where $\sigma_{\overline{X}}$ = standard error of mean of a given sample size

σ_p = standard deviation of the population

n = size of the sample.

How to find σ_p when we have the sample data only for our analysis? The answer is that we must use some best estimate of σ_p and the best estimate can be the standard deviation of the sample, σ_s. Thus, the standard error of mean can be worked out as under:[6]

$$\sigma_{\overline{X}} = \frac{\sigma_s}{\sqrt{n}}$$

where

$$\sigma_s = \sqrt{\frac{\Sigma \left(X_i - \overline{X} \right)^2}{n-1}}$$

With the help of this, one may give interval estimates about the parameter in probabilistic terms (utilising the fundamental characteristics of the normal distribution). Suppose we take one sample of 36 items and work out its mean $\left(\overline{X} \right)$ to be equal to 6.20 and its standard deviation $\left(\sigma_s \right)$ to be equal to 3.8, Then the best point estimate of population mean $\left(\mu \right)$ is 6.20. The standard error of mean $\left(\sigma_{\overline{X}} \right)$ would be $3.8/\sqrt{36} = 3.8/6 = 0.663$. If we take the interval estimate of μ to be $\overline{X} \pm 1.96 \left(\sigma_{\overline{X}} \right)$ or 6.20 ± 1.24 or from 4.96 to 7.44, it means that there is a 95 per cent chance that the population mean is within 4.96 to 7.44 interval. In other words, this means that if we were to take a complete census of all items in the population, the chances are 95 to 5 that we would find the population mean lies between 4.96 to 7.44[*]. In case we desire to have an estimate that will hold for a much smaller range, then we must either accept a smaller degree of confidence in the results or take a sample large enough to provide this smaller interval with adequate confidence levels. Usually we think of increasing the sample size till we can secure the desired interval estimate and the degree of confidence.

Illustration 1

From a random sample of 36 New Delhi civil service personnel, the mean age and the sample standard deviation were found to be 40 years and 4.5 years respectively. Construct a 95 per cent confidence interval for the mean age of civil servants in New Delhi.

Solution: The given information can be written as under:

---

[6] To make the sample standard deviation an unbiased estimate of the population, it is necessary to divide $\Sigma \left(X_i - \overline{X} \right)^2$ by $(n-1)$ and not by simply (n).

[*] In case we want to change the degree of confidence in the interval estimate, the same can be done using the table of areas under the normal curve.

$$n = 36$$
$$\overline{X} = 40 \text{ years}$$
$$\sigma_s = 4.5 \text{ years}$$

and the standard variate, z, for 95 per cent confidence is 1.96 (as per the normal curve area table).

Thus, 95 per cent confidence inteval for the mean age of population is:

$$\overline{X} \pm z \frac{\sigma_s}{\sqrt{n}}$$

or

$$40 \pm 1.96 \frac{4.5}{\sqrt{36}}$$

or

$$40 \pm (1.96)\,(0.75)$$

or

$$40 \pm 1.47 \text{ years}$$

Illustration 2

In a random selection of 64 of the 2400 intersections in a small city, the mean number of scooter accidents per year was 3.2 and the sample standard deviation was 0.8.

    (1) Make an estimate of the standard deviation of the population from the sample standard deviation.

    (2) Work out the standard error of mean for this finite population.

    (3) If the desired confidence level is .90, what will be the upper and lower limits of the confidence interval for the mean number of accidents per intersection per year?

Solution: The given information can be written as under:

    $N = 2400$ (This means that population is finite)
    $n = 64$
    $\overline{X} = 3.2$
    $\sigma_s = 0.8$

and the standard variate (z) for 90 per cent confidence is 1.645 (as per the normal curve area table).

Now we can answer the given questions thus:

    (1) The best point estimate of the standard deviation of the population is the standard deviation of the sample itself.

        Hence,

$$\hat{\sigma}_p = \sigma_s = 0.8$$

    (2) Standard error of mean for the given finite population is as follows:

$$\sigma_{\overline{X}} = \frac{\sigma_s}{\sqrt{n}} \times \sqrt{\frac{N-n}{N-1}}$$

$$= \frac{0.8}{\sqrt{64}} \times \sqrt{\frac{2400 - 64}{2400 - 1}}$$

$$= \frac{0.8}{\sqrt{64}} \times \sqrt{\frac{2336}{2399}}$$

$$= (0.1)\,(.97)$$

$$= .097$$

(3) 90 per cent confidence interval for the mean number of accidents per intersection per year is as follows:

$$\bar{X} \pm z \left\{ \frac{\sigma_s}{\sqrt{n}} \times \sqrt{\frac{N - n}{N - 1}} \right\}$$

$$= 3.2 \pm (1.645)\,(.097)$$

$$= 3.2 \pm .16 \text{ accidents per intersection.}$$

When the sample size happens to be a large one or when the population standard deviation is known, we use normal distribution for detemining confidence intervals for population mean as stated above. But how to handle estimation problem when population standard deviation is not known and the sample size is small (i.e., when $n < 30$)? In such a situation, normal distribution is not appropriate, but we can use t-distribution for our purpose. While using t-distribution, we assume that population is normal or approximately normal. There is a different t-distribution for each of the possible degrees of freedom. When we use t-distribution for estimating a population mean, we work out the degrees of freedom as equal to $n - 1$, where n means the size of the sample and then can look for cirtical value of 't' in the t-distribution table for appropriate degrees of freedom at a given level of significance. Let us illustrate this by taking an example.

Illustration 3

The foreman of *ABC* mining company has estimated the average quantity of iron ore extracted to be 36.8 tons per shift and the sample standard deviation to be 2.8 tons per shift, based upon a random selection of 4 shifts. Construct a 90 per cent confidence interval around this estimate.

Solution: As the standard deviation of population is not known and the size of the sample is small, we shall use t-distribution for finding the required confidence interval about the population mean. The given information can be written as under:

$$\bar{X} = 36.8 \text{ tons per shift}$$

$$\sigma_s = 2.8 \text{ tons per shift}$$

$$n = 4$$

degrees of freedom $= n - 1 = 4 - 1 = 3$ and the critical value of 't' for 90 per cent confidence interval or at 10 per cent level of significance is 2.353 for 3 $d.f.$ (as per the table of t-distribution).

Thus, 90 per cent confidence interval for population mean is

$$\overline{X} \pm t \frac{\sigma_s}{\sqrt{n}}$$

$$= 36.8 \pm 2.353 \frac{2.8}{\sqrt{4}} = 36.8 \pm (2.353)(1.4)$$

$$= 36.8 \pm 3.294 \text{ tons per shift.}$$

ESTIMATING POPULATION PROPORTION

So far as the point estimate is concerned, the sample proportion (p) of units that have a particular characteristic is the best estimator of the population proportion $(\hat{p})$ and its sampling distribution, so long as the sample is sufficiently large, approximates the normal distribution. Thus, if we take a random sample of 50 items and find that 10 per cent of these are defective i.e., $p = .10$, we can use this sample proportion ($p = .10$) as best estimator of the population proportion $(\hat{p} = p = .10)$. In case we want to construct confidence interval to estimate a population poportion, we should use the binomial distribution with the mean of population $(\mu) = n \cdot p$, where n = number of trials, p = probability of a success in any of the trials and population standard deviation $= \sqrt{npq}$. As the sample size increases, the binomial distribution approaches normal distribution which we can use for our purpose of estimating a population proportion. The mean of the sampling distribution of the proportion of successes (μ_p) is taken as equal to p and the standard deviation for the proportion of successes, also known as the standard error of proportion, is taken as equal to $\sqrt{pq/n}$. But when population proportion is unknown, then we can estimate the population parameters by substituting the corresponding sample statistics p and q in the formula for the standard error of proportion to obtain the estimated standard error of the proportion as shown below:

$$\sigma_p = \sqrt{\frac{pq}{n}}$$

Using the above estimated standard error of proportion, we can work out the confidence interval for population proportion thus:

$$p \pm z \cdot \sqrt{\frac{pq}{n}}$$

where

p = sample proportion of successes;

$q = 1 - p$;

n = number of trials (size of the sample);

z = standard variate for given confidence level (as per normal curve area table).

We now illustrate the use of this formula by an example.

Illustration 4

A market research survey in which 64 consumers were contacted states that 64 per cent of all consumers of a certain product were motivated by the product's advertising. Find the confidence limits for the proportion of consumers motivated by advertising in the population, given a confidence level equal to 0.95.

Solution: The given information can be written as under:

$$n = 64$$

$$p = 64\% \text{ or } .64$$

$$q = 1 - p = 1 - .64 = .36$$

and the standard variate (z) for 95 per cent confidence is 1.96 (as per the normal curve area table).

Thus, 95 per cent confidence interval for the proportion of consumers motivated by advertising in the population is:

$$p \pm z \cdot \sqrt{\frac{pq}{n}}$$

$$= .64 \pm 1.96 \sqrt{\frac{(0.64)\,(0.36)}{64}}$$

$$= .64 \pm (1.96)\,(.06)$$

$$= .64 \pm .1176$$

Thus, lower confidence limit is 52.24%

upper confidence limit is 75.76%

For the sake of convenience, we can summarise the formulae which give confidence intevals while estimating population mean (μ) and the population proportion $(\hat{p})$ as shown in the following table.

Table 8.3: Summarising Important Formulae Concerning Estimation

	In case of infinite population	In case of finite population*
Estimating population mean (μ) when we know σ_p	$\overline{X} \pm z \cdot \dfrac{\sigma_p}{\sqrt{n}}$	$\overline{X} \pm z \cdot \dfrac{\sigma_p}{\sqrt{n}} \times \sqrt{\dfrac{N-n}{N-1}}$
Estimating population mean (μ) when we do not know σ_p	$\overline{X} \pm z \cdot \dfrac{\sigma_s}{\sqrt{n}}$	$\overline{X} \pm z \cdot \dfrac{\sigma_s}{\sqrt{n}} \times \sqrt{\dfrac{N-n}{N-1}}$

Contd.

	In case of infinite population	*In case of finite population*[*]
and use σ_s as the best estimate of σ_p and sample is large (i.e., $n > 30$)		
Estimating population mean (μ) when we do not know σ_p and use σ_s as the best estimate of σ_p and sample is small (i.e., $n \le 30$)	$\overline{X} \pm t \cdot \dfrac{\sigma_s}{\sqrt{n}}$	$\overline{X} \pm t \cdot \dfrac{\sigma_s}{\sqrt{n}} \times \sqrt{\dfrac{N-n}{N-1}}$
Estimating the population proportion $(\hat{p})$ when p is not known but the sample is large.	$p \pm z \cdot \sqrt{\dfrac{pq}{n}}$	$p \pm z \cdot \sqrt{\dfrac{pq}{n}} \times \sqrt{\dfrac{N-n}{N-1}}$

[*] In case of finite population, the standard error has to be multiplied by the finite population multiplier viz., $\sqrt{(N-n)/(N-1)}$.

SAMPLE SIZE AND ITS DETERMINATION

In sampling analysis the most ticklish question is: What should be the size of the sample or how large or small should be '*n*'? If the sample size ('*n*') is too small, it may not serve to achieve the objectives and if it is too large, we may incur huge cost and waste resources. As a general rule, one can say that the sample must be of an optimum size i.e., it should neither be excessively large nor too small. Technically, the sample size should be large enough to give a confidence inerval of desired width and as such the size of the sample must be chosen by some logical process before sample is taken from the universe. Size of the sample should be determined by a researcher keeping in view the following points:

(i) *Nature of universe:* Universe may be either homogenous or heterogenous in nature. If the items of the universe are homogenous, a small sample can serve the purpose. But if the items are heteogenous, a large sample would be required. Technically, this can be termed as the dispersion factor.

(ii) *Number of classes proposed:* If many class-groups (groups and sub-groups) are to be formed, a large sample would be required because a small sample might not be able to give a reasonable number of items in each class-group.

(iii) *Nature of study:* If items are to be intensively and continuously studied, the sample should be small. For a general survey the size of the sample should be large, but a small sample is considered appropriate in technical surveys.

(iv) *Type of sampling:* Sampling technique plays an important part in determining the size of the sample. A small random sample is apt to be much superior to a larger but badly selected sample.

(v) *Standard of accuracy and acceptable confidence level:* If the standard of acuracy or the level of precision is to be kept high, we shall require relatively larger sample. For doubling the accuracy for a fixed significance level, the sample size has to be increased fourfold.

(vi) *Availability of finance:* In prctice, size of the sample depends upon the amount of money available for the study purposes. This factor should be kept in view while determining the size of sample for large samples result in increasing the cost of sampling estimates.

(vii) *Other considerations:* Nature of units, size of the population, size of questionnaire, availability of trained investigators, the conditions under which the sample is being conducted, the time available for completion of the study are a few other considerations to which a researcher must pay attention while selecting the size of the sample.

There are two alternative approaches for determining the size of the sample. The first approach is "to specify the precision of estimation desired and then to determine the sample size necessary to insure it" and the second approach "uses Bayesian statistics to weigh the cost of additional information against the expected value of the additional information."[7] The first approach is capable of giving a mathematical solution, and as such is a frequently used technique of determining '*n*'. The limitation of this technique is that it does not analyse the cost of gathering information *vis-a-vis* the expected value of information. The second approach is theoretically optimal, but it is seldom used because of the difficulty involved in measuring the value of information. Hence, we shall mainly concentrate here on the first approach.

DETERMINATION OF SAMPLE SIZE THROUGH THE APPROACH BASED ON PRECISION RATE AND CONFIDENCE LEVEL

To begin with, it can be stated that whenever a sample study is made, there arises some sampling error which can be controlled by selecting a sample of adequate size. Researcher will have to specify the precision that he wants in respect of his estimates concerning the population parameters. For instance, a researcher may like to estimate the mean of the universe within ±3 of the true mean with 95 per cent confidence. In this case we will say that the desired precision is ±3, i.e., if the sample mean is Rs 100, the true value of the mean will be no less than Rs 97 and no more than Rs 103. In other words, all this means that the acceptable error, *e*, is equal to 3. Keeping this in view, we can now explain the determination of sample size so that specified precision is ensured.

(a) *Sample size when estimating a mean:* The confidence interval for the universe mean, μ, is given by

$$\overline{X} \pm z \frac{\sigma_p}{\sqrt{n}}$$

where $\overline{X}$ = sample mean;

z = the value of the standard variate at a given confidence level (to be read from the table giving the areas under normal curve as shown in appendix) and it is 1.96 for a 95% confidence level;

n = size of the sample;

[7] Rodney D. Johnson and Bernard R. Siskih, *Quantitative Techniques for Business Decisions,* p. 374–375.

σ_p = standard deviation of the popultion (to be estimated from past experience or on the basis of a trial sample). Suppose, we have $\sigma_p = 4.8$ for our purpose.

If the difference between μ and $\overline{X}$ or the acceptable error is to be kept with in ± 3 of the sample mean with 95% confidence, then we can express the acceptable error, 'e' as equal to

$$e = z \cdot \frac{\sigma_p}{\sqrt{n}} \text{ or } 3 = 1.96 \frac{4.8}{\sqrt{n}}$$

Hence, $n = \dfrac{(1.96)^2 (4.8)^2}{(3)^2} = 9.834 \cong 10$.

In a general way, if we want to estimate μ in a population with standard deviation σ_p with an error no greater than 'e' by calculating a confidence interval with confidence corresponding to z, the necessary sample size, n, equals as under:

$$n = \frac{z^2 \sigma^2}{e^2}$$

All this is applicable whe the population happens to be infinite. Bu in case of finite population, the above stated formula for determining sample size will become

$$n = \frac{z^2 \cdot N \cdot \sigma_p^{2^*}}{(N-1)e^2 + z^2 \sigma_p^2}$$

* In case of finite population the confidence interval for μ is given by

$$\overline{X} \pm z \frac{\sigma_p}{\sqrt{n}} \times \sqrt{\frac{(N-n)}{(N-1)}}$$

where $\sqrt{(N-n)/(N-1)}$ is the finite population multiplier and all other terms mean the same thing as stated above.

If the precision is taken as equal to 'e' then we have

$$e = z \frac{\sigma_p}{\sqrt{n}} \times \sqrt{\frac{(N-n)}{(N-1)}}$$

or
$$e^2 = z^2 \frac{\sigma_p^2}{n} \times \frac{N-n}{N-1}$$

or
$$e^2 (N-1) = \frac{z^2 \sigma_p^2 N}{n} - \frac{z^2 \sigma_p^2 n}{n}$$

or
$$e^2 (N-1) + z^2 \sigma_p^2 = \frac{z^2 \sigma_p^2 N}{n}$$

or
$$n = \frac{z^2 \cdot \sigma_p^2 \cdot N}{e^2 (N-1) + z^2 \sigma_p^2}$$

or
$$n = \frac{z^2 \cdot N \cdot \sigma_p^2}{(N-1)e^2 + z^2 \sigma_p^2}$$

This is how we obtain the above stated formula for determining 'n' in the case of infinite population given the precision and confidence level.

where

N = size of population

n = size of sample

e = acceptable error (the precision)

σ_p = standard deviation of population

z = standard variate at a given confidence level.

Illustration 5

Determine the size of the sample for estimating the true weight of the cereal containers for the universe with $N = 5000$ on the basis of the following information:

(1) the variance of weight = 4 ounces on the basis of past records.

(2) estimate should be within 0.8 ounces of the true average weight with 99% probability.

Will there be a change in the size of the sample if we assume infinite population in the given case? If so, explain by how much?

Solution: In the given problem we have the following:

$N = 5000$;

σ_p = 2 ounces (since the variance of weight = 4 ounces);

$e = 0.8$ ounces (since the estimate should be within 0.8 ounces of the true average weight);

$z = 2.57$ (as per the table of area under normal curve for the given confidence level of 99%).

Hence, the confidence interval for μ is given by

$$\overline{X} \pm z \cdot \frac{\sigma_p}{\sqrt{n}} \cdot \sqrt{\frac{N-n}{N-1}}$$

and accordingly the sample size can be worked out as under:

$$n = \frac{z^2 \cdot N \cdot \sigma_p^2}{(N-1)\, e^2 + z^2\, \sigma_p^2}$$

$$= \frac{(2.57)^2 \cdot (5000) \cdot (2)^2}{(5000-1)\,(0.8)^2 + (2.57)^2\,(2)^2}$$

$$= \frac{132098}{3199.36 + 26.4196} = \frac{132098}{3225.7796} = 40.95 \cong 41$$

Hence, the sample size (or n) = 41 for the given precision and confidence level in the above question with finite population. But if we take population to be infinite, the sample size will be worked out as under:

$$n = \frac{z^2 \, \sigma_p^2}{e^2}$$

$$= \frac{(2.57)^2 \, (2)^2}{(0.8)^2} = \frac{26.4196}{0.64} = 41.28 \simeq 41$$

Thus, in the given case the sample size remains the same even if we assume infinite population.

In the above illustration, the standard deviation of the population was given, but in many cases the standard deviation of the population is not available. Since we have not yet taken the sample and are in the stage of deciding how large to make it (sample), we cannot estimate the populaion standard deviation. In such a situation, if we have an idea about the range (i.e., the difference between the highest and lowest values) of the population, we can use that to get a crude estimate of the standard deviation of the population for geting a working idea of the required sample size. We can get the said estimate of standard deviation as follows:

Since 99.7 per cent of the area under normal curve lies within the range of ± 3 standard deviations, we may say that these limits include almost all of the distribution. Accordingly, we can say that the given range equals 6 standard deviations because of ± 3. Thus, a rough estimate of the population standard deviation would be:

$$6\hat{\sigma} = \text{the given range}$$

or
$$\hat{\sigma} = \frac{\text{the given range}}{6}$$

If the range happens to be, say Rs 12, then

$$\hat{\sigma} = \frac{12}{6} = \text{Rs 2.}$$

and this estimate of standard deviation, $\hat{\sigma}$, can be used to determine the sample size in the formulae stated above.

(b) *Sample size when estimating a percentage or proportion:* If we are to find the sample size for estimating a proportion, our reasoning remains similar to what we have said in the context of estimating the mean. First of all, we shall have to specify the precision and the confidence level and then we will work out the sample size as under:

Since the confidence interval for universe proportion, $\hat{p}$ is given by

$$p \pm z \cdot \sqrt{\frac{p \cdot q}{n}}$$

where p = sample proportion, $q = 1 - p$;

      z = the value of the standard variate at a given confidence level and to be worked out from table showing area under Normal Curve;

      n = size of sample.

Since $\hat{p}$ is actually what we are trying to estimate, then what value we should assign to it ? One method may be to take the value of $p = 0.5$ in which case 'n' will be the maximum and the sample will yield at least the desired precision. This will be the most conservative sample size. The other method may be to take an initial estimate of p which may either be based on personal judgement or may be the result of a pilot study. In this context it has been suggested that a pilot study of something like 225 or more items may result in a reasonable approximation of p value.

Then with the given precision rate, the acceptable error, 'e', can be expressed as under:

$$e = z \cdot \sqrt{\frac{pq}{n}}$$

or

$$e^2 = z^2 \frac{pq}{n}$$

or

$$n = \frac{z^2 \cdot p \cdot q}{e^2}$$

The formula gives the size of the sample in case of infinite population when we are to estimate the proportion in the universe. But in case of finite population the above stated formula will be changed as under:

$$n = \frac{z^2 \cdot p \cdot q \cdot N}{e^2 (N - 1) + z^2 \cdot p \cdot q}$$

Illustration 6

What should be the size of the sample if a simple random sample from a population of 4000 items is to be drawn to estimate the per cent defective within 2 per cent of the true value with 95.5 per cent probability? What would be the size of the sample if the population is assumed to be infinite in the given case?

Solution: In the given question we have the following:

$N = 4000$;

$e = .02$ (since the estimate should be within 2% of true value);

$z = 2.005$ (as per table of area under normal curve for the given confidence level of 95.5%).

As we have not been given the p value being the proportion of defectives in the universe, let us assume it to be $p = .02$ (This may be on the basis of our experience or on the basis of past data or may be the result of a pilot study).

Now we can determine the size of the sample using all this information for the given question as follows:

$$n = \frac{z^2 \cdot p \cdot q \cdot N}{e^2 (N - 1) + z^2 \cdot p \cdot q}$$

$$= \frac{(2.005)^2 \, (.02) \, (1 - .02) \, (4000)}{(.02)^2 \, (4000 - 1) + (2.005)^2 \, (.02) \, (1 - .02)}$$

$$= \frac{315.1699}{1.5996 + .0788} = \frac{315.1699}{1.6784} = 187.78 \simeq 188$$

But if the population happens to be infinite, then our sample size will be as under:

$$n = \frac{z^2 \cdot p \cdot q}{e^2}$$

$$= \frac{(2.005)^2 \cdot (.02) \, (1 - .02)}{(.02)^2}$$

$$= \frac{.0788}{.0004} = 196.98 \simeq 197$$

Illustration 7

Suppose a certain hotel management is interested in determining the percentage of the hotel's guests who stay for more than 3 days. The reservation manager wants to be 95 per cent confident that the percentage has been estimated to be within ±3% of the true value. What is the most conservative sample size needed for this problem?

Solution: We have been given the following:

Population is infinite;

$e = .03$ (since the estimate should be within 3% of the true value);

$z = 1.96$ (as per table of area under normal curve for the given confidence level of 95%).

As we want the most conservative sample size we shall take the value of $p = .5$ and $q = .5$. Using all this information, we can determine the sample size for the given problem as under:

$$n = \frac{z^2 \, p \, q}{e^2}$$

$$= \frac{(1.96)^2 \cdot (.5) \, (1 - .5)}{(.03)^2} = \frac{.9604}{.0009} = 1067.11 \simeq 1067$$

Thus, the most conservative sample size needed for the problem is = 1067.

DETERMINATION OF SAMPLE SIZE THROUGH THE APPROACH BASED ON BAYESIAN STATISTICS

This approach of determining '*n*' utilises Bayesian statistics and as such is known as Bayesian approach. The procedure for finding the optimal value of '*n*' or the size of sample under this approach is as under:

(i) Find the expected value of the sample information (EVSI)[*] for every possible n;

(ii) Also workout reasonably approximated cost of taking a sample of every possible n;

(iii) Compare the EVSI and the cost of the sample for every possible n. In other words, workout the expected net gain (ENG) for every possible n as stated below:

For a given sample size (n):

(EVSI) – (Cost of sample) = (ENG)

(iv) Form (iii) above the optimal sample size, that value of n which maximises the difference between the EVSI and the cost of the sample, can be determined.

The computation of EVSI for every possible n and then comparing the same with the respective cost is often a very cumbersome task and is generally feasible with mechanised or computer help. Hence, this approach although being theoretically optimal is rarely used in practice.

Questions

1. Explain the meaning and significance of the concept of "Standard Error' in sampling analysis.
2. Describe briefly the commonly used sampling distributions.
3. State the reasons why sampling is used in the context of research studies.
4. Explain the meaning of the following sampling fundamentals:
   (a) Sampling frame;
   (b) Sampling error;
   (c) Central limit theorem;
   (d) Student's t distribution;
   (e) Finite population multiplier.
5. Distinguish between the following:
   (a) Statistic and parameter;
   (b) Confidence level and significance level;
   (c) Random sampling and non-random sampling;
   (d) Sampling of attributes and sampling of variables;
   (e) Point estimate and interval estimation.
6. Write a brief essay on statistical estimation.
7. 500 articles were selected at random out of a batch containing 10000 articles and 30 were found defective. How many defective articles would you reasonably expect to find in the whole batch?
8. In a sample of 400 people, 172 were males. Estimate the population proportion at 95% confidence level.
9. A smaple of 16 measurements of the diameter of a sphere gave a mean $\overline{X} = 4.58$ inches and a standard deviation $\sigma_s = 0.08$ inches. Find (a) 95%, and (b) 99% confidence limits for the actual diameter.
10. A random sample of 500 pineapples was taken from a large consignment and 65 were found to be bad. Show that the standard error of the population of bad ones in a sample of this size is 0.015 and also show that the percentage of bad pineapples in the consignment almost certainly lies between 8.5 and 17.5.

---

[*] EVSI happens to be the difference between the expected value with sampling and the expected value without sampling. For finding EVSI we have to use Bayesian statistics for which one should have a thorough knowledge of Bayesian probability analysis which can be looked into any standard text book on statistics.

11. From a packet containing iron nails, 1000 iron nails were taken at random and out of them 100 were found defective. Estimate the percentage of defective iron nails in the packet and assign limits within which the percentage probably lies.

12. A random sample of 200 measurements from an infinite population gave a mean value of 50 and a standard deviation of 9. Determine the 95% confidence interval for the mean value of the population.

13. In a random sample of 64 mangoes taken from a large consignment, some were found to be bad. Deduce that the percentage of bad mangoes in the consignment almost certainly lies between 31.25 and 68.75 given that the standard error of the proportion of bad mangoes in the sample 1/16.

14. A random sample of 900 members is found to have a mean of 4.45 cms. Can it be reasonably regarded as a sample from a large population whose mean is 5 cms and variance is 4 cms?

15. It is claimed that Americans are 16 pounds overweight on average. To test this claim, 9 randomly selected individuals were examined and the average excess weight was found to be 18 pounds. At the 5% level of significance, is there reason to believe the claim of 16 pounds to be in error?

16. The foreman of a certain mining company has estimated the average quantity of ore extracted to be 34.6 tons per shift and the sample standard deviation to be 2.8 tons per shift, based upon a random selection of 6 shifts. Construct 95% as well as 98% confidence interval for the average quantity of ore extracted per shift.

17. A sample of 16 bottles has a mean of 122 ml. (Is the sample representative of a large consignment with a mean of 130 ml.) and a standard deviation of 10 ml.? Mention the level of significance you use.

18. A sample of 900 days is taken from meteorological records of a certain district and 100 of them are found to be foggy. What are the probable limits to the percentage of foggy days in the district?

19. Suppose the following ten values represent random observations from a normal parent population:
    $$2, 6, 7, 9, 5, 1, 0, 3, 5, 4.$$
    Construct a 99 per cent confidence interval for the mean of the parent population.

20. A survey result of 1600 Playboy readers indicates that 44% finished at least three years of college. Set 98% confidence limits on the true proportion of all Playboy readers with this background.

21. (a) What are the alternative approaches of determining a sample size? Explain.

    (b) If we want to draw a simple random sample from a population of 4000 items, how large a sample do we need to draw if we desire to estimate the per cent defective within 2 % of the true value with 95.45% probability. *[M. Phil. Exam. (EAFM) RAJ. Uni. 1979]*

22. (a) Given is the following information:

    (i) Universe with $N = 10,000$.

    (ii) Variance of weight of the cereal containers on the basis of past records = 8 kg. Determine the size of the sample for estimating the true weight of the containers if the estimate should be within 0.4 kg. of the true average weight with 95% probability.

    (b) What would be the size of the sample if infinite universe is assumed in question number 22 (a) above?

23. Annual incomes of 900 salesmen employed by Hi-Fi Corporation is known to be approximately normally distributed. If the Corporation wants to be 95% confident that the true mean of this year's salesmen's income does not differ by more than 2% of the last year's mean income of Rs 12,000, what sample size would be required assuming the population standard deviation to be Rs 1500?

    [M. Phil. (EAFM) Special Exam. RAJ. Uni. 1979]

24. Mr. Alok is a purchasing agent of electronic calculators. He is interested in determining at a confidence level of 95% what proportion (within plus or minus 4%), is defective. Conservatively, how many calculators should be tested to find the proportion defective?

    (*Hint:* If he tests conservatively, then $p = .5$ and $q = .5$).

25. A team of medico research experts feels confident that a new drug they have developed will cure about 80% of the patients. How large should the sample size be for the team to be 98% certain that the sample proportion of cure is within plus and minus 2% of the proportion of all cases that the drug will cure?

26. Mr. Kishore wants to determine the average time required to complete a job with which he is concerned. As per the last studies, the population standard deviation is 8 days. How large should the sample be so that Mr. Kishore may be 99% confident that the sample average may remain within ± 2 days of the average?

9

Testing of Hypotheses I
(Parametric or Standard Tests of Hypotheses)

Hypothesis is usually considered as the principal instrument in research. Its main function is to suggest new experiments and observations. In fact, many experiments are carried out with the deliberate object of testing hypotheses. Decision-makers often face situations wherein they are interested in testing hypotheses on the basis of available information and then take decisions on the basis of such testing. In social science, where direct knowledge of population parameter(s) is rare, hypothesis testing is the often used strategy for deciding whether a sample data offer such support for a hypothesis that generalisation can be made. Thus hypothesis testing enables us to make probability statements about population parameter(s). The hypothesis may not be proved absolutely, but in practice it is accepted if it has withstood a critical testing. Before we explain how hypotheses are tested through different tests meant for the purpose, it will be appropriate to explain clearly the meaning of a hypothesis and the related concepts for better understanding of the hypothesis testing techniques.

WHAT IS A HYPOTHESIS?

Ordinarily, when one talks about hypothesis, one simply means a mere assumption or some supposition to be proved or disproved. But for a researcher hypothesis is a formal question that he intends to resolve. Thus a hypothesis may be defined as a proposition or a set of proposition set forth as an explanation for the occurrence of some specified group of phenomena either asserted merely as a provisional conjecture to guide some investigation or accepted as highly probable in the light of established facts. Quite often a research hypothesis is a predictive statement, capable of being tested by scientific methods, that relates an independent variable to some dependent variable. For example, consider statements like the following ones:

"Students who receive counselling will show a greater increase in creativity than students not receiving counselling" Or

"the automobile A is performing as well as automobile B."

These are hypotheses capable of being objectively verified and tested. Thus, we may conclude that a hypothesis states what we are looking for and it is a proposition which can be put to a test to determine its validity.

Characteristics of hypothesis: Hypothesis must possess the following characteristics:

(i) Hypothesis should be clear and precise. If the hypothesis is not clear and precise, the inferences drawn on its basis cannot be taken as reliable.

(ii) Hypothesis should be capable of being tested. In a swamp of untestable hypotheses, many a time the research programmes have bogged down. Some prior study may be done by researcher in order to make hypothesis a testable one. A hypothesis "is testable if other deductions can be made from it which, in turn, can be confirmed or disproved by observation."[1]

(iii) Hypothesis should state relationship between variables, if it happens to be a relational hypothesis.

(iv) Hypothesis should be limited in scope and must be specific. A researcher must remember that narrower hypotheses are generally more testable and he should develop such hypotheses.

(v) Hypothesis should be stated as far as possible in most simple terms so that the same is easily understandable by all concerned. But one must remember that simplicity of hypothesis has nothing to do with its significance.

(vi) Hypothesis should be consistent with most known facts i.e., it must be consistent with a substantial body of established facts. In other words, it should be one which judges accept as being the most likely.

(vii) Hypothesis should be amenable to testing within a reasonable time. One should not use even an excellent hypothesis, if the same cannot be tested in reasonable time for one cannot spend a life-time collecting data to test it.

(viii) Hypothesis must explain the facts that gave rise to the need for explanation. This means that by using the hypothesis plus other known and accepted generalizations, one should be able to deduce the original problem condition. Thus hypothesis must actually explain what it claims to explain; it should have empirical reference.

BASIC CONCEPTS CONCERNING TESTING OF HYPOTHESES

Basic concepts in the context of testing of hypotheses need to be explained.

(a) *Null hypothesis and alternative hypothesis:* In the context of statistical analysis, we often talk about null hypothesis and alternative hypothesis. If we are to compare method A with method B about its superiority and if we proceed on the assumption that both methods are equally good, then this assumption is termed as the null hypothesis. As against this, we may think that the method A is superior or the method B is inferior, we are then stating what is termed as alternative hypothesis. The null hypothesis is generally symbolized as H_0 and the alternative hypothesis as H_a. Suppose we want to test the hypothesis that the population mean (μ) is equal to the hypothesised mean $(\mu_{H_0}) = 100$.

Then we would say that the null hypothesis is that the population mean is equal to the hypothesised mean 100 and symbolically we can express as:

$$H_0 : \mu = \mu_{H_0} = 100$$

[1] C. William Emory, *Business Research Methods*, p. 33.

If our sample results do not support this null hypothesis, we should conclude that something else is true. What we conclude rejecting the null hypothesis is known as alternative hypothesis. In other words, the set of alternatives to the null hypothesis is referred to as the alternative hypothesis. If we accept H_0, then we are rejecting H_a and if we reject H_0, then we are accepting H_a. For $H_0 : \mu = \mu_{H_0} = 100$, we may consider three possible alternative hypotheses as follows[*]:

Table 9.1

Alternative hypothesis	To be read as follows
$H_a : \mu \neq \mu_{H_0}$	(The alternative hypothesis is that the population mean is not equal to 100 i.e., it may be more or less than 100)
$H_a : \mu > \mu_{H_0}$	(The alternative hypothesis is that the population mean is greater than 100)
$H_a : \mu < \mu_{H_0}$	(The alternative hypothesis is that the population mean is less than 100)

The null hypothesis and the alternative hypothesis are chosen before the sample is drawn (the researcher must avoid the error of deriving hypotheses from the data that he collects and then testing the hypotheses from the same data). In the choice of null hypothesis, the following considerations are usually kept in view:

(a) Alternative hypothesis is usually the one which one wishes to prove and the null hypothesis is the one which one wishes to disprove. Thus, a null hypothesis represents the hypothesis we are trying to reject, and alternative hypothesis represents all other possibilities.

(b) If the rejection of a certain hypothesis when it is actually true involves great risk, it is taken as null hypothesis because then the probability of rejecting it when it is true is α (the level of significance) which is chosen very small.

(c) Null hypothesis should always be specific hypothesis i.e., it should not state about or approximately a certain value.

Generally, in hypothesis testing we proceed on the basis of null hypothesis, keeping the alternative hypothesis in view. Why so? The answer is that on the assumption that null hypothesis is true, one can assign the probabilities to different possible sample results, but this cannot be done if we proceed with the alternative hypothesis. Hence the use of null hypothesis (at times also known as statistical hypothesis) is quite frequent.

(b) *The level of significance:* This is a very important concept in the context of hypothesis testing. It is always some percentage (usually 5%) which should be chosen wit great care, thought and reason. In case we take the significance level at 5 per cent, then this implies that H_0 will be rejected

---

[*]If a hypothesis is of the type $\mu = \mu_{H_0}$, then we call such a hypothesis as simple (or specific) hypothesis but if it is of the type $\mu \neq \mu_{H_0}$ or $\mu > \mu_{H_0}$ or $\mu < \mu_{H_0}$, then we call it a composite (or nonspecific) hypothesis.

when the sampling result (i.e., observed evidence) has a less than 0.05 probability of occurring if H_0 is true. In other words, the 5 per cent level of significance means that researcher is willing to take as much as a 5 per cent risk of rejecting the null hypothesis when it (H_0) happens to be true. Thus the significance level is the maximum value of the probability of rejecting H_0 when it is true and is usually determined in advance before testing the hypothesis.

(c) *Decision rule or test of hypothesis:* Given a hypothesis H_0 and an alternative hypothesis H_a, we make a rule which is known as decision rule according to which we accept H_0 (i.e., reject H_a) or reject H_0 (i.e., accept H_a). For instance, if (H_0 is that a certain lot is good (there are very few defective items in it) against H_a) that the lot is not good (there are too many defective items in it), then we must decide the number of items to be tested and the criterion for accepting or rejecting the hypothesis. We might test 10 items in the lot and plan our decision saying that if there are none or only 1 defective item among the 10, we will accept H_0 otherwise we will reject H_0 (or accept H_a). This sort of basis is known as decision rule.

(d) *Type I and Type II errors:* In the context of testing of hypotheses, there are basically two types of errors we can make. We may reject H_0 when H_0 is true and we may accept H_0 when in fact H_0 is not true. The former is known as Type I error and the latter as Type II error. In other words, Type I error means rejection of hypothesis which should have been accepted and Type II error means accepting the hypothesis which should have been rejected. Type I error is denoted by α (alpha) known as α error, also called the level of significance of test; and Type II error is denoted by β (beta) known as β error. In a tabular form the said two errors can be presented as follows:

Table 9.2

	Decision	
	Accept H_0	Reject H_0
H_0 (true)	Correct decision	Type I error (α error)
H_0 (false)	Type II error (β error)	Correct decision

The probability of Type I error is usually determined in advance and is understood as the level of significance of testing the hypothesis. If type I error is fixed at 5 per cent, it means that there are about 5 chances in 100 that we will reject H_0 when H_0 is true. We can control Type I error just by fixing it at a lower level. For instance, if we fix it at 1 per cent, we will say that the maximum probability of committing Type I error would only be 0.01.

But with a fixed sample size, n, when we try to reduce Type I error, the probability of committing Type II error increases. Both types of errors cannot be reduced simultaneously. There is a trade-off between two types of errors which means that the probability of making one type of error can only be reduced if we are willing to increase the probability of making the other type of error. To deal with this trade-off in business situations, decision-makers decide the appropriate level of Type I error by examining the costs or penalties attached to both types of errors. If Type I error involves the time and trouble of reworking a batch of chemicals that should have been accepted, whereas Type II error means taking a chance that an entire group of users of this chemical compound will be poisoned, then in such a situation one should prefer a Type I error to a Type II error. As a result one must set very high level for Type I error in one's testing technique of a given hypothesis.[2] Hence, in the testing of hypothesis, one must make all possible effort to strike an adequate balance between Type I and Type II errors.

(e) *Two-tailed and One-tailed tests:* In the context of hypothesis testing, these two terms are quite important and must be clearly understood. A two-tailed test rejects the null hypothesis if, say, the sample mean is significantly higher or lower than the hypothesised value of the mean of the population. Such a test is appropriate when the null hypothesis is some specified value and the alternative hypothesis is a value not equal to the specified value of the null hypothesis. Symbolically, the two-tailed test is appropriate when we have $H_0: \mu = \mu_{H_0}$ and $H_a: \mu \neq \mu_{H_0}$ which may mean $\mu > \mu_{H_0}$ or $\mu < \mu_{H_0}$. Thus, in a two-tailed test, there are two rejection regions[*], one on each tail of the curve which can be illustrated as under:

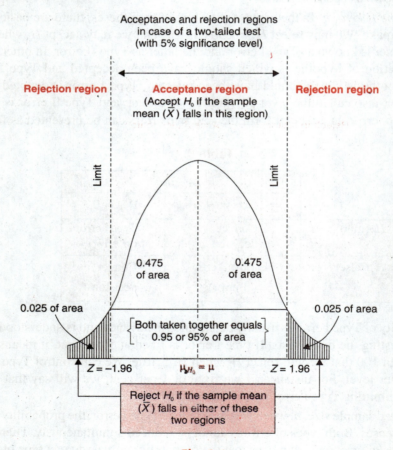

Fig. 9.1

[2] Richard I. Levin, *Statistics for Management*, p. 247–248.
[*]Also known as critical regions.

Mathematically we can state:

$$Acceptance\ Region\ \ A:|Z| < 1.96$$

$$Rejection\ Region\ \ R:|Z| > 1.96$$

If the significance level is 5 per cent and the two-tailed test is to be applied, the probability of the rejection area will be 0.05 (equally splitted on both tails of the curve as 0.025) and that of the acceptance region will be 0.95 as shown in the above curve. If we take $\mu = 100$ and if our sample mean deviates significantly from 100 in either direction, then we shall reject the null hypothesis; but if the sample mean does not deviate significantly from μ, in that case we shall accept the null hypothesis.

But there are situations when only one-tailed test is considered appropriate. A *one-tailed test* would be used when we are to test, say, whether the population mean is either lower than or higher than some hypothesised value. For instance, if our $H_0: \mu = \mu_{H_0}$ and $H_a: \mu < \mu_{H_0}$, then we are interested in what is known as left-tailed test (wherein there is one rejection region only on the left tail) which can be illustrated as below:

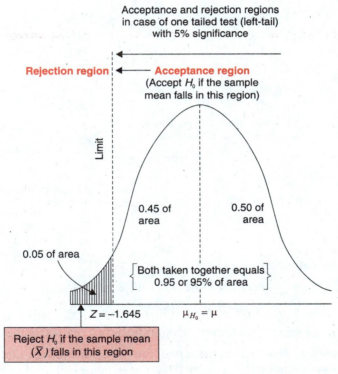

Fig. 9.2

Mathematically we can state:

$$Acceptance\ Region\ \ A: Z > -1.645$$

$$Rejection\ Region\ \ R: Z < -1.645$$

If our $\mu = 100$ and if our sample mean deviates significantly from 100 in the lower direction, we shall reject H_0, otherwise we shall accept H_0 at a certain level of significance. If the significance level in the given case is kept at 5%, then the rejection region will be equal to 0.05 of area in the left tail as has been shown in the above curve.

In case our $H_0: \mu = \mu_{H_0}$ and $H_a: \mu > \mu_{H_0}$, we are then interested in what is known as one-tailed test (right tail) and the rejection region will be on the right tail of the curve as shown below:

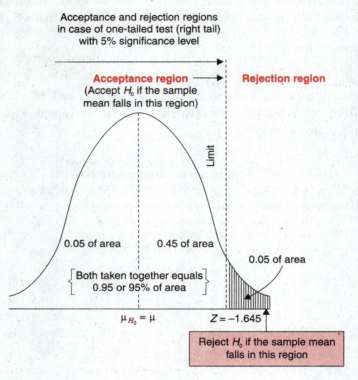

Fig. 9.3

Mathematically we can state:

$$\text{Acceptance Region } A: Z < 1.645$$

$$\text{Rejection Region } A: Z > 1.645$$

If our $\mu = 100$ and if our sample mean deviates significantly from 100 in the upward direction, we shall reject H_0, otherwise we shall accept the same. If in the given case the significance level is kept at 5%, then the rejection region will be equal to 0.05 of area in the right-tail as has been shown in the above curve.

It should always be remembered that accepting H_0 on the basis of sample information does not constitute the proof that H_0 is true. We only mean that there is no statistical evidence to reject it, but we are certainly not saying that H_0 is true (although we behave as if H_0 is true).

PROCEDURE FOR HYPOTHESIS TESTING

To test a hypothesis means to tell (on the basis of the data the researcher has collected) whether or not the hypothesis seems to be valid. In hypothesis testing the main question is: whether to accept the null hypothesis or not to accept the null hypothesis? Procedure for hypothesis testing refers to all those steps that we undertake for making a choice between the two actions i.e., rejection and acceptance of a null hypothesis. The various steps involved in hypothesis testing are stated below:

(i) *Making a formal statement:* The step consists in making a formal statement of the null hypothesis (H_0) and also of the alternative hypothesis (H_a). This means that hypotheses should be clearly stated, considering the nature of the research problem. For instance, Mr. Mohan of the Civil Engineering Department wants to test the load bearing capacity of an old bridge which must be more than 10 tons, in that case he can state his hypotheses as under:

Null hypothesis $H_0 : \mu = 10$ tons

Alternative Hypothesis $H_a : \mu > 10$ tons

Take another example. The average score in an aptitude test administered at the national level is 80. To evaluate a state's education system, the average score of 100 of the state's students selected on random basis was 75. The state wants to know if there is a significant difference between the local scores and the national scores. In such a situation the hypotheses may be stated as under:

Null hypothesis $H_0 : \mu = 80$

Alternative Hypothesis $H_a : \mu \neq 80$

The formulation of hypotheses is an important step which must be accomplished with due care in accordance with the object and nature of the problem under consideration. It also indicates whether we should use a one-tailed test or a two-tailed test. If H_a is of the type greater than (or of the type lesser than), we use a one-tailed test, but when H_a is of the type "whether greater or smaller" then we use a two-tailed test.

(ii) *Selecting a significance level:* The hypotheses are tested on a pre-determined level of significance and as such the same should be specified. Generally, in practice, either 5% level or 1% level is adopted for the purpose. The factors that affect the level of significance are: (a) the magnitude of the difference between sample means; (b) the size of the samples; (c) the variability of measurements within samples; and (d) whether the hypothesis is directional or non-directional (A directional hypothesis is one which predicts the direction of the difference between, say, means). In brief, the level of significance must be adequate in the context of the purpose and nature of enquiry.

(iii) *Deciding the distribution to use:* After deciding the level of significance, the next step in hypothesis testing is to determine the appropriate sampling distribution. The choice generally remains between normal distribution and the *t*-distribution. The rules for selecting the correct distribution are similar to those which we have stated earlier in the context of estimation.

(iv) *Selecting a random sample and computing an appropriate value:* Another step is to select a random sample(s) and compute an appropriate value from the sample data concerning the test statistic utilizing the relevant distribution. In other words, draw a sample to furnish empirical data.

(v) *Calculation of the probability:* One has then to calculate the probability that the sample result would diverge as widely as it has from expectations, if the null hypothesis were in fact true.

(vi) *Comparing the probability:* Yet another step consists in comparing the probability thus calculated with the specified value for α, the significance level. If the calculated probability is equal to or smaller than the α value in case of one-tailed test (and $\alpha/2$ in case of two-tailed test), then reject the null hypothesis (i.e., accept the alternative hypothesis), but if the calculated probability is greater, then accept the null hypothesis. In case we reject H_0 we run a risk of (at most the level of significance) committing an error of Type I, but if we accept H_0, then we run some risk (the size of which cannot be specified as long as the H_0 happens to be vague rather than specific) of committing an error of Type II.

FLOW DIAGRAM FOR HYPOTHESIS TESTING

The above stated general procedure for hypothesis testing can also be depicted in the from of a flow-chart for better understanding as shown in Fig. 9.4:[3]

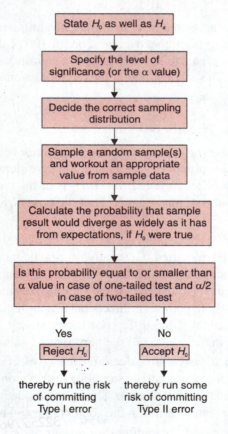

FLOW DIAGRAM FOR HYPOTHESIS TESTING

Fig. 9.4

[3] Based on the flow diagram in William A. Chance's *Statistical Methods for Decision Making,* Richard D. Irwin INC., Illinois, 1969, p.48.

MEASURING THE POWER OF A HYPOTHESIS TEST

As stated above we may commit Type I and Type II errors while testing a hypothesis. The probability of Type I error is denoted as α (the significance level of the test) and the probability of Type II error is referred to as β. Usually the significance level of a test is assigned in advance and once we decide it, there is nothing else we can do about α. But what can we say about β? We all know that hypothesis test cannot be foolproof; sometimes the test does not reject H_0 when it happens to be a false one and this way a Type II error is made. But we would certainly like that β (the probability of accepting H_0 when H_0 is not true) to be as small as possible. Alternatively, we would like that $1 - \beta$ (the probability of rejecting H_0 when H_0 is not true) to be as large as possible. If $1 - \beta$ is very much nearer to unity (i.e., nearer to 1.0), we can infer that the test is working quite well, meaning thereby that the test is rejecting H_0 when it is not true and if $1 - \beta$ is very much nearer to 0.0, then we infer that the test is poorly working, meaning thereby that it is not rejecting H_0 when H_0 is not true. Accordingly $1 - \beta$ value is the measure of how well the test is working or what is technically described as the *power of the test*. In case we plot the values of $1 - \beta$ for each possible value of the population parameter (say μ, the true population mean) for which the H_0 is not true (alternatively the H_a is true), the resulting curve is known as the power curve associated with the given test. Thus power curve of a hypothesis test is the curve that shows the conditional probability of rejecting H_0 as a function of the population parameter and size of the sample.

The function defining this curve is known as the *power function*. In other words, the power function of a test is that function defined for all values of the parameter(s) which yields the probability that H_0 is rejected and the value of the power function at a specific parameter point is called the power of the test at that point. As the population parameter gets closer and closer to hypothesised value of the population parameter, the power of the test (i.e., $1 - \beta$) must get closer and closer to the probability of rejecting H_0 when the population parameter is exactly equal to hypothesised value of the parameter. We know that this probability is simply the significance level of the test, and as such the power curve of a test terminates at a point that lies at a height of α (the significance level) directly over the population parameter.

Closely related to the power function, there is another function which is known as the *operating characteristic function* which shows the conditional probability of accepting H_0 for all values of population parameter(s) for a given sample size, whether or not the decision happens to be a correct one. If power function is represented as H and operating characteristic function as L, then we have $L = 1 - H$. However, one needs only one of these two functions for any decision rule in the context of testing hypotheses. How to compute the power of a test (i.e., $1 - \beta$) can be explained through examples.

Illustration 1

A certain chemical process is said to have produced 15 or less pounds of waste material for every 60 lbs. batch with a corresponding standard deviation of 5 lbs. A random sample of 100 batches gives an average of 16 lbs. of waste per batch. Test at 10 per cent level whether the average quantity of waste per batch has increased. Compute the power of the test for $\mu = 16$ lbs. If we raise the level of significance to 20 per cent, then how the power of the test for $\mu = 16$ lbs. would be affected?

Solution: As we want to test the hypothesis that the average quantity of waste per batch of 60 lbs. is 15 or less pounds against the hypothesis that the waste quantity is more than 15 lbs., we can write as under:

$$H_0 : \mu \leq 15 \text{ lbs.}$$
$$H_a : \mu > 15 \text{ lbs.}$$

As H_a is one-sided, we shall use the one-tailed test (in the right tail because H_a is of more than type) at 10% level for finding the value of standard deviate (z), corresponding to .4000 area of normal curve which comes to 1.28 as per normal curve area table.* From this we can find the limit of μ for accepting H_0 as under:

Accept H_0 if $\overline{X} \leq 15 + 1.28 \, (\alpha_p/\sqrt{n}\,)$

or $\overline{X} \leq 15 + 1.28 \left(5/\sqrt{100}\right)$

or $\overline{X} \leq 15.64$

at 10% level of significance otherwise accept H_a.

But the sample average is 16 lbs. which does not come in the acceptance region as above. We, therefore, reject H_0 and conclude that average quantity of waste per batch has increased. For finding the power of the test, we first calculate β and then subtract it from one. Since β is a conditional probability which depends on the value of μ, we take it as 16 as given in the question. We can now write $\beta = p$ (Accept $H_0 : \mu \leq 15 \,|\, \mu = 16$). Since we have already worked out that H_0 is accepted if $\overline{X} \leq 15.64$ (at 10% level of significance), therefore $\beta = p \, (\overline{X} \leq 15.64 \,|\, \mu = 16)$ which can be depicted as follows:

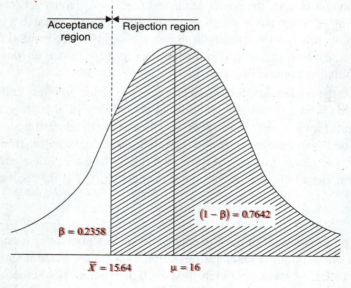

Fig. 9.5

---

* Table No. 1. given in appendix at the end of the book.

We can find out the probability of the area that lies between 15.64 and 16 in the above curve first by finding z and then using the area table for the purpose. In the given case $z = (\overline{X} - \mu)/(\sigma/\sqrt{n})$ = $(15.64 - 16)/(5/\sqrt{100}) = -0.72$ corresponding to which the area is 0.2642. Hence, $\beta = 0.5000 - 0.2642 = 0.2358$ and the power of the test = $(1 - \beta) = (1 - .2358) = 0.7642$ for $\mu = 16$.

In case the significance level is raised to 20%, then we shall have the following criteria:

Accept H_0 if $\overline{X} \lessgtr 15 + (.84)\left(5/\sqrt{100}\right)$

or $\overline{X} \lessgtr 15.42$, otherwise accept H_a

$\therefore \beta = p\left(\overline{X} \lessgtr 15.42 \,|\, \mu = 16\right)$

or $\beta = .1230$,, using normal curve area table as explained above.

Hence, $(1 - \beta) = (1 - .1230) = .8770$

TESTS OF HYPOTHESES

As has been stated above that hypothesis testing determines the validity of the assumption (technically described as null hypothesis) with a view to choose between two conflicting hypotheses about the value of a population parameter. Hypothesis testing helps to decide on the basis of a sample data, whether a hypothesis about the population is likely to be true or false. Statisticians have developed several tests of hypotheses (also known as the tests of significance) for the purpose of testing of hypotheses which can be classified as: (a) Parametric tests or standard tests of hypotheses; and (b) Non-parametric tests or distribution-free test of hypotheses.

Parametric tests usually assume certain properties of the parent population from which we draw samples. Assumptions like observations come from a normal population, sample size is large, assumptions about the population parameters like mean, variance, etc., must hold good before parametric tests can be used. But there are situations when the researcher cannot or does not want to make such assumptions. In such situations we use statistical methods for testing hypotheses which are called non-parametric tests because such tests do not depend on any assumption about the parameters of the parent population. Besides, most non-parametric tests assume only nominal or ordinal data, whereas parametric tests require measurement equivalent to at least an interval scale. As a result, non-parametric tests need more observations than parametric tests to achieve the same size of Type I and Type II errors.[4] We take up in the present chapter some of the important parametric tests, whereas non-parametric tests will be dealt with in a separate chapter later in the book.

IMPORTANT PARAMETRIC TESTS

The important parametric tests are: (1) z-test; (2) t-test; (*3) χ^2-test, and (4) F-test. All these tests are based on the assumption of normality i.e., the source of data is considered to be normally distributed.

[4] Donald L. Harnett and James L. Murphy, *Introductory Statistical Analysis,* p. 368.

* χ^2 - test is also used as a test of goodness of fit and also as a test of independence in which case it is a non-parametric test. This has been made clear in Chapter 10 entitled χ^2-test.

In some cases the population may not be normally distributed, yet the tests will be applicable on account of the fact that we mostly deal with samples and the sampling distributions closely approach normal distributions.

z-test is based on the normal probability distribution and is used for judging the significance of several statistical measures, particularly the mean. The relevant test statistic*, z, is worked out and compared with its probable value (to be read from table showing area under normal curve) at a specified level of significance for judging the significance of the measure concerned. This is a most frequently used test in research studies. This test is used even when binomial distribution or *t*-distribution is applicable on the presumption that such a distribution tends to approximate normal distribution as '*n*' becomes larger. *z*-test is generally used for comparing the mean of a sample to some hypothesised mean for the population in case of large sample, or when population variance is known. *z*-test is also used for judging he significance of difference between means of two independent samples in case of large samples, or when population variance is known. *z*-test is also used for comparing the sample proportion to a theoretical value of population proportion or for judging the difference in proportions of two independent samples when *n* happens to be large. Besides, this test may be used for judging the significance of median, mode, coefficient of correlation and several other measures.

t-test is based on *t*-distribution and is considered an appropriate test for judging the significance of a sample mean or for judging the significance of difference between the means of two samples in case of small sample(s) when population variance is not known (in which case we use variance of the sample as an estimate of the population variance). In case two samples are related, we use *paired t-test* (or what is known as difference test) for judging the significance of the mean of difference between the two related samples. It can also be used for judging the significance of the coefficients of simple and partial correlations. The relevant test statistic, *t*, is calculated from the sample data and then compared with its probable value based on *t*-distribution (to be read from the table that gives probable values of *t* for different levels of significance for different degrees of freedom) at a specified level of significance for concerning degrees of freedom for accepting or rejecting the null hypothesis. It may be noted that *t*-test applies only in case of small sample(s) when population variance is unknown.

χ^2-*test* is based on chi-square distribution and as a parametric test is used for comparing a sample variance to a theoretical population variance.

F-test is based on *F*-distribution and is used to compare the variance of the two-independent samples. This test is also used in the context of analysis of variance (ANOVA) for judging the significance of more than two sample means at one and the same time. It is also used for judging the significance of multiple correlation coefficients. Test statistic, *F*, is calculated and compared with its probable value (to be seen in the *F*-ratio tables for different degrees of freedom for greater and smaller variances at specified level of significance) for accepting or rejecting the null hypothesis.

The table on pages 198–201 summarises the important parametric tests along with test statistics and test situations for testing hypotheses relating to important parameters (often used in research studies) in the context of one sample and also in the context of two samples.

We can now explain and illustrate the use of the above stated test statistics in testing of hypotheses.

---

* The test statistic is the value obtained from the sample data that corresponds to the parameter under investigation.

HYPOTHESIS TESTING OF MEANS

Mean of the population can be tested presuming different situations such as the population may be normal or other than normal, it may be finite or infinite, sample size may be large or small, variance of the population may be known or unknown and the alternative hypothesis may be two-sided or one-sided. Our testing technique will differ in different situations. We may consider some of the important situations.

1. *Population normal, population infinite, sample size may be large or small but variance of the population is known, H_a may be one-sided or two-sided*:

   In such a situation z-test is used for testing hypothesis of mean and the test statistic z is worked our as under:

$$z = \frac{\overline{X} - \mu_{H_0}}{\sigma_p / \sqrt{n}}$$

2. *Population normal, population finite, sample size may be large or small but variance of the population is known, H_a may be one-sided or two-sided*:

   In such a situation z-test is used and the test statistic z is worked out as under (using finite population multiplier):

$$z = \frac{\overline{X} - \mu_{H_0}}{\left(\sigma_p / \sqrt{n}\right) \times \left[\sqrt{(N - n)/(N - 1)}\right]}$$

3. *Population normal, population infinite, sample size small and variance of the population unknown, H_a may be one-sided or two-sided:*

   In such a situation t-test is used and the test statistic t is worked out as under:

$$t = \frac{\overline{X} - \mu_{H_0}}{\sigma_s / \sqrt{n}} \text{ with d.f.} = (n - 1)$$

and

$$\sigma_s = \sqrt{\frac{\sum \left(X_i - \overline{X}\right)^2}{(n - 1)}}$$

4. *Population normal, population finite, sample size small and variance of the population unknown, and H_a may be one-sided or two-sided:*

   In such a situation t-test is used and the test statistic 't' is worked out as under (using finite population multiplier):

$$t = \frac{\overline{X} - \mu_{H_0}}{\left(\sigma_s / \sqrt{n}\right) \times \sqrt{(N - n)/(N - 1)}} \text{ with d.f.} = (n - 1)$$

Table 9.3: Names of Some Parametric Tests along with Test Situations and Test Statistics used in Context of Hypothesis Testing

Unknown parameter	Test situation (Population characteristics and other conditions. Random sampling is assumed in all situations along with infinite population	Name of the test and the test statistic to be used		
		One sample	Two samples	
			Independent	Related
1	*2*	*3*	*4*	*5*
Mean (μ)	Population(s) normal *or* Sample size large (i.e., $n > 30$) *or* population variance(s) known	z-test and the test statistic $$z = \frac{X - \mu_{H_0}}{\sigma_p / \sqrt{n}}$$ In case σ_p is not known, we use σ_s in its place calculating $$\sigma_s = \sqrt{\frac{\Sigma\left(X_i - \bar{X}\right)^2}{n - 1}}$$	z-test for difference in means and the test statistic $$z = \frac{\bar{X}_1 - \bar{X}_2}{\sqrt{\sigma_p^2\left(\frac{1}{n_1} + \frac{1}{n_2}\right)}}$$ is used when two samples are drawn from the same population. In case σ_p is not known, we use σ_{s12} in its place calculating $$\sigma_{s12} = \sqrt{\frac{n_1(\sigma_{s1}^2 + D_1^2) + n_2(\sigma_{s2}^2 + D_2^2)}{n_1 + n_2}}$$ where $D_1 = (\bar{X}_1 - \bar{X}_{12})$ $D_2 = (\bar{X}_2 - \bar{X}_{12})$ $$\bar{X}_{12} = \frac{n_1\,\bar{X}_1 + n_2\,\bar{X}_2}{n_1 + n_2}$$	

Contd.

1	2	3	4	5
			OR $$z = \dfrac{\bar{X}_1 - \bar{X}_2}{\sqrt{\dfrac{\sigma_{p1}^2}{n_1} + \dfrac{\sigma_{p2}^2}{n_2}}}$$ is used when two samples are drawn from different populations. In case σ_{p_1} and σ_{p_2} are not known. We use σ_{s_1} and σ_{s_2} respectively in their places calculating $$\sigma_{s1} = \sqrt{\Sigma\left(X_{1i} - \bar{X}_1\right)^2 \Big/ n_1 - 1}$$ and $$\sigma_{s2} = \sqrt{\Sigma\left(X_{2i} - \bar{X}_2\right)^2 \Big/ n_2 - 1}$$	Paired t-test or difference test and the test statistic $$t = \dfrac{\bar{D} - 0}{\sqrt{\dfrac{\Sigma D_i^2 - \bar{D}^2 \cdot n}{n-1}} \Big/ \sqrt{n}}$$ with d.f $= (n-1)$ where $n =$ number of
Mean (μ)	Populations(s) normal *and* sample size small (i.e., $n \lesssim 30$) *and* population variance(s) unknown (but the population variances assumed equal in case of test on difference between means)	t-test and the test statistic $$t = \dfrac{\bar{X} - \mu_{H_0}}{\sigma_s / \sqrt{n}}$$ with d.f. $= (n-1)$ where	t-test for difference in means and the test statistic $$t = \dfrac{\bar{X}_1 - \bar{X}_2}{\sqrt{\dfrac{\Sigma\left(X_{1i} - \bar{X}_1\right)^2 + \Sigma\left(X_{2i} - \bar{X}_2\right)^2}{n_1 + n_2 - 2}}} \times \sqrt{\dfrac{1}{n_1} + \dfrac{1}{n_2}}$$ with d.f. $= (n_1 + n_2 - 2)$	

Contd.

1	2	3	4	5
				pairs in two samples.
		$\sigma_s = \sqrt{\dfrac{\Sigma(X_i - \bar{X})^2}{n-1}}$	*Alternatively,* t can be worked out as under: $$\dfrac{\bar{X}_1 - \bar{X}_2}{\sqrt{\dfrac{(n_1-1)\sigma_{s1}^2 + (n_2-1)\sigma_{s2}^2}{n_1 + n_2 - 2}} \times \sqrt{\dfrac{1}{n_1} + \dfrac{1}{n_2}}}$$ with d.f. $= (n_1 + n_2 - 2)$	D_i = differences (i.e., $D_i = X_i - Y_i$)
Proportion (p)	Repeated independent trials, sample size large (presuming normal approximation of binomial distribution)	z-test and the test statistic $$z = \dfrac{\hat{p} - p}{\sqrt{p \cdot q/n}}$$ If p and q are not known, then we use $\bar{p}$ and $\bar{q}$ in their places	z-test for difference in proportions of two samples and the test statistic $$z = \dfrac{\hat{p}_1 - \hat{p}_2}{\sqrt{\dfrac{\hat{p}_1 \hat{q}_1}{n_1} + \dfrac{\hat{p}_2 \hat{q}_2}{n_2}}}$$ is used in case of heterogenous populations. But when populations are similar with respect to a given attribute, we work out the best estimate of the population proportion as under: $$p_0 = \dfrac{n_1 \hat{p}_1 + n_2 \hat{p}_2}{n_1 + n_2}$$	

Contd.

1	2	3	4	5
variance (σ_p^2)	Population(s) normal, observations are independent	χ^2-test and the test statistic	and $q_0 = 1 - p_0$ in which case we calculate test statistic	

$$z = \frac{\hat{p}_1 - \hat{p}_2}{\sqrt{p_0\, q_0 \left(\dfrac{1}{n_1} + \dfrac{1}{n_2}\right)}}$$

$$\chi^2 = \frac{\sigma_s^2}{\sigma_p^2}\,(n-1)$$

with d.f. $= (n-1)$

F-test and the test statistic

$$F = \frac{\sigma_{s1}^2}{\sigma_{s2}^2} = \frac{\sum\left(X_{1i} - \bar{X}_1\right)^2/n - 1}{\sum\left(X_{2i} - \bar{X}_2\right)^2/n - 1}$$

where σ_{s1}^2 is treated $> \sigma_{s2}^2$

with d.f. $= v_1 = (n_1 - 1)$ for greater variance and d.f. $= v_2 = (n_2 - 1)$ for smaller variance

In the table the various symbols stand as under:

$\bar{X}$ = mean of the sample, $\bar{X}_1$ = mean of sample one, $\bar{X}_2$ = mean of sample two, n = No. of items in a sample, n_1 = No. of items in sample one, n_2 = No. of items in sample two, μ_{H_0} = Hypothesised mean for population, σ_p = standard deviation of population, σ_s = standard deviation of sample, p = population proportion, $q = 1 - p$, $\hat{p}$ = sample proportion, $\hat{q} = 1 - \hat{p}$.

and

$$\sigma_s = \sqrt{\frac{\Sigma\left(X_i - \overline{X}\right)^2}{(n-1)}}$$

5. *Population may not be normal but sample size is large, variance of the population may be known or unknown, and H_a may be one-sided or two-sided:*

In such a situation we use z-test and work out the test statistic z as under:

$$z = \frac{\overline{X} - \mu_{H_0}}{\sigma_p/\sqrt{n}}$$

(This applies in case of infinite population when variance of the population is known but when variance is not known, we use σ_s in place of σ_p in this formula.)

$$\boxed{\text{OR}}$$

$$z = \frac{\overline{X} - \mu_{H_0}}{\left(\sigma_p/\sqrt{n}\right) \times \sqrt{(N-n)/(N-1)}}$$

(This applies in case of finite population when variance of the population is known but when variance is not known, we use σ_s in place of σ_p in this formula.)

Illustration 2

A sample of 400 male students is found to have a mean height 67.47 inches. Can it be reasonably regarded as a sample from a large population with mean height 67.39 inches and standard deviation 1.30 inches? Test at 5% level of significance.

Solution: Taking the null hypothesis that the mean height of the population is equal to 67.39 inches, we can write:

$$H_0 : \mu_{H_0} = 67.39''$$

$$H_a : \mu_{H_0} \neq 67.39''$$

and the given information as $\overline{X} = 67.47''$, $\sigma_p = 1.30''$, $n = 400$. Assuming the population to be normal, we can work out the test statistic z as under:

$$z = \frac{\overline{X} - \mu_{H_0}}{\sigma_p/\sqrt{n}} = \frac{67.47 - 67.39}{1.30/\sqrt{400}} = \frac{0.08}{0.065} = 1.231$$

As H_a is two-sided in the given question, we shall be applying a two-tailed test for determining the rejection regions at 5% level of significance which comes to as under, using normal curve area table:

$$R : |z| > 1.96$$

The observed value of z is 1.231 which is in the acceptance region since $R : |z| > 1.96$ and thus H_0 is accepted. We may conclude that the given sample (with mean height = 67.47$''$) can be regarded to have been taken from a population with mean height 67.39″ and standard deviation 1.30″ at 5% level of significance.

Illustration 3

Suppose we are interested in a population of 20 industrial units of the same size, all of which are experiencing excessive labour turnover problems. The past records show that the mean of the distribution of annual turnover is 320 employees, with a standard deviation of 75 employees. A sample of 5 of these industrial units is taken at random which gives a mean of annual turnover as 300 employees. Is the sample mean consistent with the population mean? Test at 5% level.

Solution: Taking the null hypothesis that the population mean is 320 employees, we can write:

$$H_0 : \mu_{H_0} = 320 \text{ employees}$$
$$H_a : \mu_{H_0} \neq 320 \text{ employees}$$

and the given information as under:

$$\overline{X} = 300 \text{ employees}, \ \sigma_p = 75 \text{ employees}$$
$$n = 5; N = 20$$

Assuming the population to be normal, we can work out the test statistic z as under:

$$z^* = \frac{\overline{X} - \mu_{H_0}}{\sigma_p / \sqrt{n} \times \sqrt{(N - n)/(N - 1)}}$$

$$= \frac{300 - 320}{75/\sqrt{5} \times \sqrt{(20 - 5)/(20 - 1)}} = -\frac{20}{(33.54)(.888)}$$

$$= -0.67$$

As H_a is two-sided in the given question, we shall apply a two-tailed test for determining the rejection regions at 5% level of significance which comes to as under, using normal curve area table:

$$R : |z| > 1.96$$

The observed value of z is −0.67 which is in the acceptance region since $R : |z| > 1.96$ and thus, H_0 is accepted and we may conclude that the sample mean is consistent with population mean i.e., the population mean 320 is supported by sample results.

Illustration 4

The mean of a certain production process is known to be 50 with a standard deviation of 2.5. The production manager may welcome any change is mean value towards higher side but would like to safeguard against decreasing values of mean. He takes a sample of 12 items that gives a mean value of 48.5. What inference should the manager take for the production process on the basis of sample results? Use 5 per cent level of significance for the purpose.

Solution: Taking the mean value of the population to be 50, we may write:

$$H_0 : \mu_{H_0} = 50$$

---

* Being a case of finite population.

$H_a : \mu_{H_0} < 50$ (Since the manager wants to safeguard against decreasing values of mean.)

and the given information as $\bar{X} = 48.5$, $\sigma_p = 2.5$ and $n = 12$. Assuming the population to be normal, we can work out the test statistic z as under:

$$z = \frac{\bar{X} - \mu_{H_0}}{\sigma_p / \sqrt{n}} = \frac{48.5 - 50}{2.5 / \sqrt{12}} = -\frac{1.5}{(2.5)/(3.464)} = -2.0784$$

As H_a is one-sided in the given question, we shall determine the rejection region applying one-tailed test (in the left tail because H_a is of less than type) at 5 per cent level of significance and it comes to as under, using normal curve area table:

$$R : z < -1.645$$

The observed value of z is -2.0784 which is in the rejection region and thus, H_0 is rejected at 5 per cent level of significance. We can conclude that the production process is showing mean which is significantly less than the population mean and this calls for some corrective action concerning the said process.

Illustration 5

The specimen of copper wires drawn form a large lot have the following breaking strength (in kg. weight):

578, 572, 570, 568, 572, 578, 570, 572, 596, 544

Test (using Student's *t*-statistic)whether the mean breaking strength of the lot may be taken to be 578 kg. weight (Test at 5 per cent level of significance). Verify the inference so drawn by using Sandler's *A*-statistic as well.

Solution: Taking the null hypothesis that the population mean is equal to hypothesised mean of 578 kg., we can write:

$$H_0 : \mu = \mu_{H_0} = 578 \text{ kg.}$$
$$H_a : \mu \neq \mu_{H_0}$$

As the sample size is mall (since $n = 10$) and the population standard deviation is not known, we shall use *i*-test assuming normal population and shall work out the test statistic *t* as under:

$$t = \frac{\bar{X} - \mu_{H_0}}{\sigma_s / \sqrt{n}}$$

To find $\bar{X}$ and σ_s we make the following computations:

S. No.	X_i	$\left(X_i - \bar{X} \right)$	$\left(X_i - \bar{X} \right)^2$
1	578	6	36
2	572	0	0
3	570	−2	4

Contd.

S. No.	X_i	$\left(X_i - \overline{X}\right)$	$\left(X_i - \overline{X}\right)^2$
4	568	−4	16
5	572	0	0
6	578	6	36
7	570	−2	4
8	572	0	0
9	596	24	576
10	544	−28	784
$n = 10$	$\Sigma X_i = 5720$		$\Sigma \left(X_i - \overline{X}\right)^2 = 1456$

$$\therefore \quad \overline{X} = \frac{\Sigma X_i}{n} = \frac{5720}{10} = 572 \text{ kg.}$$

and

$$\sigma_s = \sqrt{\frac{\Sigma \left(X_i - \overline{X}\right)^2}{n-1}} = \sqrt{\frac{1456}{10-1}} = 12.72 \text{ kg.}$$

Hence,

$$t = \frac{572 - 578}{12.72/\sqrt{10}} = -1.488$$

Degree of freedom $= (n - 1) = (10 - 1) = 9$

As H_a is two-sided, we shall determine the rejection region applying two-tailed test at 5 per cent level of significance, and it comes to as under, using table of t-distribution[*] for 9 d.f.:

$$R : |t| > 2.262$$

As the observed value of t (i.e., -1.488) is in the acceptance region, we accept H_0 at 5 per cent level and conclude that the mean breaking strength of copper wires lot may be taken as 578 kg. weight.

The same inference can be drawn using Sandler's A-statistic as shown below:

Table 9.3: Computations for A-Statistic

S. No.	X_i	Hypothesised mean $m_{H_0} = 578$ kg.	$D_i = \left(X_i - \mu_{H_0}\right)$	D_i^2
1	578	578	0	0
2	572	578	−6	36
3	570	578	−8	64
4	568	578	−10	100

contd.

[*] Table No. 2 given in appendix at the end of the book.

S. No.	X_i	Hypothesised mean $m_{H_0} = 578$ kg.	$D_i = \left(X_i - \mu_{H_0}\right)$	D_i^2
5	572	578	–6	36
6	578	578	0	0
7	570	578	–8	64
8	572	578	–6	36
9	596	578	18	324
10	544	578	–34	1156
$n = 10$			$\sum D_i = -60$	$\sum D_i^2 = 1816$

$$\therefore \qquad A = \sum D_i^2 / \left(\sum D_i\right)^2 = 1816 / (-60)^2 = 0.5044$$

Null hypothesis $\qquad H_0 : \mu_{H_0} = 578$ kg.

Alternate hypothesis $H_a : \mu_{H_0} \neq 578$ kg.

As H_a is two-sided, the critical value of A-statistic from the A-statistic table (Table No. 10 given in appendix at the end of the book) for $(n - 1)$ i.e., $10 - 1 = 9$ d.f. at 5% level is 0.276. Computed value of A (0.5044), being greater than 0.276 shows that A-statistic is insignificant in the given case and accordingly we accept H_0 and conclude that the mean breaking strength of copper wire' lot maybe taken as578 kg. weight. Thus, the inference on the basis of t-statistic stands verified by A-statistic.

Illustration 6

Raju Restaurant near the railway station at Falna has been having average sales of 500 tea cups per day. Because of the development of bus stand nearby, it expects to increase its sales. During the first 12 days after the start of the bus stand, the daily sales were as under:

     550, 570, 490, 615, 505, 580, 570, 460, 600, 580, 530, 526

On the basis of this sample information, can one conclude that Raju Restaurant's sales have increased? Use 5 per cent level of significance.

Solution: Taking the null hypothesis that sales average 500 tea cups per day and they have not increased unless proved, we can write:

    $H_0 : \mu = 500$ cups per day

    $H_a : \mu > 500$ (as we want to conclude that sales have increased).

As the sample size is small and the population standard deviation is not known, we shall use t-test assuming normal population and shall work out the test statistic t as:

$$t = \frac{\overline{X} - \mu}{\sigma_s / \sqrt{n}}$$

(To find $\overline{X}$ and σ_s we make the following computations:)

Table 9.4

S. No.	X_i	$(X_i - \bar{X})$	$(X_i - \bar{X})^2$
1	550	2	4
2	570	22	484
3	490	−58	3364
4	615	67	4489
5	505	−43	1849
6	580	32	1024
7	570	22	484
8	460	−88	7744
9	600	52	2704
10	580	32	1024
11	530	−18	324
12	526	−22	484
$n = 10$	$\sum X_i = 6576$		$\sum (X_i - \bar{X})^2 = 23978$

$$\therefore \quad \bar{X} = \frac{\sum X_i}{n} = \frac{6576}{12} = 548$$

and

$$\sigma_s = \sqrt{\frac{\sum (X_i - \bar{X})^2}{n-1}} = \sqrt{\frac{23978}{12-1}} = 46.68$$

Hence,

$$t = \frac{548 - 500}{46.68/\sqrt{12}} = \frac{48}{13.49} = 3.558$$

Degree of freedom $= n - 1 = 12 - 1 = 11$

As H_a is one-sided, we shall determine the rejection region applying one-tailed test (in the right tail because H_a is of more than type) at 5 per cent level of significance and it comes to as under, using table of t-distribution for 11 degrees of freedom:

$$R : t > 1.796$$

The observed value of t is 3.558 which is in the rejection region and thus H_0 is rejected at 5 per cent level of significance and we can conclude that the sample data indicate that Raju restaurant's sales have increased.

HYPOTHESIS TESTING FOR DIFFERENCES BETWEEN MEANS

In many decision-situations, we may be interested in knowing whether the parameters of two populations are alike or different. For instance, we may be interested in testing whether female workers earn less than male workers for the same job. We shall explain now the technique of hypothesis testing for differences between means. The null hypothesis for testing of difference between means is generally stated as $H_0 : \mu_1 = \mu_2$, where μ_1 is population mean of one population and μ_2 is population mean of the second population, assuming both the populations to be normal populations. Alternative hypothesis may be of not equal to or less than or greater than type as stated earlier and accordingly we shall determine the acceptance or rejection regions for testing the hypotheses. There may be different situations when we are examining the significance of difference between two means, but the following may be taken as the usual situations:

1. *Population variances are known or the samples happen to be large samples:*

   In this situation we use z-test for difference in means and work out the test statistic z as under:

$$z = \frac{\overline{X}_1 - \overline{X}_2}{\sqrt{\dfrac{\sigma_{p1}^2}{n_1} + \dfrac{\sigma_{p2}^2}{n_2}}}$$

   In case σ_{p_1} and σ_{p_2} are not known, we use σ_{s_1} and σ_{s_2} respectively in their places calculating

$$\sigma_{s_1} = \sqrt{\frac{\Sigma\left(X_{1i} - \overline{X}_1\right)^2}{n_1 - 1}} \text{ and } \sigma_{s_2} = \sqrt{\frac{\Sigma\left(X_{2i} - \overline{X}_2\right)^2}{n_2 - 1}}$$

2. *Samples happen to be large but presumed to have been drawn from the same population whose variance is known:*

   In this situation we use z test for difference in means and work out the test statistic z as under:

$$z = \frac{\overline{X}_1 - \overline{X}_2}{\sqrt{\sigma_p^2\left(\dfrac{1}{n_1} + \dfrac{1}{n_2}\right)}}$$

   In case σ_p is not known, we use $\sigma_{s_{1.2}}$ (combined standard deviation of the two samples) in its place calculating

$$\sigma_{s_{1.2}} = \sqrt{\frac{n_1\left(\sigma_{s_1}^2 + D_1^2\right) + n_2\left(\sigma_{s_2}^2 + D_2^2\right)}{n_1 + n_2}}$$

where $D_1 = \left(\overline{X}_1 - \overline{X}_{1.2}\right)$

$D_2 = \left(\overline{X}_2 - \overline{X}_{1.2}\right)$

$$\overline{X}_{1.2} = \frac{n_1 \overline{X}_1 + n_2 \overline{X}_2}{n_1 + n_2}$$

3. *Samples happen to be small samples and population variances not known but assumed to be equal:*

In this situation we use *t*-test for difference in means and work out the test statistic *t* as under:

$$t = \frac{\overline{X}_1 - \overline{X}_2}{\sqrt{\dfrac{\Sigma\left(X_{1i} - \overline{X}_1\right)^2 + \Sigma\left(X_{2i} - \overline{X}_2\right)^2}{n_1 + n_2 - 2}} \times \sqrt{\dfrac{1}{n_1} + \dfrac{1}{n_2}}}$$

with d.f. = $(n_1 + n_2 - 2)$
Alternatively, we can also state

$$t = \frac{\overline{X}_1 - \overline{X}_2}{\sqrt{\dfrac{(n_1 - 1)\sigma_{s_1}^2 + (n_2 - 1)\sigma_{s_2}^2}{n_1 + n_2 - 2}} \times \sqrt{\dfrac{1}{n_1} + \dfrac{1}{n_2}}}$$

with d.f. = $(n_1 + n_2 - 2)$

Illustration 7

The mean produce of wheat of a sample of 100 fields in 200 lbs. per acre with a standard deviation of 10 lbs. Another samples of 150 fields gives the mean of 220 lbs. with a standard deviation of 12 lbs. Can the two samples be considered to have been taken from the same population whose standard deviation is 11 lbs? Use 5 per cent level of significance.

Solution: Taking the null hypothesis that the means of two populations do not differ, we can write

$$H_0 : \mu = \mu_2$$

$$H_a : \mu_1 \neq \mu_2$$

and the given information as $n_1 = 100$; $n_2 = 150$;

$$\overline{X}_1 = 200 \text{ lbs.}; \qquad \overline{X}_2 = 220 \text{ lbs.};$$

$$\sigma_{s_1} = 10 \text{ lbs.}; \qquad \sigma_{s_2} = 12 \text{ lbs.};$$

and

$$\sigma_p = 11 \text{ lbs.}$$

Assuming the population to be normal, we can work out the test statistic *z* as under:

$$z = \frac{\overline{X}_1 - \overline{X}_2}{\sqrt{\sigma_p^2 \left(\dfrac{1}{n_1} + \dfrac{1}{n_2}\right)}} = \frac{200 - 220}{\sqrt{(11)^2 \left(\dfrac{1}{100} + \dfrac{1}{150}\right)}}$$

$$= -\frac{20}{1.42} = -14.08$$

As H_a is two-sided, we shall apply a two-tailed test for determining the rejection regions at 5 per cent level of significance which come to as under, using normal curve area table:

$$R : |z| > 1.96$$

The observed value of z is -14.08 which falls in the rejection region and thus we reject H_0 and conclude that the two samples cannot be considered to have been taken at 5 per cent level of significance from the same population whose standard deviation is 11 lbs. This means that the difference between means of two samples is statistically significant and not due to sampling fluctuations.

Illustration 8

A simple random sampling survey in respect of monthly earnings of semi-skilled workers in two cities gives the following statistical information:

Table 9.5

City	Mean monthly earnings (Rs)	Standard deviation of sample data of monthly earnings (Rs)	Size of sample
A	695	40	200
B	710	60	175

Test the hypothesis at 5 per cent level that there is no difference between monthly earnings of workers in the two cities.

Solution: Taking the null hypothesis that there is no difference in earnings of workers in the two cities, we can write:

$$H_0 : \mu_1 = \mu_2$$
$$H_a : \mu_1 \neq \mu_2$$

and the given information as

Sample 1 (City A)	Sample 2 (City B)
$\overline{X}_1 = 695$ Rs	$\overline{X}_2 = 710$ Rs
$\sigma_{s_1} = 40$ Rs	$\sigma_{s_2} = 60$ Rs
$n_1 = 200$	$n_2 = 175$

As the sample size is large, we shall use z-test for difference in means assuming the populations to be normal and shall work out the test statistic z as under:

$$z = \frac{\overline{X}_1 - \overline{X}_2}{\sqrt{\dfrac{\sigma_{s_1}^2}{n_1} + \dfrac{\sigma_{s_2}^2}{n_2}}}$$

(Since the population variances are not known, we have used the sample variances, considering the sample variances as the estimates of population variances.)

Hence $z = \dfrac{695 - 710}{\sqrt{\dfrac{(40)^2}{200} + \dfrac{(60)^2}{175}}} = -\dfrac{15}{\sqrt{8 + 20.57}} = -2.809$

As H_a is two-sided, we shall apply a two-tailed test for determining the rejection regions at 5 per cent level of significance which come to as under, using normal curve area table:

$$R : |z| > 1.96$$

The observed value of z is -2.809 which falls in the rejection region and thus we reject H_0 at 5 per cent level and conclude that earning of workers in the two cities differ significantly.

Illustration 9

Sample of sales in similar shops in two towns are taken for a new product with the following results:

Town	Mean sales	Variance	Size of sample
A	57	5.3	5
B	61	4.8	7

Is there any evidence of difference in sales in the two towns? Use 5 per cent level of significance for testing this difference between the means of two samples.

Solution: Taking the null hypothesis that the means of two populations do not differ we can write:

$$H_0 : \mu_1 = \mu_2$$
$$H_a : \mu_1 \neq \mu_2$$

and the given information as follows:

Table 9.6

Sample from town A as sample one	$\overline{X}_1 = 57$	$\sigma^2_{s_1} = 5.3$	$n_1 = 5$
Sample from town B As sample two	$\overline{X}_2 = 61$	$\sigma^2_{s_2} = 4.8$	$n_2 = 7$

Since in the given question variances of the population are not known and the size of samples is small, we shall use t-test for difference in means, assuming the populations to be normal and can work out the test statistic t as under:

$$t = \frac{\overline{X}_1 - \overline{X}_2}{\sqrt{\dfrac{(n_1 - 1)\sigma^2_{s_1} + (n_2 - 1)\sigma^2_{s_2}}{n_1 + n_2 - 2}} \times \sqrt{\dfrac{1}{n_1} + \dfrac{1}{n_2}}}$$

with d.f. $= (n_1 + n_2 - 2)$

$$= \cfrac{57 - 61}{\sqrt{\cfrac{4(5.3) + 6(4.8)}{5 + 7 - 2}} \times \sqrt{\cfrac{1}{5} + \cfrac{1}{7}}} = -3.053$$

Degrees of freedom $= (n_1 + n_2 - 2) = 5 + 7 - 2 = 10$

As H_a is two-sided, we shall apply a two-tailed test for determining the rejection regions at 5 per cent level which come to as under, using table of t-distribution for 10 degrees of freedom:

$$R : |t| > 2.228$$

The observed value of t is -3.053 which falls in the rejection region and thus, we reject H_0 and conclude that the difference in sales in the two towns is significant at 5 per cent level.

Illustration 10

A group of seven-week old chickens reared on a high protein diet weigh 12, 15, 11, 16, 14, 14, and 16 ounces; a second group of five chickens, similarly treated except that they receive a low protein diet, weigh 8, 10, 14, 10 and 13 ounces. Test at 5 per cent level whether there is significant evidence that additional protein has increased the weight of the chickens. Use assumed mean (or A_1) = 10 for the sample of 7 and assumed mean (or A_2) = 8 for the sample of 5 chickens in your calculations.

Solution: Taking the null hypothesis that additional protein has not increased the weight of the chickens we can write:

$$H_0 : \mu_1 = \mu_2$$

$H_a : \mu_1 > \mu_2$ (as we want to conclude that additional protein has increased the weight of chickens)

Since in the given question variances of the populations are not known and the size of samples is small, we shall use t-test for difference in means, assuming the populations to be normal and thus work out the test statistic t as under:

$$t = \cfrac{\overline{X}_1 - \overline{X}_2}{\sqrt{\cfrac{(n_1 - 1)\sigma_{s_1}^2 + (n_2 - 1)\sigma_{s_2}^2}{n_1 + n_2 - 2}} \times \sqrt{\cfrac{1}{n_1} + \cfrac{1}{n_2}}}$$

with d.f. $= (n_1 + n_2 - 2)$

From the sample data we work out $\overline{X}_1$, $\overline{X}_2$, $\sigma_{s_1}^2$ and $\sigma_{s_2}^2$ (taking high protein diet sample as sample one and low protein diet sample as sample two) as shown below:

Table 9.7

	Sample one				Sample two		
S.No.	X_{1i}	$X_{1i} - A_1$ $(A_1 = 10)$	$(X_{1i} - A_1)^2$	S.No.	X_{2i}	$X_{2i} - A_2$ $(A_2 = 8)$	$(X_{2i} - A_2)^2$
1.	12	2	4	1.	8	0	0
2.	15	5	25	2.	10	2	4
3.	11	1	1	3.	14	6	36
4.	16	6	36	4.	10	2	4
5.	14	4	16	5.	13	5	25
6.	14	4	16				
7.	16	6	36				
$n_1 = 7$;	$\sum(X_{1i} - A_1) = 28$;	$\sum(X_{1i} - A_1)^2$ $= 134$		$n_2 = 5$;	$\sum(X_{2i} - A_2) = 15$;	$\sum(X_{2i} - A_2)^2$ $= 69$	

$\therefore$
$$\overline{X}_1 = A_1 + \frac{\sum(X_{1i} - A_1)}{n_1} = 10 + \frac{28}{7} = 14 \text{ ounces}$$

$$\overline{X}_2 = A_2 + \frac{\sum(X_{2i} - A_2)}{n_2} = 8 + \frac{15}{5} = 11 \text{ ounces}$$

$$\sigma^2_{s_1} = \frac{\sum(X_{1i} - A_1)^2 - \left[\sum(X_{1i} - A_1)\right]^2/n_1}{(n_1 - 1)}$$

$$= \frac{134 - (28)^2/7}{7 - 1} = 3.667 \text{ ounces}$$

$$\sigma^2_{s_2} = \frac{\sum(X_{2i} - A_2)^2 - \left[\sum(X_{2i} - A_2)\right]^2/n_2}{(n_2 - 1)}$$

$$= \frac{69 - (15)^2/5}{5 - 1} = 6 \text{ ounces}$$

Hence,
$$t = \frac{14 - 11}{\sqrt{\dfrac{(7 - 1)(3.667) + (5 - 1)(6)}{7 + 5 - 2}} \times \sqrt{\dfrac{1}{7} + \dfrac{1}{5}}}$$

$$= \frac{3}{\sqrt{4.6} \times \sqrt{.345}} = \frac{3}{1.26} = 2.381$$

Degrees of freedom = $(n_1 + n_2 - 2) = 10$

As H_a is one-sided, we shall apply a one-tailed test (in the right tail because H_a is of more than type) for determining the rejection region at 5 per cent level which comes to as under, using table of *t*-distribution for 10 degrees of freedom:

$$R : t > 1.812$$

The observed value of *t* is 2.381 which falls in the rejection region and thus, we reject H_0 and conclude that additional protein has increased the weight of chickens, at 5 per cent level of significance.

HYPOTHESIS TESTING FOR COMPARING TWO RELATED SAMPLES

Paired *t*-test is a way to test for comparing two related samples, involving small values of *n* that does not require the variances of the two populations to be equal, but the assumption that the two populations are normal must continue to apply. For a paired *t*-test, it is necessary that the observations in the two samples be collected in the form of what is called matched pairs i.e., "each observation in the one sample must be paired with an observation in the other sample in such a manner that these observations are somehow "matched" or related, in an attempt to eliminate extraneous factors which are not of interest in test."[5] Such a test is generally considered appropriate in a before-and-after-treatment study. For instance, we may test a group of certain students before and after training in order to know whether the training is effective, in which situation we may use paired *t*-test. To apply this test, we first work out the difference score for each matched pair, and then find out the average of such differences, $\overline{D}$, along with the sample variance of the difference score. If the values from the two matched samples are denoted as X_i and Y_i and the differences by $D_i (D_i = X_i - Y_i)$, then the mean of the differences i.e.,

$$\overline{D} = \frac{\sum D_i}{n}$$

and the variance of the differences or

$$\left(\sigma_{diff.}\right)^2 = \frac{\sum D_i^2 - \left(\overline{D}\right)^2 \cdot n}{n-1}$$

Assuming the said differences to be normally distributed and independent, we can apply the paired *t*-test for judging the significance of mean of differences and work out the test statistic *t* as under:

$$t = \frac{\overline{D} - 0}{\sigma_{diff}/\sqrt{n}} \text{ with } (n-1) \text{ degrees of freedom}$$

where $\overline{D}$ = Mean of differences

---

[5] Donald L. Harnett and James L. Murphy, "*Introductory Statistical Analysis*", p. 364.

$\sigma_{diff.}$ = Standard deviation of differences

n = Number of matched pairs

This calculated value of t is compared with its table value at a given level of significance as usual for testing purposes. We can also use Sandler's A-test for this very purpose as stated earlier in Chapter 8.

Illustration 11

Memory capacity of 9 students was tested before and after training. State at 5 per cent level of significance whether the training was effective from the following scores:

Student	1	2	3	4	5	6	7	8	9
Before	10	15	9	3	7	12	16	17	4
After	12	17	8	5	6	11	18	20	3

Use paired t-test as well as A-test for your answer.

Solution: Take the score before training as X and the score after training as Y and then taking the null hypothesis that the mean of difference is zero, we can write:

$H_0 : \mu_1 = \mu_2$ which is equivalent to test $H_0 : \overline{D} = 0$

$H_a : \mu_1 < \mu_2$ (as we want to conclude that training has been effective)

As we are having matched pairs, we use paired t-test and work out the test statistic t as under:

$$t = \frac{\overline{D} - 0}{\sigma_{diff.}/\sqrt{n}}$$

To find the value of t, we shall first have to work out the mean and standard deviation of differences as shown below:

Table 9.8

Student	Score before training X_i	Score after training Y_i	Difference $(D_i = X_i - Y_i)$	Difference Squared D_i^2
1	10	12	−2	4
2	15	17	−2	4
3	9	8	1	1
4	3	5	−2	4
5	7	6	1	1
6	12	11	1	1
7	16	18	−2	4
8	17	20	−3	9
9	4	3	1	1
$n = 9$			$\Sigma D_i = -7$	$\Sigma D_i^2 = 29$

$\therefore$ Mean of Differences or $\overline{D} = \dfrac{\sum D_i}{n} = \dfrac{-7}{9} = -0.778$

and Standard deviation of differences or

$$\sigma_{diff.} = \sqrt{\dfrac{\sum D_i^2 - \left(\overline{D}\right)^2 \cdot n}{n-1}}$$

$$= \sqrt{\dfrac{29 - (-.778)^2 \times 9}{9-1}}$$

$$= \sqrt{2.944} = 1.715$$

Hence, $\qquad\qquad t = \dfrac{-0.778 - 0}{1.715/\sqrt{9}} = \dfrac{-.778}{0.572} = -1.361$

Degrees of freedom $= n - 1 = 9 - 1 = 8$.

As H_a is one-sided, we shall apply a one-tailed test (in the left tail because H_a is of less than type) for determining the rejection region at 5 per cent level which comes to as under, using the table of t-distribution for 8 degrees of freedom:

$$R : t < -1.860$$

The observed value of t is -1.361 which is in the acceptance region and thus, we accept H_0 and conclude that the difference in score before and after training is insignificant i.e., it is only due to sampling fluctuations. Hence we can infer that the training was not effective.

Solution using A-test: Using A-test, we workout the test statistic for the given problem thus:

$$A = \dfrac{\sum D_i^2}{\left(\sum D_i\right)^2} = \dfrac{29}{(-7)^2} = 0.592$$

Since H_a in the given problem is one-sided, we shall apply one-tailed test. Accordingly, at 5% level of significance the table value of A-statistic for $(n-1)$ or $(9-1) = 8$ d.f. in the given case is 0.368 (as per table of A-statistic given in appendix). The computed value of A i.e., 0.592 is higher than this table value and as such A-statistic is insignificant and accordingly H_0 should be accepted. In other words, we should conclude that the training was not effective. (This inference is just the same as drawn earlier using paired t-test.)

Illustration 12

The sales data of an item in six shops before and after a special promotional campaign are:

Shops	A	B	C	D	E	F
Before the promotional campaign	53	28	31	48	50	42
After the campaign	58	29	30	55	56	45

Can the campaign be judged to be a success? Test at 5 per cent level of significance. Use paired t-test as well as A-test.

Solution: Let the sales before campaign be represented as *X* and the sales after campaign as *Y* and then taking the null hypothesis that campaign does not bring any improvement in sales, we can write:

$H_0 : \mu_1 = \mu_2$ which is equivalent to test $H_0 : \overline{D} = 0$

$H_a : \mu_1 < \mu_2$ (as we want to conclude that campaign has been a success).

Because of the matched pairs we use paired *t*-test and work out the test statistic '*t*' as under:

$$t = \frac{\overline{D} - 0}{\sigma_{diff.}/\sqrt{n}}$$

To find the value of *t*, we first work out the mean and standard deviation of differences as under:

Table 9.9

Shops	Sales before campaign X_i	Sales after campaign Y_i	Difference $(D_i = X_i - Y_i)$	Difference squared D_i^2
A	53	58	−5	25
B	28	29	−1	1
C	31	30	1	1
D	48	55	−7	49
E	50	56	−6	36
F	42	45	−3	9
$n = 6$			$\sum D_i = -21$	$\sum D_i^2 = 121$

$$\overline{D} = \frac{\sum D_i}{n} = -\frac{21}{6} = -3.5$$

$$\sigma_{diff.} = \sqrt{\frac{\sum D_i^2 - (\overline{D})^2 \cdot n}{n - 1}} = \sqrt{\frac{121 - (-3.5)^2 \times 6}{6 - 1}} = 3.08$$

Hence,

$$t = \frac{-3.5 - 0}{3.08/\sqrt{6}} = \frac{-3.5}{1.257} = -2.784$$

Degrees of freedom = $(n - 1) = 6 - 1 = 5$

As H_a is one-sided, we shall apply a one-tailed test (in the left tail because H_a is of less than type) for determining the rejection region at 5 per cent level of significance which come to as under, using table of *t*-distribution for 5 degrees of freedom:

$$R : t < -2.015$$

The observed value of *t* is − 2.784 which falls in the rejection region and thus, we reject H_0 at 5 per cent level and conclude that sales promotional campaign has been a success.

Solution: *Using A-test:* Using *A*-test, we work out the test statistic for the given problem as under:

$$A = \frac{\sum D_i^2}{(\sum D_i)^2} = \frac{121}{(-21)^2} = 0.2744$$

Since H_a in the given problem is one-sided, we shall apply one-tailed test. Accordingly, at 5% level of significance the table value of *A*-statistic for $(n-1)$ or $(6-1) = 5$ d.f. in the given case is 0.372 (as per table of *A*-statistic given in appendix). The computed value of *A*, being 0.2744, is less than this table value and as such *A*-statistic is significant. This means we should reject H_0 (alternately we should accept H_a) and should infer that the sales promotional campaign has been a success.

HYPOTHESIS TESTING OF PROPORTIONS

In case of qualitative phenomena, we have data on the basis of presence or absence of an attribute(s). With such data the sampling distribution may take the form of binomial probability distribution whose mean would be equal to $n \cdot p$ and standard deviation equal to $\sqrt{n \cdot p \cdot q}$, where p represents the probability of success, q represents the probability of failure such that $p + q = 1$ and n, the size of the sample. Instead of taking mean number of successes and standard deviation of the number of successes, we may record the proportion of successes in each sample in which case the mean and standard deviation (or the standard error) of the sampling distribution may be obtained as follows:

Mean proportion of successes $= (n \cdot p)/n = p$

and standard deviation of the proportion of successes $= \sqrt{\dfrac{p \cdot q}{n}}$.

In n is large, the binomial distribution tends to become normal distribution, and as such for proportion testing purposes we make use of the test statistic z as under:

$$z = \frac{\hat{p} - p}{\sqrt{\dfrac{p \cdot q}{n}}}$$

where $\hat{p}$ is the sample proportion.

For testing of proportion, we formulate H_0 and H_a and construct rejection region, presuming normal approximation of the binomial distribution, for a predetermined level of significance and then may judge the significance of the observed sample result. The following examples make all this quite clear.

Illustration 13

A sample survey indicates that out of 3232 births, 1705 were boys and the rest were girls. Do these figures confirm the hypothesis that the sex ratio is 50 : 50? Test at 5 per cent level of significance.

Solution: Starting from the null hypothesis that the sex ratio is 50 : 50 we may write:

$$H_0 : p = p_{H_0} = \frac{1}{2}$$

$$H_a : p \neq p_{H_0}$$

Hence the probability of boy birth or $p = \frac{1}{2}$ and the probability of girl birth is also $\frac{1}{2}$.

Considering boy birth as success and the girl birth as failure, we can write as under:

the proportion success or $p = \frac{1}{2}$

the proportion of failure or $q = \frac{1}{2}$

and $n = 3232$ (given).

The standard error of proportion of success.

$$= \sqrt{\frac{p \cdot q}{n}} = \sqrt{\frac{\frac{1}{2} \times \frac{1}{2}}{3232}} = 0.0088$$

Observed sample proportion of success, or

$$\hat{p} = 1705/3232 = 0.5275$$

and the test statistic

$$z = \frac{\hat{p} - p}{\sqrt{\dfrac{p \cdot q}{n}}} = \frac{0.5275 - .5000}{.0088} = 3.125$$

As H_a is two-sided in the given question, we shall be applying the two-tailed test for determining the rejection regions at 5 per cent level which come to as under, using normal curve area table:

$$R : |z| > 1.96$$

The observed value of z is 3.125 which comes in the rejection region since $R : |z| > 1.96$ and thus, H_0 is rejected in favour of H_a. Accordingly, we conclude that the given figures do not conform the hypothesis of sex ratio being 50 : 50.

Illustration 14

The null hypothesis is that 20 per cent of the passengers go in first class, but management recognizes the possibility that this percentage could be more or less. A random sample of 400 passengers includes 70 passengers holding first class tickets. Can the null hypothesis be rejected at 10 per cent level of significance?

Solution: The null hypothesis is

$\cdot$ $H_0 : p = 20\%$ or 0.20

and $H_a : p \neq 20\%$

Hence, $\qquad\qquad\qquad\qquad p = 0.20$ and

$$q = 0.80$$

Observed sample proportion $(\hat{p}) = 70/400 = 0.175$

and the test statistic $z = \dfrac{\hat{p} - p}{\sqrt{\dfrac{p \cdot q}{n}}} = \dfrac{0.175 - .20}{\sqrt{\dfrac{.20 \times .80}{400}}} = -1.25$

As H_a is two-sided we shall determine the rejection regions applying two-tailed test at 10 per cent level which come to as under, using normal curve area table:

$$R : |z| > 1.645$$

The observed value of z is -1.25 which is in the acceptance region and as such H_0 is accepted. Thus the null hypothesis cannot be rejected at 10 per cent level of significance.

Illustration 15

A certain process produces 10 per cent defective articles. A supplier of new raw material claims that the use of his material would reduce the proportion of defectives. A random sample of 400 units using this new material was taken out of which 34 were defective units. Can the supplier's claim be accepted? Test at 1 per cent level of significance.

Solution: The null hypothesis can be written as $H_0 : p = 10\%$ or 0.10 and the alternative hypothesis $H_a : p < 0.10$ (because the supplier claims that new material will reduce proportion of defectives). Hence,

$$p = 0.10 \text{ and } q = 0.90$$

Observed sample proportion $\hat{p} = 34/400 = 0.085$ and test statistic

$$z = \frac{\hat{p} - p}{\sqrt{\dfrac{p \cdot q}{n}}} = \frac{.085 - .10}{\sqrt{\dfrac{.10 \times .90}{400}}} = \frac{.015}{.015} = -1.00$$

As H_a is one-sided, we shall determine the rejection region applying one-tailed test (in the left tail because H_a is of less than type) at 1% level of significance and it comes to as under, using normal curve area table:

$$R : z < -2.32$$

As the computed value of z does not fall in the rejection region, H_0 is accepted at 1% level of significance and we can conclude that on the basis of sample information, the supplier's claim cannot be accepted at 1% level.

HYPOTHESIS TESTING FOR DIFFERENCE BETWEEN PROPORTIONS

If two samples are drawn from different populations, one may be interested in knowing whether the difference between the proportion of successes is significant or not. In such a case, we start with the hypothesis that the difference between the proportion of success in sample one $(\hat{p}_1)$ and the proportion of success in sample two $(\hat{p}_2)$ is due to fluctuations of random sampling. In other words, we take the null hypothesis as $H_0: \hat{p}_1 = \hat{p}_2$ and for testing the significance of difference, we work out the test statistic as under:

$$z = \frac{\hat{p}_1 - \hat{p}_2}{\sqrt{\dfrac{\hat{p}_1 \cdot \hat{q}_1}{n_1} + \dfrac{\hat{p}_2 \cdot \hat{q}_2}{n_2}}}$$

where $\hat{p}_1$ = proportion of success in sample one

$\hat{p}_2$ = proportion of success in sample two

$\hat{q}_1 = 1 - \hat{p}_1$

$\hat{q}_2 = 1 - \hat{p}_2$

n_1 = size of sample one

n_2 = size of sample two

and

$$\sqrt{\frac{\hat{p}_1 \hat{q}_1}{n_1} + \frac{\hat{p}_2 \hat{q}_2}{n_2}} = \text{the standard error of difference between two sample proportions.}^*$$

Then, we construct the rejection region(s) depending upon the H_a for a given level of significance and on its basis we judge the significance of the sample result for accepting or rejecting H_0. We can now illustrate all this by examples.

Illustration 6

A drug research experimental unit is testing two drugs newly developed to reduce blood pressure levels. The drugs are administered to two different sets of animals. In group one, 350 of 600 animals tested respond to drug one and in group two, 260 of 500 animals tested respond to drug two. The research unit wants to test whether there is a difference between the efficacy of the said two drugs at 5 per cent level of significance. How will you deal with this problem?

---

* This formula is used when samples are drawn from two heterogeneous populations where we cannot have the best estimate of the common value of the proportion of the attribute in the population from the given sample information. But on the assumption that the populations are similar as regards the given attribute, we make use of the following formula for working out the standard error of difference between proportions of the two samples:

$$\text{S.E.}_{Diff \cdot p_1 - p_2} = \sqrt{\frac{p_0 \cdot q_0}{n_1} + \frac{p_0 \cdot q_0}{n_2}}$$

where $p_0 = \dfrac{n_1 \cdot \hat{p}_1 + n_2 \cdot \hat{p}_2}{n_1 + n_2}$ = best estimate of proportion in the population

$q_0 = 1 - p_0$

Solution: We take the null hypothesis that there is no difference between the two drugs i.e., $H_0 : \hat{p}_1 = \hat{p}_2$

The alternative hypothesis can be taken as that there is a difference between the drugs i.e., $H_a : \hat{p}_1 \neq \hat{p}_2$ and the given information can be stated as:

$$\hat{p}_1 = 350/600 = 0.583$$

$$\hat{q}_1 = 1 - \hat{p}_1 = 0.417$$

$$n_1 = 600$$

$$\hat{p}_2 = 260/500 = 0.520$$

$$\hat{q}_2 = 1 - \hat{p}_2 = 0.480$$

$$n_2 = 500$$

We can work out the test statistic z thus:

$$z = \frac{\hat{p}_1 - \hat{p}_2}{\sqrt{\dfrac{\hat{p}_1 \hat{q}_1}{n_1} + \dfrac{\hat{p}_2 \hat{q}_2}{n_2}}} = \frac{0.583 - 0.520}{\sqrt{\dfrac{(.583)(.417)}{600} + \dfrac{(.520)(.480)}{500}}}$$

$$= 2.093$$

As H_a is two-sided, we shall determine the rejection regions applying two-tailed test at 5% level which comes as under using normal curve area table:

$$R : |z| > 1.96$$

The observed value of z is 2.093 which is in the rejection region and thus, H_0 is rejected in favour of H_a and as such we conclude that the difference between the efficacy of the two drugs is significant.

Illustration 17

At a certain date in a large city 400 out of a random sample of 500 men were found to be smokers. After the tax on tobacco had been heavily increased, another random sample of 600 men in the same city included 400 smokers. Was the observed decrease in the proportion of smokers significant? Test at 5 per cent level of significance.

Solution: We start with the null hypothesis that the proportion of smokers even after the heavy tax on tobacco remains unchanged i.e. $H_0 : \hat{p}_1 = \hat{p}_2$ and the alternative hypothesis that proportion of smokers after tax has decreased i.e.,

$$H_a : \hat{p}_1 > \hat{p}_2$$

On the presumption that the given populations are similar as regards the given attribute, we work out the best estimate of proportion of smokers (p_0) in the population as under, using the given information:

$$p_0 = \frac{n_1 \hat{p}_1 + n_2 \hat{p}_2}{n_1 + n_2} = \frac{500\left(\dfrac{400}{500}\right) + 600\left(\dfrac{400}{600}\right)}{500 + 600} = \frac{800}{1100} = \frac{8}{11} = .7273$$

Thus, $q_0 = 1 - p_0 = .2727$

The test statistic z can be worked out as under:

$$z = \frac{\hat{p}_1 - \hat{p}_2}{\sqrt{\dfrac{p_0 q_0}{n_1} + \dfrac{p_0 q_0}{n_2}}} = \frac{\dfrac{400}{500} - \dfrac{400}{600}}{\sqrt{\dfrac{(.7273)(.2727)}{500} + \dfrac{(.7273)(.2727)}{600}}}$$

$$= \frac{0.133}{0.027} = 4.926$$

As the H_a is one-sided we shall determine the rejection region applying one-tailed test (in the right tail because H_a is of greater than type) at 5 per cent level and the same works out to as under, using normal curve area table:

$$R : z > 1.645$$

The observed value of z is 4.926 which is in the rejection region and so we reject H_0 in favour of H_a and conclude that the proportion of smokers after tax has decreased significantly.

Testing the difference between proportion based on the sample and the proportion given for the whole population: In such a situation we work out the standard error of difference between proportion of persons possessing an attribute in a sample and the proportion given for the population as under:

Standard error of difference between sample proportion and

population proportion or $\text{S.E.}_{diff.\,\hat{p}-p} = \sqrt{p \cdot q \dfrac{N - n}{nN}}$

where p = population proportion

$q = 1 - p$

n = number of items in the sample

N = number of items in population

and the test statistic z can be worked out as under:

$$z = \frac{\hat{p} - p}{\sqrt{p \cdot q \dfrac{N - n}{nN}}}$$

All other steps remain the same as explained above in the context of testing of proportions. We take an example to illustrate the same.

Illustration 18

There are 100 students in a university college and in the whole university, inclusive of this college, the number of students is 2000. In a random sample study 20 were found smokers in the college and the proportion of smokers in the university is 0.05. Is there a significant difference between the proportion of smokers in the college and university? Test at 5 per cent level.

Solution: Let $H_0 : \hat{p} = p$ (there is no difference between sample proportion and population proportion)

and $\qquad\qquad H_a : \hat{p} \neq p$ (there is difference between the two proportions)

and on the basis of the given information, the test statistic z can be worked out as under:

$$z = \frac{\hat{p} - p}{\sqrt{p \cdot q \dfrac{N - n}{nN}}} = \frac{\dfrac{20}{100} - .05}{\sqrt{(.05)(.95)\dfrac{2000 - 100}{(100)(2000)}}}$$

$$= \frac{0.150}{0.021} = 7.143$$

As the H_a is two-sided, we shall determine the rejection regions applying two-tailed test at 5 per cent level and the same works out to as under, using normal curve area table:

$$R : |z| > 1.96$$

The observed value of z is 7.143 which is in the rejection region and as such we reject H_0 and conclude that there is a significant difference between the proportion of smokers in the college and university.

HYPOTHESIS TESTING FOR COMPARING A VARIANCE TO SOME HYPOTHESISED POPULATION VARIANCE

The test we use for comparing a sample variance to some theoretical or hypothesised variance of population is different than z-test or the t-test. The test we use for this purpose is known as chi-square test and the test statistic symbolised as χ^2, known as the chi-square value, is worked out. The chi-square value to test the null hypothesis viz, $H_0 : \sigma_s^2 = \sigma_p^2$ worked out as under:

$$\chi^2 = \frac{\sigma_s^2}{\sigma_p^2}(n - 1)$$

where $\quad \sigma_s^2$ = variance of the sample

$\qquad \sigma_p^2$ = variance of the population

$(n - 1)$ = degree of freedom, n being the number of items in the sample.

Then by comparing the calculated value of χ^2 with its table value for $(n - 1)$ degrees of freedom at a given level of significance, we may either accept H_0 or reject it. If the calculated value of χ^2 is equal to or less than the table value, the null hypothesis is accepted; otherwise the null hypothesis is rejected. This test is based on chi-square distribution which is not symmetrical and all the values happen to be positive; one must simply know the degrees of freedom for using such a distribution.[*]

TESTING THE EQUALITY OF VARIANCES OF TWO NORMAL POPULATIONS

When we want to test the equality of variances of two normal populations, we make use of *F*-test based on *F*-distribution. In such a situation, the null hypothesis happens to be $H_0 : \sigma^2_{p_1} = \sigma^2_{p_2}$, $\sigma^2_{p_1}$ and $\sigma^2_{p_2}$ representing the variances of two normal populations. This hypothesis is tested on the basis of sample data and the test statistic *F* is found, using $\sigma^2_{s_1}$ and $\sigma^2_{s_2}$ the sample estimates for $\sigma^2_{p_1}$ and $\sigma^2_{p_2}$ respectively, as stated below:

$$F = \frac{\sigma^2_{s_1}}{\sigma^2_{s_2}}$$

where $\sigma^2_{s_1} = \dfrac{\Sigma\left(X_{1i} - \overline{X}_1\right)^2}{(n_1 - 1)}$ and $\sigma^2_{s_2} = \dfrac{\Sigma\left(X_{2i} - \overline{X}_2\right)^2}{(n_2 - 1)}$

While calculating *F*, $\sigma^2_{s_1}$ is treated $> \sigma^2_{s_2}$ which means that the numerator is always the greater variance. Tables for *F*-distribution[**] have been prepared by statisticians for different values of *F* at different levels of significance for different degrees of freedom for the greater and the smaller variances. By comparing the observed value of *F* with the corresponding table value, we can infer whether the difference between the variances of samples could have arisen due to sampling fluctuations. If the calculated value of *F* is greater than table value of *F* at a certain level of significance for $(n_1 - 1)$ and $(n_2 - 2)$ degrees of freedom, we regard the *F*-ratio as significant. Degrees of freedom for greater variance is represented as v_1 and for smaller variance as v_2. On the other hand, if the calculated value of *F* is smaller than its table value, we conclude that *F*-ratio is not significant. If *F*-ratio is considered non-significant, we accept the null hypothesis, but if *F*-ratio is considered significant, we then reject H_0 (i.e., we accept H_a).

When we use the *F*-test, we presume that

    (i) the populations are normal;

    (ii) samples have been drawn randomly;

    (iii) observations are independent; and

    (iv) there is no measurement error.

The object of *F*-test is to test the hypothesis whether the two samples are from the same normal population with equal variance or from two normal populations with equal variances. *F*-test was initially used to verify the hypothesis of equality between two variances, but is now mostly used in the

---

[*]See Chapter 10 entitled Chi-square test for details.

[**] *F*-distribution tables [Table 4(a) and Table 4(b)] have been given in appendix at the end of the book.

context of analysis of variance. The following examples illustrate the use of *F*-test for testing the equality of variances of two normal populations.

Illustration 19

Two random samples drawn from two normal populations are:

| Sample 1 | 20 | 16 | 26 | 27 | 23 | 22 | 18 | 24 | 25 | 19 | | |
| Sample 2 | 27 | 33 | 42 | 35 | 32 | 34 | 38 | 28 | 41 | 43 | 30 | 37 |

Test using variance ratio at 5 per cent and 1 per cent level of significance whether the two populations have the same variances.

Solution: We take the null hypothesis that the two populations from where the samples have been drawn have the same variances i.e., $H_0 : \sigma^2_{p_1} = \sigma^2_{p_2}$. From the sample data we work out $\sigma^2_{s_1}$ and $\sigma^2_{s_2}$ as under:

Table 9.10

	Sample 1			Sample 2		
X_{1i}	$(X_{1i} - \overline{X}_1)$	$(X_{1i} - \overline{X}_1)^2$	X_{2i}	$(X_{2i} - \overline{X}_2)$	$(X_{2i} - \overline{X}_2)^2$
20	−2	4	27	−8	64
16	−6	36	33	−2	4
26	4	16	42	7	49
27	5	25	35	0	0
23	1	1	32	−3	9
22	0	0	34	−1	1
18	−4	16	38	3	9
24	2	4	28	−7	49
25	3	9	41	6	36
19	−3	9	43	8	64
			30	−5	25
			37	2	4
$\sum X_{1i} = 220$		$\sum (X_{1i} - \overline{X}_1)^2 = 120$	$\sum X_{2i} = 420$		$\sum (X_{2i} - \overline{X}_2)^2 = 314$
$n_1 = 10$			$n_2 = 12$		

$$\overline{X}_1 = \frac{\sum X_{1i}}{n_1} = \frac{220}{10} = 22; \qquad \overline{X}_2 = \frac{\sum X_{2i}}{n_2} = \frac{420}{12} = 35$$

$$\sigma^2_{s_1} = \frac{\sum (X_{1i} - \overline{X}_1)^2}{n_1 - 1} = \frac{120}{10 - 1} = 13.33$$

and
$$\sigma^2_{s_2} = \frac{\Sigma\left(X_{2i} - \bar{X}_2\right)^2}{n_2 - 1} = \frac{314}{12 - 1} = 28.55$$

Hence,
$$F = \frac{\sigma^2_{s_2}}{\sigma^2_{s_1}} \qquad \left(\because \sigma^2_{s_2} > \sigma^2_{s_1}\right)$$

$$= \frac{28.55}{13.33} = 2.14$$

Degrees of freedom in sample 1 = $(n_1 - 1) = 10 - 1 = 9$

Degrees of freedom in sample 2 = $(n_2 - 1) = 12 - 1 = 11$

As the variance of sample 2 is greater variance, hence
$$v_1 = 11;\ v_2 = 9$$

The table value of F at 5 per cent level of significance for $v_1 = 11$ and $v_2 = 9$ is 3.11 and the table value of F at 1 per cent level of significance for $v_1 = 11$ and $v_2 = 9$ is 5.20.

Since the calculated value of $F = 2.14$ which is less than 3.11 and also less than 5.20, the F ratio is insignificant at 5 per cent as well as at 1 per cent level of significance and as such we accept the null hypothesis and conclude that samples have been drawn from two populations having the same variances.

Illustration 20

Given $n_1 = 9;\ n_2 = 8$

$$\Sigma\left(X_{1i} - \bar{X}_1\right)^2 = 184$$

$$\Sigma\left(X_{2i} - \bar{X}_2\right)^2 = 38$$

Apply F-test to judge whether this difference is significant at 5 per cent level.

Solution: We start with the hypothesis that the difference is not significant and hence, $H_0 : \sigma^2_{p_1} = \sigma^2_{p_2}$.

To test this, we work out the F-ratio as under:

$$F = \frac{\sigma^2_{s_1}}{\sigma^2_{s_2}} = \frac{\Sigma\left(X_{1i} - \bar{X}_1\right)^2 / (n_1 - 1)}{\Sigma\left(X_{2i} - \bar{X}_2\right)^2 / (n_2 - 1)}$$

$$= \frac{184/8}{38/7} = \frac{23}{5.43} = 4.25$$

$v_1 = 8$ being the number of d.f. for greater variance

$v_2 = 7$ being the number of d.f. for smaller variance.

The table value of F at 5 per cent level for $v_1 = 8$ and $v_2 = 7$ is 3.73. Since the calculated value of F is greater than the table value, the F ratio is significant at 5 per cent level. Accordingly we reject H_0 and conclude that the difference is significant.

HYPOTHESIS TESTING OF CORRELATION COEFFICIENTS*

We may be interested in knowing whether the correlation coefficient that we calculate on the basis of sample data is indicative of significant correlation. For this purpose we may use (in the context of small samples) normally either the t-test or the F-test depending upon the type of correlation coefficient. We use the following tests for the purpose:

(a) *In case of simple correlation coefficient:* We use t-test and calculate the test statistic as under:

$$t = r_{yx} \sqrt{\frac{n-2}{1-r_{yx}^2}}$$

with $(n-2)$ degrees of freedom r_{yx} being coefficient of simple correlation between x and y.

This calculated value of t is then compared with its table value and if the calculated value is less than the table value, we accept the null hypothesis at the given level of significance and may infer that there is no relationship of statistical significance between the two variables.

(b) *In case of partial correlation coefficient:* We use t-test and calculate the test statistic as under:

$$t = r_p \sqrt{\frac{(n-k)}{1-r_p^2}}$$

with $(n-k)$ degrees of freedom, n being the number of paired observations and k being the number of variables involved, r_p happens to be the coefficient of partial correlation.

If the value of t in the table is greater than the calculated value, we may accept null hypothesis and infer that there is no correlation.

(c) *In case of multiple correlation coefficient:* We use F-test and work out the test statistic as under:

$$F = \frac{R^2/(k-1)}{\left(1-R^2\right)/(n-k)}$$

where R is any multiple coefficient of correlation, k being the number of variables involved and n being the number of paired observations. The test is performed by entering tables of the F-distribution with

$v_1 = k - 1 =$ degrees of freedom for variance in numerator.

$v_2 = n - k =$ degrees of freedom for variance in denominator.

If the calculated value of F is less than the table value, then we may infer that there is no statistical evidence of significant correlation.

---

*Only the outline of testing procedure has been given here. Readers may look into standard tests for further details.

LIMITATIONS OF THE TESTS OF HYPOTHESES

We have described above some important test often used for testing hypotheses on the basis of which important decisions may be based. But there are several limitations of the said tests which should always be borne in mind by a researcher. Important limitations are as follows:

   (i) The tests should not be used in a mechanical fashion. It should be kept in view that testing is not decision-making itself; the tests are only useful aids for decision-making. Hence "proper interpretation of statistical evidence is important to intelligent decisions."[6]

   (ii) Test do not explain the reasons as to why does the difference exist, say between the means of the two samples. They simply indicate whether the difference is due to fluctuations of sampling or because of other reasons but the tests do not tell us as to which is/are the other reason(s) causing the difference.

   (iii) Results of significance tests are based on probabilities and as such cannot be expressed with full certainty. When a test shows that a difference is statistically significant, then it simply suggests that the difference is probably not due to chance.

   (iv) Statistical inferences based on the significance tests cannot be said to be entirely correct evidences concerning the truth of the hypotheses. This is specially so in case of small samples where the probability of drawing erring inferences happens to be generally higher. For greater reliability, the size of samples be sufficiently enlarged.

   All these limitations suggest that in problems of statistical significance, the inference techniques (or the tests) must be combined with adequate knowledge of the subject-matter along with the ability of good judgement.

Questions

1. Distinguish between the following:
   (i) Simple hypothesis and composite hypothesis;
   (ii) Null hypothesis and alternative hypothesis;
   (iii) One-tailed test and two-tailed test;
   (iv) Type I error and Type II error;
   (v) Acceptance region and rejection region;
   (vi) Power function and operating characteristic function.

2. What is a hypothesis? What characteristics it must possess in order to be a good research hypothesis? A manufacturer considers his production process to be working properly if the mean length of the rods the manufactures is 8.5″. The standard deviation of the rods always runs about 0.26″. Suppose a sample of 64 rods is taken and this gives a mean length of rods equal to 8.6″. What are the null and alternative hypotheses for this problem? Can you infer at 5% level of significance that the process is working properly?

3. The procedure of testing hypothesis requires a researcher to adopt several steps. Describe in brief all such steps.

---

[6] Ya-Lun-Chou, "Applied Business and Economic Statistics".

4. What do you mean by the power of a hypothesis test? How can it be measured? Describe and illustrate by an example.

5. Briefly describe the important parametric tests used in context of testing hypotheses. How such tests differ from non-parametric tests? Explain.

6. Clearly explain how will you test the equality of variances of two normal populations.

7. (a) What is a *t*-test? When it is used and for what purpose(s)? Explain by means of examples.

   (b) Write a brief note on "Sandler's *A*-test" explaining its superiority over *t*-test.

8. Point out the important limitations of tests of hypotheses. What precaution the researcher must take while drawing inferences as per the results of the said tests?

9. A coin is tossed 10,000 times and head turns up 5,195 times. Is the coin unbiased?

10. In some dice throwing experiments, *A* threw dice 41952 times and of these 25145 yielded a 4 or 5 or 6. Is this consistent with the hypothesis that the dice were unbiased?

11. A machine puts out 16 imperfect articles in a sample of 500. After machine is overhauled, it puts out three imperfect articles in a batch of 100. Has the machine improved? Test at 5% level of significance.

12. In two large populations, there are 35% and 30% respectively fair haired people. Is this difference likely to be revealed by simple sample of 1500 and 1000 respectively from the two populations?

13. In a certain association table the following frequencies were obtained:

    $(AB) = 309$, $(Ab) = 214$, $(aB) = 132$, $(ab) = 119$.

    Can the association between *AB* as per the above data can be said to have arisen as a fluctuation of simple sampling?

14. A sample of 900 members is found to have a mean of 3.47 cm. Can it be reasonably regarded as a simple sample from a large population with mean 3.23 cm. and standard deviation 2.31 cm.?

15. The means of the two random samples of 1000 and 2000 are 67.5 and 68.0 inches respectively. Can the samples be regarded to have been drawn from the same population of standard deviation 9.5 inches? Test at 5% level of significance.

16. A large corporation uses thousands of light bulbs every year. The brand that has been used in the past has an average life of 1000 hours with a standard deviation of 100 hours. A new brand is offered to the corporation at a price far lower than one they are paying for the old brand. It is decided that they will switch to the new brand unless it is proved with a level of significance of 5% that the new brand has smaller average life than the old brand. A random sample of 100 new brand bulbs is tested yielding an observed sample mean of 985 hours. Assuming that the standard deviation of the new brand is the same as that of the old brand,

    (a) What conclusion should be drawn and what decision should be made?

    (b) What is the probability of accepting the new brand if it has the mean life of 950 hours?

17. Ten students are selected at random from a school and their heights are found to be, in inches, 50, 52, 52, 53, 55, 56, 57, 58, 58 and 59. In the light of these data, discuss the suggestion that the mean height of the students of the school is 54 inches. You may use 5% level of significance (Apply *t*-test as well as *A*-test).

18. In a test given to two groups of students, the marks obtained were as follows:

First Group	18	20	36	50	49	36	34	49	41
Second Group	29	28	26	35	30	44	46		

    Examine the significance of difference between mean marks obtained by students of the above two groups. Test at five per cent level of significance.

19. The heights of six randomly chosen sailors are, in inches, 63, 65, 58, 69, 71 and 72. The heights of 10 randomly chosen soldiers are, in inches, 61, 62, 65, 66, 69, 69, 70, 71, 72 and 73. Do these figures indicate that soldiers are on an average shorter than sailors? Test at 5% level of significance.

20. Ten young recruits were put through a strenuous physical training programme by the army. Their weights (in kg) were recorded before and after with the following results:

Recruit	1	2	3	4	5	6	7	8	9	10
Weight before	127	195	162	170	143	205	168	175	197	136
Weight after	135	200	160	182	147	200	172	186	194	141

Using 5% level of significance, should we conclude that the programme affects the average weight of young recruits (Answer using *t*-test as well as *A*-test)?

21. Suppose a test on the hypotheses $H_0 : \mu = 200$ against $H_a : \mu > 200$ is done with 1% level of significance, $\sigma_p = 40$ and $n = 16$.

(a) What is the probability that the null hypothesis might be accepted when the true mean is really 210? What is the power of the test for $\mu = 210$? How these values of β and $1 - \beta$ change if the test had used 5% level of significance?

(b) Which is more serious, a Type I and Type II error?

22. The following nine observations were drawn from a normal population:

$$27 \ 19 \ 20 \ 24 \ 23 \ 29 \ 21 \ 17 \ 27$$

(i) Test the null hypothesis $H_0 : \mu = 26$ against the alternative hypothesis $H_a : \mu \neq 26$. At what level of significance can H_0 be rejected?

(ii) At what level of significance can $H_0 : \mu = 26$ be rejected when tested against $H_a : \mu < 26$?

23. Suppose that a public corporation has agreed to advertise through a local newspaper if it can be established that the newspaper circulation reaches more than 60% of the corporation's customers. What H_0 and H_a should be established for this problem while deciding on the basis of a sample of customers whether or not the corporation should advertise in the local newspaper? If a sample of size 100 is collected and 1% level of significance is taken, what is the critical value for making a decision whether or not to advertise? Would it make any difference if we take a sample of 25 in place of 100 for our purpose? If so, explain.

24. Answer using *F*-test whether the following two samples have come from the same population:

Sample 1   17 27 18 25 27 29 27 23 17

Sample 2   16 16 20 16 20 17 15 21

Use 5% level of significance.

25. The following table gives the number of units produced per day by two workers *A* and *B* for a number of days:

$$A \ 40 \ 30 \ 38 \ 41 \ 38 \ 35$$
$$B \ 39 \ 38 \ 41 \ 33 \ 32 \ 49 \ 49 \ 34$$

Should these results be accepted as evidence that *B* is the more stable worker? Use *F*-test at 5% level.

26. A sample of 600 persons selected at random from a large city gives the result that males are 53%. Is there reason to doubt the hypothesis that males and females are in equal numbers in the city? Use 1% level of significance.

27. 12 students were given intensive coaching and 5 tests were conducted in a month. The scores of tests 1 and 5 are given below. Does the score from Test 1 to Test 5 show an improvement? Use 5% level of significance.

No. of students	1	2	3	4	5	6	7	8	9	10	11	12
Marks in 1st Test	50	42	51	26	35	42	60	41	70	55	62	38
Marks in 5th test	62	40	61	35	30	52	68	51	84	63	72	50

28. (i) A random sample from 200 villages was taken from Kanpur district and the average population per village was found to be 420 with a standard deviation of 50. Another random sample of 200 villages from the same district gave an average population of 480 per village with a standard deviation of 60. Is the difference between the averages of the two samples statistically significant? Take 1% level of significance.

(ii) The means of the random samples of sizes 9 and 7 are 196.42 and 198.42 respectively. The sums of he squares of the deviations from the mean are 26.94 and 18.73 respectively. Can the samples be constituted to have been drawn from the same normal population? Use 5% level of significance.

29. A farmer grows crops on two fields *A* and *B*. On *A* he puts Rs. 10 worth of manure per acre and on *B* Rs 20 worth. The net returns per acre exclusive of the cost of manure on the two fields in the five years are:

Year	1	2	3	4	5
Field A, Rs per acre	34	28	42	37	44
Field B, Rs per acre	36	33	48	38	50

Other things being equal, discuss the question whether it is likely to pay the farmer to continue the more expensive dressing. Test at 5% level of significance.

30. *ABC* Company is considering a site for locating their another plant. The company insists that any location they choose must have an average auto traffic of more than 2000 trucks per day passing the site. They take a traffic sample of 20 days and find an average volume per day of 2140 with standard deviation equal to 100 trucks.

Answer the following:

(i) If $\alpha = .05$, should they purchase the site?

(ii) If we assume the population mean to be 2140, what is the β error?

Chi-Square Test

The chi-square test is an important test amongst the several tests of significance developed by statisticians. Chi-square, symbolically written as χ^2 (Pronounced as Ki-square), is a statistical measure used in the context of sampling analysis for comparing a variance to a theoretical variance. As a non-parametric[*] test, it "can be used to determine if categorical data shows dependency or the two classifications are independent. It can also be used to make comparisons between theoretical populations and actual data when categories are used."[1] Thus, the chi-square test is applicable in large number of problems. The test is, in fact, a technique through the use of which it is possible for all researchers to (i) test the goodness of fit; (ii) test the significance of association between two attributes, and (iii) test the homogeneity or the significance of population variance.

CHI-SQUARE AS A TEST FOR COMPARING VARIANCE

The chi-square value is often used to judge the significance of population variance i.e., we can use the test to judge if a random sample has been drawn from a normal population with mean (μ) and with a specified variance (σ_p^2). The test is based on χ^2-distribution. Such a distribution we encounter when we deal with collections of values that involve adding up squares. Variances of samples require us to add a collection of squared quantities and, thus, have distributions that are related to χ^2-distribution. If we take each one of a collection of sample variances, divided them by the known population variance and multiply these quotients by $(n - 1)$, where n means the number of items in the sample, we shall obtain a χ^2-distribution. Thus, $\dfrac{\sigma_s^2}{\sigma_p^2}(n - 1) = \dfrac{\sigma_s^2}{\sigma_p^2}$ (d.f.) would have the same distribution as χ^2-distribution with $(n - 1)$ degrees of freedom.

---

[*] See Chapter 12 Testing of Hypotheses-II for more details.
[1] Neil R. Ullman, *Elementary Statistics—An Applied Approach*, p. 234.

The χ^2-distribution is not symmetrical and all the values are positive. For making use of this distribution, one is required to know the degrees of freedom since for different degrees of freedom we have different curves. The smaller the number of degrees of freedom, the more skewed is the distribution which is illustrated in Fig. 10.1:

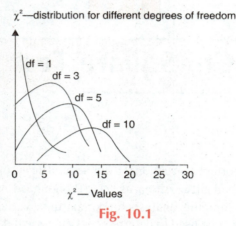

Fig. 10.1

Table given in the Appendix gives selected critical values of χ^2 for the different degrees of freedom. χ^2-values are the quantities indicated on the *x*-axis of the above diagram and in the table are areas below that value.

In brief, when we have to use chi-square as a test of population variance, we have to work out the value of χ^2 to test the null hypothesis (viz., $H_0 : \sigma_s^2 = \sigma_p^2$) as under:

$$\chi^2 = \frac{\sigma_s^2}{\sigma_p^2}(n-1)$$

where σ_s^2 = variance of the sample;

σ_p^2 = variance of the population;

$(n-1)$ = degrees of freedom, *n* being the number of items in the sample.

Then by comparing the calculated value with the table value of χ^2 for $(n-1)$ degrees of freedom at a given level of significance, we may either accept or reject the null hypothesis. If the calculated value of χ^2 is less than the table value, the null hypothesis is accepted, but if the calculated value is equal or greater than the table value, the hypothesis is rejected. All this can be made clear by an example.

Illustration 1

Weight of 10 students is as follows:

S. No.	1	2	3	4	5	6	7	8	9	10
Weight (kg.)	38	40	45	53	47	43	55	48	52	49

Can we say that the variance of the distribution of weight of all students from which the above sample of 10 students was drawn is equal to 20 kgs? Test this at 5 per cent and 1 per cent level of significance.

Solution: First of all we should work out the variance of the sample data or σ_s^2 and the same has been worked out as under:

Table 10.1

S. No.	X_i (Weight in kgs.)	$(X_i - \overline{X})$	$(X_i - \overline{X})^2$
1	38	-9	81
2	40	-7	49
3	45	-2	04
4	53	$+6$	36
5	47	$+0$	00
6	43	-4	16
7	55	$+8$	64
8	48	$+1$	01
9	52	$+5$	25
10	49	$+2$	04
$n = 10$	$\Sigma X_i = 470$		$\Sigma(X_i - \overline{X})^2 = 280$

$$\overline{X} = \frac{\Sigma X_i}{n} = \frac{470}{10} = 47 \text{ kgs.}$$

$\therefore$

$$\sigma_s = \sqrt{\frac{\Sigma(X_i - \overline{X})^2}{n-1}} = \sqrt{\frac{280}{10-1}} = \sqrt{31.11}$$

or

$$\sigma_s^2 = 31.11.$$

Let the null hypothesis be $H_0 : \sigma_p^2 = \sigma_s^2$. In order to test this hypothesis we work out the χ^2 value as under:

$$\chi^2 = \frac{\sigma_s^2}{\sigma_p^2}(n-1)$$

$$= \frac{31.11}{20}(10 - 1) = 13.999.$$

Degrees of freedom in the given case is $(n - 1) = (10 - 1) = 9$. At 5 per cent level of significance the table value of $\chi^2 = 16.92$ and at 1 per cent level of significance, it is 21.67 for 9 d.f. and both these values are greater than the calculated value of χ^2 which is 13.999. Hence we accept the null hypothesis and conclude that the variance of the given distribution can be taken as 20 kgs at 5 per cent as also at 1 per cent level of significance. In other words, the sample can be said to have been taken from a population with variance 20 kgs.

Illustration 2

A sample of 10 is drawn randomly from a certain population. The sum of the squared deviations from the mean of the given sample is 50. Test the hypothesis that the variance of the population is 5 at 5 per cent level of significance.

Solution: Given information is

$$n = 10$$

$$\Sigma \left(X_i - \bar{X} \right)^2 = 50$$

$$\therefore \quad \sigma_s^2 = \frac{\Sigma \left(X_i - \bar{X} \right)^2}{n - 1} = \frac{50}{9}$$

Take the null hypothesis as $H_0 : \sigma_p^2 = \sigma_s^2$. In order to test this hypothesis, we work out the χ^2 value as under:

$$\chi^2 = \frac{\sigma_s^2}{\sigma_p^2}(n - 1) = \frac{\frac{50}{9}}{5}(10 - 1) = \frac{50}{9} \times \frac{1}{5} \times \frac{9}{1} = 10$$

Degrees of freedom $= (10 - 1) = 9$.

The table value of χ^2 at 5 per cent level for 9 d.f. is 16.92. The calculated value of χ^2 is less than this table value, so we accept the null hypothesis and conclude that the variance of the population is 5 as given in the question.

CHI-SQUARE AS A NON-PARAMETRIC TEST

Chi-square is an important non-parametric test and as such no rigid assumptions are necessary in respect of the type of population. We require only the degrees of freedom (implicitly of course the size of the sample) for using this test. As a non-parametric test, chi-square can be used (i) as a test of goodness of fit and (ii) as a test of independence.

As a test of goodness of fit, χ^2 test enables us to see how well does the assumed theoretical distribution (such as Binomial distribution, Poisson distribution or Normal distribution) fit to the observed data. When some theoretical distribution is fitted to the given data, we are always interested in knowing as to how well this distribution fits with the observed data. The chi-square test can give answer to this. If the calculated value of χ^2 is less than the table value at a certain level of significance, the fit is considered to be a good one which means that the divergence between the observed and expected frequencies is attributable to fluctuations of sampling. But if the calculated value of χ^2 is greater than its table value, the fit is not considered to be a good one.

As a test of independence, χ^2 test enables us to explain whether or not two attributes are associated. For instance, we may be interested in knowing whether a new medicine is effective in controlling fever or not, χ^2 test will helps us in deciding this issue. In such a situation, we proceed with the null hypothesis that the two attributes (viz., new medicine and control of fever) are independent which means that new medicine is not effective in controlling fever. On this basis we first calculate the expected frequencies and then work out the value of χ^2. If the calculated value of χ^2 is less than the table value at a certain level of significance for given degrees of freedom, we conclude that null hypothesis stands which means that the two attributes are independent or not associated (i.e., the new medicine is not effective in controlling the fever). But if the calculated value of χ^2 is greater than its table value, our inference then would be that null hypothesis does not hold good which means the two attributes are associated and the association is not because of some chance factor but it exists in reality (i.e., the new medicine is effective in controlling the fever and as such may be prescribed). It may, however, be stated here that χ^2 is not a measure of the degree of relationship or the form of relationship between two attributes, but is simply a technique of judging the significance of such association or relationship between two attributes.

In order that we may apply the chi-square test either as a test of goodness of fit or as a test to judge the significance of association between attributes, it is necessary that the observed as well as theoretical or expected frequencies must be grouped in the same way and the theoretical distribution must be adjusted to give the same total frequency as we find in case of observed distribution. χ^2 is then calculated as follows:

$$\chi^2 = \sum \frac{\left(O_{ij} - E_{ij}\right)^2}{E_{ij}}$$

where

O_{ij} = observed frequency of the cell in ith row and jth column.

E_{ij} = expected frequency of the cell in ith row and jth column.

If two distributions (observed and theoretical) are exactly alike, $\chi^2 = 0$; but generally due to sampling errors, χ^2 is not equal to zero and as such we must know the sampling distribution of χ^2 so that we may find the probability of an observed χ^2 being given by a random sample from the hypothetical universe. Instead of working out the probabilities, we can use ready table which gives probabilities for given values of χ^2. Whether or not a calculated value of χ^2 is significant can be ascertained by looking at the tabulated values of χ^2 for given degrees of freedom at a certain level of significance. If the calculated value of χ^2 is equal to or exceeds the table value, the difference between the observed and expected frequencies is taken as significant, but if the table value is more than the calculated value of χ^2, then the difference is considered as insignificant i.e., considered to have arisen as a result of chance and as such can be ignored.

As already stated, degrees of freedom[*] play an important part in using the chi-square distribution and the test based on it, one must correctly determine the degrees of freedom. If there are 10 frequency classes and there is one independent constraint, then there are $(10 - 1) = 9$ degrees of freedom. Thus, if 'n' is the number of groups and one constraint is placed by making the totals of observed and expected frequencies equal, the d.f. would be equal to $(n - 1)$. In the case of a contingency table (i.e., a table with 2 columns and 2 rows or a table with two columns and more than two rows or a table with two rows but more than two columns or a table with more than two rows and more than two columns), the d.f. is worked out as follows:

$$d.f. = (c - 1)(r - 1)$$

where 'c' means the number of columns and 'r' means the number of rows.

CONDITIONS FOR THE APPLICATION OF χ^2 TEST

The following conditions should be satisfied before χ^2 test can be applied:

(i) Observations recorded and used are collected on a random basis.

(ii) All the itmes in the sample must be independent.

(iii) No group should contain very few items, say less than 10. In case where the frequencies are less than 10, regrouping is done by combining the frequencies of adjoining groups so that the new frequencies become greater than 10. Some statisticians take this number as 5, but 10 is regarded as better by most of the statisticians.

(iv) The overall number of items must also be reasonably large. It should normally be at least 50, howsoever small the number of groups may be.

(v) The constraints must be linear. Constraints which involve linear equations in the cell frequencies of a contingency table (i.e., equations containing no squares or higher powers of the frequencies) are known are know as linear constraints.

STEPS INVOLVED IN APPLYING CHI-SQUARE TEST

The various steps involved are as follows:

---

[*] For d.f. greater than 30, the distribution of $\sqrt{2\chi^2}$ approximates the normal distribution wherein the mean of $\sqrt{2\chi^2}$ distribution is $\sqrt{2 d.f. - 1}$ and the standard deviation = 1. Accordingly, when d.f. exceeds 30, the quantity $\left[\sqrt{2\chi^2} - \sqrt{2 d.f. - 1} \right]$ may be used as a normal variate with unit variance, i.e.,

$$z_\alpha = \sqrt{2\chi^2} - \sqrt{2 d.f. - 1}$$

(i) First of all calculate the expected frequencies on the basis of given hypothesis or on the basis of null hypothesis. Usually in case of a 2 × 2 or any contingency table, the expected frequency for any given cell is worked out as under:

$$\text{Expected frequency of any cell} = \left[\frac{\substack{(\text{Row total for the row of that cell}) \times \\ (\text{Column total for the column of that cell})}}{(\text{Grand total})} \right]$$

(ii) Obtain the difference between observed and expected frequencies and find out the squares of such differences i.e., calculate $(O_{ij} - E_{ij})^2$.

(iii) Divide the quantity $(O_{ij} - E_{ij})^2$ obtained as stated above by the corresponding expected frequency to get $(O_{ij} - E_{ij})^2/E_{ij}$ and this should be done for all the cell frequencies or the group frequencies.

(iv) Find the summation of $(O_{ij} - E_{ij})^2/E_{ij}$ values or what we call $\sum \frac{\left(O_{ij} - E_{ij}\right)^2}{E_{ij}}$. This is the required χ^2 value.

The χ^2 value obtained as such should be compared with relevant table value of χ^2 and then inference be drawn as stated above.

We now give few examples to illustrate the use of χ^2 test.

Illustration 3

A die is thrown 132 times with following results:

Number turned up	1	2	3	4	5	6
Frequency	16	20	25	14	29	28

Is the die unbiased?

Solution: Let us take the hypothesis that the die is unbiased. If that is so, the probability of obtaining any one of the six numbers is 1/6 and as such the expected frequency of any one number coming upward is $132 \times 1/6 = 22$. Now we can write the observed frequencies along with expected frequencies and work out the value of χ^2 as follows:

Table 10.2

No. turned up	Observed frequency O_i	Expected frequency E_i	$(O_i - E_i)$	$(O_i - E_i)^2$	$(O_i - E_i)^2/E_i$
1	16	22	–6	36	36/22
2	20	22	–2	4	4/22
3	25	22	3	9	9/22
4	14	22	–8	64	64/22
5	29	22	7	49	49/22
6	28	22	6	36	36/22

$$\therefore \qquad \qquad \sum [(O_i - E_i)^2/E_i] = 9.$$

Hence, the calculated value of $\chi^2 = 9$.

$\because$ Degrees of freedom in the given problem is

$(n - 1) = (6 - 1) = 5$.

The table value* of χ^2 for 5 degrees of freedom at 5 per cent level of significance is 11.071. Comparing calculated and table values of χ^2, we find that calculated value is less than the table value and as such could have arisen due to fluctuations of sampling. The result, thus, supports the hypothesis and it can be concluded that the die is unbiased.

Illustration 4

Find the value of χ^2 for the following information:

Class	A	B	C	D	E
Observed frequency	8	29	44	15	4
Theoretical (or expected) frequency	7	24	38	24	7

Solution: Since some of the frequencies less than 10, we shall first re-group the given data as follows and then will work out the value of χ^2:

Table 10.3

Class	Observed frequency O_i	Expected frequency E_i	$O_i - E_i$	$(O_i - E_i)^2/E_i$
A and B	(8+29)=37	(7+24)=31	6	36/31
C	44	38	6	36/38
D and E	(15+4)=19	(24+7)=31	−12	144/31

$$\therefore \qquad \qquad \chi^2 = \sum \frac{(O_i - E_i)^2}{E_i} = 6.76 \text{ app.}$$

Illustration 5

Genetic theory states that children having one parent of blood type A and the other of blood type B will always be of one of three types, A, AB, B and that the proportion of three types will on an average be as 1 : 2 : 1. A report states that out of 300 children having one A parent and B parent, 30 per cent were found to be types A, 45 per cent per cent type AB and remainder type B. Test the hypothesis by χ^2 test.

Solution: The observed frequencies of type A, AB and B is given in the question are 90, 135 and 75 respectively.

*Table No. 3 showing some critical values of χ^2 for specified degrees of freedom has been given in Appendix at the end of the book.

The expected frequencies of type *A*, *AB* and *B* (as per the genetic theory) should have been 75, 150 and 75 respectively.

We now calculate the value of χ^2 as follows:

Table 10.4

Type	Observed frequency O_i	Expected frequency E_i	$(O_i - E_i)$	$(O_i - E_i)^2$	$(O_i - E_i)^2/E_i$
A	90	75	15	225	225/75 = 3
AB	135	150	−15	225	225/150 = 1.5
B	75	75	0	0	0/75 = 0

$$\therefore \qquad \chi^2 = \Sigma \frac{\left(O_i - E_i\right)^2}{E_i} = 3 + 1.5 + 0 = 4.5$$

$$\because \qquad \text{d.f.} = (n - 1) = (3 - 1) = 2.$$

Table value of χ^2 for 2 d.f. at 5 per cent level of significance is 5.991.

The calculated value of χ^2 is 4.5 which is less than the table value and hence can be ascribed to have taken place because of chance. This supports the theoretical hypothesis of the genetic theory that on an average type *A*, *AB* and *B* stand in the proportion of 1 : 2 : 1.

Illustration 6

The table given below shows the data obtained during outbreak of smallpox:

	Attacked	Not attacked	Total
Vaccinated	31	469	500
Not vaccinated	185	1315	1500
Total	216	1784	2000

Test the effectiveness of vaccination in preventing the attack from smallpox. Test your result with the help of χ^2 at 5 per cent level of significance.

Solution: Let us take the hypothesis that vaccination is not effective in preventing the attack from smallpox i.e., vaccination and attack are independent. On the basis of this hypothesis, the expected frequency corresponding to the number of persons vaccinated and attacked would be:

$$\text{Expectation of } (AB) = \frac{(A) \times (B)}{N}$$

when *A* represents vaccination and *B* represents attack.

$$\therefore \quad (A) = 500$$
$$(B) = 216$$
$$N = 2000$$

$$\text{Expectation of } (AB) = \frac{500 \times 216}{2000} = 54$$

Now using the expectation of (AB), we can write the table of expected values as follows:

	Attacked: B	*Not attacked: b*	*Total*
Vaccinated: A	(AB) = 54	(Ab) = 446	500
Not vaccinated: a	(aB) = 162	(ab) = 1338	1500
Total	216	1784	2000

Table 10.5:   Calculation of Chi-Square

Group	Observed frequency O_{ij}	Expected frequency E_{ij}	$(O_{ij} - E_{ij})$	$(O_{ij} - E_{ij})^2$	$(O_{ij} - E_{ij})^2/E_{ij}$
AB	31	54	–23	529	529/54 = 9.796
Ab	469	446	+23	529	529/44 = 1.186
aB	158	162	+23	529	529/162 = 3.265
ab	1315	1338	–23	529	529/1338 = 0.395

$$\chi^2 = \Sigma \frac{\left(O_{ij} - E_{ij}\right)^2}{E_{ij}} = 14.642$$

$\because$ Degrees of freedom in this case = $(r - 1)(c - 1) = (2 - 1)(2 - 1) = 1$.

The table value of χ^2 for 1 degree of freedom at 5 per cent level of significance is 3.841. The calculated value of χ^2 is much higher than this table value and hence the result of the experiment does not support the hypothesis. We can, thus, conclude that vaccination is effective in preventing the attack from smallpox.

Illustration 7

Two research workers classified some people in income groups on the basis of sampling studies. Their results are as follows:

Investigators	Income groups			Total
	Poor	*Middle*	*Rich*	
A	160	30	10	200
B	140	120	40	300
Total	300	150	50	500

Show that the sampling technique of at least one research worker is defective.

Solution: Let us take the hypothesis that the sampling techniques adopted by research workers are similar (i.e., there is no difference between the techniques adopted by research workers). This being so, the expectation of *A* investigator classifying the people in

(i) Poor income group $= \dfrac{200 \times 300}{500} = 120$

(ii) Middle income group $= \dfrac{200 \times 150}{500} = 60$

(iii) Rich income group $= \dfrac{200 \times 50}{500} = 20$

Similarly the expectation of *B* investigator classifying the people in

(i) Poor income group $= \dfrac{300 \times 300}{500} = 180$

(ii) Middle income group $= \dfrac{300 \times 150}{500} = 90$

(iii) Rich income group $= \dfrac{300 \times 50}{500} = 30$

We can now calculate value of χ^2 as follows:

Table 10.6

Groups	Observed frequency O_{ij}	Expected frequency E_{ij}	$O_{ij} - E_{ij}$	$(O_{ij} - E_{ij})^2 E_{ij}$
Investigator A classifies people as poor	160	120	40	1600/120 = 13.33
classifies people as middle class people	30	60	−30	900/60 = 15.00
classifies people as rich	10	20	−10	100/20 = 5.00
Investigator B classifies people as poor	140	180	−40	1600/180 = 8.88
classifies people as middle class people	120	90	30	900/90 = 10.00
classifies people as rich	40	30	10	100/30 = 3.33

Hence,
$$\chi^2 = \Sigma \frac{\left(O_{ij} - E_{ij}\right)^2}{E_{ij}} = 55.54$$

$\because$ Degrees of freedom $= (c-1)\,(r-1)$
$$= (3-1)\,(2-1) = 2.$$

The table value of χ^2 for two degrees of freedom at 5 per cent level of significance is 5.991.

The calculated value of χ^2 is much higher than this table value which means that the calculated value cannot be said to have arisen just because of chance. It is significant. Hence, the hypothesis does not hold good. This means that the sampling techniques adopted by two investigators differ and are not similar. Naturally, then the technique of one must be superior than that of the other.

Illustration 8

Eight coins were tossed 256 times and the following results were obtained:

Numbers of heads	0	1	2	3	4	5	6	7	8
Frequency	2	6	30	52	67	56	32	10	1

Are the coins biased? Use χ^2 test.

Solution: Let us take the hypothesis that the coins are not biased. If that is so, the probability of any one coin falling with head upward is 1/2 and with tail upward is 1/2 and it remains the same whatever be the number of throws. In such a case the expected values of getting 0, 1, 2, … heads in a single throw in 256 throws of eight coins will be worked out as follows[*].

Table 10.7

Events or No. of heads	Expected frequencies
0	$^8C_0\left(\frac{1}{2}\right)^0\left(\frac{1}{2}\right)^8 \times 256 = 1$
1	$^8C_1\left(\frac{1}{2}\right)^1\left(\frac{1}{2}\right)^7 \times 256 = 8$
2	$^8C_2\left(\frac{1}{2}\right)^2\left(\frac{1}{2}\right)^6 \times 256 = 28$

contd.

[*]The probabilities of random variable i.e., various possible events have been worked out on the binomial principle viz., through the expansion of $(p + q)^n$ where $p = 1/2$ and $q = 1/2$ and $n = 8$ in the given case. The expansion of the term $^nC_r\,p^r\,q^{n-r}$ has given the required probabilities which have been multiplied by 256 to obtain the expected frequencies.

Events or No. of heads	Expected frequencies
3	$^8C_3\left(\dfrac{1}{2}\right)^3\left(\dfrac{1}{2}\right)^5 \times 256 = 56$
4	$^8C_4\left(\dfrac{1}{2}\right)^4\left(\dfrac{1}{2}\right)^4 \times 256 = 70$
5	$^8C_5\left(\dfrac{1}{2}\right)^5\left(\dfrac{1}{2}\right)^3 \times 256 = 56$
6	$^8C_6\left(\dfrac{1}{2}\right)^6\left(\dfrac{1}{2}\right)^2 \times 256 = 28$
7	$^8C_7\left(\dfrac{1}{2}\right)^7\left(\dfrac{1}{2}\right)^1 \times 256 = 8$
8	$^8C_8\left(\dfrac{1}{2}\right)^8\left(\dfrac{1}{2}\right)^0 \times 256 = 1$

The value of χ^2 can be worked out as follows:

Table 10.8

No. of heads	Observed frequency O_i	Expected frequency E_i	$O_i - E_i$	$(O_i - E_i)^2/E_i$
0	2	1	1	$1/1 = 1.00$
1	6	8	−2	$4/8 = 0.50$
2	30	28	2	$4/28 = 0.14$
3	52	56	−4	$16/56 = 0.29$
4	67	70	−3	$9/70 = 0.13$
5	56	56	0	$0/56 = 0.00$
6	32	28	4	$16/28 = 0.57$
7	10	8	2	$4/8 = 0.50$
8	1	1	0	$0/1 = 0.00$

$$\therefore \quad \chi^2 = \Sigma \frac{(O_i - E_i)^2}{E_i} = 3.13$$

$\therefore$ Degrees of freedom $= (n-1) = (9-1) = 8$

The table value of χ^2 for eight degrees of freedom at 5 per cent level of significance is 15.507.

The calculated value of χ^2 is much less than this table and hence it is insignificant and can be ascribed due to fluctuations of sampling. The result, thus, supports the hypothesis and we may say that the coins are not biased.

ALTERNATIVE FORMULA

There is an alternative method of calculating the value of χ^2 in the case of a (2×2) table. If we write the cell frequencies and marginal totals in case of a (2×2) table thus,

a	b	$(a+b)$
c	d	$(c+d)$
$(a+c)\ (b+d)$		N

then the formula for calculating the value of χ^2 will be stated as follows:

$$\chi^2 = \frac{(ad-bc)^2 \cdot N}{(a+c)\ (b+d)\ (a+b)\ (c+d)}$$

where N means the total frequency, ad means the larger cross product, bc means the smaller cross product and $(a+c)$, $(b+d)$, $(a+b)$, and $(c+d)$ are the marginal totals. The alternative formula is rarely used in finding out the value of chi-square as it is not applicable uniformly in all cases but can be used only in a (2×2) contingency table.

YATES' CORRECTION

F. Yates has suggested a correction for continuity in χ^2 value calculated in connection with a (2×2) table, particularly when cell frequencies are small (since no cell frequency should be less than 5 in any case, through 10 is better as stated earlier) and χ^2 is just on the significance level. The correction suggested by Yates is popularly known as Yates' correction. It involves the reduction of the deviation of observed from expected frequencies which of course reduces the value of χ^2. The rule for correction is to adjust the observed frequency in each cell of a (2×2) table in such a way as to reduce the deviation of the observed from the expected frequency for that cell by 0.5, but this adjustment is made in all the cells without disturbing the marginal totals. The formula for finding the value of χ^2 after applying Yates' correction can be stated thus:

$$\chi^2 \text{(corrected)} = \frac{N \cdot \left(\left|ad - bc\right| - 0.5N\right)^2}{(a + b)\,(c + d)\,(a + c)\,(b + d)}$$

In case we use the usual formula for calculating the value of chi-square viz.,

$$\chi^2 = \Sigma \frac{\left(O_{ij} - E_{ij}\right)^2}{E_{ij}},$$

then Yates' correction can be applied as under:

$$\chi^2 \text{(corrected)} = \frac{\left[\left|O_1 - E_1\right| - 0.5\right]^2}{E_1} + \frac{\left[\left|O_2 - E_2\right| - 0.5\right]^2}{E_2} + \ldots$$

It may again be emphasised that Yates' correction is made only in case of (2×2) table and that too when cell frequencies are small.

Illustration 9

The following information is obtained concerning an investigation of 50 ordinary shops of small size:

	Shops		Total
	In towns	*In villages*	
Run by men	17	18	35
Run by women	3	12	15
Total	20	30	50

Can it be inferred that shops run by women are relatively more in villages than in towns? Use χ^2 test.

Solution: Take the hypothesis that there is no difference so far as shops run by men and women in towns and villages. With this hypothesis the expectation of shops run by men in towns would be:

$$\text{Expectation of } (AB) = \frac{(A) \times (B)}{N}$$

where A = shops run by men

  B = shops in towns

  (A) = 35; (B) = 20 and N = 50

Thus, expectation of $(AB) = \dfrac{35 \times 20}{50} = 14$

Hence, table of expected frequencies would be

	Shops in towns	Shops in villages	Total
Run by men	14 (AB)	21 (Ab)	35
Run by women	6 (aB)	9 (ab)	15
Total	20	30	50

Calculation of χ^2 value:

Table 10.9

Groups	Observed frequency O_{ij}	Expected frequency E_{ij}	$(O_{ij} - E_{ij})$	$(O_{ij} - E_{ij})^2/E_{ij}$
(AB)	17	14	3	9/14 = 0.64
(Ab)	18	21	-3	9/21 = 0.43
(aB)	3	6	-3	9/6 = 1.50
(ab)	12	9	3	9/9 = 1.00

$$\therefore \qquad \chi^2 = \Sigma \frac{\left(O_{ij} - E_{ij}\right)^2}{E_{ij}} = 3.57$$

As one cell frequency is only 3 in the given 2×2 table, we also work out χ^2 value applying Yates' correction and this is as under:

$$\chi^2 \text{(corrected)} = \frac{\left[|17 - 14| - 0.5\right]^2}{14} + \frac{\left[|18 - 21| - 0.5\right]^2}{21} + \frac{\left[|3 - 6| - 0.5\right]^2}{6} + \frac{\left[|12 - 9| - 0.5\right]^2}{9}$$

$$= \frac{(2.5)^2}{14} + \frac{(2.5)^2}{21} + \frac{(2.5)^2}{6} + \frac{(2.5)^2}{9}$$

$$= 0.446 + 0.298 + 1.040 + 0.694$$

$$= 2.478$$

$$\because \text{ Degrees of freedom} = (c - 1)(r - 1) = (2 - 1)(2 - 1) = 1$$

Table value of χ^2 for one degree of freedom at 5 per cent level of significance is 3.841. The calculated value of χ^2 by both methods (i.e., before correction and after Yates' correction) is less than its table value. Hence the hypothesis stands. We can conclude that there is no difference between shops run by men and women in villages and towns.

Additive property: An important property of χ^2 is its additive nature. This means that several values of χ^2 can be added together and if the degrees of freedom are also added, this number gives the degrees of freedom of the total value of χ^2. Thus, if a number of χ^2 values have been obtained from a number of samples of similar data, then because of the additive nature of χ^2 we can combine the various values of χ^2 by just simply adding them. Such addition of various values of χ^2 gives one value of χ^2 which helps in forming a better idea about the significance of the problem under consideration. The following example illustrates the additive property of χ^2.

Illustration 10

The following values of χ^2 from different investigations carried to examine the effectiveness of a recently invented medicine for checking malaria are obtained:

Investigation	χ^2	*d.f.*
1	2.5	1
2	3.2	1
3	4.1	1
4	3.7	1
5	4.5	1

What conclusion would you draw about the effectiveness of the new medicine on the basis of the five investigations taken together?

Solution: By adding all the values of χ^2, we obtain a value equal to 18.0. Also by adding the various d.f., as given in the question, we obtain the value 5. We can now state that the value of χ^2 for 5 degrees of freedom (when all the five investigations are taken together) is 18.0.

Let us take the hypothesis that the new medicine is not effective. The table value of χ^2 for 5 degrees of freedom at 5 per cent level of significance is 11.070. But our calculated value is higher than this table value which means that the difference is significant and is not due to chance. As such the hypothesis is rejected and it can be concluded that the new medicine is effective in checking malaria.

CONVERSION OF CHI-SQUARE INTO PHI COEFFICIENT (ϕ)

Since χ^2 does not by itself provide an estimate of the magnitude of association between two attributes, any obtained χ^2 value may be converted into Phi coefficient (symbolized as ϕ) for the purpose. In other words, chi-square tells us about the significance of a relation between variables; it provides no answer regarding the magnitude of the relation. This can be achieved by computing the Phi coefficient, which is a non-parametric measure of coefficient of correlation, as under:

$$\phi = \sqrt{\frac{\chi^2}{N}}$$

CONVERSION OF CHI-SQUARE INTO COEFFICIENT OF CONTINGENCY (*C*)

Chi-square value may also be converted into coefficient of contingency, especially in case of a contingency table of higher order than 2×2 table to study the magnitude of the relation or the degree of association between two attributes, as shown below:

$$C = \sqrt{\frac{\chi^2}{\chi^2 + N}}$$

While finding out the value of *C* we proceed on the assumption of null hypothesis that the two attributes are independent and exhibit no association. Coefficient of contingency is also known as coefficient of Mean Square contingency. This measure also comes under the category of non-parametric measure of relationship.

IMPORTANT CHARACTERISTICS OF χ^2 TEST

(i) This test (as a non-parametric test) is based on frequencies and not on the parameters like mean and standard deviation.

(ii) The test is used for testing the hypothesis and is not useful for estimation.

(iii) This test possesses the additive property as has already been explained.

(iv) This test can also be applied to a complex contingency table with several classes and as such is a very useful test in research work.

(v) This test is an important non-parametric test as no rigid assumptions are necessary in regard to the type of population, no need of parameter values and relatively less mathematical details are involved.

CAUTION IN USING χ^2 TEST

The chi-square test is no doubt a most frequently used test, but its correct application is equally an uphill task. It should be borne in mind that the test is to be applied only when the individual observations of sample are independent which means that the occurrence of one individual observation (event) has no effect upon the occurrence of any other observation (event) in the sample under consideration. Small theoretical frequencies, if these occur in certain groups, should be dealt with under special care. The other possible reasons concerning the improper application or misuse of this test can be (i) neglect of frequencies of non-occurrence; (ii) failure to equalise the sum of observed and the sum of the expected frequencies; (iii) wrong determination of the degrees of freedom; (iv) wrong computations, and the like. The researcher while applying this test must remain careful about all these things and must thoroughly understand the rationale of this important test before using it and drawing inferences in respect of his hypothesis.

Questions

1. What is Chi-square text? Explain its significance in statistical analysis.

2. Write short notes on the following:
   (i) Additive property of Chi-square;
   (ii) Chi-square as a test of 'goodness of fit';
   (iii) Precautions in applying Chi-square test;
   (iv) Conditions for applying Chi-square test.

3. An experiment was conducted to test the efficacy of chloromycetin in checking typhoid. In a certain hospital chloromycetin was given to 285 out of the 392 patients suffering from typhoid. The number of typhoid cases were as follows:

	Typhoid	No Typhoid	Total
Chloromycetin	35	250	285
No chloromycetin	50	57	107
Total	85	307	392

With the help of χ^2, test the effectiveness of chloromycetin in checking typhoid.

(The χ^2 value at 5 per cent level of significance for one degree of freedom is 3.841).

(M. Com., Rajasthan University, 1966)

4. On the basis of information given below about the treatment of 200 patients suffering from a disease, state whether the new treatment is comparatively superior to the conventional treatment.

Treatment	No. of patients	
	Favourable Response	No Response
New	60	20
Conventional	70	50

For drawing your inference, use the value of χ^2 for one degree of freedom at the 5 per cent level of significance, viz., 3.84.

5. 200 digits were chosen at random from a set of tables. The frequencies of the digits were:

Digit	0	1	2	3	4	5	6	7	8	9
Frequency	18	19	23	21	16	25	22	20	21	15

Calculate χ^2.

6. Five dice were thrown 96 times and the number of times 4, 5, or 6 was thrown were

Number of dice throwing

4, 5 or 6	5	4	3	2	1	0
Frequency	8	18	35	24	10	1

Find the value of Chi-square.

7. Find Chi-square from the following information:

Condition of child	Condition of home		Total
	Clean	Dirty	
Clean	70	50	120
Fairly clean	80	20	100
Dirty	35	45	80
Total	185	115	300

State whether the two attributes viz., condition of home and condition of child are independent (Use Chi-square test for the purpose).

8. In a certain cross the types represented by XY, Xy, xY and xy are expected to occur in a $9:5:4:2$ ratio. The actual frequencies were:

XY	Xy	xY	xy
180	110	60	50

Test the goodness of fit of observation to theory.

9. The normal rate of infection for a certain disease in cattle is known to be 50 per cent. In an experiment with seven animals injected with a new vaccine it was found that none of the animals caught infection. Can the evidence be regarded as conclusive (at 1 per cent level of significance) to prove the value of the new vaccine?

10. Result of throwing die were recorded as follows:

Number falling upwards	1	2	3	4	5	6
Frequency	27	33	31	29	30	24

Is the die unbiased? Answer on the basis of Chi-square test.

11. The Theory predicts the proportion of beans, in the four groups A, B, C and D should be $9:3:3:1$. In an experiment among 1600 beans, the number in the four groups were 882, 313, 287 and 118. Does the experimental result support the theory? Apply χ^2 test.

(M.B.A., Delhi University, 1975)

12. You are given a sample of 150 observations classified by two attributes A and B as follows:

	A_1	A_2	A_3	Total
B_1	40	25	15	80
B_2	11	26	8	45
B_3	9	9	7	25
Total	60	60	30	150

Use the χ^2 test to examine whether A and B are associated.

(M.A. Eco., Patiala University, 1975)

13. A survey of 320 families with five children each revealed the following distribution:

No. of boys	5	4	3	2	1	0
No. of girls	0	1	2	3	4	5
No. of families	14	56	110	88	40	12

Is this distribution consistent with the hypothesis that male and female births are equally probable? Apply Chi-square test.

14. What is Yates' correction? Find the value of Chi-square applying Yates' correction to the following data:

	Passed	*Failed*	*Total*
Day classes	10	20	30
Evening classes	4	66	70
Total	14	86	100

Also state whether the association, if any, between passing in the examination and studying in day classes is significant using Chi-square test.

15. (a) 1000 babies were born during a certain week in a city of which 600 were boys and 400 girls. Use χ^2 test to examine the correctness of the hypothesis that the sex-ratio is 1 : 1 in newly born babies.

(b) The percentage of smokers in a certain city was 90. A random sample of 100 persons was selected in which 85 persons were found to be smokers. Is the sample proportion significantly different from the proportion of smokers in the city? Answer on the basis of Chi-square test.

16. A college is running post-graduate classes in five subjects with equal number of students. The total number of absentees in these five classes is 75. Test the hypothesis that these classes are alike in absenteeism if the actual absentees in each are as follows:

History = 19
Philosophy = 18
Economics = 15
Commerce = 12
Chemistry = 11

(M.Phil. (EAFM) Exam. Raj. Uni., 1978)

17. The number of automobile accidents per week in a certain community were as follows:

12, 8, 20, 2, 14, 10, 15, 6, 9, 4

Are these frequencies in agreement with the belief that accident conditions were the same during the 10 week period under consideration?

18. A certain chemical plant processes sea water to collect sodium chloride and magnesium. From scientific analysis, sea water is known to contain sodium chloride, magnesium and other elements in the ratio of 62 : 4 : 34. A sample of 200 tons of sea water has resulted in 130 tons of sodium chloride and 6 tons of magnesium. Are these data consistent with the scientific model at 5 per cent level of significance?

19. An oil company has explored three different areas for possible oil reserves. The results of the test were as given below:

	Area			Total
	A	B	C	
Strikes	7	10	8	25
Dry holes	10	18	9	37
Total number of test wells	17	28	17	62

Do the three areas have the same potential, at the 10 per cent level of significance?

20. While conducting an air traffic study, a record was made of the number of aircraft arrivals, at a certain airport, during 250 half hour time intervals. The following tables gives the observed number of periods in which there were 0, 1, 2, 3, 4, or more arrivals as well as the expected number of such periods if arrivals per half hour have a Poisson distribution $\lambda = 2$. Does this Poisson distribution describe the observed arrivals at 5 per cent level of significance.

Number of observed arrivals (per half hour)	Number of periods observed	Number of periods expected (Poisson, $\lambda = 2$)
0	47	34
1	56	68
2	71	68
3	44	45
4 or more	32	35

21. A marketing researcher interested in the business publication reading habits of purchasing agents has assembled the following data:

Business Publication Preferences (First Choice Mentions)

Business Publication	Frequency of first choice
A	35
B	30
C	45
D	55

(i) Test the null hypothesis ($\alpha = 0.05$) that there are no differences among frequencies of first choice of tested publications.

(ii) If the choice of A and C and that of B and D are aggregated, test the null hypothesis at $\alpha = 0.05$ that there are no differences.

22. A group of 150 College students were asked to indicate their most liked film star from among six different well known film actors viz., A, B, C, D, E and F in order to ascertain their relative popularity. The observed frequency data were as follows:

Actors	A	B	C	D	E	F	Total
Frequencies	24	20	32	25	28	21	150

Test at 5 per cent whether all actors are equally popular.

23. For the data in question 12, find the coefficient of contingency to measure the magnitude of relationship between A and B.

24. (a) What purpose is served by calculating the Phi coefficient (ϕ)? Explain.

(b) If $\chi^2 = 16$ and $N = 4$, find the value of Phi coefficient.

11

Analysis of Variance and Co-variance

ANALYSIS OF VARIANCE (ANOVA)

Analysis of variance (abbreviated as ANOVA) is an extremely useful technique concerning researches in the fields of economics, biology, education, psychology, sociology, business/industry and in researches of several other disciplines. This technique is used when multiple sample cases are involved. As stated earlier, the significance of the difference between the means of two samples can be judged through either z-test or the t-test, but the difficulty arises when we happen to examine the significance of the difference amongst more than two sample means at the same time. The ANOVA technique enables us to perform this simultaneous test and as such is considered to be an important tool of analysis in the hands of a researcher. Using this technique, one can draw inferences about whether the samples have been drawn from populations having the same mean.

The ANOVA technique is important in the context of all those situations where we want to compare more than two populations such as in comparing the yield of crop from several varieties of seeds, the gasoline mileage of four automobiles, the smoking habits of five groups of university students and so on. In such circumstances one generally does not want to consider all possible combinations of two populations at a time for that would require a great number of tests before we would be able to arrive at a decision. This would also consume lot of time and money, and even then certain relationships may be left unidentified (particularly the interaction effects). Therefore, one quite often utilizes the ANOVA technique and through it investigates the differences among the means of all the populations simultaneously.

WHAT IS ANOVA?

Professor R.A. Fisher was the first man to use the term 'Variance'* and, in fact, it was he who developed a very elaborate theory concerning ANOVA, explaining its usefulness in practical field.

---

* Variance is an important statistical measure and is described as the mean of the squares of deviations taken from the mean of the given series of data. It is a frequently used measure of variation. Its squareroot is known as standard deviation, i.e., Standard deviation = $\sqrt{\text{Variance}}$.

Later on Professor Snedecor and many others contributed to the development of this technique. ANOVA is essentially a procedure for testing the difference among different groups of data for homogeneity. "The essence of ANOVA is that the total amount of variation in a set of data is broken down into two types, that amount which can be attributed to chance and that amount which can be attributed to specified causes."[1] There may be variation between samples and also within sample items. ANOVA consists in splitting the variance for analytical purposes. Hence, it is a method of analysing the variance to which a response is subject into its various components corresponding to various sources of variation. Through this technique one can explain whether various varieties of seeds or fertilizers or soils differ significantly so that a policy decision could be taken accordingly, concerning a particular variety in the context of agriculture researches. Similarly, the differences in various types of feed prepared for a particular class of animal or various types of drugs manufactured for curing a specific disease may be studied and judged to be significant or not through the application of ANOVA technique. Likewise, a manager of a big concern can analyse the performance of various salesmen of his concern in order to know whether their performances differ significantly.

Thus, through ANOVA technique one can, in general, investigate any number of factors which are hypothesized or said to influence the dependent variable. One may as well investigate the differences amongst various categories within each of these factors which may have a large number of possible values. If we take only one factor and investigate the differences amongst its various categories having numerous possible values, we are said to use one-way ANOVA and in case we investigate two factors at the same time, then we use two-way ANOVA. In a two or more way ANOVA, the interaction (i.e., inter-relation between two independent variables/factors), if any, between two independent variables affecting a dependent variable can as well be studied for better decisions.

THE BASIC PRINCIPLE OF ANOVA

The basic principle of ANOVA is to test for differences among the means of the populations by examining the amount of variation within each of these samples, relative to the amount of variation between the samples. In terms of variation within the given population, it is assumed that the values of (X_{ij}) differ from the mean of this population only because of random effects i.e., there are influences on (X_{ij}) which are unexplainable, whereas in examining differences between populations we assume that the difference between the mean of the jth population and the grand mean is attributable to what is called a 'specific factor' or what is technically described as treatment effect. Thus while using ANOVA, we assume that each of the samples is drawn from a normal population and that each of these populations has the same variance. We also assume that all factors other than the one or more being tested are effectively controlled. This, in other words, means that we assume the absence of many factors that might affect our conclusions concerning the factor(s) to be studied.

In short, we have to make two estimates of population variance viz., one based on between samples variance and the other based on within samples variance. Then the said two estimates of population variance are compared with F-test, wherein we work out.

$$F = \frac{\text{Estimate of population variance based on between samples variance}}{\text{Estimate of population variance based on within samples variance}}$$

---

[1] Donald L. Harnett and James L. Murphy, *Introductory Statistical Analysis*, p. 376.

This value of F is to be compared to the F-limit for given degrees of freedom. If the F value we work out is equal or exceeds[*] the F-limit value (to be seen from F tables No. 4(a) and 4(b) given in appendix), we may say that there are significant differences between the sample means.

ANOVA TECHNIQUE

One-way (or single factor) ANOVA: Under the one-way ANOVA, we consider only one factor and then observe that the reason for said factor to be important is that several possible types of samples can occur within that factor. We then determine if there are differences within that factor. The technique involves the following steps:

(i) Obtain the mean of each sample i.e., obtain

$$\bar{X}_1, \bar{X}_2, \bar{X}_3, ..., \bar{X}_k$$

when there are k samples.

(ii) Work out the mean of the sample means as follows:

$$\bar{\bar{X}} = \frac{\bar{X}_1 + \bar{X}_2 + \bar{X}_3 + ... + \bar{X}_k}{\text{No. of samples } (k)}$$

(iii) Take the deviations of the sample means from the mean of the sample means and calculate the square of such deviations which may be multiplied by the number of items in the corresponding sample, and then obtain their total. This is known as the sum of squares for variance between the samples (or *SS* between). Symbolically, this can be written:

$$SS \text{ between} = n_1\left(\bar{X}_1 - \bar{\bar{X}}\right)^2 + n_2\left(\bar{X}_2 - \bar{\bar{X}}\right)^2 + ... + n_k\left(\bar{X}_k - \bar{\bar{X}}\right)^2$$

(iv) Divide the result of the (iii) step by the degrees of freedom between the samples to obtain variance or mean square (*MS*) between samples. Symbolically, this can be written:

$$MS \text{ between} = \frac{SS \text{ between}}{(k - 1)}$$

where $(k - 1)$ represents degrees of freedom (d.f.) between samples.

(v) Obtain the deviations of the values of the sample items for all the samples from corresponding means of the samples and calculate the squares of such deviations and then obtain their total. This total is known as the sum of squares for variance within samples (or *SS* within). Symbolically this can be written:

$$SS \text{ within} = \Sigma\left(X_{1i} - \bar{X}_1\right)^2 + \Sigma\left(X_{2i} - \bar{X}_2\right)^2 + ... + \Sigma\left(X_{ki} - \bar{X}_k\right)^2$$
$$i = 1, 2, 3, ...$$

(vi) Divide the result of (v) step by the degrees of freedom within samples to obtain the variance or mean square (*MS*) within samples. Symbolically, this can be written:

---

[*]It should be remembered that ANOVA test is always a one-tailed test, since a low calculated value of F from the sample data would mean that the fit of the sample means to the null hypothesis (viz., $\bar{X}_1 = \bar{X}_2 ... = \bar{X}_k$) is a very good fit.

$$MS \text{ within} = \frac{SS \text{ within}}{(n-k)}$$

where $(n-k)$ represents degrees of freedom within samples,

n = total number of items in all the samples i.e., $n_1 + n_2 + \ldots + n_k$

k = number of samples.

(vii) For a check, the sum of squares of deviations for total variance can also be worked out by adding the squares of deviations when the deviations for the individual items in all the samples have been taken from the mean of the sample means. Symbolically, this can be written:

$$SS \text{ for total variance} = \Sigma \left(X_{ij} - \overline{\overline{X}} \right)^2 \qquad i = 1, 2, 3, \ldots$$

$$j = 1, 2, 3, \ldots$$

This total should be equal to the total of the result of the (iii) and (v) steps explained above i.e.,

$$SS \text{ for total variance} = SS \text{ between} + SS \text{ within}.$$

The degrees of freedom for total variance will be equal to the number of items in all samples minus one i.e., $(n-1)$. The degrees of freedom for between and within must add up to the degrees of freedom for total variance i.e.,

$$(n-1) = (k-1) + (n-k)$$

This fact explains the additive property of the ANOVA technique.

(viii) Finally, F-ratio may be worked out as under:

$$F\text{-ratio} = \frac{MS \text{ between}}{MS \text{ within}}$$

This ratio is used to judge whether the difference among several sample means is significant or is just a matter of sampling fluctuations. For this purpose we look into the table*, giving the values of F for given degrees of freedom at different levels of significance. If the worked out value of F, as stated above, is less than the table value of F, the difference is taken as insignificant i.e., due to chance and the null-hypothesis of no difference between sample means stands. In case the calculated value of F happens to be either equal or more than its table value, the difference is considered as significant (which means the samples could not have come from the same universe) and accordingly the conclusion may be drawn. The higher the calculated value of F is above the table value, the more definite and sure one can be about his conclusions.

SETTING UP ANALYSIS OF VARIANCE TABLE

For the sake of convenience the information obtained through various steps stated above can be put as under:

---

*An extract of table giving F-values has been given in Appendix at the end of the book in Tables 4 (a) and 4 (b).

Table 11.1: Analysis of Variance Table for One-way Anova
(There are k samples having in all n items)

Source of variation	Sum of squares (SS)	Degrees of freedom (d.f.)	Mean Square (MS) (This is SS divided by d.f.) and is an estimation of variance to be used in F-ratio	F-ratio
Between samples or categories	$n_1\left(\overline{X}_1 - \overline{\overline{X}}\right)^2 + \ldots$ $+ n_k\left(\overline{X}_k - \overline{\overline{X}}\right)^2$	$(k-1)$	$\dfrac{SS \text{ between}}{(k-1)}$	$\dfrac{MS \text{ between}}{MS \text{ within}}$
Within samples or categories	$\Sigma\left(X_{1i} - \overline{X}_1\right)^2 + \ldots$ $+ \Sigma\left(X_{ki} - \overline{X}_k\right)^2$ $i = 1, 2, 3, \ldots$	$(n-k)$	$\dfrac{SS \text{ within}}{(n-k)}$	
Total	$\Sigma\left(X_{ij} - \overline{\overline{X}}\right)^2$ $i = 1, 2, \ldots$ $j = 1, 2, \ldots$	$(n-1)$		

SHORT-CUT METHOD FOR ONE-WAY ANOVA

ANOVA can be performed by following the short-cut method which is usually used in practice since the same happens to be a very convenient method, particularly when means of the samples and/or mean of the sample means happen to be non-integer values. The various steps involved in the short-cut method are as under:

(i) Take the total of the values of individual items in all the samples i.e., work out ΣX_{ij}
$i = 1, 2, 3, \ldots$
$j = 1, 2, 3, \ldots$
and call it as T.

(ii) Work out the correction factor as under:

$$\text{Correction factor} = \frac{(T)^2}{n}$$

(iii) Find out the square of all the item values one by one and then take its total. Subtract the correction factor from this total and the result is the sum of squares for total variance. Symbolically, we can write:

$$\text{Total } SS = \Sigma X_{ij}^2 - \frac{(T)^2}{n} \qquad i = 1, 2, 3, \ldots$$

$$j = 1, 2, 3, \ldots$$

(iv) Obtain the square of each sample total $(T_j)^2$ and divide such square value of each sample by the number of items in the concerning sample and take the total of the result thus obtained. Subtract the correction factor from this total and the result is the sum of squares for variance between the samples. Symbolically, we can write:

$$SS \text{ between} = \Sigma \frac{(T_j)^2}{n_j} - \frac{(T)^2}{n} \qquad j = 1, 2, 3, \ldots$$

where subscript j represents different samples or categories.

(v) The sum of squares within the samples can be found out by subtracting the result of (iv) step from the result of (iii) step stated above and can be written as under:

$$SS \text{ within} = \left\{ \Sigma X_{ij}^2 - \frac{(T)^2}{n} \right\} - \left\{ \Sigma \frac{(T_j)^2}{n_j} - \frac{(T)^2}{n} \right\}$$

$$= \Sigma X_{ij}^2 - \Sigma \frac{(T_j)^2}{n_j}$$

After doing all this, the table of ANOVA can be set up in the same way as explained earlier.

CODING METHOD

Coding method is furtherance of the short-cut method. This is based on an important property of F-ratio that its value does not change if all the n item values are either multiplied or divided by a common figure or if a common figure is either added or subtracted from each of the given n item values. Through this method big figures are reduced in magnitude by division or subtraction and computation work is simplified without any disturbance on the F-ratio. This method should be used specially when given figures are big or otherwise inconvenient. Once the given figures are converted with the help of some common figure, then all the steps of the short-cut method stated above can be adopted for obtaining and interpreting F-ratio.

Illustration 1

Set up an analysis of variance table for the following per acre production data for three varieties of wheat, each grown on 4 plots and state if the variety differences are significant.

Plot of land	Per acre production data		
	Variety of wheat		
	A	B	C
1	6	5	5
2	7	5	4
3	3	3	3
4	8	7	4

Solution: We can solve the problem by the direct method or by short-cut method, but in each case we shall get the same result. We try below both the methods.

Solution through direct method: First we calculate the mean of each of these samples:

$$\overline{X}_1 = \frac{6 + 7 + 3 + 8}{4} = 6$$

$$\overline{X}_2 = \frac{5 + 5 + 3 + 7}{4} = 5$$

$$\overline{X}_3 = \frac{5 + 4 + 3 + 4}{4} = 4$$

Mean of the sample means or $\quad \overline{\overline{X}} = \dfrac{\overline{X}_1 + \overline{X}_2 + \overline{X}_3}{k}$

$$= \frac{6 + 5 + 4}{3} = 5$$

Now we work out *SS* between and *SS* within samples:

$$SS \text{ between} = n_1\left(\overline{X}_1 - \overline{\overline{X}}\right)^2 + n_2\left(\overline{X}_2 - \overline{\overline{X}}\right)^2 + n_3\left(\overline{X}_3 - \overline{\overline{X}}\right)^2$$

$$= 4(6 - 5)^2 + 4(5 - 5)^2 + 4(4 - 5)^2$$

$$= 4 + 0 + 4$$

$$= 8$$

$$SS \text{ within} = \Sigma\left(X_{1i} - \overline{X}_1\right)^2 + \Sigma\left(X_{2i} - \overline{X}_2\right)^2 + \Sigma\left(X_{3i} - \overline{X}_3\right)^2, \qquad i = 1, 2, 3, 4$$

$$= \{(6 - 6)^2 + (7 - 6)^2 + (3 - 6)^2 + (8 - 6)^2\}$$

$$+ \{(5 - 5)^2 + (5 - 5)^2 + (3 - 5)^2 + (7 - 5)^2\}$$

$$+ \{(5 - 4)^2 + (4 - 4)^2 + (3 - 4)^2 + (4 - 4)^2\}$$

$$= \{0 + 1 + 9 + 4\} + \{0 + 0 + 4 + 4\} + \{1 + 0 + 1 + 0\}$$

$$= 14 + 8 + 2$$

$$= 24$$

$$SS \text{ for total variance } = \Sigma\left(X_{ij} - \overline{\overline{X}}\right)^2 \qquad i = 1, 2, 3\ldots$$

$$j = 1, 2, 3\ldots$$

$$= (6-5)^2 + (7-5)^2 + (3-5)^2 + (8-5)^2$$
$$+ (5-5)^2 + (5-5)^2 + (3-5)^2$$
$$+ (7-5)^2 + (5-5)^2 + (4-5)^2$$
$$+ (3-5)^2 + (4-5)^2$$
$$= 1 + 4 + 4 + 9 + 0 + 0 + 4 + 4 + 0 + 1 + 4 + 1$$
$$= 32$$

Alternatively, it (*SS* for total variance) can also be worked out thus:

SS for total = *SS* between + *SS* within
$$= 8 + 24$$
$$= 32$$

We can now set up the ANOVA table for this problem:

Table 11.2

Source of variation	SS	d.f.	MS	F-ratio	5% F-limit (from the F-table)
Between sample	8	$(3-1) = 2$	$8/2 = 4.00$	$4.00/2.67 = 1.5$	$F(2, 9) = 4.26$
Within sample	24	$(12-3) = 9$	$24/9 = 2.67$		
Total	32	$(12-1) = 11$			

The above table shows that the calculated value of *F* is 1.5 which is less than the table value of 4.26 at 5% level with d.f. being $v_1 = 2$ and $v_2 = 9$ and hence could have arisen due to chance. This analysis supports the null-hypothesis of no difference is sample means. We may, therefore, conclude that the difference in wheat output due to varieties is insignificant and is just a matter of chance.

Solution through short-cut method: In this case we first take the total of all the individual values of *n* items and call it as *T*.

T in the given case = 60

and
$$n = 12$$

Hence, the correction factor = $(T)^2/n = 60 \times 60/12 = 300$. Now total *SS*, *SS* between and *SS* within can be worked out as under:

$$\text{Total } SS = \Sigma X_{ij}^2 - \frac{(T)^2}{n} \qquad i = 1, 2, 3, \ldots$$

$$j = 1, 2, 3, \ldots$$

$$= (6)^2 + (7)^2 + (3)^2 + (8)^2 + (5)^2 + (5)^2 + (3)^2$$

$$+ (7)^2 + (5)^2 + (4)^2 + (3)^2 + (4)^2 - \left(\frac{60 \times 60}{12} \right)$$

$$= 332 - 300 = 32$$

$$SS \text{ between} = \sum \frac{\left(T_j \right)^2}{n_j} - \frac{(T)^2}{n}$$

$$= \left(\frac{24 \times 24}{4} \right) + \left(\frac{20 \times 20}{4} \right) + \left(\frac{16 \times 16}{4} \right) - \left(\frac{60 \times 60}{12} \right)$$

$$= 144 + 100 + 64 - 300$$

$$= 8$$

$$SS \text{ within} = \sum X_{ij}^2 - \sum \frac{\left(T_j \right)^2}{n_j}$$

$$= 332 - 308$$

$$= 24$$

It may be noted that we get exactly the same result as we had obtained in the case of direct method. From now onwards we can set up ANOVA table and interpret *F*-ratio in the same manner as we have already done under the direct method.

TWO-WAY ANOVA

Two-way ANOVA technique is used when the data are classified on the basis of two factors. For example, the agricultural output may be classified on the basis of different varieties of seeds and also on the basis of different varieties of fertilizers used. A business firm may have its sales data classified on the basis of different salesmen and also on the basis of sales in different regions. In a factory, the various units of a product produced during a certain period may be classified on the basis of different varieties of machines used and also on the basis of different grades of labour. Such a two-way design may have repeated measurements of each factor or may not have repeated values. The ANOVA technique is little different in case of repeated measurements where we also compute the interaction variation. We shall now explain the two-way ANOVA technique in the context of both the said designs with the help of examples.

(a) *ANOVA technique in context of two-way design when repeated values are not there:* As we do not have repeated values, we cannot directly compute the sum of squares within samples as we had done in the case of one-way ANOVA. Therefore, we have to calculate this residual or error variation by subtraction, once we have calculated (just on the same lines as we did in the case of one-way ANOVA) the sum of squares for total variance and for variance between varieties of one treatment as also for variance between varieties of the other treatment.

The various steps involved are as follows:

(i) Use the coding device, if the same simplifies the task.

(ii) Take the total of the values of individual items (or their coded values as the case may be) in all the samples and call it T.

(iii) Work out the correction factor as under:

$$\text{Correction factor} = \frac{(T)^2}{n}$$

(iv) Find out the square of all the item values (or their coded values as the case may be) one by one and then take its total. Subtract the correction factor from this total to obtain the sum of squares of deviations for total variance. Symbolically, we can write it as:

Sum of squares of deviations for total variance or total SS

$$= \Sigma X_{ij}^2 - \frac{(T)^2}{n}$$

(v) Take the total of different columns and then obtain the square of each column total and divide such squared values of each column by the number of items in the concerning column and take the total of the result thus obtained. Finally, subtract the correction factor from this total to obtain the sum of squares of deviations for variance between columns or (SS between columns).

(vi) Take the total of different rows and then obtain the square of each row total and divide such squared values of each row by the number of items in the corresponding row and take the total of the result thus obtained. Finally, subtract the correction factor from this total to obtain the sum of squares of deviations for variance between rows (or SS between rows).

(vii) Sum of squares of deviations for residual or error variance can be worked out by subtracting the result of the sum of (v)th and (vi)th steps from the result of (iv)th step stated above. In other words,

Total SS – (SS between columns + SS between rows)

= SS for residual or error variance.

(viii) Degrees of freedom (d.f.) can be worked out as under:

d.f. for total variance $= (c . r - 1)$

d.f. for variance between columns $= (c - 1)$

d.f. for variance between rows $= (r - 1)$

d.f. for residual variance $= (c - 1)(r - 1)$

where c = number of columns

r = number of rows

(ix) ANOVA table can be set up in the usual fashion as shown below:

Table 11.3: Analysis of Variance Table for Two-way Anova

Source of variation	Sum of squares (SS)	Degrees of freedom (d.f.)	Mean square (MS)	F-ratio
Between columns treatment	$\sum \dfrac{(T_j)^2}{n_j} - \dfrac{(T)^2}{n}$	$(c-1)$	$\dfrac{SS \text{ between columns}}{(c-1)}$	$\dfrac{MS \text{ between columns}}{MS \text{ residual}}$
Between rows treatment	$\sum \dfrac{(T_i)^2}{n_i} - \dfrac{(T)^2}{n}$	$(r-1)$	$\dfrac{SS \text{ between rows}}{(r-1)}$	$\dfrac{MS \text{ between rows}}{MS \text{ residual}}$
Residual or error	Total SS − (SS between columns + SS between rows)	$(c-1)(r-1)$	$\dfrac{SS \text{ residual}}{(c-1)(r-1)}$	
Total	$\sum X_{ij}^2 - \dfrac{(T)^2}{n}$	$(c.r-1)$		

In the table c = number of columns

                r = number of rows

      SS residual = Total SS − (SS between columns + SS between rows).

Thus, MS residual or the residual variance provides the basis for the F-ratios concerning variation between columns treatment and between rows treatment. MS residual is always due to the fluctuations of sampling, and hence serves as the basis for the significance test. Both the F-ratios are compared with their corresponding table values, for given degrees of freedom at a specified level of significance, as usual and if it is found that the calculated F-ratio concerning variation between columns is equal to or greater than its table value, then the difference among columns means is considered significant. Similarly, the F-ratio concerning variation between rows can be interpreted.

Illustration 2

Set up an analysis of variance table for the following two-way design results:

Per Acre Production Data of Wheat

(in metric tonnes)

Varieties of seeds	A	B	C
Varieties of fertilizers			
W	6	5	5
X	7	5	4
Y	3	3	3
Z	8	7	4

Also state whether variety differences are significant at 5% level.

Solution: As the given problem is a two-way design of experiment without repeated values, we shall adopt all the above stated steps while setting up the ANOVA table as is illustrated on the following page.

ANOVA table can be set up for the given problem as shown in Table 11.5.

From the said ANOVA table, we find that differences concerning varieties of seeds are insignificant at 5% level as the calculated *F*-ratio of 4 is less than the table value of 5.14, but the variety differences concerning fertilizers are significant as the calculated *F*-ratio of 6 is more than its table value of 4.76.

(b) *ANOVA technique in context of two-way design when repeated values are there:* In case of a two-way design with repeated measurements for all of the categories, we can obtain a separate independent measure of inherent or smallest variations. For this measure we can calculate the sum of squares and degrees of freedom in the same way as we had worked out the sum of squares for variance within samples in the case of one-way ANOVA. Total *SS*, *SS* between columns and *SS* between rows can also be worked out as stated above. We then find left-over sums of squares and left-over degrees of freedom which are used for what is known as '*interaction variation*' (Interaction is the measure of inter relationship among the two different classifications). After making all these computations, ANOVA table can be set up for drawing inferences. We illustrate the same with an example.

Table 11.4: Computations for Two-way Anova (in a design without repeated values)

Step (i) $T = 60, n = 12, \therefore$ Correction factor $= \dfrac{(T)^2}{n} = \dfrac{60 \times 60}{12} = 300$

Step (ii)   Total $SS = (36 + 25 + 25 + 49 + 25 + 16 + 9 + 9 + 9 + 64 + 49 + 16) - \left(\dfrac{60 \times 60}{12}\right)$

$= 332 - 300$

$= 32$

Step (iii) SS between columns treatment $= \left[\dfrac{24 \times 24}{4} + \dfrac{20 \times 20}{4} + \dfrac{16 \times 16}{4}\right] - \left[\dfrac{60 \times 60}{12}\right]$

$= 144 + 100 + 64 - 300$

$= 8$

Step (iv) SS between rows treatment $= \left[\dfrac{16 \times 16}{3} + \dfrac{16 \times 16}{3} + \dfrac{9 \times 9}{3} + \dfrac{19 \times 19}{3}\right] - \left[\dfrac{60 \times 60}{12}\right]$

$= 85.33 + 85.33 + 27.00 + 120.33 - 300$

$= 18$

Step (v) SS residual or error $=$ Total $SS - (SS$ between columns $+ SS$ between rows$)$

$= 32 - (8 + 18)$

$= 6$

Table 11.5: The Anova Table

Source of variation	SS	d.f.	MS	F-ratio	5% F-limit (or the tables values)
Between columns (i.e., between varieties of seeds)	8	$(3-1) = 2$	$8/2 = 4$	$4/1 = 4$	$F(2, 6) = 5.14$
Between rows (i.e., between varieties of fertilizers)	18	$(4-1) = 3$	$18/3 = 6$	$6/1 = 6$	$F(3, 6) = 4.76$
Residual or error	6	$(3-1) \times (4-1) = 6$	$6/6 = 1$		
Total	32	$(3 \times 4) - 1 = 11$			

Illustration 3

Set up ANOVA table for the following information relating to three drugs testing to judge the effectiveness in reducing blood pressure for three different groups of people:

Amount of Blood Pressure Reduction in Millimeters of Mercury

	Drug		
	X	Y	Z
Group of People A	14	10	11
	15	9	11
B	12	7	10
	11	8	11
C	10	11	8
	11	11	7

Do the drugs act differently?

Are the different groups of people affected differently?

Is the interaction term significant?

Answer the above questions taking a significant level of 5%.

Solution: We first make all the required computations as shown below:

We can set up ANOVA table shown in Table 11.7 (Page 269).

Table 11.6: Computations for Two-way Anova (in design with repeated values)

Step (i) $T = 187, n = 18$, thus, the correction factor $= \dfrac{187 \times 187}{18} = 1942.72$

Step (ii) Total $SS = [(14)^2 + (15)^2 + (12)^2 + (11)^2 + (10)^2 + (11)^2 + (10)^2 + (9)^2 + (7)^2 + (8)^2 + (11)^2 + (11)^2 + (11)^2$

$$+ (11)^2 + (10)^2 + (11)^2 + (8)^2 + (7)^2] - \left[\dfrac{(187)^2}{18}\right]$$

$$= (2019 - 1942.72)$$

$$= 76.28$$

Step (iii) SS between columns (i.e., between drugs) $= \left[\dfrac{73 \times 73}{6} + \dfrac{56 \times 56}{6} + \dfrac{58 \times 58}{6}\right] - \left[\dfrac{(187)^2}{18}\right]$

$$= 888.16 + 522.66 + 560.67 - 1942.72$$

$$= 28.77$$

Step (iv) SS between rows (i.e., between people) $= \left[\dfrac{70 \times 70}{6} + \dfrac{59 \times 59}{6} + \dfrac{58 \times 58}{6}\right] - \left[\dfrac{(187)^2}{18}\right]$

$$= 816.67 + 580.16 + 560.67 - 1942.72$$

$$= 14.78$$

Step (v) SS within samples $= (14 - 14.5)^2 + (15 - 14.5)^2 + (10 - 9.5)^2 + (9 - 9.5)^2 + (11 - 11)^2 + (11 - 11)^2$

$$+ (12 - 11.5)^2 + (11 - 11.5)^2 + (7 - 7.5)^2 + (8 - 7.5)^2$$

$$+ (10 - 10.5)^2 + (11 - 10.5)^2 + (10 - 10.5)^2 + (11 - 10.5)^2$$

$$+ (11 - 11)^2 + (11 - 11)^2 + (8 - 7.5)^2 + (7 - 7.5)^2$$

$$= 3.50$$

Step (vi) SS for interaction variation $= 76.28 - [28.77 + 14.78 + 3.50]$

$$= 29.23$$

Table 11.7: The Anova Table

Source of variation	*SS*	*d.f.*	*MS*	*F-ratio*	*5% F-limit*
Between columns (i.e., between drugs)	28.77	$(3-1) = 2$	$\dfrac{28.77}{2}$ $= 14.385$	$\dfrac{14.385}{0.389}$ $= 36.9$	$F(2, 9) = 4.26$
Between rows (i.e., between people)	14.78	$(3-1) = 2$	$\dfrac{14.78}{2}$ $= 7.390$	$\dfrac{7.390}{0.389}$ $= 19.0$	$F(2, 9) = 4.26$

Contd.

Source of variation	SS	d.f.	MS	F-ratio	5% F-limit
Interaction	29.23*	4*	$\dfrac{29.23}{4}$	$\dfrac{7.308}{0.389}$	$F(4, 9) = 3.63$
Within samples (Error)	3.50	$(18 - 9) = 9$	$\dfrac{3.50}{9}$ $= 0.389$		
Total	76.28	$(18 - 1) = 17$			

*These figures are left-over figures and have been obtained by subtracting from the column total the total of all other value in the said column. Thus, interaction $SS = (76.28) - (28.77 + 14.78 + 3.50) = 29.23$ and interaction degrees of freedom $= (17) - (2 + 2 + 9) = 4$.

The above table shows that all the three *F*-ratios are significant of 5% level which means that the drugs act differently, different groups of people are affected differently and the interaction term is significant. In fact, if the interaction term happens to be significant, it is pointless to talk about the differences between various treatments i.e., differences between drugs or differences between groups of people in the given case.

Graphic method of studying interaction in a two-way design: Interaction can be studied in a two-way design with repeated measurements through graphic method also. For such a graph we shall select one of the factors to be used as the *X*-axis. Then we plot the averages for all the samples on the graph and connect the averages for each variety of the other factor by a distinct mark (or a coloured line). If the connecting lines do not cross over each other, then the graph indicates that there is no interaction, but if the lines do cross, they indicate definite interaction or inter-relation between the two factors. Let us draw such a graph for the data of illustration 3 of this chapter to see whether there is any interaction between the two factors viz., the drugs and the groups of people.

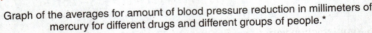

Graph of the averages for amount of blood pressure reduction in millimeters of mercury for different drugs and different groups of people.*

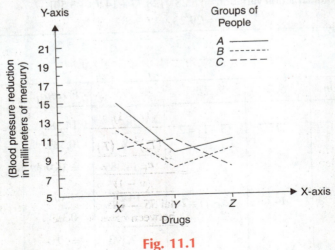

Fig. 11.1

*Alternatively, the graph can be drawn by taking different group of people on *X*-axis and drawing lines for various drugs through the averages.

The graph indicates that there is a significant interaction because the different connecting lines for groups of people do cross over each other. We find that A and B are affected very similarly, but C is affected differently. The highest reduction in blood pressure in case of C is with drug Y and the lowest reduction is with drug Z, whereas the highest reduction in blood pressure in case of A and B is with drug X and the lowest reduction is with drug Y. Thus, there is definite inter-relation between the drugs and the groups of people and one cannot make any strong statements about drugs unless he also qualifies his conclusions by stating which group of people he is dealing with. In such a situation, performing F-tests is meaningless. But if the lines do not cross over each other (and remain more or less identical), then there is no interaction or the interaction is not considered a significantly large value, in which case the researcher should proceed to test the main effects, drugs and people in the given case, as stated earlier.

ANOVA IN LATIN-SQUARE DESIGN

Latin-square design is an experimental design used frequently in agricultural research. In such a design the treatments are so allocated among the plots that no treatment occurs, more than once in any one row or any one column. The ANOVA technique in case of Latin-square design remains more or less the same as we have already stated in case of a two-way design, excepting the fact that the variance is splitted into four parts as under:

(i) variance between columns;

(ii) variance between rows;

(iii) variance between varieties;

(iv) residual variance.

All these above stated variances are worked out as under:

Table 11.8

Variance between columns or *MS* between columns	$= \dfrac{\sum \dfrac{\left(T_j\right)^2}{n_j} - \dfrac{(T)^2}{n}}{(c-1)} = \dfrac{SS \text{ between columns}}{\text{d.f.}}$
Variance between rows or *MS* between rows	$= \dfrac{\sum \dfrac{\left(T_i\right)^2}{n_i} - \dfrac{(T)^2}{n}}{(r-1)} = \dfrac{SS \text{ between rows}}{\text{d.f.}}$
Variance between varieties or *MS* between varieties	$= \dfrac{\sum \dfrac{\left(T_v\right)^2}{n_v} - \dfrac{(T)^2}{n}}{(v-1)} = \dfrac{SS \text{ between varieties}}{\text{d.f.}}$
Residual or error variance or *MS* residual	$= \dfrac{\text{Total } SS - (SS \text{ between columns} + SS \text{ between rows} + SS \text{ between varieties})}{(c-1)(c-2)^*}$

Contd.

*In place of c we can as well write r or v since in Latin-square design $c = r = v$.

where total
$$SS = \Sigma\left(x_{ij}\right)^2 - \frac{(T)^2}{n}$$
c = number of columns
r = number of rows
v = number of varieties

Illustration 4

Analyse and interpret the following statistics concerning output of wheat per field obtained as a result of experiment conducted to test four varieties of wheat viz., A, B, C and D under a Latin-square design.

C 25	B 23	A 20	D 20
A 19	D 19	C 21	B 18
B 19	A 14	D 17	C 20
D 17	C 20	B 21	A 15

Solution: Using the coding method, we subtract 20 from the figures given in each of the small squares and obtain the coded figures as under:

Rows		Columns				Row totals
		1	2	3	4	
	1	C 5	B 3	A 0	D 0	8
	2	A −1	D −1	C 1	B −2	−2
	3	B −1	A −6	D −3	C 0	−10
	4	D −3	C 0	B 1	A −5	−7
Column totals		0	−4	−1	−7	T = −12

Fig. 11.2 (a)

Squaring these coded figures in various columns and rows we have:

		\multicolumn{4}{c}{Squares of coded figures}	Sum of squares
		\multicolumn{4}{c}{Columns}	
		1	2	3	4	
Rows	1	C 25	B 9	A 0	D 0	34
	2	A 1	D 1	C 1	B 4	7
	3	B 1	A 36	D 9	C 0	46
	4	D 9	C 0	B 1	A 25	35
Sum of squares		36	46	11	29	T = 122

Fig. 11.2 (b)

$$\text{Correction factor} = \frac{(T)^2}{n} = \frac{(-12)(-12)}{16} = 9$$

$$SS \text{ for total variance} = \Sigma\left(X_{ij}\right)^2 - \frac{(T)^2}{n} = 122 - 9 = 113$$

$$SS \text{ for variance between columns} = \Sigma\frac{\left(T_j\right)^2}{n_j} - \frac{(T)^2}{n}$$

$$= \left\{\frac{(0)^2}{4} + \frac{(-4)^2}{4} + \frac{(-1)^2}{4} + \frac{(-7)^2}{4}\right\} - 9$$

$$= \frac{66}{4} - 9 = 7.5$$

SS for variance between rows

$$= \Sigma\frac{\left(T_i\right)^2}{n_i} - \frac{(T)^2}{n}\left\{\frac{(8)^2}{4} + \frac{(-3)^2}{4} + \frac{(-10)^2}{4} + \frac{(-7)^2}{4}\right\} - 9$$

$$= \frac{222}{4} - 9 = 46.5$$

SS for variance between varieties would be worked out as under:

For finding *SS* for variance between varieties, we would first rearrange the coded data in the following form:

Table 11. 9

Varieties of wheat	Yield in different parts of field				Total (T_v)
	I	II	III	IV	
A	–1	–6	0	–5	–12
B	–1	3	1	–2	1
C	5	0	1	0	6
D	–3	–1	–3	0	–7

Now we can work out *SS* for variance between varieties as under:

$$SS \text{ for variance between varieties} = \sum \frac{(T_v)^2}{n_v} - \frac{(T)^2}{n}$$

$$= \left\{ \frac{(-12)^2}{4} + \frac{(1)^2}{4} + \frac{(6)^2}{4} + \frac{(-7)^2}{4} \right\} - 9$$

$$= \frac{230}{4} - 9 = 48.5$$

∴ Sum of squares for residual variance will work out to

$$113 - (7.5 + 46.5 + 48.5) = 10.50$$

d.f. for variance between columns	$= (c - 1) = (4 - 1) = 3$
d.f. for variance between rows	$= (r - 1) = (4 - 1) = 3$
d.f. for variance between varieties	$= (v - 1) = (4 - 1) = 3$
d.f. for total variance	$= (n - 1) = (16 - 1) = 15$
d.f. for residual variance	$= (c - 1)(c - 2) = (4 - 1)(4 - 2) = 6$

ANOVA table can now be set up as shown below:

Table 11. 10: The Ánova Table in Latin-square Design

Source of variation	SS	d.f.	MS	F-ratio	5% F-limit
Between columns	7.50	3	$\frac{7.50}{3} = 2.50$	$\frac{2.50}{1.75} = 1.43$	$F(3,6) = 4.76$
Between rows	46.50	3	$\frac{46.50}{3} = 15.50$	$\frac{15.50}{1.75} = 8.85$	$F(3,6) = 4.76$

contd.

Source of variation	SS	d.f.	MS	F-ratio	5% F-limit
Between varieties	48.50	3	$\dfrac{48.50}{3} = 16.17$	$\dfrac{16.17}{1.75} = 9.24$	$F(3, 6) = 4.76$
Residual or error	10.50	6	$\dfrac{10.50}{6} = 1.75$		
Total	113.00	15			

The above table shows that variance between rows and variance between varieties are significant and not due to chance factor at 5% level of significance as the calculated values of the said two variances are 8.85 and 9.24 respectively which are greater than the table value of 4.76. But variance between columns is insignificant and is due to chance because the calculated value of 1.43 is less than the table value of 4.76.

ANALYSIS OF CO-VARIANCE (ANOCOVA)
WHY ANOCOVA?

The object of experimental design in general happens to be to ensure that the results observed may be attributed to the treatment variable and to no other causal circumstances. For instance, the researcher studying one independent variable, X, may wish to control the influence of some uncontrolled variable (sometimes called the covariate or the concomitant variables), Z, which is known to be correlated with the dependent variable, Y, then he should use the technique of analysis of covariance for a valid evaluation of the outcome of the experiment. "In psychology and education primary interest in the analysis of covariance rests in its use as a procedure for the statistical control of an uncontrolled variable."[2]

ANOCOVA TECHNIQUE

While applying the ANOCOVA technique, the influence of uncontrolled variable is usually removed by simple linear regression method and the residual sums of squares are used to provide variance estimates which in turn are used to make tests of significance. In other words, covariance analysis consists in subtracting from each individual score (Y_i) that portion of it Y_i' that is predictable from uncontrolled variable (Z_i) and then computing the usual analysis of variance on the resulting $(Y - Y')$'s, of course making the due adjustment to the degrees of freedom because of the fact that estimation using regression method required loss of degrees of freedom.[*]

---

[2] George A-Ferguson, *Statistical Analysis in Psychology and Education*, 4th ed., p. 347.

[*] Degrees of freedom associated with adjusted sums of squares will be as under:

Between	$k - 1$
within	$N - k - 1$
Total	$N - 2$

ASSUMPTIONS IN ANOCOVA

The ANOCOVA technique requires one to assume that there is some sort of relationship between the dependent variable and the uncontrolled variable. We also assume that this form of relationship is the same in the various treatment groups. Other assumptions are:

   (i) Various treatment groups are selected at random from the population.
   (ii) The groups are homogeneous in variability.
   (iii) The regression is linear and is same from group to group.

   The *short-cut method for ANOCOVA* can be explained by means of an example as shown below:

Illustration 5

The following are paired observations for three experimental groups:

Group I		Group II		Group III	
X	Y	X	Y	X	Y
7	2	15	8	30	15
6	5	24	12	35	16
9	7	25	15	32	20
15	9	19	18	38	24
12	10	31	19	40	30

   Y is the covariate (or concomitant) variable. Calculate the adjusted total, within groups and between groups, sums of squares on *X* and test the significance of differences between the adjusted means on *X* by using the appropriate *F*-ratio. Also calculate the adjusted means on *X*.

Solution: We apply the technique of analysis of covariance and work out the related measures as under:

Table 11.11

	Group I		Group II		Group III	
	X	Y	X	Y	X	Y
	7	2	15	8	30	15
	6	5	24	12	35	16
	9	7	25	15	32	20
	15	9	19	18	38	24
	12	10	31	19	40	30
Total	49	33	114	72	175	105
Mean	9.80	6.60	22.80	14.40	35.00	21.00

$$\Sigma X = 49 + 114 + 175 = 338$$

$$\text{Correction factor for } X = \frac{(\Sigma X)^2}{N} = 7616.27$$

$$\Sigma Y = 33 + 72 + 105 = 210$$

$$\text{Correction factor for } Y = \frac{(\Sigma Y)^2}{N} = 2940$$

$$\Sigma X^2 = 9476 \quad \Sigma Y^2 = 3734 \quad \Sigma XY = 5838$$

$$\text{Correction factor for } XY = \frac{\Sigma X \cdot \Sigma Y}{N} = 4732$$

Hence, total SS for $X = \Sigma X^2 -$ correction factor for X

$$= 9476 - 7616.27 = 1859.73$$

$$SS \text{ between for } X = \left\{ \frac{(49)^2}{5} + \frac{(114)^2}{5} + \frac{(175)^2}{5} \right\} - \left\{ \text{correction factor for } X \right\}$$

$$= (480.2 + 2599.2 + 6125) - (7616.27)$$

$$= 1588.13$$

$$SS \text{ within for } X = (\text{total } SS \text{ for } X) - (SS \text{ between for } X)$$

$$= (1859.73) - (1588.13) = 271.60$$

Similarly we work out the following values in respect of Y

$$\text{total } SS \text{ for } Y = \Sigma Y^2 - \text{correction factor for } Y$$

$$= 3734 - 2940 = 794$$

$$SS \text{ between for } Y = \left\{ \frac{(33)^2}{5} + \frac{(72)^2}{5} + \frac{(105)^2}{5} \right\} - \left\{ \text{correction factor for } Y \right\}$$

$$= (217.8 + 1036.8 + 2205) - (2940) = 519.6$$

$$SS \text{ within for } Y = (\text{total } SS \text{ for } Y) - (SS \text{ between for } Y)$$

$$= (794) - (519.6) = 274.4$$

Then, we work out the following values in respect of both X and Y

$$\text{Total sum of product of } XY = \Sigma XY - \text{correction factor for } XY$$

$$= 5838 - 4732 = 1106$$

$$SS \text{ between for } XY = \left\{ \frac{(49)(33)}{5} + \frac{(114)(72)}{5} + \frac{(175)(105)}{5} \right\} - \text{correction factor for } XY$$

$$= (323.4 + 1641.6 + 3675) - (4732) = 908$$

$$SS \text{ within for } XY = (\text{Total sum of product}) - (SS \text{ between for } XY)$$

$$= (1106) - (908) = 198$$

ANOVA table for *X*, *Y* and *XY* can now be set up as shown below:

Anova Table for *X*, *Y* and *XY*

Source	d.f.	SS for X	SS for Y	Sum of product XY
Between groups	2	1588.13	519.60	908
Within groups	12	E_{XX} 271.60	E_{YY} 274.40	E_{XY} 198
Total	14	T_{XX} 1859.73	T_{YY} 794.00	T_{XY} 1106

$$\text{Adjusted total } SS = T_{XX} - \frac{(T_{XY})^2}{T_{YY}}$$

$$= 1859.73 - \frac{(1106)^2}{794}$$

$$= (1859.73) - (1540.60)$$

$$= 319.13$$

$$\text{Adjusted } SS \text{ within group} = E_{XX} - \frac{(E_{XY})^2}{E_{YY}}$$

$$= 271.60 - \frac{(198)^2}{274.40}$$

$$= (271.60) - (142.87)) = 128.73$$

Adjusted *SS* between groups = (adjusted total *SS*) – (Adjusted *SS* within group)

$$= (319.13 - 128.73)$$

$$= 190.40$$

Anova Table for Adjusted *X*

Source	d.f.	SS	MS	F-ratio
Between groups	2	190.40	95.2	8.14
Within group	11	128.73	11.7	
Total	13	319.13		

At 5% level, the table value of *F* for $v_1 = 2$ and $v_2 = 11$ is 3.98 and at 1% level the table value of *F* is 7.21. Both these values are less than the calculated value (i.e., calculated value of 8.14 is greater than table values) and accordingly we infer that *F*-ratio is significant at both levels which means the difference in group means is significant.

Adjusted means on X will be worked out as follows:

Regression coefficient for *X* on *Y* i.e., $b = \dfrac{\text{Sum of product within group}}{\text{Sum of squares within groups for } Y}$

$$= \frac{198}{274.40} = 0.7216$$

Deviation of initial group means from general mean (= 14) in case of Y		Final means of groups in X (unadjusted)
Group I	−7.40	9.80
Group II	0.40	22.80
Group III	7.00	35.00

Adjusted means of groups in X = (Final mean) – b (deviation of initial mean from general mean in case of Y)

Hence,

Adjusted mean for Group I $\quad = (9.80) – 0.7216 \,(–7.4) = 15.14$

Adjusted mean for Group II $\quad = (22.80) – 0.7216 \,(0.40) = 22.51$

Adjusted mean for Group III $= (35.00) – 0.7216 \,(7.00) = 29.95$

Questions

1. (a) Explain the meaning of analysis of variance. Describe briefly the technique of analysis of variance for one-way and two-way classifications.

   (b) State the basic assumptions of the analysis of variance.

2. What do you mean by the additive property of the technique of the analysis of variance? Explain how this technique is superior in comparison to sampling.

3. Write short notes on the following:

   (i) Latin-square design.

   (ii) Coding in context of analysis of variance.

   (iii) F-ratio and its interpretation.

   (iv) Significance of the analysis of variance.

4. Below are given the yields per acre of wheat for six plots entering a crop competition, there of the plots being sown with wheat of variety A and three with B.

Variety	Yields in fields per acre		
	1	2	3
A	30	32	22
B	20	18	16

Set up a table of analysis of variance and calculate F. State whether the difference between the yields of two varieties is significant taking 7.71 as the table value of F at 5% level for $v_1 = 1$ and $v_2 = 4$.

(*M.Com. II Semester EAFM Exam., Rajasthan University, 1976*)

5. A certain manure was used on four plots of land A, B, C and D. Four beds were prepared in each plot and the manure used. The output of the crop in the beds of plots A, B, C and D is given below:

Output on Plots

A	B	C	D
8	9	3	3
12	4	8	7
1	7	2	8
3	1	5	2

Find out whether the difference in the means of the production of crops of the plots is significant or not.

6. Present your conclusions after doing analysis of variance to the following results of the Latin-square design experiment conducted in respect of five fertilizers which were used on plots of different fertility.

A 16	B 10	C 11	D 09	E 09
E 10	C 09	A 14	B 12	D 11
B 15	D 08	E 08	C 10	A 18
D 12	E 06	B 13	A 13	C 12
C 13	A 11	D 10	E 07	B 14

7. Test the hypothesis at the 0.05 level of significance that $\mu_1 = \mu_2 = \mu_3$ for the following data:

Samples

	No. one (1)	No. two (2)	No. three (3)
	6	2	6
	7	4	8
	6	5	9
	–	3	5
	–	4	–
Total	19	18	28

8. Three varieties of wheat W_1, W_2 and W_3 are treated with four different fertilizers viz., f_1, f_2, f_3 and f_4. The yields of wheat per acre were as under:

Fertilizer treatment	Varieties of wheat			Total
	W_1	W_2	W_3	
f_1	55	72	47	174
f_2	64	66	53	183
f_3	58	57	74	189
f_4	59	57	58	174
Total	236	252	232	720

Set up a table for the analysis of variance and work out the *F*-ratios in respect of the above. Are the *F*-ratios significant?

9. The following table gives the monthly sales (in thousand rupees) of a certain firm in three states by its four salesmen:

States	Salesmen				Total
	A	*B*	*C*	*D*	
X	5	4	4	7	20
Y	7	8	5	4	24
Z	9	6	6	7	28
Total	21	18	15	18	72

Set up an analysis of variance table for the above information. Calculate *F*-coefficients and state whether the difference between sales affected by the four salesmen and difference between sales affected in three States are significant.

10. The following table illustrates the sample psychological health ratings of corporate executives in the field of Banking. Manufacturing and Fashion retailing:

Banking	41	53	54	55	43
Manufacturing	45	51	48	43	39
Fashion retailing	34	44	46	45	51

Can we consider the psychological health of corporate executives in the given three fields to be equal at 5% level of significance?

11. The following table shows the lives in hours of randomly selected electric lamps from four batches:

Batch	Lives in hours							
1	1600	1610	1650	1680	1700	1720	1800	
2	1580	1640	1640	1700	1750			
3	1450	1550	1600	1620	1640	1660	1740	1820
4	1510	1520	1530	1570	1600	1680		

Perform an analysis of variance of these data and show that a significance test does not reject their homogeneity. *(M.Phil. (EAFM) Exam., Raj. University, 1979)*

12. Is the interaction variation significant in case of the following information concerning mileage based on different brands of gasoline and cars?

			Brands of gasoline		
		W	X	Y	Z
Cars	A	13	12	12	11
		11	10	11	13
	B	12	10	11	9
		13	11	12	10
	C	14	11	13	10
		13	10	14	8

13. The following are paired observations for three experimental groups concerning an experimental involving three methods of teaching performed on a single class.

Method A to Group I		Method B to Group II		Method C to Group III	
X	Y	X	Y	X	Y
33	20	35	31	15	15
40	32	50	45	10	20
40	22	10	5	5	10
32	24	50	33	35	15

X represents initial measurement of achievement in a subject and Y the final measurement after subject has been taught. 12 pupils were assigned at random to 3 groups of 4 pupils each, one group from one method as shown in the table.

Apply the technique of analysis of covariance for analyzing the experimental results and then state whether the teaching methods differ significantly at 5% level. Also calculate the adjusted means on Y.

[**Ans:** F-ratio is not significant and hence there is no difference due to teaching methods.

Adjusted means on Y will be as under:

For Group I	20.70
For Group II	24.70
For Group III	22.60]

12

Testing of Hypotheses-II
(Nonparametric or Distribution-free Tests)

It has already been stated in earlier chapters that a statistical test is a formal technique, based on some probability distribution, for arriving at a decision about the reasonableness of an assertion or hypothesis. The test technique makes use of one or more values obtained from sample data [often called test statistic(s)] to arrive at a probability statement about the hypothesis. But such a test technique also makes use of some more assertions about the population from which the sample is drawn. For instance, it may assume that population is normally distributed, sample drawn is a random sample and similar other assumptions. The normality of the population distribution forms the basis for making statistical inferences about the sample drawn from the population. But no such assumptions are made in case of non-parametric tests.

In a statistical test, two kinds of assertions are involved viz., an assertion directly related to the purpose of investigation and other assertions to make a probability statement. The former is an assertion to be tested and is technically called a hypothesis, whereas the set of all other assertions is called the model. When we apply a test (to test the hypothesis) without a model, it is known as distribution-free test, or the nonparametric test. Non-parametric tests do not make an assumption about the parameters of the population and thus do not make use of the parameters of the distribution. In other words, under non-parametric or distribution-free tests we do not assume that a particular distribution is applicable, or that a certain value is attached to a parameter of the population. For instance, while testing the two training methods, say A and B, for determining the superiority of one over the other, if we do not assume that the scores of the trainees are normally distributed or that the mean score of all trainees taking method A would be a certain value, then the testing method is known as a distribution-free or nonparametric method. In fact, there is a growing use of such tests in situations when the normality assumption is open to doubt. As a result many distribution-free tests have been developed that do not depend on the shape of the distribution or deal with the parameters of the underlying population. The present chapter discusses few such tests.

IMPORTANT NONPARAMETRIC OR DISTRIBUTION-FREE TESTS

Tests of hypotheses with 'order statistics' or 'nonparametric statistics' or 'distribution-free' statistics are known as nonparametric or distribution-free tests. The following distribution-free tests are important and generally used:

(i) Test of a hypothesis concerning some single value for the given data (such as one-sample sign test).

(ii) Test of a hypothesis concerning no difference among two or more sets of data (such as two-sample sign test, Fisher-Irwin test, Rank sum test, etc.).

(iii) Test of a hypothesis of a relationship between variables (such as Rank correlation, *Kendall's coefficient of concordance* and other tests for dependence.

(iv) Test of a hypothesis concerning variation in the given data i.e., test analogous to ANOVA viz., Kruskal-Wallis test.

(v) Tests of randomness of a sample based on the theory of runs viz., one sample runs test.

(vi) Test of hypothesis to determine if categorical data shows dependency or if two classifications are independent viz., the chi-square test. (The chi-square test has already been dealt with in Chapter 10.) The chi-square test can as well be used to make comparison between theoretical populations and actual data when categories are used.

Let us explain and illustrate some of the above stated tests which are often used in practice.

1. *Sign Tests*

The sign test is one of the easiest parametric tests. Its name comes from the fact that it is based on the direction of the plus or minus signs of observations in a sample and not on their numerical magnitudes. The sign test may be one of the following two types:

(a) One sample sign test;
(b) Two sample sign test.

(a) *One sample sign test:* The one sample sign test is a very simple non-parametric test applicable when we sample a continuous symmetrical population in which case the probability of getting a sample value less than mean is 1/2 and the probability of getting a sample value greater than mean is also 1/2. To test the null hypothesis $\mu = \mu_{H_0}$ against an appropriate alternative on the basis of a random sample of size 'n', we replace the value of each and every item of the sample with a plus (+) sign if it is greater than μ_{H_0}, and with a minus (–) sign if it is less than μ_{H_0}. But if the value happens to be equal to μ_{H_0}, then we simply discard it. After doing this, we test the null hypothesis that these + and – signs are values of a random variable, having a binomial distribution with $p = 1/2^*$. For performing one sample sign test when the sample is small, we can use tables of binomial probabilities, but when sample happens to be large, we use normal approximation to binomial distribution. Let us take an illustration to apply one sample sign test.

---

*If it is not possible for one reason or another to assume a symmetrical population, even then we can use the one sample sign test, but we shall then be testing the null hypothesis $\tilde{\mu} = \tilde{\mu}_{H_0}$, where $\tilde{\mu}$ is the population median.

Illustration 1

Suppose playing four rounds of golf at the City Club 11 professionals totalled 280, 282, 290, 273, 283, 283, 275, 284, 282, 279, and 281. Use the sign test at 5% level of significance to test the null hypothesis that professional golfers average $\mu_{H_0} = 284$ for four rounds against the alternative hypothesis $\mu_{H_0} < 284$.

Solution: To test the null hypothesis $\mu_{H_0} = 284$ against the alternative hypothesis $\mu_{H_0} < 284$ at 5% (or 0.05) level of significance, we first replace each value greater than 284 with a plus sign and each value less than 284 with a minus sign and discard the one value which actually equals 284. If we do this we get

$$-,-,+,-,-,-,-,-,-,-.$$

Now we can examine whether the one plus sign observed in 10 trials support the null hypothesis $p = 1/2$ or the alternative hypothesis $p < 1/2$. The probability of one or fewer successes with $n = 10$ and $p = 1/2$ can be worked out as under:

$$^{10}C_1 p^1 q^9 + {}^{10}C_0 p^0 q^{10} = 10\left(\frac{1}{2}\right)^1 \left(\frac{1}{2}\right)^9 + 1\left(\frac{1}{2}\right)^0 \left(\frac{1}{2}\right)^{10}$$

$$= 0.010 + 0.001$$

(These values can also be seen from the table of binomial probabilities[*] when $p = 1/2$ and $n = 10$)

$$= 0.011$$

Since this value is less than $\alpha = 0.05$, the null hypothesis must be rejected. In other words, we conclude that professional golfers' average is less than 284 for four rounds of golf.

Alternatively, we can as well use normal approximation to the binomial distribution. If we do that, we find the observed proportion of success, on the basis of signs that we obtain, is 1/10 and that of failure is 9/10. The. standard error of proportion assuming null hypothesis $p = 1/2$ is as under:

$$\sigma_{\text{prop.}} = \sqrt{\frac{p \cdot q}{n}} = \sqrt{\frac{\frac{1}{2} \times \frac{1}{2}}{10}} = 0.1581$$

For testing the null hypothesis i.e., $p = 1/2$ against the alternative hypothesis $p < 1/2$, a one-tailed test is appropriate which can be indicated as shown in the Fig. 12.1.

By using table of area under normal curve, we find the appropriate z value for 0.45 of the area under normal curve and it is 1.64. Using this, we now work out the limit (on the lower side as the alternative hypothesis is of < type) of the acceptance region as under:

$$p - z \cdot \sigma_{(\text{prop.})}$$

or
$$p - (1.64)\,(0.1581)$$

or
$$\frac{1}{2} - 0.2593$$

or
$$0.2407$$

---

[*] Table No. 8 given in appendix at the end of the book.

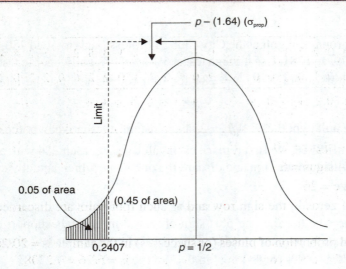

(Shaded portion indicates rejection region)

Fig. 12.1

As the observed proportion of success is only 1/10 or 0.1 which comes in the rejection region, we reject the null hypothesis at 5% level of significance and accept the alternative hypothesis. Thus, we conclude that professional golfers' average is less than 284 for four rounds of golf.

(b) *Two sample sign test (or the sign test for paired data):* The sign test has important applications in problems where we deal with paired data. In such problems, each pair of values can be replaced with a plus (+) sign if the first value of the first sample (say *X*) is greater than the first value of the second sample (say *Y*) and we take minus (–) sign if the first value of *X* is less than the first value of *Y*. In case the two values are equal, the concerning pair is discarded. (In case the two samples are not of equal size, then some of the values of the larger sample left over after the random pairing will have to be discarded.) The testing technique remains the same as started in case of one sample sign test. An example can be taken to explain and illustrate the two sample sign test.

Illustration 2

The following are the numbers of artifacts dug up by two archaeologists at an ancient cliff dwelling on 30 days.

By *X*	1 0 2 3 1 0 2 2 3 0 1 1 4 1 2 1 3 5 2 1 3 2 4 1 3 2 0 2 4 2
By *Y*	0 0 1 0 2 0 0 1 1 2 0 1 2 1 1 0 2 2 6 0 2 3 0 2 1 0 1 0 1 0

Use the sign test at 1% level of significance to test the null hypothesis that the two archaeologists, *X* and *Y*, are equally good at finding artifacts against the alternative hypothesis that *X* is better.

Solution: First of all the given paired values are changed into signs (+ or –) as under:

Table 12.1

By X	1 0 2 3 1 0 2 2 3 0 1 1 4 1 2 1 3 5 2 1 3 2 4 1 3 2 0 2 4 2
By Y	0 0 1 0 2 0 0 1 1 2 0 1 2 1 1 0 2 2 6 0 2 3 0 2 1 0 1 0 1 0
Sign (X − Y)	+ 0 + + − 0 + + + − + 0 + 0 + + + + − + + − + − + + − + +

Total Number of + signs = 20

Total Number of − signs = 6

Hence, sample size = 26

(Since there are 4 zeros in the sign row and as such four pairs are discarded, we are left with 30 − 4 = 26.)

Thus the observed proportion of pluses (or successes) in the sample is = 20/26 = 0.7692 and the observed proportion of minuses (or failures) in the sample is = 6/26 = 0.2308.

As we are to test the null hypothesis that the two archaeologists X and Y are equally good and if that is so, the number of pluses and minuses should be equal and as such $p = 1/2$ and $q = 1/2$. Hence, the standard error of proportion of successes, given the null hypothesis and the size of the sample, we have:

$$\sigma_{\text{prop.}} = \sqrt{\frac{p \cdot q}{n}} = \sqrt{\frac{\frac{1}{2} \times \frac{1}{2}}{26}} = 0.0981$$

Since the alternative hypothesis is that the archaeologists X is better (or $p > 1/2$), we find one tailed test is appropriate. This can be indicated as under, applying normal approximation to binomial distribution in the given case:

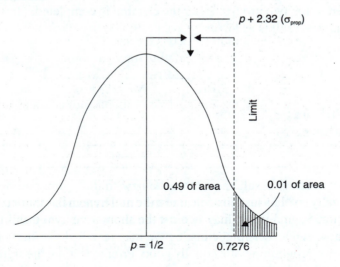

(Shaded area represents rejection region)

Fig. 12.2

By using the table of area under normal curve, we find the appropriate z value for 0.49 of the area under normal curve and it is 2.32. Using this, we now work out the limit (on the upper side as the alternative hypothesis is of > type) of the acceptance region as under:

$$p + 2.32\sigma_{prop.} = 0.5 + 2.32(0.0981)$$

$$= 0.5 + 0.2276 = 0.7276$$

and we now find the observed proportion of successes is 0.7692 and this comes in the rejection region and as such we reject the null hypothesis, at 1% level of significance, that two archaeologists X and Y are equally good. In other words, we accept the alternative hypothesis, and thus conclude that archaeologist X is better.

Sign tests, as explained above, are quite simple and they can be applied in the context of both one-tailed and two-tailed tests. They are generally based on binomial distribution, but when the sample size happens to be large enough (such that $n \cdot p$ and $n \cdot q$ both happen to be greater than 5), we can as well make use of normal approximation to binomial distribution.

2. *Fisher-Irwin Test*

Fisher-Irwin test is a distribution-free test used in testing a hypothesis concerning no difference among two sets of data. It is employed to determine whether one can reasonably assume, for example, that two supposedly different treatments are in fact different in terms of the results they produce. Suppose the management of a business unit has designed a new training programme which is now ready and as such it wishes to test its performance against that of the old training programme. For this purpose a test is performed as follows:

Twelve newly selected workers are chosen for an experiment through a standard selection procedure so that we presume that they are of equal ability prior to the experiment. This group of twelve is then divided into two groups of six each, one group for each training programme. Workers are randomly assigned to the two groups. After the training is completed, all workers are given the same examination and the result is as under:

Table 12.2

	No. passed	No. failed	Total
New Training (*A*)	5	1	6
Old Training (*B*)	3	3	6
Total	8	4	12

A casual look of the above result shows that the new training programme is superior. But the question arises: Is it really so? It is just possible that the difference in the result of the two groups may be due to chance factor. Such a result may occur even though the two training programmes were equally good. Then how can a decision be made? We may test the hypothesis for the purpose. The hypothesis is that the two programmes are equally good. Prior to testing, the significance level (or the α value) must be specified and supposing the management fixes 5% level for the purpose, which must invariably be respected following the test to guard against bias entering into the result and to avoid the possibility of vacillation oil the part of the decision maker. The required probability that the particular result or a better one for A Group would occur if the two training programmes were, in fact, equally good, (alternatively the probability that the particular result or worse for *B* group would occur) be worked out. This should be done keeping in view the probability principles. For the given case, the probability that Group *A* has the particular result or a better one, given the null hypothesis that the two programmes are equally good, is as follows:

Pr. of Group *A* doing as well or better

$$= \text{Pr. (5 passing and 1 failing)} + \text{Pr. (6 passing and 0 failing)}$$

$$= \frac{{}^8C_5 \times {}^4C_1}{{}^{12}C_6} + \frac{{}^8C_6 \times {}^4C_0}{{}^{12}C_6}$$

$$= \frac{224}{924} + \frac{28}{924} = 0.24 + 0.03 = 0.27$$

Alternatively, we can work out as under:

Pr. of Group *B* doing as well or worse

$$= \text{Pr. (3 passing and 3 failing)} + \text{Pr. (2 passing and 4 failing)}$$

$$= \frac{{}^8C_3 \times {}^4C_3}{{}^{12}C_6} + \frac{{}^8C_2 \times {}^4C_4}{{}^{12}C_6}$$

$$= \frac{224}{924} + \frac{28}{924} = 0.24 + 0.03 = 0.27$$

Now we have to compare this calculated probability with the significance level of 5% or 0.05 already specified by the management. If we do so, we notice that the calculated value is greater than 0.05 and hence, we must accept the null hypothesis. This means that at a significance level of 5% the result obtained in the above table is not significant. Hence, we can infer that both training programmes are equally good.

This test (Fisher-Irwin test), illustrated above, is applicable for those situations where the observed result for each item in the sample can be classified into one of the two mutually exclusive categories. For instance, in the given example the worker's performance was classified as fail or pass and accordingly numbers failed and passed in each group were obtained. But supposing the score of each worker is also given and we only apply the Fisher-Irwin test as above, then certainly we are discarding the useful information concerning how well a worker scored. This in fact is the limitation of the Fisher-Irwin test which can be removed if we apply some other test, say, Wilcoxon test as stated in the pages that follow.

3. *McNemer Test*

McNemer test is one of the important nonparametric tests often used when the data happen to be nominal and relate to two related samples. As such this test is specially useful with before-after measurement of the same subjects. The experiment is designed for the use of this test in such a way that the subjects initially are divided into equal groups as to their favourable and unfavourable views about, say, any system. After some treatment, the same number of subjects are asked to express their views about the given system whether they favour it or do not favour it. Through McNemer test we in fact try to judge the significance of any observed change in views of the same subjects before and after the treatment by setting up a table in the following form in respect of the first and second set of responses:

Table 12.3

Before treatment	After treatment	
	Do not favour	*Favour*
Favour	A	B
Do not favour	C	D

Since $A + D$ indicates change in people's responses ($B + C$ shows no change in responses), the expectation under null hypothesis H_0 is that $(A + D)/2$ cases change in one direction and the same proportion in other direction. The test statistic under McNemer Test is worked out as under (as it uses the under-mentioned transformation of Chi-square test):

$$\chi^2 = \frac{\left(\left| A - D \right| - 1\right)^2}{(A + D)} \text{ with d.f. } = 1$$

The minus 1 in the above equation is a correction for continuity as the Chi-square test happens to be a continuous distribution, whereas the observed data represent a discrete distribution. We illustrate this test by an example given below:

Illustration 3

In a certain before-after experiment the responses obtained from 1000 respondents, when classified, gave the following information:

Before treatment	After treatment	
	Unfavourable Response	*Favourable Response*
Favourable response	200 =A	300 =B
Unfavourable response	400 = C	100 = D

Test at 5% level of significance, whether there has been a significant change in people's attitude before and after the concerning experiment.

Solution: In the given question we have nominal data and the study involves before-after measurements of the two related samples, we can use appropriately the McNemer test.

We take the null hypothesis (H_0) that there has been no change in people's attitude before and after the experiment. This, in other words, means that the probability of favourable response before and unfavourable response after is equal to the probability of unfavourable response before and favourable response after i.e.,

$$H_0: P(A) = P(D)$$

We can test this hypothesis against the alternative hypothesis (H_a) viz.,

$$H_a: P(A) \neq P(D)$$

The test statistic, utilising the McNemer test, can be worked out as under:

$$\chi^2 = \frac{\left(\left|A - D\right| - 1\right)^2}{(A + D)} = \frac{\left(\left|200 - 100\right| - 1\right)^2}{(200 + 100)}$$

$$= \frac{99 \times 99}{300} = 32.67$$

Degree of freedom = 1.

From the Chi-square distribution table, the value of χ^2 for 1 degree of freedom at 5% level of significance is 3.84. The calculated value of χ^2 is 32.67 which is greater than the table value, indicating that we should reject the null hypothesis. As such we conclude that the change in people's attitude before and after the experiment is significant.

4. *Wilcoxon Matched-pairs Test (or Signed Rank Test)*

In various research situations in the context of two-related samples (i.e., case of matched paires such as a study where husband and wife are matched or when we compare the output of two similar machines or where some subjects are studied in context of before-after experiment) when we can determine both direction and magnitude of difference between matched values, we can use an important non-parametric test viz., Wilcoxon matched-paires test. While applying this test, we first find the differences (d_i) between each pair of values and assign rank to the differences from the smallest to the largest without regard to sign. The actual signs of each difference are then put to corresponding ranks and the test statistic T is calculated which happens to be the smaller of the two sums viz., the sum of the negative ranks and the sum of the positive ranks.

While using this test, we may come across two types of tie situations. One situation arises when the two values of some matched pair(s) are equal i.e., the difference between values is zero in which case we drop out the pair(s) from our calculations. The other situation arises when two or more pairs have the same difference value in which case we assign ranks to such pairs by averaging their rank positions. For instance, if two pairs have rank score of 5, we assign the rank of 5.5 i.e., $(5 + 6)/2 = 5.5$ to each pair and rank the next largest difference as 7.

When the given number of matched pairs after considering the number of dropped out pair(s), if any, as stated above is equal to or less than 25, we use the table of critical values of T (Table No. 7 given in appendix at the end of the book) for the purpose of accepting or rejecting the null hypothesis of no difference between the values of the given pairs of observations at a desired level of significance. For this test, the calculated value of T must be equal to or smaller than the table value in order to reject the null hypothesis. In case the number exceeds 25, the sampling distribution of T is taken as approximately normal with mean $U_T = n(n + 1)/4$ and standard deviation

$$\sigma_T = \sqrt{n(n + 1)(2n + 1)/24} \,,$$

where $n = $ [(number of given matched pairs) – (number of dropped out pairs, if any)] and in such situation the test statistic z is worked out as under:

$$z = \frac{T - U_T}{\sigma_T}$$

We may now explain the use of this test by an example.

Illustration 4

An experiment is conducted to judge the effect of brand name on quality perception. 16 subjects are recruited for the purpose and are asked to taste and compare two samples of product on a set of scale items judged to be ordinal. The following data are obtained:

Pair	Brand A	Brand B
1	73	51
2	43	41
3	47	43
4	53	41
5	58	47
6	47	32
7	52	24
8	58	58
9	38	43
10	61	53
11	56	52
12	56	57
13	34	44
14	55	57
15	65	40
16	75	68

Test the hypothesis, using Wilcoxon matched-pairs test, that there is no difference between the perceived quality of the two samples. Use 5% level of significance.

Solution: Let us first write the null and alternative hypotheses as under:

H_0: There is no difference between the perceived quality of two samples.

H_a: There is difference between the perceived quality of the two samples.

Using Wilcoxon matched-pairs test, we work out the value of the test statistic T as under:

Table 12.4

Pair	Brand A	Brand B	Difference d_i	Rank of $|d_i|$	Rank with signs +	Rank with signs –
1	73	51	22	13	13	...
2	43	41	2	2.5	2.5	...

Contd.

Pair	Brand A	Brand B	Difference d_i	Rank of $|d_i|$	Rank with signs +	Rank with signs −
3	47	43	4	4.5	4.5	...
4	53	41	12	11	11	...
5	58	47	11	10	10	...
6	47	32	15	12	12	...
7	52	24	28	15	15	...
8	58	58	0	–	–	–
9	38	43	–5	6	...	–6
10	61	53	8	8	8	...
11	56	52	4	4.5	4.5	...
12	56	57	–1	1	...	–1
13	34	44	–10	9	...	–9
14	55	57	–2	2.5	...	–2.5
15	65	40	25	14	14	...
16	75	68	7	7	7	...
				TOTAL	101.5	–18.5
				Hence,	$T = 18.5$	

We drop out pair 8 as 'd' value for this is zero and as such our $n = (16 - 1) = 15$ in the given problem.

The table value of T at five percent level of significance when $n = 15$ is 25 (using a two-tailed test because our alternative hypothesis is that there is difference between the perceived quality of the two samples). The calculated value of T is 18.5 which is less than the table value of 25. As such we reject the null hypothesis and conclude that there is difference between the perceived quality of the two samples.

5. Rank Sum Tests

Rank sum tests are a whole family of test, but we shall describe only two such tests commonly used viz., the U test and the H test. U test is popularly known as Wilcoxon-Mann-Whitney test, whereas H test is also known as Kruskal-Wallis test. A brief description of the said two tests is given below:

(a) *Wilcoxon-Mann-Whitney test (or U-test):* This is a very popular test amongst the rank sum tests. This test is used to determine whether two independent samples have been drawn from the same population. It uses more information than the sign test or the Fisher-Irwin test. This test applies under very general conditions and requires only that the populations sampled are continuous. However, in practice even the violation of this assumption does not affect the results very much.

To perform this test, we first of all rank the data jointly, taking them as belonging to a single sample in either an increasing or decreasing order of magnitude. We usually adopt low to high ranking process which means we assign rank 1 to an item with lowest value, rank 2 to the next higher item and so on. In case there are ties, then we would assign each of the tied observation the mean of the ranks which they jointly occupy. For example, if sixth, seventh and eighth values are identical, we would assign each the rank $(6 + 7 + 8)/3 = 7$. After this we find the sum of the ranks assigned to the values of the first sample (and call it R_1) and also the sum of the ranks assigned to the values of the second sample (and call it R_2). Then we work out the test statistic i.e., U, which is a measurement of the difference between the ranked observations of the two samples as under:

$$U = n_1 \cdot n_2 + \frac{n_1(n_1 + 1)}{2} - R_1$$

where n_1, and n_2 are the sample sizes and R_1 is the sum of ranks assigned to the values of the first sample. (In practice, whichever rank sum can be conveniently obtained can be taken as R_1, since it is immaterial which sample is called the first sample.)

In applying U-test we take the null hypothesis that the two samples come from identical populations. If this hypothesis is true, it seems reasonable to suppose that the means of the ranks assigned to the values of the two samples should be more or less the same. Under the alternative hypothesis, the means of the two populations are not equal and if this is so, then most of the smaller ranks will go to the values of one sample while most of the higher ranks will go to those of the other sample.

If the null hypothesis that the $n_1 + n_2$ observations came from identical populations is true, the said 'U' statistic has a sampling distribution with

$$\text{Mean} = \mu_U = \frac{n_1 \cdot n_2}{2}$$

and   Standard deviation (or the standard error)

$$= \sigma_U = \sqrt{\frac{n_1 n_2 (n_1 + n_2 + 1)}{12}}$$

If n_1 and n_2 are sufficiently large (i.e., both greater than 8), the sampling distribution of U can be approximated closely with normal distribution and the limits of the acceptance region can be determined in the usual way at a given level of significance. But if either n_1 or n_2 is so small that the normal curve approximation to the sampling distribution of U cannot be used, then exact tests may be based on special tables such as one given in the, appendix,[*] showing selected values of Wilcoxon's (unpaired) distribution. We now can take an example to explain the operation of U test.

Illustration 5

The values in one sample are 53, 38, 69, 57, 46, 39, 73, 48, 73, 74, 60 and 78. In another sample they are 44, 40, 61, 52, 32, 44, 70, 41, 67, 72, 53 and 72. Test at the 10% level the hypothesis that they come from populations with the same mean. Apply U-test.

Solution: First of all we assign ranks to all observations, adopting low to high ranking process on the presumption that all given items belong to a single sample. By doing so we get the following:

[*]Table No. 6 given in appendix at the end of the book.

Table 12.5

Size of sample item in ascending order	Rank	Name of related sample: [A for sample one and B for sample two]
32	1	B
38	2	A
39	3	A
40	4	B
41	5	B
44	6.5	B
44	6.5	B
46	8	A
48	9	A
52	10	B
53	11.5	B
53	11.5	A
57	13	A
60	14	A
61	15	B
67	16	B
69	17	A
70	18	B
72	19.5	B
72	19.5	B
73	21.5	A
73	21.5	A
74	23	A
78	24	A

From the above we find that the sum of the ranks assigned to sample one items or $R_1 = 2 + 3 + 8 + 9 + 11.5 + 13 + 14 + 17 + 21.5 + 21.5 + 23 + 24 = 167.5$ and similarly we find that the sum of ranks assigned to sample two items or $R_2 = 1 + 4 + 5 + 6.5 + 6.5 + 10 + 11.5 + 15 + 16 + 18 + 19.5 + 19.5 = 132.5$ and we have $n_1 = 12$ and $n_2 = 12$

Hence, test statistic $U = n_1 \cdot n_2 + \dfrac{n_1(n_1 + 1)}{2} - R_1$

$$= (12)\,(12) + \frac{12(12 + 1)}{2} - 167.5$$

$$= 144 + 78 - 167.5 = 54.5$$

Since in the given problem n_1 and n_2 both are greater than 8, so the sampling distribution of U approximates closely with normal curve. Keeping this in view, we work out the mean and standard deviation taking the null hypothesis that the two samples come from identical populations as under:

$$\mu_U = \frac{n_1 \times n_2}{2} = \frac{(12)\,(12)}{2} = 72$$

$$\sigma_U = \sqrt{\frac{n_1 n_2 (n_1 + n_2 + 1)}{12}} = \sqrt{\frac{(12)\,(12)\,(12 + 12 + 1)}{12}}$$

$$= 17.32$$

As the alternative hypothesis is that the means of the two populations are not equal, a two-tailed test is appropriate. Accordingly the limits of acceptance region, keeping in view 10% level of significance as given, can be worked out as under:

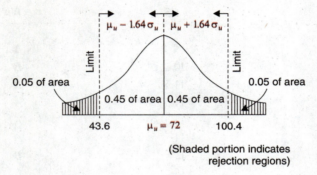

(Shaded portion indicates
rejection regions)

Fig. 12.3

As the z value for 0.45 of the area under the normal curve is 1.64, we have the following limits of acceptance region:

Upper limit $= \mu_U + 1.64\ \sigma_U = 72 + 1.64(17.32) = 100.40$

Lower limit $= \mu_U - 1.64\ \sigma_U = 72 - 1.64(17.32) = 43.60$

As the observed value of U is 54.5 which is in the acceptance region, we accept the null hypothesis and conclude that the two samples come from identical populations (or that the two populations have the same mean) at 10% level.

We can as well calculate the U statistic as under using R_2 value:

$$U = n_1 \cdot n_2 + \frac{n_2 (n_2 + 1)}{2} - R_2$$

$$= (12)\,(12) + \frac{12(12 + 1)}{2} - 132.5$$

$$= 144 + 78 - 132.5 = 89.5$$

The value of U also lies in the acceptance region and as such our conclusion remains the same, even if we adopt this alternative way of finding U.

We can take one more example concerning U test wherein n_1 and n_2 are both less than 8 and as such we see the use of table given in the appendix concerning values of Wilcoxon's distribution (unpaired distribution).

Illustration 6

Two samples with values 90, 94, 36 and 44 in one case and the other with values 53, 39, 6, 24, and 33 are given. Test applying Wilcoxon test whether the two samples come from populations with the same mean at 10% level against the alternative hypothesis that these samples come from populations with different means.

Solution: Let us first assign ranks as stated earlier and we get:

Table 12.6

Size of sample item in ascending order	Rank	Name of related sample (Sample one as A Sample two as B)
6	1	B
24	2	B
33	3	B
36	4	A
39	5	B
44	6	A
53	7	B
90	8	A
94	9	A

Sum of ranks assigned to items of sample one = 4 + 6 + 8 + 9 = 27
No. of items in this sample = 4
Sum of ranks assigned to items of sample two = 1 + 2 + 3 + 5 + 7 = 18
No. of items in this sample = 5

As the number of items in the two samples is less than 8, we cannot use the normal curve approximation technique as stated above and shall use the table giving values of Wilcoxon's distribution. To use this table, we denote 'W_s' as the smaller of the two sums and 'W_l' the larger. Also, let 's' be the number of items in the sample with smaller sum and let 'l' be the number of items in the sample with the larger sum. Taking these notations we have for our question the following values:

$$W_s = 18; \; s = 5; \; W_l = 27; \; l = 4$$

The value of W_s is 18 for sample two which has five items and as such $s = 5$. We now find the difference between W_s and the minimum value it might have taken, given the value of s. The minimum value that W_s could have taken, given that $s = 5$, is the sum of ranks 1 through 5 and this comes as equal to $1 + 2 + 3 + 4 + 5 = 15$. Thus, $(W_s - \text{Minimum } W_s) = 18 - 15 = 3$. To determine the probability that a result as extreme as this or more so would occur, we find the cell of the table which is in the column headed by the number 3 and in the row for $s = 5$ and $l = 4$ (the specified values of l are given in the second column of the table). The entry in this cell is 0.056 which is the required probability of getting a value as small as or smaller than 3 and now we should compare it with the significance level of 10%. Since the alternative hypothesis is that the two samples come from populations with different means, a two-tailed test is appropriate and accordingly 10% significance level will mean 5% in the left tail and 5% in the right tail. In other words, we should compare the calculated probability with the probability of 0.05, given the null hypothesis and the significance level. If the calculated probability happens to be greater than 0.05 (which actually is so in the given case as 0.056 > 0.05), then we should accept the null hypothesis. Hence, in the given problem, we must conclude that the two samples come from populations with the same mean.

(The same result we can get by using the value of W_l. The only difference is that the value maximum $W_l - W_l$ is required. Since for this problem, the maximum value of W_l (given $s = 5$ and $l = 4$) is the sum of 6 through 9 i.e., $6 + 7 + 8 + 9 = 30$, we have Max. $W_l - W_l = 30 - 27 = 3$ which is the same value that we worked out earlier as W_s, – Minimum W_s. All other things then remain the same as we have stated above).

(b) *The Kruskal-Wallis test (or H test):* This test is conducted in a way similar to the *U* test described above. This test is used to test the null hypothesis that '*k*' independent random samples come from identical universes against the alternative hypothesis that the means of these universes are not equal. This test is analogous to the one-way analysis of variance, but unlike the latter it does not require the assumption that the samples come from approximately normal populations or the universes having the same standard deviation.

In this test, like the *U* test, the data are ranked jointly from low to high or high to low as if they constituted a single sample. The test statistic is *H* for this test which is worked out as under:

$$H = \frac{12}{n(n + 1)} \sum_{i=1}^{k} \frac{R_i^2}{n_i} - 3(n + 1)$$

where $n = n_1 + n_2 + ... + n_k$ and R_i being the sum of the ranks assigned to n_i observations in the *i*th sample.

If the null hypothesis is true that there is no difference between the sample means and each sample has at least five items[*], then the sampling distribution of *H* can be approximated with a chi-square distribution with $(k - 1)$ degrees of freedom. As such we can reject the null hypothesis at a given level of significance if *H* value calculated, as stated above, exceeds the concerned table value of chi-square. Let us take an example to explain the operation of this test:

Illustration 7

Use the Kruskal-Wallis test at 5% level of significance to test the null hypothesis that a professional bowler performs equally well with the four bowling balls, given the following results:

Bowling Results in Five Games

With Ball No. *A*	271	282	257	248	262
With Ball No. *B*	252	275	302	268	276
With Ball No. *C*	260	255	239	246	266
With Ball No. *D*	279	242	297	270	258

[*] If any of the given samples has less than five items then chi-square distribution approximation can not be used and the exact tests may be based on table meant for it given in the book "Non-parametric statistics for the behavioural sciences" by S. Siegel.

Solution: To apply the *H* test or the Kruskal-Wallis test to this problem, we begin by ranking all the given figures from the highest to the lowest, indicating besides each the name of the ball as under:

Table 12.7

Bowling results	Rank	Name of the ball associated
302	1	B
297	2	D
282	3	A
279	4	D
276	5	B
275	6	B
271	7	A
270	8	D
268	9	B
266	10	C
262	11	A
260	12	C
258	13	D
257	14	A
255	15	C
252	16	B
248	17	A
246	18	C
242	19	D
239	20	C

For finding the values of R_i, we arrange the above table as under:

Table 12.7 (a): Bowling Results with Different Balls and Corresponding Rank

Ball A	Rank	Ball B	Rank	Ball C	Rank	Ball D	Rank
271	7	252	16	260	12	279	4
282	3	275	6	255	15	242	19
257	14	302	1	239	20	297	2
248	17	268	9	246	18	270	8
262	11	276	5	266	10	158	13
$n_1 = 5$	$R_1 = 52$	$n_2 = 5$	$R_2 = 37$	$n_3 = 5$	$R_3 = 75$	$n_4 = 5$	$R_4 = 46$

Now we calculate *H* statistic as under:

$$H = \frac{12}{n(n+1)} \sum_{i=1}^{k} \frac{R_i^2}{n_i} - 3(n+1)$$

$$= \frac{12}{20(20+1)} \left\{ \frac{52^2}{5} + \frac{37^2}{5} + \frac{75^2}{5} + \frac{46^2}{5} \right\} - 3(20+1)$$

$$= (0.02857)\,(2362.8) - 63 = 67.51 - 63 = 4.51$$

As the four samples have five items[*] each, the sampling distribution of H approximates closely with χ^2 distribution. Now taking the null hypothesis that the bowler performs equally well with the four balls, we have the value of $\chi^2 = 7.815$ for $(k-1)$ or $4-1 = 3$ degrees of freedom at 5% level of significance. Since the calculated value of H is only 4.51 and does not exceed the χ^2 value of 7.815, so we accept the null hypothesis and conclude that bowler performs equally well with the four bowling balls.

6. *One Sample Runs Test*

One sample runs test is a test used to judge the randomness of a sample on the basis of the order in which the observations are taken. There are many applications in which it is difficult to decide whether the sample used is a random one or not. This is particularly true when we have little or no control over the selection of the data. For instance, if we want to predict a retail store's sales volume for a given month, we have no choice but to use past sales data and perhaps prevailing conditions in general. None of this information constitutes a random sample in the strict sense. To allow us to test samples for the randomness of their order, statisticians have developed the theory of runs. A run is a succession of identical letters (or other kinds of symbols) which is followed and preceded by different letters or no letters at all. To illustrate, we take the following arrangement of healthy, H, and diseased, D, mango trees that were planted many years ago along a certain road:

HH	DD	HHHHH	DDD	HHHH	DDDDD	HHHHHHHHH
1st	2nd	3rd	4th	5th	6th	7th

Using underlines to combine the letters which constitute the runs, we find that first there is a run of two H's, then a run of two D's, then a run of five H's, then a run of three D's, then a run of four H's, then a run of five D's and finally a run of nine H's. In this way there are 7 runs in all or $r = 7$. If there are too few runs, we might suspect a definite grouping or a trend; if there are too many runs, we might suspect some sort of repeated alternating patterns. In the given case there seems some grouping i.e., the diseased trees seem to come in groups. Through one sample runs test which is based on the idea that too few or too many runs show that the items were not chosen randomly, we can say whether the apparently seen grouping is significant or whether it can be attributed to chance. We shall use the following symbols for a test of runs:

n_1 = number of occurrences of type 1 (say H in the given case)

n_2 = number of occurrences of type 2 (say D in the given case)

---

[*] For the application of H test, it is not necessary that all samples should have equal number of items.

r = number of runs.

In the given case the values of n_1, n_2 and r would be as follows:

$$n_1 = 20; \; n_2 = 10; \; r = 7$$

The sampling distribution of 'r' statistic, the number of runs, is to be used and this distribution has its mean

$$\mu_r = \frac{2n_1 n_2}{n_1 + n_2} + 1$$

and the standard deviation $\sigma_r = \sqrt{2n_1 n_2 \dfrac{2n_1 n_2 - n_1 - n_2}{(n_1 + n_2)^2 \, (n_1 + n_2 - 1)}}$

In the given case, we work out the values of μ_r and σ_r as follows:

$$\mu_r = \frac{(2)\,(20)\,(10)}{20 + 10} + 1 = 14.33$$

and

$$\sigma_r = \sqrt{\frac{(2)\,(20)\,(10)\,(2 \times 20 \times 10 - 20 - 10)}{(20 + 10)^2 \,(20 + 10 - 1)}} = 2.38$$

For testing the null hypothesis concerning the randomness of the planted trees, we should have been given the level of significance. Suppose it is 1% or 0.01. Since too many or too few runs would indicate that the process by which the trees were planted was not random, a two-tailed test is appropriate which can be indicated as follows on the assumption* that the sampling distribution of r can be closely approximated by the normal distribution.

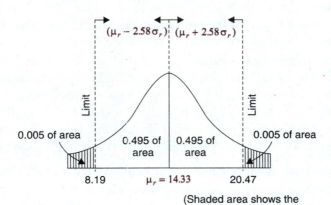

Fig. 12.4

*This assumption can be applied when n_1 and n_2 are sufficiently large i.e., they should not be less than 10. But in case n_1 or n_2 is so small that the normal curve approximation assumption cannot be used, then exact tests may be based on special tables which can be seen in the book *Non-parametric Statistics for the Behavioural Science* by S. Siegel.

By using the table of area under normal curve, we find the appropriate z value for 0.495 of the area under the curve and it is 2.58. Using this we now calculate the limits of the acceptance region:

Upper limit $= \mu_r + (2.58)(2.38) = 14.33 + 6.14 = 20.47$ and

Lower limit $= \mu_r - (2.58)(2.38) = 14.33 - 6.14 = 8.19$

We now find that the observed number of runs (i.e., $r = 7$) lies outside the acceptance region i.e., in the rejection region. Therefore, we cannot accept the null hypothesis of randomness at the given level of significance viz., $\alpha = 0.01$. As such we conclude that there is a strong indication that the diseased trees come in non-random grouping.

One sample runs test, as explained above, is not limited only to test the randomness of series of attributes. Even a sample consisting of numerical values can be treated similarly by using the letters say 'a' and 'b' to denote respectively the values falling above and below the median of the sample. Numbers equal to the median are omitted. The resulting series of a's and b's (representing the data in their original order) can be tested for randomness on the basis of the total number of runs above and below the median, as per the procedure explained above.

(The method of runs above and below the median is helpful in testing for trends or cyclical patterns concerning economic data. In case of an upward trend, there will be first mostly b's and later mostly a's, but in case of a downward trend, there will be first mostly a's and later mostly b's. In case of a cyclical pattern, there will be a systematic alternating of a's and b's and probably many runs.)

7. Spearman's Rank Correlation

When the data are not available to use in numerical form for doing correlation analysis but when the information is sufficient to rank the data as first, second, third, and so forth, we quite often use the rank correlation method and work out the coefficient of rank correlation. In fact, the rank correlation coefficient is a measure of correlation that exists between the two sets of ranks. In other words, it is a measure of association that is based on the ranks of the observations and not on the numerical values of the data. It was developed by famous statistician Charles Spearman in the early 1900s and as such it is also known as Spearman's rank correlation coefficient.

For calculating rank correlation coefficient, first of all the actual observations be replaced by their ranks, giving rank 1 to the highest value, rank 2 to the next highest value and following this very order ranks are assigned for all values. If two or more values happen to be equal, then the average of the ranks which should have been assigned to such values had they been all different, is taken and the same rank (equal to the said average) is given to concerning values. The second step is to record the difference between ranks (or 'd') for each pair of observations, then square these differences to obtain a total of such differences which can symbolically be stated as $\sum d_i^2$. Finally, Spearman's rank correlation coefficient, r^*, is worked out as under:

$$\text{Spearman's '} r \text{'} = 1 - \left\{ \frac{6 \sum d_i^2}{n(n^2 - 1)} \right\}$$

---

[*]Some authors use the symbol Rho (ρ) for this coefficient. Rho is to be used when the sample size does not exceed 30.

where n = number of paired observations.

The value of Spearman's rank correlation coefficient will always vary between ± 1, +1, indicating a perfect positive correlation and –1 indicating perfect negative correlation between two variables. All other values of correlation coefficient will show different degrees of correlation.

Suppose we get $r = 0.756$ which suggests a substantial positive relationship between the concerning two variables. But how we should test this value of 0.756? The testing device depends upon the value of n. For small values of n (i.e., n less than 30), the distribution of r is not normal and as such we use the table showing the values for Spearman's Rank correlation (Table No. 5 given in Appendix at the end of the book) to determine the acceptance and rejection regions. Suppose we get $r = 0.756$ for a problem where $n = 15$ and want to test at 5% level of significance the null hypothesis that there is zero correlation in the concerning ranked data. In this case our problem is reduced to test the null hypothesis that there is no correlation i.e., $u_r = 0$ against the alternative hypothesis that there is a correlation i.e., $\mu_r \neq 0$ at 5% level. In this case a two-tailed test is appropriate and we look in the said table in row for $n = 15$ and the column for a significance level of 0.05 and find that the critical values for r are ± 0.5179 i.e., the upper limit of the acceptance region is 0.5179 and the lower limit of the acceptance region is –0.5179. And since our calculated $r = 0.756$ is outside the limits of the acceptance region, we reject the null hypothesis and accept the alternative hypothesis that there is a correlation in the ranked data.

In case the sample consists of more than 30 items, then the sampling distribution of r is approximately normal with a mean of zero and a standard deviation of $1/\sqrt{n-1}$ and thus, the standard error of r is:

$$\sigma_r = \frac{1}{\sqrt{n-1}}$$

We can use the table of area under normal curve to find the appropriate z values for testing hypotheses about the population rank correlation and draw inference as usual. We can illustrate it, by an example.

Illustration 8

Personnel manager of a certain company wants to hire 30 additional programmers for his corporation. In the past, hiring decisions had been made on the basis of interview and also on the basis of an aptitude test. The agency doing aptitude test had charged Rs. 100 for each test, but now wants Rs. 200 for a test. Performance on the test has been a good predictor of a programmer's ability and Rs. 100 for a test was a reasonable price. But now the personnel manager is not sure that the test results are worth Rs. 200. However, he has kept over the past few years records of the scores assigned to applicants for programming positions on the basis of interviews taken by him. If he becomes confident (using 0.01 level of significance) that the rank correlation between his interview scores and the applicants' scores on aptitude test is positive, then he will feel justified in discontinuing the aptitude test in view of the increased cost of the test. What decision should he take on the basis of the following sample data concerning 35 applicants?

Sample Data Concerning 35 Applicants

Serial Number	Interview score	Aptitude test score
1	81	113
2	88	88
3	55	76
4	83	129
5	78	99
6	93	142
7	65	93
8	87	136
9	95	82
10	76	91
11	60	83
12	85	96
13	93	126
14	66	108
15	90	95
16	69	65
17	87	96
18	68	101
19	81	111
20	84	121
21	82	83
22	90	79
23	63	71
24	78	109
25	73	68
26	79	121
27	72	109
28	95	121
29	81	140
30	87	132
31	93	135
32	85	143
33	91	118
34	94	147
35	94	138

Solution: To solve this problem we should first work out the value of Spearman's *r* as under:

Table 12.8: Calculation of Spearman's

S. No.	Interview score X	Aptitude test score Y	Rank X	Rank Y	Rank Difference 'd_i' (Rank X) − (Rank Y)	Differences squared d_i^2
1	81	113	21	15	6	36
2	88	88	11	27	−16	256
3	55	76	35	32	3	9
4	83	129	18	9	9	81
5	78	99	24.5	21	3.5	12.25
6	93	142	6	3	3	9
7	65	93	32	25	7	49
8	87	136	13	6	7	49
9	95	82	1.5	30	−28.5	812.25
10	76	91	26	26	0	0
11	60	83	34	28.5	5.5	30.25
12	85	96	15.5	22.5	−7	49
13	93	126	6	10	−4	16
14	66	108	31	18.5	12.5	156.25
15	90	95	9.5	24	−14.5	210.25
16	69	65	29	35	−6	36
17	87	96	13	22.5	−9.5	90.25
18	68	101	30	20	10	100
19	81	111	21	16	5	25
20	84	121	17	12	5	25
21	82	83	19	28.5	−9.5	90.25
22	90	79	9.5	31	−21.5	462.25
23	63	71	33	33	0	0
24	78	108	24.5	18.5	6	36
25	73	68	27	34	−7	49
26	79	121	23	12	11	121
27	72	109	28	17	11	121
28	95	121	1.5	12	−10.5	110.25
29	81	140	21	4	17	289
30	87	132	13	8	5	25
31	93	135	6	7	−1	1
32	85	143	15.5	2	13.5	182.25
33	91	118	8	14	−6	36
34	94	147	3.5	1	2.5	6.25
35	94	138	3.5	5	−1.5	225
$n = 35$						$\sum d_i^2 = 3583$

$$\text{Spearman's } `r' = 1 - \left\{ \frac{6\sum d_i^2}{n(n^2 - 1)} \right\} = 1 - \left\{ \frac{6 \times 3583}{35(35^2 - 1)} \right\}$$

$$= 1 - \frac{21498}{42840} = 0.498$$

Since $n = 35$ the sampling distribution of r is approximately normal with a mean of zero and a standard deviation of $1/\sqrt{n-1}$. Hence the standard error of r is

$$\sigma_r = \frac{1}{\sqrt{n-1}} = \frac{1}{\sqrt{35-1}} = 0.1715$$

As the personnel manager wishes to test his hypothesis at 0.01 level of significance, the problem can be stated:

Null hypothesis that there is no correlation between interview score and aptitude test score i.e., $\mu_r = 0$.

Alternative hypothesis that there is positive correlation between interview score and aptitude test score i.e., $\mu_r > 0$.

As such one-tailed test is appropriate which can be indicated as under in the given case:

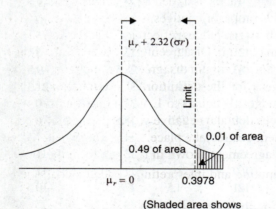

Fig. 12.5

By using the table of area under normal curve, we find the appropriate z value for 0.49 of the area under normal curve and it is 2.32. Using this we now work out the limit (on the upper side as alternative hypothesis is of > type) of the acceptance region as under:

$$\mu_r + (2.32)\,(0.1715)$$
$$= 0 + 0.3978$$
$$= 0.3978$$

We now find the observed $r = 0.498$ and as such it comes in the rejection region and, therefore, we reject the null hypothesis at 1% level and accept the alternative hypothesis. Hence we conclude that correlation between interview score and aptitude test score is positive. Accordingly personnel manager should decide that the aptitude test be discontinued.

8. *Kendall's Coefficient of Concordance*

Kendall's coefficient of concordance, represented by the symbol *W*, *is* an important non-parametric measure of relationship. It is used for determining the degree of association among several (*k*) sets of ranking of *N* objects or individuals. When there are only two sets of rankings of *N* objects, we generally work out Spearman's coefficient of correlation, but Kendall's coefficient of concordance (*W*) is considered an appropriate measure of studying the degree of association among three or more sets of rankings. This descriptive measure of the agreement has special applications in providing a standard method of ordering objects according to consensus when we do not have an objective order of the objects.

The basis of Kendall's coefficient of concordance is to imagine how the given data would look if there were no agreement among the several sets of rankings, and then to imagine how it would look if there were perfect agreement among the several sets. For instance, in case of, say, four interviewers interviewing, say, six job applicants and assigning rank order on suitability for employment, if there is observed perfect agreement amongst the interviewers, then one applicant would be assigned rank 1 by all the four and sum of his ranks would be $1 + 1 + 1 + 1 = 4$. Another applicant would be assigned a rank 2 by all four and the sum of his ranks will be $2 + 2 + 2 + 2 = 8$. The sum of ranks for the six applicants would be 4, 8, 12, 16, 20 and 24 (not necessarily in this very order). In general, when perfect agreement exists among ranks assigned by *k* judges to *N* objects, the rank sums are k, $2k$, $3k$, … Nk. The, total sum of *N* ranks for *k* judges is $kN(N + 1)/2$ and the mean rank sum *is* $k(N + 1)/2$. The degree of agreement between judges reflects itself in the variation in the rank sums. When all judges agree, this sum is a maximum. Disagreement between judges reflects itself in a reduction in the variation of rank sums. For maximum disagreement, the rank sums will tend to be more or less equal. This provides the basis for the definition of a coefficient of concordance. When perfect agreement exists between judges, *W* equals to 1. When maximum disagreement exists, *W* equals to 0. It may be noted that *W* does not take negative values because of the fact that with more than two judges complete disagreement cannot take place. Thus, coefficient of concordance (*W*) is an index of divergence of the actual agreement shown in the data from the perfect agreement.

The procedure for computing and interpreting Kendall's coefficient of concordance (*W*) is as follows:

(a) All the objects, *N*, should be ranked by all *k* judges in the usual fashion and this information may be put in the form of a *k* by *N* matrix;

(b) For each object determine the sum of ranks (R_j) assigned by all the *k* judges;

(c) Determine $\overline{R}_j$ and then obtain the value of *s* as under:

$$s = \Sigma \left(R_j - \overline{R}_j \right)^2$$

(d) Work out the value of *W* using the following formula:

$$W = \frac{s}{\frac{1}{12} k^2 \left(N^3 - N\right)}$$

where $s = \Sigma \left(R_j - \bar{R}_j\right)^2$;

k = no. of sets of rankings i.e., the number of judges;

N = number of objects ranked;

$\frac{1}{12} k^2 \left(N^3 - N\right)$ = maximum possible sum of the squared deviations i.e., the sum s which

would occur with perfect agreement among k rankings.

Case of Tied Ranks

Where tied ranks occur, the average method of assigning ranks be adopted i.e., assign to each member the average rank which the tied observations occupy. If the ties are not numerous, we may compute 'W' as stated above without making any adjustment in the formula; but if the ties are numerous, a correction factor is calculated for each set of ranks. This correction fact is

$$T = \frac{\Sigma \left(t^3 - t\right)}{12}$$

where t = number of observations in a group tied for a given rank.

For instance, if the ranks on X are 1, 2, 3.5, 5, 6, 3.5, 8, 10, 8, 8, we have two groups of ties, one of two ranks and one of three ranks. The correction factor for this set of ranks for X would be

$$T = \frac{\left(2^3 - 2\right) + \left(3^3 - 3\right)}{12} = 2.5$$

A correction factor T is calculated for each of the k sets of ranks and these are added together over the k sets to obtain ΣT. We then use the formula for finding the value of 'W' as under:

$$W = \frac{s}{\frac{1}{12} k^2 \left(N^3 - N\right) - k \Sigma T}$$

The application of the correction in this formula tends to increase the size of W, but the correction factor has a very limited effect unless the ties are quite numerous.

   (e) The method for judging whether the calculated value of W is significantly different from zero depends on the size of N as stated below:

   (i) If N is 7 or smaller, Table No. 9 given in appendix at the end of the book gives critical values of s associated with W's significance at 5% and 1% levels. If an observed s is equal to or greater than that shown in the table for a particular level of significance, then $H_0 T$ (i.e., k sets of rankings are independent) may be rejected at that level of significance.

(ii) If N is larger than 7, we may use χ^2 value to be worked out as: $\chi^2 = k(N-1)$. W with d.f. $= (N-1)$ for judging W's significance at a given level in the usual way of using χ^2 values.

(f) Significant value of W may be interpreted and understood as if the judges are applying essentially the same standard in ranking the N objects under consideration, but this should never mean that the orderings observed are correct for the simple reason that all judges can agree in ordering objects because they all might employ 'wrong' criterion. Kendall, therefore, suggests that the best estimate of the 'true' rankings of N objects is provided, when W is significant, by the order of the various sums of ranks, R_j. If one accepts the criterion which the various judges have agreed upon, then the best estimate of the 'true' ranking is provided by the order of the sums of ranks. The best estimate is related to the lowest value observed amongst R_j.

This can be illustrated with the help of an example.

Illustration 9

Seven individuals have been assigned ranks by four judges at a certain music competition as shown in the following matrix:

	Individuals						
	A	*B*	*C*	*D*	*E*	*F*	*G*
Judge 1	1	3	2	5	7	4	6
Judge 2	2	4	1	3	7	5	6
Judge 3	3	4	1	2	7	6	5
Judge 4	1	2	5	4	6	3	7

Is there significant agreement in ranking assigned by different judges? Test at 5% level. Also point out the best estimate of the true rankings.

Solution: As there are four sets of rankings, we can work out the coefficient of concordance (W) for judging significant agreement in ranking by different judges. For this purpose we first develop the given matrix as under:

Table 12.9

$K = 4$	Individuals							$\therefore N = 7$
	A	*B*	*C*	*D*	*E*	*F*	*G*	
Judge 1	1	3	2	5	7	4	6	
Judge 2	2	4	1	3	7	5	6	
Judge 3	3	4	1	2	7	6	5	
Judge 4	1	2	5	4	6	3	7	
Sum of ranks (R_j)	7	13	9	14	27	18	24	$\Sigma R_j = 112$
$\left(R_j - \bar{R}_j\right)^2$	81	9	49	4	121	4	64	$\therefore s = 332$

$$\therefore \quad \bar{R}_j = \frac{\sum R_j}{N} = \frac{112}{7} = 16$$

$$\therefore \quad s = 332$$

$$\therefore \quad W = \frac{s}{\frac{1}{12}k^2\left(N^3 - N\right)} = \frac{332}{\frac{1}{12}(4)^2\left(7^3 - 7\right)} = \frac{332}{\frac{16}{12}(336)} = \frac{332}{448} = 0.741$$

To judge the significance of this W, we look into the Table No. 9 given in appendix for finding the value of s at 5% level for $k = 4$ and $N = 7$. This value is 217.0 and thus for accepting the null hypothesis (H_0) that k sets of rankings are independent) our calculated value of s should be less than 217. But the worked out value of s is 332 which is higher than the table value which fact shows that $W = 0.741$ is significant. Hence, we reject the null hypothesis and infer that the judges are applying essentially the same standard in ranking the N objects i.e., there is significant agreement in ranking by different judges at 5% level in the given case. The lowest value observed amongst R_j is 7 and as such the best estimate of true rankings is in the case of individual A i.e., all judges on the whole place the individual A as first in the said music competition.

Illustration 10

Given is the following information:

$$k = 13$$
$$N = 20$$
$$W = 0.577$$

Determine the significance of W at 5% level.

Solution: As N is larger than 7, we shall workout the value of χ^2 for determining W's significance as under:

$$\chi^2 = k(N - 1)W \text{ with } N - \quad \text{degrees of freedom}$$

$$\therefore \qquad \chi^2 = 13(20 - 1)\,(0.577)$$

or $\qquad \chi^2 = (247)\,(0.577) = 142.52$

Table value of χ^2 at 5% level for $N - 1 = 20 - 1 = 19$ d.f. is 30.144 but the calculated value of χ^2 is 142.52 and this is considerably higher than the table value. This does not support the null hypothesis of independence and as such we can infer that W is significant at 5% level.

RELATIONSHIP BETWEEN SPEARMAN'S *r*'s AND KENDALL'S *W*

As stated above, W is an appropriate measure of studying the degree of association among three or more sets of ranks, but we can as well determine the degree of association among k sets of rankings by averaging the Spearman's correlation coefficients (r's) between all possible pairs (i.e., $^kC_2$ or $k\,(k-1)/2$) of rankings keeping in view that W bears a linear relation to the average r's taken over all possible pairs. The relationship between the average of Spearman's r's and Kendall's W can be put in the following form:

$$\text{average of } r\text{'s} = (kW - 1)/(k - 1)$$

But the method of finding W using average of Spearman's r's between all possible pairs is quite tedious, particularly when k happens to be a big figure and as such this method is rarely used in practice for finding W.

Illustration 11

Using data of illustration No. 9 above, find W using average of Spearman's r's.

Solution: As $k = 4$ in the given question, the possible pairs are equal to $k(k-1)/2 = 4(4-1)/2 = 6$ and we work out Spearman's r for each of these pairs as shown in Table 12.10.

Now we can find W using the following relationship formula between r's average and W

$$\text{Average of } r\text{'s} = (kW - 1)/(k - 1)$$

or
$$0.655 = (4W - 1)/(4 - 1)$$

or
$$(0.655)(3) = 4W - 1$$

or
$$W = \frac{(0.655)(3) + 1}{4} = \frac{2.965}{4} = 0.741$$

[*Note:* This value of W is exactly the same as we had worked out using the formula:

$$W = s/[(1/12)(k^2)(N^3 - N)]]$$

CHARACTERISTICS OF DISTRIBUTION-FREE OR NON-PARAMETRIC TESTS

From what has been stated above in respect of important non-parametric tests, we can say that these tests share in main the following characteristics:

1. They do not suppose any particular distribution and the consequential assumptions.

2. They are rather quick and easy to use i.e., they do not require laborious computations since in many cases the observations are replaced by their rank order and in many others we simply use signs.

3. They are often not as efficient or 'sharp' as tests of significance or the parametric tests. An interval estimate with 95% confidence may be twice as large with the use of non-parametric tests as with regular standard methods. The reason being that these tests do not use all the available information but rather use groupings or rankings and the price we pay is a loss in efficiency. In fact, when we use non-parametric tests, we make a trade-off: we loose sharpness in estimating intervals, but we gain the ability to use less information and to calculate faster.

4. When our measurements are not as accurate as is necessary for standard tests of significance, then non-parametric methods come to our rescue which can be used fairly satisfactorily.

5. Parametric tests cannot apply to ordinal or nominal scale data but non-parametric tests do not suffer from any such limitation.

6. The parametric tests of difference like 't' or 'F' make assumption about the homogeneity of the variances whereas this is not necessary for non-parametric tests of difference.

Table 12.10: Difference between Ranks $|d_i|$ Assigned by $k = 4$ Judges and the Square Values of such Differences (d_i^2) for all Possible Pairs of Judges

Individuals	Pair 1 – 2		Pair 1 – 3		Pair 1 – 4		Pair 2 – 3		Pair 2 – 4		Pair 3 – 4	
	$|d|$	d^2	$|d|$	d^2	$|d|$	d^2	$|d|$	d^2	$|d|$	d^2	$|d|$	d^2
A	1	1	2	4	0	0	1	1	1	1	2	4
B	1	1	1	1	1	1	0	0	2	4	2	4
C	–1	1	–1	1	3	9	0	0	4	16	4	16
D	–2	4	3	9	1	1	1	1	1	1	2	4
E	0	0	0	0	1	1	0	0	1	1	1	1
F	1	1	2	4	1	1	1	1	2	4	3	9
G	0	0	1	1	1	1	1	1	1	1	2	4
	$\Sigma d_i^2 = 8$		$\Sigma d_i^2 = 20$		$\Sigma d_i^2 = 14$		$\Sigma d_i^2 = 4$		$\Sigma d_i^2 = 28$		$\Sigma d_i^2 = 42$	
Spearman's Coefficient of Correlation $r = 1 - \dfrac{6\Sigma d_i^2}{N(N^2-1)}$	$r_{12} = 0.857$		$r_{13} = 0.643$		$r_{14} = 0.750$		$r_{23} = 0.929$		$r_{24} = 0.500$		$r_{34} = 0.250$	

$$\text{Average of Spearman's } r\text{'s} = \frac{0.857 + 0.643 + 0.750 + 0.929 + 0.500 + 0.250}{6}$$

$$= \frac{3.929}{6} = 0.655$$

CONCLUSION

There are many situations in which the various assumptions required for standard tests of significance (such as that population is normal, samples are independent, standard deviation is known, etc.) cannot be met, then we can use non-parametric methods. Moreover, they are easier to explain and easier to understand. This is the reason why such tests have become popular. But one should not forget the fact that they are usually less efficient/powerful as they are based on no assumption (or virtually no assumption) and we all know that the less one assumes, the less one can infer from a set of data. But then the other side must also be kept in view that the more one assumes, the more one limits the applicability of one's methods.

Questions

1. Give your understanding of non-parametric or distribution free methods explaining their important characteristics.
2. Narrate the various advantages of using non-parametric tests. Also point out their limitations.
3. Briefly describe the different non-parametric tests explaining the significance of each such test.
4. On 15 occasions Mr. Kalicharan had to wait 4, 8, 2, 7, 7, 5, 8, 6, 1, 9, 6, 6, 5, 9 and 5 minutes for the bus he takes to reach his office. Use the sign test at 5% level of significance to test the bus company's claim that on the average Mr. Kalicharan should not have to wait more than 5 minutes for a bus.
5. The following are the numbers of tickets issued by two policemen on 20 days:

   By first policeman: 7, 10, 14, 12, 6, 9, 11, 13, 7, 6, 10, 8, 14, 8, 12, 11, 9, 8, 10 and 15.
   By second policeman: 10, 13, 14, 11, 10, 7, 15, 11, 10, 9, 8, 12, 16, 10, 10, 14, 10, 12, 8 and 14.

   Use the sign test at 1% level of significance to test the null hypothesis that on the average the two policemen issue equal number of tickets against the alternative hypothesis that on the average the second policeman issues more tickets than the first one.
6. (a) Under what circumstances is the Fisher-Irwin test used? Explain. What is the main limitation of this test?

   (b) A housing contractor plans to build a large number of brick homes in the coming year. Two brick manufacturing concerns have given him nearly identical rates for supplying the bricks. But before placing his order, he wants to apply a test at 5% level of significance. The nature of the test is to subject each sampled brick to a force of 900 pounds. The test is performed on 8 bricks randomly chosen from a day's production of concern *A* and on the same number of bricks randomly chosen from a day's production of concern *B*. The results were as follows:

   Of the 8 bricks from concern *A*, two were broken and of the 8 bricks from concern *B*, five were broken.

   On the basis of these test results, determine whether the contractor should place order with concern *A* or with concern *B* if he prefers significantly stronger bricks.
7. Suppose that the breaking test described in problem 6(b) above is modified so that each brick is subjected to an increasing force until it breaks. The force applied at the time the brick breaks (calling it the breaking point) is recorded as under:

	Breaking-points							
Bricks of concern A	880,	950,	990,	975	895,	1030,	1025,	1010
Bricks of concern B	915,	790,	905,	900,	890,	825,	810	885.

On the basis of the above test results, determine whether the contractor should place order for bricks with concern *A* or with concern *B* (You should answer using *U* test or Wilcoxon-Mann-Whitney test).

8. The following are the kilometres per gallon which a test driver got for ten tankfuls each of three kinds of gasoline:

Gasoline *A*	30,	41,	34,	43,	33,	34,	38,	26,	29,	36
Gasoline *B*	39,	28,	39,	29,	30,	31,	44,	43,	40,	33
Gasoline *C*	29,	41,	26,	36,	41,	43,	38,	38,	35,	40.

Use the Kruskal-Wallis test at the level of significance $\alpha = 0.05$ to test the null hypothesis that there is no difference in the average kilometre yield of the three types of gasoline.

9. (a) The following are the number of students absent from a college on 24 consecutive days:

29, 25, 31, 28, 30, 28, 33, 31, 35, 29, 31, 33, 35, 28, 36, 30, 33, 26, 30, 28, 32, 31, 38 and 27. Test for randomness at 1% level of significance.

(b) The following arrangement indicates whether 25 consecutive persons interviewed by a social scientist are for (*F*) or against (*A*) an increase in the number of crimes in a certain locality:

F, *F*, *F*, *F*, *F*, *F*, *A*, *F*, *F*, *F*, *F*, *F*, *A*, *F*, *F*, *F*, *F*, *A*, *A*, *F*, *F*, *F*, *F*, *F*, *F*.

Test whether this arrangement of *A*'s and *F*'s may be regarded as random at 5% as well as at 10% level of significance.

10. Use a rank correlation at the 1% significance level and determine if there is significant positive correlation between the two samples on the basis of the following information:

Blender model	A1	A2	A3	B	C1	C2	D1	D2	E	F1	F2	G1	G2	H
Sample 1	1	11	12	2	13	10	3	4	14	5	6	9	7	8
Sample 2	4	12	11	2	13	10	1	3	14	8	6	5	9	7

11. Three interviewers rank-order a group of 10 applicants as follows:

Interviewers	*Applicants*									
	a	*b*	*c*	*d*	*e*	*f*	*g*	*h*	*i*	*j*
A	1	2	3	4	5	6	7	8	9	10
B	2	3	4	5	1	7	6	9	8	10
C	5	4	1	2	3	6	7	10	9	8

Compute the coefficient of concordance (*W*) and verify the same by using the relationship between average of Spearman's *r*'s and the coefficient of concordance. Test the significance of *W* at 5% and 1% levels of significance and state what should be inferred from the same. Also point out the best estimate of true rankings.

12. Given are the values of Spearman's *r*'s as under:

$$r_{ab} = 0.607$$
$$r_{ac} = 0.429$$
$$r_{bc} = 0.393$$

Calculate Kendall's coefficient of concordance *W* from the above information and test its significance at 5% level.

13

Multivariate Analysis Techniques

All statistical techniques which simultaneously analyse more than two variables on a sample of observations can be categorized as multivariate techniques. We may as well use the term 'multivariate analysis' which is a collection of methods for analyzing data in which a number of observations are available for each object. In the analysis of many problems, it is helpful to have a number of scores for each object. For instance, in the field of intelligence testing if we start with the theory that general intelligence is reflected in a variety of specific performance measures, then to study intelligence in the context of this theory one must administer many tests of mental skills, such as vocabulary, speed of recall, mental arithmetic, verbal analogies and so on. The score on each test is one variable, X_i, and there are several, k, of such scores for each object, represented as $X_1, X_2 \ldots X_k$. Most of the research studies involve more than two variables in which situation analysis is desired of the association between one (at times many) criterion variable and several independent variables, or we may be required to study the association between variables having no dependency relationships. All such analyses are termed as multivariate analyses or multivariate techniques. In brief, techniques that take account of the various relationships among variables are termed multivariate analyses or multivariate techniques.

GROWTH OF MULTIVARIATE TECHNIQUES

Of late, multivariate techniques have emerged as a powerful tool to analyse data represented in terms of many variables. The main reason being that a series of univariate analysis carried out separately for each variable may, at times, lead to incorrect interpretation of the result. This is so because univariate analysis does not consider the correlation or inter-dependence among the variables. As a result, during the last fifty years, a number of statisticians have contributed to the development of several multivariate techniques. Today, these techniques are being applied in many fields such as economics, sociology, psychology, agriculture, anthropology, biology and medicine. These techniques are used in analyzing social, psychological, medical and economic data, specially when the variables concerning research studies of these fields are supposed to be correlated with each other and when rigorous probabilistic models cannot be appropriately used. Applications of multivariate techniques in practice have been accelerated in modern times because of the advent of high speed electronic computers.

CHARACTERISTICS AND APPLICATIONS

Multivariate techniques are largely empirical and deal with the reality; they possess the ability to analyse complex data. Accordingly in most of the applied and behavioural researches, we generally resort to multivariate analysis techniques for realistic results. Besides being a tool for analyzing the data, multivariate techniques also help in various types of decision-making. For example, take the case of college entrance examination wherein a number of tests are administered to candidates, and the candidates scoring high total marks based on many subjects are admitted. This system, though apparently fair, may at times be biased in favour of some subjects with the larger standard deviations. Multivariate techniques may be appropriately used in such situations for developing norms as to who should be admitted in college. We may also cite an example from medical field. Many medical examinations such as blood pressure and cholesterol tests are administered to patients. Each of the results of such examinations has significance of its own, but it is also important to consider relationships between different test results or results of the same tests at different occasions in order to draw proper diagnostic conclusions and to determine an appropriate therapy. Multivariate techniques can assist us in such a situation. In view of all this, we can state that "if the researcher is interested in making probability statements on the basis of sampled multiple measurements, then the best strategy of data analysis is to use some suitable multivariate statistical technique."[1]

The basic objective underlying multivariate techniques is to represent a collection of massive data in a simplified way. In other words, multivariate techniques transform a mass of observations into a smaller number of composite scores in such a way that they may reflect as much information as possible contained in the raw data obtained concerning a research study. Thus, the main contribution of these techniques is in arranging a large amount of complex information involved in the real data into a simplified visible form. Mathematically, multivariate techniques consist in "forming a linear composite vector in a vector subspace, which can be represented in terms of projection of a vector onto certain specified subspaces."[2]

For better appreciation and understanding of multivariate techniques, one must be familiar with fundamental concepts of linear algebra, vector spaces, orthogonal and oblique projections and univariate analysis. Even then before applying multivariate techniques for meaningful results, one must consider the nature and structure of the data and the real aim of the analysis. We should also not forget that multivariate techniques do involve several complex mathematical computations and as such can be utilized largely with the availability of computer facility.

CLASSIFICATION OF MULTIVARIATE TECHNIQUES

Today, there exist a great variety of multivariate techniques which can be conveniently classified into two broad categories viz., dependence methods and interdependence methods. This sort of classification depends upon the question: Are some of the involved variables dependent upon others? If the answer is 'yes', we have dependence methods; but in case the answer is 'no', we have interdependence methods. Two more questions are relevant for understanding the nature of multivariate techniques. Firstly, in case some variables are dependent, the question is how many variables are dependent? The other question is, whether the data are metric or non-metric? This means whether

[1] K. Takeuchi, H. Yanai and B.N. Mukherji, *The Foundations of Multivariate Analysis,* p. 54.

[2] Ibid., p. iii.

the data are quantitative, collected on interval or ratio scale, or whether the data are qualitative, collected on nominal or ordinal scale. The technique to be used for a given situation depends upon the answers to all these very questions. Jadish N. Sheth in his article on "The multivariate revolution in marketing research"[3] has given the flow chart that clearly exhibits the nature of some important multivariate techniques as shown in Fig. 13.1.

Thus, we have two types of multivariate techniques: one type for data containing both dependent and independent variables, and the other type for data containing several variables without dependency relationship. In the former category are included techniques like multiple regression analysis, multiple discriminant analysis, multivariate analysis of variance and canonical analysis, whereas in the latter category we put techniques like factor analysis, cluster analysis, multidimensional scaling or MDS (both metric and non-metric) and the latent structure analysis.

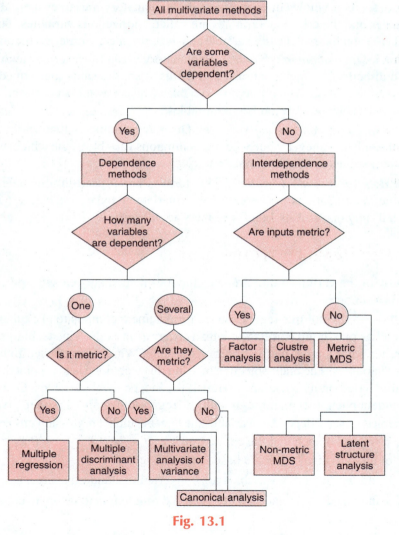

Fig. 13.1

VARIABLES IN MULTIVARIATE ANALYSIS

Before we describe the various multivariate techniques, it seems appropriate to have a clear idea about the term, 'variables' used in the context of multivariate analysis. Many variables used in multivariate analysis can be classified into different categories from several points of view. Important ones are as under:

(i) *Explanatory variable and criterion variable:* If X may be considered to be the cause of Y, then X is described as explanatory variable (also termed as causal or independent variable) and Y is described as criterion variable (also termed as resultant or dependent variable). In some cases both explanatory variable and criterion variable may consist of a set of many variables in which case set $(X_1, X_2, X_3, ..., X_p)$ may be called a set of explanatory variables and the set $(Y_1, Y_2, Y_3, ..., Y_q)$ may be called a set of criterion variables if the variation of the former may be supposed to cause the variation of the latter as a whole. In economics, the explanatory variables are called external or exogenous variables and the criterion variables are called endogenous variables. Some people use the term external criterion for explanatory variable and the term internal criterion for criterion variable.

(ii) *Observable variables and latent variables:* Explanatory variables described above are supposed to be observable directly in some situations, and if this is so, the same are termed as observable variables. However, there are some unobservable variables which may influence the criterion variables. We call such unobservable variables as latent variables.

(iii) *Discrete variable and continuous variable:* Discrete variable is that variable which when measured may take only the integer value whereas continuous variable is one which, when measured, can assume any real value (even in decimal points).

(iv) *Dummy variable* (*or Pseudo variable*): This term is being used in a technical sense and is useful in algebraic manipulations in context of multivariate analysis. We call X_i ($i = 1, ..., m$) a dummy variable, if only one of X_i is 1 and the others are all zero.

IMPORTANT MULTIVARIATE TECHNIQUES

A brief description of the various multivariate techniques named above (with special emphasis on factor analysis) is as under:

(i) *Multiple regression*[*]: In multiple regression we form a linear composite of explanatory variables in such way that it has maximum correlation with a criterion variable. This technique is appropriate when the researcher has a single, metric criterion variable. Which is supposed to be a function of other explanatory variables. The main objective in using this technique is to predict the variability the dependent variable based on its covariance with all the independent variables. One can predict the level of the dependent phenomenon through multiple regression analysis model, given the levels of independent variables. Given a dependent variable, the linear-multiple regression problem is to estimate constants $B_1, B_2, ... B_k$ and A such that the expression $Y = B_1X_1 + B_2X_2 + ... + B_kX_k + A$ pare rovides a good estimate of an individual's Y score based on his X scores.

In practice, Y and the several X variables are converted to standard scores; $z_y, z_1, z_2, ... z_k$; each z has a mean of 0 and standard deviation of 1. Then the problem is to estimate constants, β_i, such that

$$z'_y = \beta_1 z_1 + \beta_2 z_2 + ... + \beta_k z_k$$

[*] See Chapter 7 also for other relevant information about multiple regression.

where z'_y stands for the predicted value of the standardized Y score, z_y. The expression on the right side of the above equation is the linear combination of explanatory variables. The constant A is eliminated in the process of converting X's to z's. The least-squares-method is used, to estimate the beta weights in such a way that the sum of the squared prediction errors is kept as small as possible i.e., the expression $\Sigma \left(z_y - z'_y\right)^2$ is minimized. The predictive adequacy of a set of beta weights is indicated by the size of the correlation coefficient $r_{zy \cdot z'y}$ between the predicted z'_y scores and the actual z_y scores. This special correlation coefficient from Karl Pearson is termed the multiple correlation coefficient (R). The squared multiple correlation, R^2, represents the proportion of criterion (z_y) variance accounted for by the explanatory variables, i.e., the proportion of total variance that is 'Common Variance'.

Sometimes the researcher may use step-wise regression techniques to have a better idea of the independent contribution of each explanatory variable. Under these techniques, the investigator adds the independent contribution of each explanatory variable into the prediction equation one by one, computing betas and R^2 at each step. Formal computerized techniques are available for the purpose and the same can be used in the context of a particular problem being studied by the researcher.

(ii) *Multiple discriminant analysis:* Through discriminant analysis technique, researcher may classify individuals or objects into one of two or more mutually exclusive and exhaustive groups on the basis of a set of independent variables. Discriminant analysis requires interval independent variables and a nominal dependent variable. For example, suppose that brand preference (say brand x or y) is the dependent variable of interest and its relationship to an individual's income, age, education, etc. is being investigated, then we should use the technique of discriminant analysis. Regression analysis in such a situation is not suitable because the dependent variable is, not intervally scaled. Thus discriminant analysis is considered an appropriate technique when the single dependent variable happens to be non-metric and is to be classified into two or more groups, depending upon its relationship with several independent variables which all happen to be metric. The objective in discriminant analysis happens to be to predict an object's likelihood of belonging to a particular group based on several independent variables. In case we classify the dependent variable in more than two groups, then we use the name multiple discriminant analysis; but in case only two groups are to be formed, we simply use the term discriminant analysis.

We may briefly refer to the technical aspects[*] relating to discriminant analysis.

(i) There happens to be a simple scoring system that assigns a score to each individual or object. This score is a weighted average of the individual's numerical values of his independent variables. On the basis of this score, the individual is assigned to the 'most likely' category. For example, an individual is 20 years old, has an annual income of Rs 12,000,and has 10 years of formal education. Let b_1, b_2, and b_3 be the weights attached to the independent variables of age, income and education respectively. The individual's score (z), assuming linear score, would be:

$$z = b_1 (20) + b_2 (12000) + b_3 (10)$$

---

[*] Based on Robert Ferber, ed., *Handbook of Marketing Research.*

This numerical value of z can then be transformed into the probability that the individual is an early user, a late user or a non-user of the newly marketed consumer product (here we are making three categories viz. early user, late user or a non-user).

(ii) The numerical values and signs of the b's indicate the importance of the independent variables in their ability to discriminate among the different classes of individuals. Thus, through the discriminant analysis, the researcher can as well determine which independent variables are most useful in predicting whether the respondent is to be put into one group or the other. In other words, discriminant analysis reveals which specific variables in the profile account for the largest proportion of inter-group differences.

(iii) In case only two groups of the individuals are to be formed on the basis of several independent variables, we can then have a model like this

$$z_i = b_0 + b_1 X_{1i} + b_2 X_{2i} + \dots + b_n X_{ni}$$

where X_{ji} = the ith individual's value of the jth independent variable;

     b_j = the discriminant coefficient of the jth variable;

     z_i = the ith individual's discriminant score;

     $z_{\text{crit.}}$ = the critical value for the discriminant score.

The classification procedure in such a case would be

If $z_i > z_{\text{crit.}}$, classify individual i as belonging to Group I

If $z_i < z_{\text{crit}}$, classify individual i as belonging to Group II.

When n (the number of independent variables) is equal to 2, we have a straight line classification boundary. Every individual on one side of the line is classified as Group I and on the other side, every one is classified as belonging to Group II. When $n = 3$, the classification boundary is a two-dimensional plane in 3 space and in general the classification boundary is an $n - 1$ dimensional hyper-plane in n space.

(iv) In n-group discriminant analysis, a discriminant function is formed for each pair of groups. If there are 6 groups to be formed, we would have $6(6 - 1)/2 = 15$ pairs of groups, and hence 15 discriminant functions. The b values for each function tell which variables are important for discriminating between particular pairs of groups. The z score for each discriminant function tells in which of these two groups the individual is more likely to belong. Then use is made of the transitivity of the relation "more likely than". For example, if group II is more likely than group I and group III is more likely than group II, then group III is also more likely than group I. This way all necessary comparisons are made and the individual is assigned to the most likely of all the groups. Thus, the multiple-group discriminant analysis is just like the two-group discriminant analysis for the multiple groups are simply examined two at a time.

(v) For judging the statistical significance between two groups, we work out the Mahalanobis statistic, D^2, which happens to be a generalized distance between two groups, where each group is characterized by the same set of n variables and where it is assumed that variance-covariance structure is identical for both groups. It is worked out thus:

$$D^2 = (U_1 - U_2)v^{-1}(U_1 - U_2)'$$

where U_1 = the mean vector for group I

U_2 = the mean vector for group II

v = the common variance matrix

By transformation procedure, this D^2 statistic becomes an F statistic which can be used to see if the two groups are statistically different from each other.

From all this, we can conclude that the discriminant analysis provides a predictive equation, measures the relative importance of each variable and is also a measure of the ability of the equation to predict actual class-groups (two or more) concerning the dependent variable.

(iii) *Multivariate analysis of variance:* Multivariate analysis of variance is an extension of bivariate analysis of variance in which the ratio of among-groups variance to within-groups variance is calculated on a set of variables instead of a single variable. This technique is considered appropriate when several metric dependent variables are involved in a research study along with many non-metric explanatory variables. (But if the study has only one metric dependent variable and several non-metric explanatory variables, then we use the ANOVA technique as explained earlier in the book.) In other words, multivariate analysis of variance is specially applied whenever the researcher wants to test hypotheses concerning multivariate differences in group responses to experimental manipulations. For instance, the market researcher may be interested in using one test market and one control market to examine the effect of an advertising campaign on sales as well as awareness, knowledge and attitudes. In that case he should use the technique of multivariate analysis of variance for meeting his objective.

(iv) *Canonical correlation analysis:* This technique was first developed by Hotelling wherein an effort is made to simultaneously predict a set of criterion variables from their joint co-variance with a set of explanatory variables. Both metric and non-metric data can be used in the context of this multivariate technique. The procedure followed is to obtain a set of weights for the dependent and independent variables in such a way that linear composite of the criterion variables has a maximum correlation with the linear composite of the explanatory variables. For example, if we want to relate grade school adjustment to health and physical maturity of the child, we can then use canonical correlation analysis, provided we have for each child a number of adjustment scores (such as tests, teacher's ratings, parent's ratings and so on) and also we have for each child a number of health and physical maturity scores (such as heart rate, height, weight, index of intensity of illness and so on). The main objective of canonical correlation analysis is to discover factors separately in the two sets of variables such that the multiple correlation between sets of factors will be the maximum possible. Mathematically, in canonical correlation analysis, the weights of the two sets viz., $a_1, a_2, \ldots a_k$ and y_1, $y_2, y_3, \ldots y_j$ are so determined that the variables $X = a_1X_1 + a_2X_2 + \ldots + a_kX_k + a$ and $Y = y_1Y_1 + y_2Y_2 + \ldots y_jY_j + y$ have a maximum common variance. The process of finding the weights requires factor analyses with two matrices.[*] The resulting canonical correlation solution then gives an over all description of the presence or absence of a relationship between the two sets of variables.

(v) *Factor analysis:* Factor analysis is by far the most often used multivariate technique of research studies, specially pertaining to social and behavioural sciences. It is a technique applicable when there is a systematic interdependence among a set of observed or manifest variables and the researcher is interested in finding out something more fundamental or latent which creates this commonality. For instance, we might have data, say, about an individual's income, education, occupation and dwelling

[*] See, Eleanor W. Willemsen, *Understanding Statistical Reasoning,* p. 167–168.

area and want to infer from these some factor (such as social class) which summarises the commonality of all the said four variables. The technique used for such purpose is generally described as factor analysis. Factor analysis, thus, seeks to resolve a large set of measured variables in terms of relatively few categories, known as factors. This technique allows the researcher to group variables into factors (based on correlation between variables) and the factors so derived may be treated as new variables (often termed as latent variables) and their value derived by summing the values of the original variables which have been grouped into the factor. The meaning and name of such new variable is subjectively determined by the researcher. Since the factors happen to be linear combinations of data, the coordinates of each observation or variable is measured to obtain what are called factor loadings. Such factor loadings represent the correlation between the particular variable and the factor, and are usually place in a matrix of correlations between the variable and the factors.

The mathematical basis of factor analysis concerns a data matrix* (also termed as score matrix), symbolized as S. The matrix contains the scores of N persons of k measures. Thus a_1 is the score of person 1 on measure a, a_2 is the score of person 2 on measure a, and k_N is the score of person N on measure k. The score matrix then take the form as shown following:

SCORE MATRIX (or Matrix S)

Measures (variables)

	a	b	c	k
1	a_1	b_1	c_1	k_1
2	a_2	b_2	c_2	k_2
3	a_3	b_3	c_3	k_3
.	.	.	.	
.	.	.	.	
.	.	.	.	
N	a_N	b_N	c_N	k_N

Persons (objects)

It is assumed that scores on each measure are standardized [i.e., $x_i = (X - \overline{X}_i)^2/\sigma_i$]. This being so, the sum of scores in any column of the matrix, S, is zero and the variance of scores in any column is 1.0. Then factors (a factor is any linear combination of the variables in a data matrix and can be stated in a general way like: $A = W_a a + W_b b + \ldots + W_k k$) are obtained (by any method of factoring). After this, we work out factor loadings (i.e., factor-variable correlations). Then communality, symbolized as h^2, the eigen value and the total sum of squares are obtained and the results interpreted. For realistic results, we resort to the technique of rotation, because such rotations reveal different structures in the data. Finally, factor scores are obtained which help in explaining what the factors mean. They also facilitate comparison among groups of items as groups. With factor scores, one can also perform several other multivariate analyses such as multiple regression, cluster analysis, multiple discriminant analysis, etc.

*Alternatively the technique can be applied through the matrix of correlations, R as stated later on.

IMPORTANT METHODS OF FACTOR ANALYSIS

There are several methods of factor analysis, but they do not necessarily give same results. As such factor analysis is not a single unique method but a set of techniques. Important methods of factor analysis are:

    (i) the centroid method;

    (ii) the principal components method;

    (ii) the maximum likelihood method.

Before we describe these different methods of factor analysis, it seems appropriate that some basic terms relating to factor analysis be well understood.

(i) *Factor:* A factor is an underlying dimension that account for several observed variables. There can be one or more factors, depending upon the nature of the study and the number of variables involved in it.

(ii) *Factor-loadings:* Factor-loadings are those values which explain how closely the variables are related to each one of the factors discovered. They are also known as factor-variable correlations. In fact, factor-loadings work as key to understanding what the factors mean. It is the absolute size (rather than the signs, plus or minus) of the loadings that is important in the interpretation of a factor.

(iii) *Communality* (h^2): Communality, symbolized as h^2, shows how much of each variable is accounted for by the underlying factor taken together. A high value of communality means that not much of the variable is left over after whatever the factors represent is taken into consideration. It is worked out in respect of each variable as under:

$$h^2 \text{ of the } i\text{th variable } = (i\text{th factor loading of factor } A)^2$$
$$+ (i\text{th factor loading of factor } B)^2 + \ldots$$

(iv) *Eigen value (or latent root):* When we take the sum of squared values of factor loadings relating to a factor, then such sum is referred to as Eigen Value or latent root. Eigen value indicates the relative importance of each factor in accounting for the particular set of variables being analysed.

(v) *Total sum of squares:* When eigen values of all factors are totalled, the resulting value is termed as the total sum of squares. This value, when divided by the number of variables (involved in a study), results in an index that shows how the particular solution accounts for what all the variables taken together represent. If the variables are all very different from each other, this index will be low. If they fall into one or more highly redundant groups, and if the extracted factors account for all the groups, the index will then approach unity.

(vi) *Rotation:* Rotation, in the context of factor analysis, is something like staining a microscope slide. Just as different stains on it reveal different structures in the tissue, different rotations reveal different structures in the data. Though different rotations give results that appear to be entirely different, but from a statistical point of view, all results are taken as equal, none superior or inferior to others. However, from the standpoint of making sense of the results of factor analysis, one must select the right rotation. If the factors are independent orthogonal rotation is done and if the factors are correlated, an oblique rotation is made. Communality for each variables will remain undisturbed regardless of rotation but the eigen values will change as result of rotation.

(vii) *Factor scores:* Factor score represents the degree to which each respondent gets high scores on the group of items that load high on each factor. Factor scores can help explain what the factors mean. With such scores, several other multivariate analyses can be performed.

We can now take up the important methods of factor analysis.

(A) Centroid Method of Factor Analysis

This method of factor analysis, developed by L.L. Thurstone, was quite frequently used until about 1950 before the advent of large capacity high speed computers.[*] The centroid method tends to maximize the sum of loadings, disregarding signs; it is the method which extracts the largest sum of absolute loadings for each factor in turn. It is defined by linear combinations in which all weights are either + 1.0 or − 1.0. The main merit of this method is that it is relatively simple, can be easily understood and involves simpler computations. If one understands this method, it becomes easy to understand the mechanics involved in other methods of factor analysis.

Various steps[**] involved in this method are as follows:

(i) This method starts with the computation of a matrix of correlations, *R*, wherein unities are place in the diagonal spaces. The product moment formula is used for working out the correlation coefficients.

(ii) If the correlation matrix so obtained happens to be positive manifold (i.e., disregarding the diagonal elements each variable has a large sum of positive correlations than of negative correlations), the centroid method requires that the weights for all variables be +1.0. In other words, the variables are not weighted; they are simply summed. But in case the correlation matrix is not a positive manifold, then reflections must be made before the first centroid factor is obtained.

(iii) The first centroid factor is determined as under:

(a) The sum of the coefficients (including the diagonal unity) in each column of the correlation matrix is worked out.

(b) Then the sum of these column sums (*T*) is obtained.

(c) The sum of each column obtained as per (a) above is divided by the square root of *T* obtained in (b) above, resulting in what are called centroid loadings. This way each centroid loading (one loading for one variable) is computed. The full set of loadings so obtained constitute the first centroid factor (say *A*).

(iv) To obtain second centroid factor (say *B*), one must first obtain a matrix of residual coefficients. For this purpose, the loadings for the two variables on the first centroid factor are multiplied. This is done for all possible pairs of variables (in each diagonal space is the square of the particular factor loading). The resulting matrix of factor cross products may be named as Q_1. Then Q_1 is subtracted clement by element from the original matrix of

---

[*]But since 1950, Principal components method, to be discussed a little later, is being popularly used.

[**]See, Jum C. Nunnally, *Psychometric Theory*, 2nd ed., p. 349–357, for details.

correlation, R, and the result is the first matrix of residual coefficients, R_1.[*] After obtaining R_1, one must *reflect* some of the variables in it, meaning thereby that some of the variables are given negative signs in the sum [This is usually done by inspection. The aim in doing this should be to obtain a reflected matrix, R'_1, which will have the highest possible sum of coefficients (T)]. For any variable which is so reflected, the signs of all coefficients in that column and row of the residual matrix are changed. When this is done, the matrix is named as 'reflected matrix' form which the loadings are obtained in the usual way (already explained in the context of first centroid factor), but the loadings of the variables which were reflected must be given negative signs. The full set of loadings so obtained constitutes the second centroid factor (say B). Thus loadings on the second centroid factor are obtained from R'_1.

(v) For subsequent factors (C, D, etc.) the same process outlined above is repeated. After the second centroid factor is obtained, cross products are computed forming, matrix, Q_2. This is then subtracted from R_1 (and not from R'_1) resulting in R_2. To obtain a third factor (C), one should operate on R_2 in the same way as on R_1. First, some of the variables would have to be reflected to maximize the sum of loadings, which would produce R'_2. Loadings would be computed from R'_2 as they were from R'_1. Again, it would be necessary to give negative signs to the loadings of variables which were reflected which would result in third centroid factor (C).

We may now illustrate this method by an example.

Illustration 1

Given is the following correlation matrix, R, relating to eight variables with unities in the diagonal spaces:

		1	2	3	4	5	6	7	8
	1	1.000	.709	.204	.081	.626	.113	.155	.774
	2	.709	1.000	.051	.089	.581	.098	.083	.652
	3	.204	.051	1.000	.671	.123	.689	.582	.072
Variables	4	.081	.089	.671	1.000	.022	.798	.613	.111
	5	.626	.581	.123	.022	1.000	.047	.201	.724
	6	.113	.098	.689	.798	.047	1.000	.801	.120
	7	.155	.083	.582	.613	.201	.801	1.000	.152
	8	.774	.652	.072	.111	.724	.120	.152	1.000

(Variables across the top)

Using the centroid method of factor analysis, work out the first and second centroid factors from the above information.

---

[*] One should understand the nature of the elements in R_1 matrix. Each diagonal element is a partial variance i.e., the variance that remains after the influence of the first factor is partialed. Each off-diagonal element is a partial co-variance i.e., the covariance between two variables after the influence of the first factor is removed. This can be verified by looking at the partial correlation coefficient between any two variables say 1 and 2 when factor A is held constant

$$r_{12 \cdot A} = \frac{r_{12} - r_{1A} \cdot r_{2A}}{\sqrt{1 - r_{1A}^2} \sqrt{1 - r_{2A}^2}}$$

(The numerator in the above formula is what is found in R_1 corresponding to the entry for variables 1 and 2. In the denominator, the square of the term on the left is exactly what is found in the diagonal element for variable 1 in R_1. Likewise the partial variance for 2 is found in the diagonal space for that variable in the residual matrix.)   *contd.*

Solution: Given correlation matrix, R, is a positive manifold and as such the weights for all variables be +1.0. Accordingly, we calculate the first centroid factor (A) as under:

Table 13.1(a)

Variables

		1	2	3	4	5	6	7	8
	1	1.000	.709	.204	.081	.626	.113	.155	.774
	2	.709	1.000	.051	.089	.581	.098	.083	.652
	3	.204	.051	1.000	.671	.123	.689	.582	.072
Variables	4	.081	.089	.671	1.000	.022	.798	.613	.111
	5	.626	.581	.123	.022	1.000	.047	.201	.724
	6	.113	.098	.689	.798	.047	1.000	.801	.120
	7	.155	.083	.582	.613	.201	.801	1.000	.152
	8	.774	.652	.072	.111	.724	.120	.152	1.000
Column sums		3.662	3.263	3.392	3.385	3.324	3.666	3.587	3.605

Sum of the column sums $(T) = 27.884$ $\therefore \sqrt{T} = 5.281$

First centroid factor $A = \dfrac{3.662}{5.281}, \dfrac{3.263}{5.281}, \dfrac{3.392}{5.281}, \dfrac{3.385}{5.281}, \dfrac{3.324}{5.281}, \dfrac{3.666}{5.281}, \dfrac{3.587}{5.281}, \dfrac{3.605}{5.281}$

$= .693, .618, .642, .641, .629, .694, .679, .683$

We can also state this information as under:

Table 13.1 (b)

Variables	Factor loadings concerning first Centroid factor A
1	.693
2	.618
3	.642
4	.641
5	.629
6	.694
7	.679
8	.683

To obtain the second centroid factor B, we first of all develop (as shown on the next page) the first matrix of factor cross product, Q_1:

Since in R_1 the diagonal terms are partial variances and the off-diagonal terms are partial covariances, it is easy to convert the entire table to a matrix of partial correlations. For this purpose one has to divide the elements in each row by the square-root of the diagonal element for that row and then dividing the elements in each column by the square-root of the diagonal element for that column.

First Matrix of Factor Cross Product (Q_1)

First centroid factor A → .693 .618 .642 .641 .629 .694 .679 .683

.693	.480	.428	.445	.444	.436	.481	.471	.473
.618	.428	.382	.397	.396	.389	.429	.420	.422
.642	.445	.397	.412	.412	.404	.446	.436	.438
.641	.444	.396	.412	.411	.403	.445	.435	.438
.629	.436	.389	.404	.403	.396	.437	.427	.430
.694	.481	.429	.446	.445	.437	.482	.471	.474
.679	.471	.420	.436	.435	.427	.471	.461	.464
.683	.473	.422	.438	.438	.430	.474	.464	.466

Now we obtain first matrix of residual coefficient (R_1) by subtracting Q_1 from R as shown below:

First Matrix of Residual Coefficient (R_1)

Variables

Variables	1	2	3	4	5	6	7	8
1	.520	.281	–.241	–.363	.190	–.368	–.316	.301
2	.281	.618	–.346	–.307	.192	–.331	–.337	.230
3	–.241	–.346	.588	.259	–.281	.243	.146	–.366
4	–.363	–.307	.259	.589	–.381	.353	.178	–.327
5	.190	.192	–.281	–.381	.604	–.390	–.217	.294
6	–.368	–.331	.243	.353	–.390	.518	.330	–.354
7	–.316	–.337	.146	.178	–.226	.330	.539	–.312
8	.301	.230	–.366	–.327	.294	–.354	–.312	.534

Reflecting the variables 3, 4, 6 and 7, we obtain reflected matrix of residual coefficient (R'_1) as under and then we can extract the second centroid factor (B) from it as shown on the next page.

Reflected Matrix of Residual Coefficients (R'_1)
and Extraction of 2nd Centroid Factor (B)

Variables

Variables	1	2	3*	4*	5	6*	7*	8
1	.520	.281	.241	.363	.190	.368	.316	.301
2	.281	.618	.346	.307	.192	.331	.337	.230
3*	.241	.346	.588	.259	.281	.243	.146	.366
4*	.363	.307	.259	.589	.381	.353	.178	.327
5	.190	.192	.281	.381	.604	.390	.217	.294
6*	.368	.331	.243	.353	.390	.518	.330	.354
7*	.316	.337	.146	.178	.226	.330	.539	.312

Contd.

	Variables							
	1	2	3*	4*	5	6*	7*	8
8	.301	.230	.366	.327	.294	.354	.312	.534
Column sums:	2.580	2.642	2.470	2.757	2.558	2.887	2.375	2.718

Sum of column sums $(T) = 20.987$ $\therefore$ $\sqrt{T} = 4.581$

Second centroid factor B = .563   .577   −.539   −.602   .558   −.630   −.518   .593

*These variables were reflected.

Now we can write the matrix of factor loadings as under:

Variables	Factor loadings	
	Centroid Factor A	Centroid Factor B
1	.693	.563
2	.618	.577
3	.642	−.539
4	.641	−.602
5	.629	.558
6	.694	−.630
7	.679	−.518
8	.683	.593

Illustration 2

Work out the communality and eigen values from the final results obtained in illustration No. 1 of this chapter. Also explain what they (along with the said two factors) indicate.

Solution: We work out the communality and eigen values for the given problem as under:

Table 13.2

Variables	Factor loadings		Communality (h^2)
	Centroid Factor A	Centroid Factor B	
1	.693	.563	$(.693)^2 + (.563)^2 = .797$
2	.618	.577	$(.618)^2 + (.577)^2 = .715$
3	.642	−.539	$(.642)^2 + (−.539)^2 = .703$
4	.641	−.602	$(.641)^2 + (−.602)^2 = .773$
5	.629	.558	$(.629)^2 + (.558)^2 = .707$
6	.694	−.630	$(.694)^2 + (−.630)^2 = .879$
7	.679	−.518	$(.679)^2 + (−.518)^2 = .729$
8	.683	.593	$(.683)^2 + (.593)^2 = .818$

Contd.

Variables	Factor loadings		Communality (h^2)
	Centroid Factor A	Centroid Factor B	
Eigen value (Variance accounted for i.e., common variance)	3.490	2.631	6.121
Proportion of total variance	.44 (44%)	.33 (33%)	.77 (77%)
Proportion of common variance	.57 (57%)	.43 (43%)	1.00 (100%)

Each communality in the above table represents the proportion of variance in the corresponding (row) variable and is accounted for by the two factors (*A* and *B*). For instance, 79.7% of the variance in variable one is accounted for by the centroid factor *A* and *B* and the remaining 20.3% of the total variance in variable one scores is thought of as being made up of two parts: a factor specific to the attribute represented by variable one, and a portion due to errors of measurement involved in the assessment of variable one (but there is no mention of these portions in the above table because we usually concentrate on common variance in factor analysis).

It has become customary in factor analysis literature for a loading of 0.33 to be the minimum absolute value to be interpreted. The portion of a variable's variance accounted for by this minimum loading is approximately 10%. This criterion, though arbitrary, is being used more or less by way of convention, and as such must be kept in view when one reads and interprets the multivariate research results. In our example, factor *A* has loading in excess of 0.33 on all variables; such a factor is usually called "*the general factor*" and is taken to represent whatever it is that all of the variables have in common. We might consider all the eight variables to be product of some unobserved variable (which can be named subjectively by the researcher considering the nature of his study). The factor name is chosen in such a way that it conveys what it is that all variables that correlate with it (that "load on it") have in common. Factor *B* in our example has all loadings in excess of 0.33, but half of them are with negative signs. Such a factor is called a "*bipolar factor*" and is taken to represent a single dimension with two poles. Each of these poles is defined by a cluster of variables—one pole by those with positive loadings and the other pole with negative loadings.

We can give different names to the said two groups to help us interpret and name factor *B*. The rows at the bottom of the above table give us further information about the usefulness of the two factors in explaining the relations among the eight variables. The total variance (*V*) in the analysis is taken as equal to the number of variables involved (on the presumption that variables are standardized). In this present example, then *V* = 8.0. The row labeled "Eigen value" or "Common variance" gives the numerical value of that portion of the variance attributed to the factor in the concerning column above it. These are found by summing up the squared values of the corresponding factor loadings. Thus the total value, 8.0, is partitioned into 3.490 as eigen value for factor *A* and 2.631 as eigen value for factor *B* and the total 6.121 as the sum of eigen values for these two factors. The corresponding proportion of the total variance, 8.0, are shown in the next row; there we can notice that 77% of the total variance is related to these two factors, i.e., approximately 77% of the total variance is common variance whereas remaining 23% of it is made up of portions unique to individual variables and the techniques used to measure them. The last row shows that of the common variance approximately 57% is accounted for by factor *A* and the other 43% by factor *B*. Thus it can be concluded that the two factors together "explain" the common variance.

(B) Principal-components Method of Factor Analysis

Principal-components method (or simply P.C. method) of factor analysis, developed by H. Hotelling, seeks to maximize the sum of squared loadings of each factor extracted in turn. Accordingly PC factor explains more variance than would the loadings obtained from any other method of factoring.

The aim of the principal components method is the construction out of a given set of variables X_j's $(j = 1, 2, …, k)$ of new variables (p_i), called principal components which are linear combinations of the X_s

$$p_1 = a_{11} X_1 + a_{12} X_2 + … + a_{1k} X_k$$
$$p_2 = a_{21} X_1 + a_{22} X_2 + … + a_{2k} X_k$$
$$\cdot \qquad \cdot \qquad \cdot \qquad \cdot$$
$$\cdot \qquad \cdot \qquad \cdot \qquad \cdot$$
$$p_k = a_{k1} X_1 + a_{k2} X_2 + … + a_{kk} X_k$$

The method is being applied mostly by using standardized variables, i.e., $z_j = \left(X_j - \bar{X}_j \right)^2 / \sigma_j$.

The a_{ij}'s are called loadings and are worked out in such a way that the extracted principal components satisfy two conditions: (i) principal components are uncorrelated (orthogonal) and (ii) the first principal component (p_1) has the maximum variance, the second principal component (p_2) has the next maximum variance and so on.

Following steps are usually involved in principal components method

(i) Estimates of a_{ij}'s are obtained with which *X*'s are transformed into orthogonal variables i.e., the principal components. A decision is also taken with regard to the question: how many of the components to retain into the analysis?

(ii) We then proceed with the regression of *Y* on these principal components i.e.,

$$Y = \hat{y}_1 p_1 + \hat{y}_2 p_2 + … + \hat{y}_m p_m \ (m < k)$$

(iii) From the $\hat{a}_{ij}$ and $\hat{y}_{ij}$, we may find b_{ij} of the original model, transferring back from the *p*'s into the standardized *X*'s.

Alternative method for finding the factor loadings is as under:

(i) Correlation coefficients (by the product moment method) between the pairs of *k* variables are worked out and may be arranged in the form of a correlation matrix, *R*, as under:

Correlation Matrix, R

Variables

		X_1	X_2	X_3	....	X_k
	X_1	r_{11}	r_{12}	r_{13}	....	r_{1k}
	X_2	r_{21}	r_{22}	r_{23}	....	r_{3k}
Variables X_3		r_{31}	r_{32}	r_{33}	....	r_{3k}
	.	.	.	.		
	.	.	.	.		
	X_k	r_{k1}	r_{k2}	r_{k3}	....	r_{kk}

The main diagonal spaces include unities since such elements are self-correlations. The correlation matrix happens to be a symmetrical matrix.

(ii) Presuming the correlation matrix to be positive manifold (if this is not so, then reflections as mentioned in case of centroid method must be made), the first step is to obtain the sum of coefficients in each column, including the diagonal element. The vector of column sums is referred to as U_{a1} and when U_{a1} is normalized, we call it V_{a1}. This is done by squaring and summing the column sums in U_{a1} and then dividing each element in U_{a1} by the square root of the sum of squares (which may be termed as normalizing factor). Then elements in V_{a1} are accumulatively multiplied by the first row of R to obtain the first element in a new vector U_{a2}. For instance, in multiplying V_{a1} by the first row of R, the first element in V_{a1} would be multiplied by the r_{11} value and this would be added to the product of the second element in V_{a1} multiplied by the r_{12} value, which would be added to the product of third element in V_{a1} multiplied by the r_{13} value, and so on for all the corresponding elements in V_{a1} and the first row of R. To obtain the second element of U_{a2}, the same process would be repeated i.e., the elements in V_{a1} are accumulatively multiplied by the 2nd row of R. The same process would be repeated for each row of R and the result would be a new vector U_{a2}. Then U_{a2} would be normalized to obtain V_{a2}. One would then compare V_{a1} and V_{a2}. If they are nearly identical, then convergence is said to have occurred (If convergence does not occur, one should go on using these trial vectors again and again till convergence occurs). Suppose the convergence occurs when we work out V_{a8} in which case V_{a7} will be taken as V_a (the characteristic vector) which can be converted into loadings on the first principal component when we multiply the said vector (i.e., each element of V_a) by the square root of the number we obtain for normalizing U_{a8}.

(iii) To obtain factor B, one seeks solutions for V_b, and the actual factor loadings for second component factor, B. The same procedures are used as we had adopted for finding the first factor, except that one operates off the first residual matrix, R_1 rather than the original correlation matrix R (We operate on R_1 in just the same way as we did in case of centroid method stated earlier).

(iv) This very procedure is repeated over and over again to obtain the successive PC factors (viz. C, D, etc.).

Other steps involved in factor analysis

(a) Next the question is: How many principal components to retain in a particular study? Various criteria for this purpose have been suggested, but one often used is Kaiser's criterion. According to this criterion only the principal components, having latent root greater than one, are considered as essential and should be retained.

(b) The principal components so extracted and retained are then rotated from their beginning position to enhance the interpretability of the factors.

(c) Communality, symbolized, h^2, is then worked out which shows how much of each variable is accounted for by the underlying factors taken together. A high communality figure means that not much of the variable is left over after whatever the factors represent is taken into consideration. It is worked out in respect of each variable as under:

$$h^2 \text{ of the } i\text{th variable} = (i\text{th factor loading of factor } A)^2$$
$$+ (i\text{th factor loading of factor } B)^2 + \ldots$$

Then follows the task of interpretation. The amount of variance explained (sum of squared loadings) by each PC factor is equal to the corresponding characteristic root. When these roots are divided by the number of variables, they show the characteristic roots as proportions of total variance explained.

(d) The variables are then regressed against each factor loading and the resulting regression coefficients are used to generate what are known as factor scores which are then used in further analysis and can also be used as inputs in several other multivariate analyses.

Illustration 3

Take the correlation matrix, R, for eight variables of illustration 1 of this chapter and then compute:

  (i) the first two principal component factors;
 (ii) the communality for each variable on the basis of said two component factors;
(iii) the proportion of total variance as well as the proportion of common variance explained by each of the two component factors.

Solution: Since the given correlation matrix is a positive manifold, we work out the first principal component factor (using trial vectors) as under:

Table 13.3

Variables

		1	2	3	4	5	6	7	8
	1	1.000	.709	.204	.081	.626	.113	.155	.774
	2	.709	1.000	.051	.089	.581	.098	.083	.652
	3	.204	.051	1.000	.671	.123	.689	.582	.072
	4	.081	.089	.671	1.000	.022	.798	.613	.111
Variables	5	.626	.581	.123	.022	1.000	.047	.201	.724
	6	.113	.098	.689	.798	.047	1.000	.801	.120

Contd.

	1	2	3	4	5	6	7	8
7	.155	.083	.582	.613	.201	.801	1.000	.152
8	.774	.652	.072	.111	.724	.120	.152	1.000
Column sums U_{a1}	3.662	3.263	3.392	3.385	3.324	3.666	3.587	3.605
Normalizing U_{a1} we obtain V_{a1} i.e., $V_{a1} =$ U_a/Normalizing factor*	.371	.331	.344	.343	.337	.372	.363	.365

*Normalizing factor $= \sqrt{(3.662)^2 + (3.263)^2 + (3.392)^2 + (3.385)^2 + (3.324)^2 + (3.666)^2 + (3.587)^2 + (3.605)^2}$

$$= \sqrt{97.372} = 9.868$$

Then we obtain U_{a2} by accumulatively multiplying V_{a1} row by row into R and the result comes as under:

$$U_{a2} : [1.296, 1.143, 1.201, 1.201, 1.165, 1.308, 1.280, 1.275]$$

Normalizing it we obtain (normalizing factor for U_{a2} will be worked out as above and will be $= 3.493$):

$$V_{a2} : [.371, .327, .344, .344, .334, .374, .366, .365]$$

Comparing V_{a1} and V_{a2}, we find the two vectors are almost equal and this shows convergence has occurred. Hence V_{a1} is taken as the characteristic vector, V_a. Finally, we compute the loadings on the first principal component by multiplying V_a by the square root of the number that we obtain for normalizing U_{a2}. The result is as under:

Variables	(Characteristic vector V_a)	×	$\sqrt{normalizing\ factor\ of\ U_{a2}}$	=	Principal Component I
1	.371	×	1.868	=	.69
2	.331	×	1.868	=	.62
3	.344	×	1.868	=	.64
4	.343	×	1.868	=	.64
5	.337	×	1.868	=	.63
6	.372	×	1.868	=	.70
7	.363	×	1.868	=	.68
8	.365	×	1.868	=	.68

For finding principal component II, we have to proceed on similar lines (as stated in the context of obtaining centroid factor *B* earlier in this chapter) to obtain the following result[*]:

Variables	Principal Component II
1	+.57
2	+.59
3	−.52
4	−.59
5	+.57
6	−.61
7	−.49
8	−.61

The other parts of the question can now be worked out (after first putting the above information in a matrix form) as given below:

Variables	Principal Components		Communality, h^2
	I	*II*	
1	.69	+.57	$(.69)^2 + (.57)^2 = .801$
2	.62	+.59	$(.62)^2 + (.59)^2 = .733$
3	.64	−.52	$(.64)^2 + (−.52)^2 = .680$
4	.64	−.59	$(.64)^2 + (−.59)^2 = .758$
5	.63	+.57	$(.63)^2 + (.57)^2 = .722$
6	.70	−.61	$(.70)^2 + (−.61)^2 = .862$
7	.68	−.49	$(.68)^2 + (−.49)^2 = .703$
8	.68	−.61	$(.68)^2 + (−.61)^2 = .835$
Eigen value i.e., common variance	3.4914	2.6007	6.0921
Proportion of total variance	.436 (43.6%)	.325 (32.5%)	.761 (76%)
Proportion of common variance	.573 (57%)	.427 (43%)	1.000 (100%)

All these values can be interpreted in the same manner as stated earlier.

[*]This can easily be worked out. Actual working has been left as an exercise for the students.

(C) Maximum Likelihood (ML) Method of Factor Analysis

The ML method consists in obtaining sets of factor loadings successively in such a way that each, in turn, explains as much as possible of the population correlation matrix as estimated from the sample correlation matrix. If R_s stands for the correlation matrix actually obtained from the data in a sample, R_p stands for the correlation matrix that would be obtained if the entire population were tested, then the ML method seeks to extrapolate what is known from R_s in the best possible way to estimate R_p (but the PC method only maximizes the variance explained in R_s). Thus, the ML method is a statistical approach in which one maximizes some relationship between the sample of data and the population from which the sample was drawn.

The arithmetic underlying the ML method is relatively difficult in comparison to that involved in the PC method and as such is understandable when one has adequate grounding in calculus, higher algebra and matrix algebra in particular. Iterative approach is employed in ML method also to find each factor, but the iterative procedures have proved much more difficult than what we find in the case of PC method. Hence the ML method is generally not used for factor analysis in practice.[*]

The loadings obtained on the first factor are employed in the usual way to obtain a matrix of the residual coefficients. A significance test is then applied to indicate whether it would be reasonable to extract a second factor. This goes on repeatedly in search of one factor after another. One stops factoring after the significance test fails to reject the null hypothesis for the residual matrix. The final product is a matrix of factor loadings. The ML factor loadings can be interpreted in a similar fashion as we have explained in case of the centroid or the PC method.

ROTATION IN FACTOR ANALYSIS

One often talks about the rotated solutions in the context of factor analysis. This is done (i.e., a factor matrix is subjected to rotation) to attain what is technically called "simple structure" in data. Simple structure according to L.L. Thurstone is obtained by rotating the axes[**] until:

(i) Each row of the factor matrix has one zero.

(ii) Each column of the factor matrix has p zeros, where p is the number of factors.

(iii) For each pair of factors, there are several variables for which the loading on one is virtually zero and the loading on the other is substantial.

(iv) If there are many factors, then for each pair of factors there are many variables for which both loadings are zero.

(v) For every pair of factors, the number of variables with non-vanishing loadings on both of them is small.

All these criteria simply imply that the factor analysis should reduce the complexity of all the variables.

---

[*] The basic mathematical derivations of the ML method are well explained in S.A. Mulaik's, *The Foundations of Factor Analysis.*

[**] Rotation constitutes the geometric aspects of factor analysis. Only the axes of the graph (wherein the points representing variables have been shown) are rotated keeping the location of these points relative to each other undisturbed.

There are several methods of rotating the initial factor matrix (obtained by any of the methods of factor analysis) to attain this simple structure. *Varimax rotation* is one such method that maximizes (simultaneously for all factors) the variance of the loadings within each factor. The variance of a factor is largest when its smallest loadings tend towards zero and its largest loadings tend towards unity. In essence, the solution obtained through varimax rotation produces factors that are characterized by large loadings on relatively few variables. The other method of rotation is known as *quartimax rotation* wherein the factor loadings are transformed until the variance of the squared factor loadings throughout the matrix is maximized. As a result, the solution obtained through this method permits a general factor to emerge, whereas in case of varimax solution such a thing is not possible. But both solutions produce orthogonal factors i.e., uncorrelated factors. It should, however, be emphasised that right rotation must be selected for making sense of the results of factor analysis.

R-TYPE AND *Q*-TYPE FACTOR ANALYSES

Factor analysis may be R-type factor analysis or it may be Q-type factor analysis. In *R-type factor analysis,* high correlations occur when respondents who score high on variable 1 also score high on variable 2 and respondents who score low on variable 1 also score low on variable 2. Factors emerge when there are high correlations within groups of variables. In *Q-type factor analysis,* the correlations are computed between pairs of respondents instead of pairs of variables. High correlations occur when respondent 1's pattern of responses on all the variables is much like respondent 2's pattern of responses. Factors emerge when there are high correlations within groups of people. Q-type analysis is useful when the object is to sort out people into groups based on their simultaneous responses to all the variables.

Factor analysis has been mainly used in developing psychological tests (such as *IQ* tests, personality tests, and the like) in the realm of psychology. In marketing, this technique has been used to look at media readership profiles of people.

Merits: The main merits of factor analysis can be stated thus:

(i) The technique of factor analysis is quite useful when we want to condense and simplify the multivariate data.

(ii) The technique is helpful in pointing out important and interesting, relationships among observed data that were there all the time, but not easy to see from the data alone.

(iii) The technique can reveal the latent factors (i.e., underlying factors not directly observed) that determine relationships among several variables concerning a research study. For example, if people are asked to rate different cold drinks (say, Limca, Nova-cola, Gold Spot and so on) according to preference, a factor analysis may reveal some salient characteristics of cold drinks that underlie the relative preferences.

(iv) The technique may be used in the context of empirical clustering of products, media or people i.e., for providing a classification scheme when data scored on various rating scales have to be grouped together.

Limitations: One should also be aware of several limitations of factor analysis. Important ones are as follows:

(i) Factor analysis, like all multivariate techniques, involves laborious computations involving heavy cost burden. With computer facility available these days, there is no doubt that factor analysis has become relatively faster and easier, but the cost factor continues to be the same i.e., large factor analyses are still bound to be quite expensive.

(ii) The results of a single factor analysis are considered generally less reliable and dependable for very often a factor analysis starts with a set of imperfect data. "The factors are nothing but blurred averages, difficult to be identified."[4] To overcome this difficulty, it has been realised that analysis should at least be done twice. If we get more or less similar results from all rounds of analyses, our confidence concerning such results increases.

(iii) Factor-analysis is a complicated decision tool that can be used only when one has thorough knowledge and enough experience of handling this tool. Even then, at times it may not work well and may even disappoint the user.

To conclude, we can state that in spite of all the said limitations "when it works well, factor analysis helps the investigator make sense of large bodies of intertwined data. When it works unusually well, it also points out some interesting relationships that might not have been obvious from examination of the input data alone".[5]

(vi) *Cluster Analysis*

Cluster analysis consists of methods of classifying variables into clusters. Technically, a cluster consists of variables that correlate highly with one another and have comparatively low correlations with variables in other clusters. The basic objective of cluster analysis is to determine how many mutually and exhaustive groups or clusters, based on the similarities of profiles among entities, really exist in the population and then to state the composition of such groups. Various groups to be determined in cluster analysis are not predefined as happens to be the case in discriminant analysis.

Steps: In general, cluster analysis contains the following steps to be performed:

(i) First of all, if some variables have a negative sum of correlations in the correlation matrix, one must reflect variables so as to obtain a maximum sum of positive correlations for the matrix as a whole.

(ii) The second step consists in finding out the highest correlation in the correlation matrix and the two variables involved (i.e., having the highest correlation in the matrix) form the nucleus of the first cluster.

(iii) Then one looks for those variables that correlate highly with the said two variables and includes them in the cluster. This is how the first cluster is formed.

(iv) To obtain the nucleus of the second cluster, we find two variables that correlate highly but have low correlations with members of the first cluster. Variables that correlate highly with the said two variables are then found. Such variables along the said two variables thus constitute the second cluster.

(v) One proceeds on similar lines to search for a third cluster and so on.

---

[4] Srinibas Bhattacharya, *Psychometrics and Behavioural Research,* p. 177.

[5] William D. Wells and Jagdish N. Sheth in their article on "Factor Analysis" forming chapter 9 in Robert Ferber, (ed.), *Handbook of Marketing Research,* p. 2–471.

From the above description we find that clustering methods in general are judgemental and are devoid of statistical inferences. For problems concerning large number of variables, various cut-and-try methods have been proposed for locating clusters. McQuitty has specially developed a number of rather elaborate computational routines[*] for that purpose.

In spite of the above stated limitation, cluster analysis has been found useful in context of market research studies. Through the use of this technique we can make segments of market of a product on the basis of several characteristics of the customers such as personality, socio-economic considerations, psychological factors, purchasing habits and like ones.

(vii) *Multidimensional Scaling*[**]

Multidimensional scaling (MDS) allows a researcher to measure an item in more than one dimension at a time. The basic assumption is that people perceive a set of objects as being more or less similar to one another on a number of dimensions (usually uncorrelated with one another) instead of only one.

There are several MDS techniques (also known as techniques for dimensional reduction) often used for the purpose of revealing patterns of one sort or another in interdependent data structures. If data happen to be non-metric, MDS involves rank ordering each pair of objects in terms of similarity. Then the judged similarities are transformed into distances through statistical manipulations and are consequently shown in *n*-dimensional space in a way that the interpoint distances best preserve the original interpoint proximities. After this sort of mapping is performed, the dimensions are usually interpreted and labeled by the researcher.

The significance of MDS lies in the fact that it enables the researcher to study "The perceptual structure of a set of stimuli and the cognitive processes underlying the development of this structure.... MDS provides a mechanism for determining the truly salient attributes without forcing the judge to appear irrational."[6] With MDS, one can scale objects, individuals or both with a minimum of information. The MDS analysis will reveal the most salient attributes which happen to be the primary determinants for making a specific decision.

(viii) *Latent Structure Analysis*

This type of analysis shares both of the objectives of factor analysis viz., to extract latent factors and express relationship of observed (manifest) variables with these factors as their indicators and to classify a population of respondents into pure types. This type of analysis is appropriate when the variables involved in a study do not possess dependency relationship and happen to be non-metric.

In addition to the above stated multivariate techniques, we may also describe the salient features of what is known as "Path analysis", a technique useful for decomposing the total correlation between any two variables in a causal system.

---

[*] These are beyond the scope of this book and hence have been omitted. Readers interested in such methods are referred to "Cluster Analysis" by R. C. Tryon and D. E. Bailey.

[**] See, Chapter No. 5 of this book for other details about MDS.

[6] Robert Ferber, ed., *Handbook of Marketing Research*, p. 3–52.

PATH ANALYSIS

The term 'path analysis' was first introduced by the biologist Sewall Wright in 1934 in connection with decomposing the total correlation between any two variables in a causal system. The technique of path analysis is based on a series of multiple regression analyses with the added assumption of causal relationship between independent and dependent variables. This technique lays relatively heavier emphasis on the heuristic use of visual diagram, technically described as a path diagram. An illustrative path diagram showing interrelationships between Fathers' education, Fathers' occupation, Sons' education, Sons' first and Sons' present occupation can be shown in the Fig. 13.2.

Path analysis makes use of standardized partial regression coefficients (known as beta weights) as effect coefficients. In linear additive effects are assumed, then through path analysis a simple set of equations can be built up showing how each variable depends on preceding variables. "The main principle of path analysis is that any correlation coefficient between two variables, or a gross or overall measure of empirical relationship can be decomposed into a series of parts: separate paths of influence leading through chronologically intermediate variable to which both the correlated variables have links."[7]

The merit of path analysis in comparison to correlational analysis is that it makes possible the assessment of the relative influence of each antecedent or explanatory variable on the consequent or criterion variables by first making explicit the assumptions underlying the causal connections and then by elucidating the indirect effect of the explanatory variables.

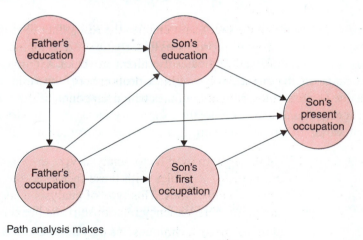

Path analysis makes

Fig.13.2

"The use of the path analysis technique requires the assumption that there are linear additive, a symmetric relationships among a set of variables which can be measured at least on a quasi-interval scale. Each dependent variable is regarded as determined by the variables preceding it in the path diagram, and a residual variable, defined as uncorrelated with the other variables, is postulated to account for the unexplained portion of the variance in the dependent variable. The determining variables are assumed for the analysis to be given (exogenous in the model)."[8]

[7] K. Takeuchi, *et al. op. cit.*, *The Foundations of Multivariate Analysis*, p. 122.

[8] *Ibid.*, p. 121–122.

We may illustrate the path analysis technique in connection with a simple problem of testing a causal model with three explicit variables as shown in the following path diagram:

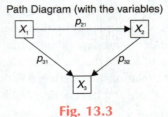

Path Diagram (with the variables)

Fig. 13.3

The structural equation for the above can be written as:

$$\begin{bmatrix} X_1 \\ X_2 \\ X_3 \end{bmatrix} = \begin{bmatrix} e_1 \\ p_{21}X_1 + e_2 \\ p_{31}X_2 + p_{32}X_2 + e_3 \end{bmatrix} = pX + e$$

where the X variables are measured as deviations from their respective means. p_{21} may be estimated from the simple regression of X_2 on X_1 i.e., $X_2 = b_{21}X_1$ and p_{31} and p_{32} may be estimated from the regression of X_3 on X_2 and X_1 as under:

$$\hat{X}_3 = b_{31.2} X_1 + b_{2.1} X_2$$

where $b_{31.2}$ means the standardized partial regression coefficient for predicting variable 3 from variable 1 when the effect of variable 2 is held constant.

In path analysis the beta coefficient indicates the direct effect of X_j ($j = 1, 2, 3, ..., p$) on the dependent variable. Squaring the direct effect yields the proportion of the variance in the dependent variable Y which is due to each of the p number of independent variables X_j ($i = 1, 2, 3, ..., p$). After calculating the direct effect, one may then obtain a summary measure of the total indirect effect of X_j on the dependent variable Y by subtracting from the zero correlation coefficient r_{yxj}, the beta coefficient b_j i.e.,

$$\text{Indirect effect of } X_j \text{ on } Y = c_{jy} = r_{yxj} - b_j$$
$$\text{for all } j = 1, 2, ..., p.$$

Such indirect effects include the unanalysed effects and spurious relationships due to antecedent variables.

In the end, it may again be emphasised that the main virtue of path analysis lies in making explicit the assumptions underlying the causal connections and in elucidating the indirect effects due to antecedent variables of the given system.

CONCLUSION

From the brief account of multivariate techniques presented above, we may conclude that such techniques are important for they make it possible to encompass all the data from an investigation in one analysis. They in fact result in a clearer and better account of the research effort than do the piecemeal analyses of portions of data. These techniques yield more realistic probability statements in hypothesis testing and interval estimation studies. Multivariate analysis (consequently the use of multivariate techniques) is specially important in behavioural sciences and applied researches for most of such studies involve problems in which several response variables are observed simultaneously. The common source of each individual observation generally results into dependence or correlation among the dimensions and it is this feature that distinguishes multivariate data and techniques from their univariate prototypes.

In spite of all this, multivariate techniques are expensive and involve laborious computations. As such their applications in the context of research studies have been accelerated only with the advent of high speed electronic computers since 1950's.

Questions

1. What do you mean by multivariate techniques? Explain their significance in context of research studies.
2. Write a brief essay on "Factor analysis" particularly pointing out its merits and limitations.
3. Name the important multivariate techniques and explain the important characteristic of each one of such techniques.
4. Enumerate the steps involved in Thurstone's centroid method of factor analysis.
5. Write a short note on '*rotation*' in context of factor analysis.
6. Work out the first two centroid factors as well as first two principal components from the following correlation matrix, *R*, *relating* to six variables:

Variables

	1	2	3	4	5	6
1	1.00	.55	.43	.32	.28	.36
2		1.00	.50	.25	.31	.32
3			1.00	.39	.25	.33
4				1.00	.43	.49
5					1.00	.44
6						1.00

Variables (row label at left)

Answers:

Variables	Centroid factors		Principal Components	
	I	*II*	*I*	*II*
1	.71	.40	.71	.39
2	.70	.46	.71	.48
3	.70	.37	.70	.32
4	.69	−.41	.69	−.42
5	.65	−.43	.64	−.45
6	.71	−.39	.71	−.38

7. Compute communality for each of the variable based on first two centroid factors in question six above and state what does it indicate.

8. Compute the proportion of total variance explained by the two factors worked out in question six above by the principal components method. Also point out the proportion of common variance explained by each of the two factors. '

9. What is the significance of using multiple discriminant analysis? Explain in brief the technical details involved in such a technique.

10. Write short notes on:

   (i) Cluster analysis;   (ii) Multidimensional scaling;

  (iii) Reflections in context of factor analysis;

  (iv) Maximum likelihood method of factor analysis;   (v) Path analysis.

Summary Chart:
Showing the Appropriateness of a Particular Multivariate Technique

Techniques of multivariate analysis	Number of			
	Explanatory variables		Criterion variables	
1. Multiple regression analysis (along with path analysis)		many		one
2. Multiple discriminant analysis		many	one (to be classified into many groups)	
3. Multivariate analysis of variance	many			many
4. Canonical correlation analysis		many	many[1]	many[2]
5. Factor analysis		many		
6. Cluster analysis		many		
7. Multidimensional scaling (MDS)	many	many		
8. Latent structure analysis	many			
Nature of data	↑ Non-metric	↑ metric	↑ Non-metric	↑ metric

[1] Any one of the two.

[2] Any one of the two.

14

Interpretation and Report Writing

After collecting and analyzing the data, the researcher has to accomplish the task of drawing inferences followed by report writing. This has to be done very carefully, otherwise misleading conclusions may be drawn and the whole purpose of doing research may get vitiated. It is only through interpretation that the researcher can expose relations and processes that underlie his findings. In case of hypotheses testing studies, if hypotheses are tested and upheld several times, the researcher may arrive at generalizations. But in case the researcher had no hypothesis to start with, he would try to explain his findings on the basis of some theory. This may at times result in new questions, leading to further researches. All this analytical information and consequential inference(s) may well be communicated, preferably through research report, to the consumers of research results who may be either an individual or a group of individuals or some public/private organisation.

MEANING OF INTERPRETATION

Interpretation refers to the task of drawing inferences from the collected facts after an analytical and/or experimental study. In fact, it is a search for broader meaning of research findings. The task of interpretation has two major aspects viz., (i) the effort to establish continuity in research through linking the results of a given study with those of another, and (ii) the establishment of some explanatory concepts. "In one sense, interpretation is concerned with relationships within the collected data, partially overlapping analysis. Interpretation also extends beyond the data of the study to include the results of other research, theory and hypotheses."[1] Thus, interpretation is the device through which the factors that seem to explain what has been observed by researcher in the course of the study can be better understood and it also provides a theoretical conception which can serve as a guide for further researches.

WHY INTERPRETATION?

Interpretation is essential for the simple reason that the usefulness and utility of research findings lie in proper interpretation. It is being considered a basic component of research process because of the following reasons:

[1] C. William Emory, *Business Research Methods,* p. 336.

(i) It is through interpretation that the researcher can well understand the abstract principle that works beneath his findings. Through this he can link up his findings with those of other studies, having the same abstract principle, and thereby can predict about the concrete world of events. Fresh inquiries can test these predictions later on. This way the continuity in research can be maintained.

(ii) Interpretation leads to the establishment of explanatory concepts that can serve as a guide for future research studies; it opens new avenues of intellectual adventure and stimulates the quest for more knowledge.

(iii) Researcher can better appreciate only through interpretation why his findings are what they are and can make others to understand the real significance of his research findings.

(iv) The interpretation of the findings of exploratory research study often results into hypotheses for experimental research and as such interpretation is involved in the transition from exploratory to experimental research. Since an exploratory study does not have a hypothesis to start with, the findings of such a study have to be interpreted on a *post-factum* basis in which case the interpretation is technically described as '*post factum*' interpretation.

TECHNIQUE OF INTERPRETATION

The task of interpretation is not an easy job, rather it requires a great skill and dexterity on the part of researcher. Interpretation is an art that one learns through practice and experience. The researcher may, at times, seek the guidance from experts for accomplishing the task of interpretation.

The technique of interpretation often involves the following steps:

(i) Researcher must give reasonable explanations of the relations which he has found and he must interpret the lines of relationship in terms of the underlying processes and must try to find out the thread of uniformity that lies under the surface layer of his diversified research findings. In fact, this is the technique of how generalization should be done and concepts be formulated.

(ii) Extraneous information, if collected during the study, must be considered while interpreting the final results of research study, for it may prove to be a key factor in understanding the problem under consideration.

(iii) It is advisable, before embarking upon final interpretation, to consult someone having insight into the study and who is frank and honest and will not hesitate to point out omissions and errors in logical argumentation. Such a consultation will result in correct interpretation and, thus, will enhance the utility of research results.

(iv) Researcher must accomplish the task of interpretation only after considering all relevant factors affecting the problem to avoid false generalization. He must be in no hurry while interpreting results, for quite often the conclusions, which appear to be all right at the beginning, may not at all be accurate.

PRECAUTIONS IN INTERPRETATION

One should always remember that even if the data are properly collected and analysed, wrong interpretation would lead to inaccurate conclusions. It is, therefore, absolutely essential that the task of interpretation be accomplished with patience in an impartial manner and also in correct perspective. Researcher must pay attention to the following points for correct interpretation:

(i) At the outset, researcher must invariably satisfy himself that (a) the data are appropriate, trustworthy and adequate for drawing inferences; (b) the data reflect good homogeneity; and that (c) proper analysis has been done through statistical methods.

(ii) The researcher must remain cautious about the errors that can possibly arise in the process of interpreting results. Errors can arise due to false generalization and/or due to wrong interpretation of statistical measures, such as the application of findings beyond the range of observations, identification of correlation with causation and the like. Another major pitfall is the tendency to affirm that definite relationships exist on the basis of confirmation of particular hypotheses. In fact, the positive test results accepting the hypothesis must be interpreted as "being in accord" with the hypothesis, rather than as "confirming the validity of the hypothesis". The researcher must remain vigilant about all such things so that false generalization may not take place. He should be well equipped with and must know the correct use of statistical measures for drawing inferences concerning his study.

(iii) He must always keep in view that the task of interpretation is very much intertwined with analysis and cannot be distinctly separated. As such he must take the task of interpretation as a special aspect of analysis and accordingly must take all those precautions that one usually observes while going through the process of analysis viz., precautions concerning the reliability of data, computational checks, validation and comparison of results.

(iv) He must never lose sight of the fact that his task is not only to make sensitive observations of relevant occurrences, but also to identify and disengage the factors that are initially hidden to the eye. This will enable him to do his job of interpretation on proper lines. Broad generalisation should be avoided as most research is not amenable to it because the coverage may be restricted to a particular time, a particular area and particular conditions. Such restrictions, if any, must invariably be specified and the results must be framed within their limits.

(v) The researcher must remember that "ideally in the course of a research study, there should be constant interaction between initial hypothesis, empirical observation and theoretical conceptions. It is exactly in this area of interaction between theoretical orientation and empirical observation that opportunities for originality and creativity lie."[2] He must pay special attention to this aspect while engaged in the task of interpretation.

SIGNIFICANCE OF REPORT WRITING

Research report is considered a major component of the research study for the research task remains incomplete till the report has been presented and/or written. As a matter of fact even the most brilliant hypothesis, highly well designed and conducted research study, and the most striking generalizations and findings are of little value unless they are effectively communicated to others. The purpose of research is not well served unless the findings are made known to others. Research results must invariably enter the general store of knowledge. All this explains the significance of

[2] Pauline V. Young, *Scientific Social Surveys and Research,* 4th ed., p. 488.

writing research report. There are people who do not consider writing of report as an integral part of the research process. But the general opinion is in favour of treating the presentation of research results or the writing of report as part and parcel of the research project. Writing of report is the last step in a research study and requires a set of skills somewhat different from those called for in respect of the earlier stages of research. This task should be accomplished by the researcher with utmost care; he may seek the assistance and guidance of experts for the purpose.

DIFFERENT STEPS IN WRITING REPORT

Research reports are the product of slow, painstaking, accurate inductive work. The usual steps involved in writing report are: (a) logical analysis of the subject-matter; (b) preparation of the final outline; (c) preparation of the rough draft; (d) rewriting and polishing; (c) preparation of the final bibliography; and (f) writing the final draft. Though all these steps are self explanatory, yet a brief mention of each one of these will be appropriate for better understanding.

Logical analysis of the subject matter: It is the first step which is primarily concerned with the development of a subject. There are two ways in which to develop a subject (a) logically and (b) chronologically. The logical development is made on the basis of mental connections and associations between the one thing and another by means of analysis. Logical treatment often consists in developing the material from the simple possible to the most complex structures. Chronological development is based on a connection or sequence in time or occurrence. The directions for doing or making something usually follow the chronological order.

Preparation of the final outline: It is the next step in writing the research report "Outlines are the framework upon which long written works are constructed. They are an aid to the logical organisation of the material and a reminder of the points to be stressed in the report."[3]

Preparation of the rough draft: This follows the logical analysis of the subject and the preparation of the final outline. Such a step is of utmost importance for the researcher now sits to write down what he has done in the context of his research study. He will write down the procedure adopted by him in collecting the material for his study along with various limitations faced by him, the technique of analysis adopted by him, the broad findings and generalizations and the various suggestions he wants to offer regarding the problem concerned.

Rewriting and polishing of the rough draft: This step happens to be most difficult part of all formal writing. Usually this step requires more time than the writing of the rough draft. The careful revision makes the difference between a mediocre and a good piece of writing. While rewriting and polishing, one should check the report for weaknesses in logical development or presentation. The researcher should also "see whether or not the material, as it is presented, has unity and cohesion; does the report stand upright and firm and exhibit a definite pattern, like a marble arch? Or does it resemble an old wall of moldering cement and loose brick."[4] In addition the researcher should give due attention to the fact that in his rough draft he has been consistent or not. He should check the mechanics of writing—grammar, spelling and usage.

Preparation of the final bibliography: Next in order comes the task of the preparation of the final bibliography. The bibliography, which is generally appended to the research report, is a list of books

---

[3] Elliott S.M. Gatner and Francesco Cordasco, *Research and Report Writing,* p. 37.

[4] *Ibid.,* p. 50.

in some way pertinent to the research which has been done. It should contain all those works which the researcher has consulted. The bibliography should be arranged alphabetically and may be divided into two parts; the first part may contain the names of books and pamphlets, and the second part may contain the names of magazine and newspaper articles. Generally, this pattern of bibliography is considered convenient and satisfactory from the point of view of reader, though it is not the only way of presenting bibliography. The entries in bibliography should be made adopting the following order:

For books and pamphlets the order may be as under:

1. Name of author, last name first.
2. Title, underlined to indicate italics.
3. Place, publisher, and date of publication.
4. Number of volumes.

Example

Kothari, C.R., *Quantitative Techniques,* New Delhi, Vikas Publishing House Pvt. Ltd., 1978.

For magazines and newspapers the order may be as under:

1. Name of the author, last name first.
2. Title of article, in quotation marks.
3. Name of periodical, underlined to indicate italics.
4. The volume or volume and number.
5. The date of the issue.
6. The pagination.

Example

Robert V. Roosa, "Coping with Short-term International Money Flows", *The Banker,* London, September, 1971, p. 995.

The above examples are just the samples for bibliography entries and may be used, but one should also remember that they are not the only acceptable forms. The only thing important is that, whatever method one selects, it must remain consistent.

Writing the final draft: This constitutes the last step. The final draft should be written in a concise and objective style and in simple language, avoiding vague expressions such as "it seems", "there may be", and the like ones. While writing the final draft, the researcher must avoid abstract terminology and technical jargon. Illustrations and examples based on common experiences must be incorporated in the final draft as they happen to be most effective in communicating the research findings to others. A research report should not be dull, but must enthuse people and maintain interest and must show originality. It must be remembered that every report should be an attempt to solve some intellectual problem and must contribute to the solution of a problem and must add to the knowledge of both the researcher and the reader.

LAYOUT OF THE RESEARCH REPORT

Anybody, who is reading the research report, must necessarily be conveyed enough about the study so that he can place it in its general scientific context, judge the adequacy of its methods and thus form an opinion of how seriously the findings are to be taken. For this purpose there is the need of proper layout of the report. The layout of the report means as to what the research report should contain. A comprehensive layout of the research report should comprise (A) preliminary pages; (B) the main text; and (C) the end matter. Let us deal with them separately.

(A) Preliminary Pages

In its preliminary pages the report should carry a *title and date,* followed by acknowledgements in the form of 'Preface' or 'Foreword'. Then there should be a *table of contents* followed by *list of tables and illustrations* so that the decision-maker or anybody interested in reading the report can easily locate the required information in the report.

(B) Main Text

The main text provides the complete outline of the research report along with all details. Title of the research study is repeated at the top of the first page of the main text and then follows the other details on pages numbered consecutively, beginning with the second page. Each main section of the report should begin on a new page. The main text of the report should have the following sections: (i) Introduction; (ii) Statement of findings and recommendations; (iii) The results; (iv) The implications drawn from the results; and (v) The summary.

(i) *Introduction:* The purpose of introduction is to introduce the research project to the readers. It should contain a clear statement of the objectives of research i.e., enough background should be given to make clear to the reader why the problem was considered worth investigating. A brief summary of other relevant research may also be stated so that the present study can be seen in that context. The hypotheses of study, if any, and the definitions of the major concepts employed in the study should be explicitly stated in the introduction of the report.

The methodology adopted in conducting the study must be fully explained. The scientific reader would like to know in detail about such thing: How was the study carried out? What was its basic design? If the study was an experimental one, then what were the experimental manipulations? If the data were collected by means of questionnaires or interviews, then exactly what questions were asked (The questionnaire or interview schedule is usually given in an appendix)? If measurements were based on observation, then what instructions were given to the observers? Regarding the sample used in the study the reader should be told: Who were the subjects? How many were there? How were they selected? All these questions are crucial for estimating the probable limits of generalizability of the findings. The statistical analysis adopted must also be clearly stated. In addition to all this, the scope of the study should be stated and the boundary lines be demarcated. The various limitations, under which the research project was completed, must also be narrated.

(ii) *Statement of findings and recommendations:* After introduction, the research report must contain a statement of findings and recommendations in non-technical language so that it can be easily understood by all concerned. If the findings happen to be extensive, at this point they should be put in the summarised form.

(iii) *Results:* A detailed presentation of the findings of the study, with supporting data in the form of tables and charts together with a validation of results, is the next step in writing the main text of the report. This generally comprises the main body of the report, extending over several chapters. The result section of the report should contain statistical summaries and reductions of the data rather than the raw data. All the results should be presented in logical sequence and splitted into readily identifiable sections. All relevant results must find a place in the report. But how one is to decide about what is relevant is the basic question. Quite often guidance comes primarily from the research problem and from the hypotheses, if any, with which the study was concerned. But ultimately the researcher must rely on his own judgement in deciding the outline of his report. "Nevertheless, it is still necessary that he states clearly the problem with which he was concerned, the procedure by which he worked on the problem, the conclusions at which he arrived, and the bases for his conclusions."[5]

(iv) *Implications of the results:* Toward the end of the main text, the researcher should again put down the results of his research clearly and precisely. He should, state the implications that flow from the results of the study, for the general reader is interested in the implications for understanding the human behaviour. Such implications may have three aspects as stated below:

(a) A statement of the inferences drawn from the present study which may be expected to apply in similar circumstances.

(b) The conditions of the present study which may limit the extent of legitimate generalizations of the inferences drawn from the study.

(c) The relevant questions that still remain unanswered or new questions raised by the study along with suggestions for the kind of research that would provide answers for them.

It is considered a good practice to finish the report with a short conclusion which summarises and recapitulates the main points of the study. The conclusion drawn from the study should be clearly related to the hypotheses that were stated in the introductory section. At the same time, a forecast of the probable future of the subject and an indication of the kind of research which needs to be done in that particular field is useful and desirable.

(v) *Summary:* It has become customary to conclude the research report with a very brief summary, resting in brief the research problem, the methodology, the major findings and the major conclusions drawn from the research results.

(C) End Matter

At the end of the report, appendices should be enlisted in respect of all technical data such as questionnaires, sample information, mathematical derivations and the like ones. Bibliography of sources consulted should also be given. Index (an alphabetical listing of names, places and topics along with the numbers of the pages in a book or report on which they are mentioned or discussed) should invariably be given at the end of the report. The value of index lies in the fact that it works as a guide to the reader for the contents in the report.

[5] Selltiz, Jahoda, Deutsch and Cook, *Research Methods in Social Relations*, p. 448.

TYPES OF REPORTS

Research reports vary greatly in length and type. In each individual case, both the length and the form are largely dictated by the problems at hand. For instance, business firms prefer reports in the letter form, just one or two pages in length. Banks, insurance organisations and financial institutions are generally fond of the short balance-sheet type of tabulation for their annual reports to their customers and shareholders. Mathematicians prefer to write the results of their investigations in the form of algebraic notations. Chemists report their results in symbols and formulae. Students of literature usually write long reports presenting the critical analysis of some writer or period or the like with a liberal use of quotations from the works of the author under discussion. In the field of education and psychology, the favourite form is the report on the results of experimentation accompanied by the detailed statistical tabulations. Clinical psychologists and social pathologists frequently find it necessary to make use of the case-history form.

News items in the daily papers are also forms of report writing. They represent firsthand on-the-scene accounts of the events described or compilations of interviews with persons who were on the scene. In such reports the first paragraph usually contains the important information in detail and the succeeding paragraphs contain material which is progressively less and less important.

Book-reviews which analyze the content of the book and report on the author's intentions, his success or failure in achieving his aims, his language, his style, scholarship, bias or his point of view. Such reviews also happen to be a kind of short report. The reports prepared by governmental bureaus, special commissions, and similar other organisations are generally very comprehensive reports on the issues involved. Such reports are usually considered as important research products. Similarly, Ph.D. theses and dissertations are also a form of report-writing, usually completed by students in academic institutions.

The above narration throws light on the fact that the results of a research investigation can be presented in a number of ways viz., a technical report, a popular report, an article, a monograph or at times even in the form of oral presentation. Which method(s) of presentation to be used in a particular study depends on the circumstances under which the study arose and the nature of the results. A *technical report* is used whenever a full written report of the study is required whether for record-keeping or for public dissemination. A *popular report* is used if the research results have policy implications. We give below a few details about the said two types of reports:

(A) Technical Report

In the technical report the main emphasis is on (i) the methods employed, (it) assumptions made in the course of the study, (iii) the detailed presentation of the findings including their limitations and supporting data.

A general outline of a technical report can be as follows:

1. *Summary of results:* A brief review of the main findings just in two or three pages.

2. *Nature of the study:* Description of the general objectives of study, formulation of the problem in operational terms, the working hypothesis, the type of analysis and data required, etc.

3. *Methods employed:* Specific methods used in the study and their limitations. For instance, in sampling studies we should give details of sample design viz., sample size, sample selection, etc.

4. *Data:* Discussion of data collected, their sources, characteristics and limitations. If secondary data are used, their suitability to the problem at hand be fully assessed. In case of a survey, the manner in which data were collected should be fully described.

5. *Analysis of data and presentation of findings:* The analysis of data and presentation of the findings of the study with supporting data in the form of tables and charts be fully narrated. This, in fact, happens to be the main body of the report usually extending over several chapters.

6. *Conclusions:* A detailed summary of the findings and the policy implications drawn from the results be explained.

7. *Bibliography:* Bibliography of various sources consulted be prepared and attached.

8. *Technical appendices:* Appendices be given for all technical matters relating to questionnaire, mathematical derivations, elaboration on particular technique of analysis and the like ones.

9. *Index:* Index must be prepared and be given invariably in the report at the end.

The order presented above only gives a general idea of the nature of a technical report; the order of presentation may not necessarily be the same in all the technical reports. This, in other words, means that the presentation may vary in different reports; even the different sections outlined above will not always be the same, nor will all these sections appear in any particular report.

It should, however, be remembered that even in a technical report, simple presentation and ready availability of the findings remain an important consideration and as such the liberal use of charts and diagrams is considered desirable.

(B) Popular Report

The popular report is one which gives emphasis on simplicity and attractiveness. The simplification should be sought through clear writing, minimization of technical, particularly mathematical, details and liberal use of charts and diagrams. Attractive layout along with large print, many subheadings, even an occasional cartoon now and then is another characteristic feature of the popular report. Besides, in such a report emphasis is given on practical aspects and policy implications.

We give below a general outline of a popular report.

1. *The findings and their implications:* Emphasis in the report is given on the findings of most practical interest and on the implications of these findings.

2. *Recommendations for action:* Recommendations for action on the basis of the findings of the study is made in this section of the report.

3. *Objective of the study:* A general review of how the problem arise is presented along with the specific objectives of the project under study.

4. *Methods employed:* A brief and non-technical description of the methods and techniques used, including a short review of the data on which the study is based, is given in this part of the report.

5. *Results:* This section constitutes the main body of the report wherein the results of the study are presented in clear and non-technical terms with liberal use of all sorts of illustrations such as charts, diagrams and the like ones.

6. *Technical appendices:* More detailed information on methods used, forms, etc. is presented in the form of appendices. But the appendices are often not detailed if the report is entirely meant for general public.

There can be several variations of the form in which a popular report can be prepared. The only important thing about such a report is that it gives emphasis on simplicity and policy implications from the operational point of view, avoiding the technical details of all sorts to the extent possible.

ORAL PRESENTATION

At times oral presentation of the results of the study is considered effective, particularly in cases where policy recommendations are indicated by project results. The merit of this approach lies in the fact that it provides an opportunity for give-and-take decisions which generally lead to a better understanding of the findings and their implications. But the main demerit of this sort of presentation is the lack of any permanent record concerning the research details and it may be just possible that the findings may fade away from people's memory even before an action is taken. In order to overcome this difficulty, a written report may be circulated before the oral presentation and referred to frequently during the discussion. Oral presentation is effective when supplemented by various visual devices. Use of slides, wall charts and blackboards is quite helpful in contributing to clarity and in reducing the boredom, if any. Distributing a board outline, with a few important tables and charts concerning the research results, makes the listeners attentive who have a ready outline on which to focus their thinking. This very often happens in academic institutions where the researcher discusses his research findings and policy implications with others either in a seminar or in a group discussion.

Thus, research results can be reported in more than one ways, but the usual practice adopted, in academic institutions particularly, is that of writing the Technical Report and then preparing several research papers to be discussed at various forums in one form or the other. But in practical field and with problems having policy implications, the technique followed is that of writing a popular report. Researches done on governmental account or on behalf of some major public or private organisations are usually presented in the form of technical reports.

MECHANICS OF WRITING A RESEARCH REPORT

There are very definite and set rules which should be followed in the actual preparation of the research report or paper. Once the techniques are finally decided, they should be scrupulously adhered to, and no deviation permitted. The criteria of format should be decided as soon as the materials for the research paper have been assembled. The following points deserve mention so far as the mechanics of writing a report are concerned:

1. *Size and physical design:* The manuscript should be written on unruled paper 8 1/2$''$ × 11$''$ in size. If it is to be written by hand, then black or blue-black ink should be used. A margin of at least one and one-half inches should be allowed at the left hand and of at least half an inch at the right hand of the paper. There should also be one-inch margins, top and bottom. The paper should be neat and legible. If the manuscript is to be typed, then all typing should be double-spaced on one side of the page only except for the insertion of the long quotations.

2. *Procedure:* Various steps in writing the report should be strictly adhered (All such steps have already been explained earlier in this chapter).

3. *Layout:* Keeping in view the objective and nature of the problem, the layout of the report should be thought of and decided and accordingly adopted (The layout of the research report and various

types of reports have been described in this chapter earlier which should be taken as a guide for report-writing in case of a particular problem).

4. *Treatment of quotations:* Quotations should be placed in quotation marks and double spaced, forming an immediate part of the text. But if a quotation is of a considerable length (more than four or five type written lines) then it should be single-spaced and indented at least half an inch to the right of the normal text margin.

5. *The footnotes:* Regarding footnotes one should keep in view the followings:

(a) The footnotes serve two purposes viz., the identification of materials used in quotations in the report and the notice of materials not immediately necessary to the body of the research text but still of supplemental value. In other words, footnotes are meant for cross references, citation of authorities and sources, acknowledgement and elucidation or explanation of a point of view. It should always be kept in view that footnote is not an end nor a means of the display of scholarship. The modern tendency is to make the minimum use of footnotes for scholarship does not need to be displayed.

(b) Footnotes are placed at the bottom of the page on which the reference or quotation which they identify or supplement ends. Footnotes are customarily separated from the textual material by a space of half an inch and a line about one and a half inches long.

(c) Footnotes should be numbered consecutively, usually beginning with 1 in each chapter separately. The number should be put slightly above the line, say at the end of a quotation. At the foot of the page, again, the footnote number should be indented and typed a little above the line. Thus, consecutive numbers must be used to correlate the reference in the text with its corresponding note at the bottom of the page, except in case of statistical tables and other numerical material, where symbols such as the asterisk (*) or the like one may be used to prevent confusion.

(d) Footnotes are always typed in single space though they are divided from one another by double space.

6. *Documentation style:* Regarding documentation, the first footnote reference to any given work should be complete in its documentation, giving all the essential facts about the edition used. Such documentary footnotes follow a general sequence. The common order may be described as under:

(i) *Regarding the single-volume reference*

1. Author's name in normal order (and not beginning with the last name as in a bibliography) followed by a comma;
2. Title of work, underlined to indicate italics;
3. Place and date of publication;
4. Pagination references (The page number).

Example

John Gassner, *Masters of the Drama,* New York: Dover Publications, Inc. 1954, p. 315.

(ii) *Regarding multivolumed reference*

1. Author's name in the normal order;

2. Title of work, underlined to indicate italics;

3. Place and date of publication;

4. Number of volume;

5. Pagination references (The page number).

(iii) *Regarding works arranged alphabetically*

For works arranged alphabetically such as encyclopedias and dictionaries, no pagination reference is usually needed. In such cases the order is illustrated as under:

Example 1

"Salamanca," *Encyclopaedia Britannica,* 14th Edition.

Example 2

"Mary Wollstonecraft Godwin," *Dictionary of national biography.*

But if there should be a detailed reference to a long encyclopedia article, volume and pagination reference may be found necessary.

(iv) *Regarding periodicals reference*

1. Name of the author in normal order;

2. Title of article, in quotation marks;

3. Name of periodical, underlined to indicate italics;

4. Volume number;

5. Date of issuance;

6. Pagination.

(v) *Regarding anthologies and collections reference*

Quotations from anthologies or collections of literary works must be acknowledged not only by author, but also by the name of the collector.

(vi) *Regarding second-hand quotations reference*

In such cases the documentation should be handled as follows:

1. Original author and title;

2. "quoted or cited in,";

3. Second author and work.

Example

J.F. Jones, *Life in Ploynesia,* p. 16, quoted in *History of the Pacific Ocean area,* by R.B. Abel, p. 191.

(vii) *Case of multiple authorship*

If there are more than two authors or editors, then in the documentation the name of only the first is given and the multiple authorship is indicated by "et al." or "and others".

Subsequent references to the same work need not be so detailed as stated above. If the work is cited again without any other work intervening, it may be indicated as *ibid,* followed by a comma and the page number. A single page should be referred to as p., but more than one page be referred to as pp. If there are several pages referred to at a stretch, the practice is to use often the page number, for example, pp. 190ff, which means page number 190 and the following pages; but only for page 190 and the following page '190f'. Roman numerical is generally used to indicate the number of the volume of a book. Op. cit. (opera citato, in the work cited) or Loc. cit. (loco citato, in the place cited) are two of the very convenient abbreviations used in the footnotes. Op. cit. or Loc. cit. after the writer's name would suggest that the reference is to work by the writer which has been cited in detail in an earlier footnote but intervened by some other references.

7. Punctuation and abbreviations in footnotes: The first item after the number in the footnote is the author's name, given in the normal signature order. This is followed by a comma. After the comma, the title of the book is given: the article (such as "A", "An", "The" etc.) is omitted and only the first word and proper nouns and adjectives are capitalized. The title is followed by a comma. Information concerning the edition is given next. This entry is followed by a comma. The place of publication is then stated; it may be mentioned in an abbreviated form, if the place happens to be a famous one such as Lond. for London, N.Y. for New York, N.D. for New Delhi and so on. This entry is followed by a comma. Then the name of the publisher is mentioned and this entry is closed by a comma. It is followed by the date of publication if the date is given on the title page. If the date appears in the copyright notice on the reverse side of the title page or elsewhere in the volume, the comma should be omitted and the date enclosed in square brackets [c 1978], [1978]. The entry is followed by a comma. Then follow the volume and page references and are separated by a comma if both are given. A period closes the complete documentary reference. But one should remember that the documentation regarding acknowledgements from magazine articles and periodical literature follow a different form as stated earlier while explaining the entries in the bibliography.

Certain English and Latin abbreviations are quite often used in bibliographies and footnotes to eliminate tedious repetition. The following is a partial list of the most common abbreviations frequently used in report-writing (the researcher should learn to recognise them as well as he should learn to use them):

anon.,	anonymous
ante.,	before
art.,	article
aug.,	augmented
bk.,	book
bull.,	bulletin
cf.,	compare
ch.,	chapter
col.,	column
diss.,	dissertation
ed.,	editor, edition, edited.
ed. cit.,	edition cited
e.g.,	exempli gratia: for example
eng.,	enlarged
et.al.,	and others

et seq.,	et sequens: and the following
ex.,	example
f., ff.,	and the following
fig(s).,	figure(s)
fn.,	footnote
ibid., ibidem:	in the same place (when two or more successive footnotes refer to the same work, it is not necessary to repeat complete reference for the second footnote. Ibid. may be used. If different pages are referred to, pagination must be shown).
id., idem:	the same
ill., illus., or illust(s).	illustrated, illustration(s)
Intro., intro.,	introduction
l, or *ll*,	line(s)
loc. cit., loco citato:	in the place cited; used as op.cit., (when new reference is made to the same pagination as cited in the previous note)
MS., MSS.,	Manuscript or Manuscripts
N.B., nota bene:	note well
n.d.,	no date
n.p.,	no place
no pub.,	no publisher
no(s).,	number(s)
o.p.,	out of print
op. cit: opera citato	in the work cited (If reference has been made to a work and new reference is to be made, ibid., may be used, if intervening reference has been made to different works, op.cit. must be used. The name of the author must precede.
p. or pp.,	page(s)
passim:	here and there
post:	after
rev.,	revised
tr., trans.,	translator, translated, translation
vid or vide:	see, refer to
viz.,	namely
vol. or vol(s).,	volume(s)
vs., versus:	against

8. *Use of statistics, charts and graphs:* A judicious use of statistics in research reports is often considered a virtue for it contributes a great deal towards the clarification and simplification of the material and research results. One may well remember that a good picture is often worth more than

a thousand words. Statistics are usually presented in the form of tables, charts, bars and line-graphs and pictograms. Such presentation should be self explanatory and complete in itself. It should be suitable and appropriate looking to the problem at hand. Finally, statistical presentation should be neat and attractive.

9. The final draft: Revising and rewriting the rough draft of the report should be done with great care before writing the final draft. For the purpose, the researcher should put to himself questions like: Are the sentences written in the report clear? Are they grammatically correct? Do they say what is meant'? Do the various points incorporated in the report fit together logically? "Having at least one colleague read the report just before the final revision is extremely helpful. Sentences that seem crystal-clear to the writer may prove quite confusing to other people; a connection that had seemed self evident may strike others as a *non-sequitur.* A friendly critic, by pointing out passages that seem unclear or illogical, and perhaps suggesting ways of remedying the difficulties, can be an invaluable aid in achieving the goal of adequate communication."[6]

10. Bibliography: Bibliography should be prepared and appended to the research report as discussed earlier.

11. Preparation of the index: At the end of the report, an index should invariably be given, the value of which lies in the fact that it acts as a good guide, to the reader. Index may be prepared both as subject index and as author index. The former gives the names of the subject-topics or concepts along with the number of pages on which they have appeared or discussed in the report, whereas the latter gives the similar information regarding the names of authors. The index should always be arranged alphabetically. Some people prefer to prepare only one index common for names of authors, subject-topics, concepts and the like ones.

PRECAUTIONS FOR WRITING RESEARCH REPORTS

Research report is a channel of communicating the research findings to the readers of the report. A good research report is one which does this task efficiently and effectively. As such it must be prepared keeping the following precautions in view:

1. While determining the length of the report (since research reports vary greatly in length), one should keep in view the fact that it should be long enough to cover the subject but short enough to maintain interest. In fact, report-writing should not be a means to learning more and more about less and less.

2. A research report should not, if this can be avoided, be dull; it should be such as to sustain reader's interest.

3. Abstract terminology and technical jargon should be avoided in a research report. The report should be able to convey the matter as simply as possible. This, in other words, means that report should be written in an objective style in simple language, avoiding expressions such as "it seems," "there may be" and the like.

4. Readers are often interested in acquiring a quick knowledge of the main findings and as such the report must provide a ready availability of the findings. For this purpose, charts,

[6] Claire Selltiz and others, *Research Methods in Social Relations* rev., Methuen & Co. Ltd., London, 1959, p. 454.

graphs and the statistical tables may be used for the various results in the main report in addition to the summary of important findings.

5. The layout of the report should be well thought out and must be appropriate and in accordance with the objective of the research problem.

6. The reports should be free from grammatical mistakes and must be prepared strictly in accordance with the techniques of composition of report-writing such as the use of quotations, footnotes, documentation, proper punctuation and use of abbreviations in footnotes and the like.

7. The report must present the logical analysis of the subject matter. It must reflect a structure wherein the different pieces of analysis relating to the research problem fit well.

8. A research report should show originality and should necessarily be an attempt to solve some intellectual problem. It must contribute to the solution of a problem and must add to the store of knowledge.

9. Towards the end, the report must also state the policy implications relating to the problem under consideration. It is usually considered desirable if the report makes a forecast of the probable future of the subject concerned and indicates the kinds of research still needs to be done in that particular field.

10. Appendices should be enlisted in respect of all the technical data in the report.

11. Bibliography of sources consulted is a must for a good report and must necessarily be given.

12. Index is also considered an essential part of a good report and as such must be prepared and appended at the end.

13. Report must be attractive in appearance, neat and clean, whether typed or printed.

14. Calculated confidence limits must be mentioned and the various constraints experienced in conducting the research study may also be stated in the report.

15. Objective of the study, the nature of the problem, the methods employed and the analysis techniques adopted must all be clearly stated in the beginning of the report in the form of introduction.

CONCLUSION

In spite of all that has been stated above, one should always keep in view the fact report-writing is an art which is learnt by practice and experience, rather than by mere doctrination.

Questions

1. Write a brief note on the 'task of interpretation' in the context of research methodology.
2. "Interpretation is a fundamental component of research process", Explain. Why so?
3. Describe the precautions that the researcher should take while interpreting his findings.
4. "Interpretation is an art of drawing inferences, depending upon the skill of the researcher". Elucidate the given statement explaining the technique of interpretation.

5. "It is only through interpretation the researcher can expose the relations and processes that underlie his findings". Explain, giving examples.

6. Explain the significance of a research report and narrate the various steps involved in writing such a report.

7. Describe, in brief, the layout of a research report, covering all relevant points.

8. Write a short note on 'Documentation' in the context of a research report.

9. Mention the different types of report, particularly pointing out the difference between a technical report and a popular report.

10. Explain the technique and importance of oral presentation of research findings. Is only oral presentation sufficient? If not, why?

11. (a) What points will you keep in mind while preparing a research report? Explain.

    (b) What are the different forms in which a research work may be reported. Describe.

    (M. Phil. Exam. (EAFM) 1979, Uni. of Rajasthan)

12. "We can teach methods of analysis, yet any extensive research... requires something equally important: an organisation or synthesis which provides the essential structure into which the pieces of analysis fit." Examine this statement and show how a good research report may be prepared.

    (M. Phil. Exam. (EAFM) 1978, Uni. of Rajasthan)

13. Write short notes on the following:

    (a) The techniques of writing report;

    (b) Characteristics of a good research report;

    (c) Bibliography and its importance in context of research report;

    (d) Rewriting and polishing of report.

14. "Report writing is more an art that hinges upon practice and experience". Discuss.

15

The Computer: Its Role in Research

INTRODUCTION

Problem solving is an age old activity. The development of electronic devices, specially the computers, has given added impetus to this activity. Problems which could not be solved earlier due to sheer amount of computations involved can now be tackled with the aid of computers accurately and rapidly. Computer is certainly one of the most versatile and ingenious developments of the modern technological age. Today people use computers in almost every walk of life. No longer are they just big boxes with flashing lights whose sole purpose is to do arithmetic at high speed but they make use of studies in philosophy, psychology, mathematics and linguistics to produce output that mimics the human mind. The sophistication in computer technology has reached the stage that it will not be longer before it is impossible to tell whether you are talking to man or machine. Indeed, the advancement in computers is astonishing.

To the researcher, the use of computer to analyse complex data has made complicated research designs practical. Electronic computers have by now become an indispensable part of research students in the physical and behavioural sciences as well as in the humanities. The research student, in this age of computer technology, must be exposed to the methods and use of computers. A basic understanding of the manner in which a computer works helps a person to appreciate the utility of this powerful tool. Keeping all this in view, the present chapter introduces the basics of computers, especially it. answers questions like: What is a computer? How does it function? How does one communicate with it? How does it help in analysing data?

THE COMPUTER AND COMPUTER TECHNOLOGY

A computer, as the name indicates, is nothing but a device that computes. In this sense, any device, however crude or sophisticated, that enables one to carry out mathematical manipulations becomes a computer. But what has made this term conspicuous today and, what we normally imply when we speak of computers, are electronically operating machines which are used to carry out computations.

In brief, computer is a machine capable of receiving, storing, manipulating and yielding information such as numbers, words, pictures.

The computer can be a digital computer or it can be a analogue computer. A *digital computer* is one which operates essentially by counting (using information, including letters and symbols, in coded form) where as *the analogue computer* operates by measuring rather than counting. Digital computer handles information as strings of binary numbers i.e., zeros and ones, with the help of counting process but analogue computer converts varying quantities such as temperature and pressure into corresponding electrical voltages and then performs specified functions on the given signals. Thus, analogue computers are used for certain specialised engineering and scientific applications. Most computers are digital, so much so that the word computer is generally accepted as being synonymous with the term 'digital computer'.

Computer technology has undergone a significant change over a period of four decades. The present day microcomputer is far more powerful and costs very little, compared to the world's first electronic computer viz. Electronic Numerical Integrator and Calculator (ENIAC) completed in 1946. The microcomputer works many times faster, is thousands of times more reliable and has a large memory.

The advances in computer technology are usually talked in terms of 'generations'.* Today we have the fourth generation computer in service and efforts are being made to develop the fifth generation computer, which is expected to be ready by 1990. *The first generation computer* started in 1945 contained 18000 small bottle-sized valves which constituted its central processing unit (CPU). This machine did not have any facility for storing programs and the instructions had to be fed into it by a readjustment of switches and wires. *The second generation computer* found the way for development with the invention of the transistor in 1947. The transistor replaced the valve in all electronic devices and made them much smaller and more reliable. Such computers appeared in the market in the early sixties. *The third generation computer* followed the invention of integrated circuit (IC) in 1959. Such machines, with their CPU and main store made of IC chips, appeared in the market in the second half of the sixties. *The fourth generation computers* owe their birth to the advent of microprocessor—the king of chips—in 1972. The use of microprocessor as CPU in a computer has made real the dream of 'computer for the masses'. This device has enabled the development of microcomputers, personal computers, portable computers and the like. *The fifth generation computer,* which is presently in the developing stage, may use new switch (such as the High Electron Mobility Transistor) instead of the present one and it may herald the era of superconducting computer. It is said that fifth generation computer will be 50 times or so more faster than the present day superfast machines.

So far as input devices in computers are concerned, the card or tape-based data entry system has almost been replaced by direct entry devices, such as Visual Display Unit (VDU) which consist of a TV-like screen and a typewriter-like key board which is used for feeding data into the computer. Regarding output devices, the teleprinter has been substituted by various types of low-cost high speed printers. VDU is also used as an output device. For storing data, the magnetic tapes and discs

---

* (i) First generation computers were those produced between 1945–60 such as IBM 650, IBM 701.

 (ii) Second generation computers were those produced between 1960–65 such as IBM 1401 Honeywell 40.

 (iii) Third generation computers were those produced between 1965–70 such as IBM System 360, 370.

 (iv) Fourth generation computers are those produced between 1971 to this date such as IBM 3033, HP 3000, Burroughs B 7700.

are being replaced by devices such as bubble memories and optical video discs. In brief, computer technology has become highly sophisticated and is being developed further at a very rapid speed.

THE COMPUTER SYSTEM

In general, all computer systems can be described as containing some kind of input devices, the CPU and some kind of output devices. Figure 15.1 depicts the components of a computer system and their inter-relationship:

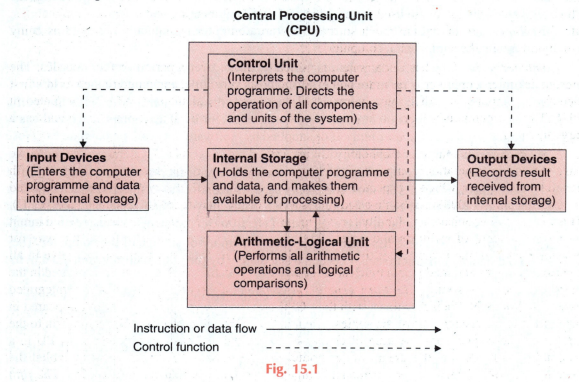

Fig. 15.1

The function of the input-output devices is to get information into, and out of, the CPU. The input devices translate the characters into binary, understandable by the CPU, and the output devices retranslate them back into the familiar character i.e., in a human readable form. In other words, the purpose of the input-output devices is to act as translating devices between our external world and the internal world of the CPU i.e., they act as an interface between man and the machine. So far as CPU is concerned, it has three segments viz. (i) internal storage, (ii) control unit, and (iii) arithmetic logical unit. When a computer program or data is input into the CPU, it is in fact input into the internal storage of the CPU. The control unit serves to direct the sequence of computer system operation. Its function extends to the input and output devices as well and does not just remain confined to the sequence of operation within the CPU. The arithmetic logical unit is concerned with performing the arithmetic operations and logical comparisons designated in the computer program.

In terms of overall sequence of events, a computer program is input into the internal storage and then transmitted to the control unit, where it becomes the basis for overall sequencing and control of computer system operations. Data that is input into the internal storage of the CPU is available for processing by the arithmetic logical unit, which conveys the result of the calculations and comparisons back to the internal storage. After the designated calculations and comparisons have been completed, output is obtained from the internal storage of the CPU.

It would be appropriate to become familiar with the following terms as well in context of computers:

(a) *Hardware:* All the physical components (such as CPU, Input-output devices, storage devices, etc.) of computer are collectively called hardware.

(b) *Software:* It consists of computer programs written by the user which allow the computer to execute instructions.

(c) *Firmware:* It is that software which is incorporated by the manufacturer into the electronic circuitry of computer.

(d) *System software:* It is that program which tells the computer how to function. It is also known as operating software and is normally supplied by the computer manufacturer.

(e) *Application software:* It is that program which tells the computer how to perform specific tasks such as preparation of company pay roll or inventory management. This software is either written by the user himself or supplied by 'software houses', the companies whose business is to produce and sell software.

(f) *Integrated circuit (IC):* It is a complete electronic circuit fabricated on a single piece of pure silicon. Silicon is the most commonly used semiconductor—a material which is neither a good conductor of electricity nor a bad one. An IC may be small-scale, medium-scale or a large-scale depending upon the number of electronic components fabricated on the chip.

(g) *Memory chips:* These ICs form the secondary memory or storage of the computer. They hold data and instructions not needed immediately by the main memory contained in the CPU.

(h) *Two-state devices:* The transistors on an IC Chip take only two states—they are either on or off, conducting or non-conducting. The on-state is represented by 1 and the off-state by zero. These two binary digits are called bits. A string of eight bits is termed byte and a group of bits constitute a word. A chip is called 8-bit, 16-bit, 32-bit and so on, depending on the number of bits contained in its standard word.

IMPORTANT CHARACTERISTICS

The following characteristics of computers are note worthy:

(i) *Speed:* Computers can perform calculations in just a few seconds that human beings would need weeks to do by hand. This has led to many scientific projects which were previously impossible.

(ii) *Diligence:* Being a machine, a computer does not suffer from the human traits of tireness and lack of concentration. If two million calculations have to be performed, it will perform the two millionth with exactly the same accuracy and speed as the first.

(iii) *Storage:* Although the storage capacity of the present day computer is much more than its earlier counterpart but even then the internal memory of the CPU is only large enough to retain a certain amount of information just as the human brain selects and retains what it feels to be important and relegates unimportant details to the back of the mind or just forgets them. Hence, it is impossible to store all types of information inside the computer records. If need be, all unimportant information/data can be stored in auxiliary storage devices and the same may be brought into the main internal memory of the computer, as and when required for processing.

(iv) *Accuracy:* The computer's accuracy is consistently high. Errors in the machinery can occur but, due to increased efficiency in error-detecting techniques, these seldom lead to false results. Almost without exception, the errors in computing are due to human rather than to technological weaknesses, i.e., due to imprecise thinking by the programmer or due to inaccurate data or due to poorly designed systems.

(v) *Automation:* Once a program is in the computer's memory, all that is needed is the individual instructions to it which are transferred one after the other, to the control unit for execution. The CPU follows these instructions until it meets a last instruction which says 'stop program execution'.

(vi) *Binary digits:* Computers use only the binary number system (a system in which all the numbers are represented by a combination of two digits—one and zero) and thus operates to the base of two, compared to the ordinary decimal arithmetic which operates on a base of ten. (Binary system has been described in further details under separate heading in this chapter.) Computers use binary system because the electrical devices can understand only 'on' (1) or 'off' (0).

THE BINARY NUMBER SYSTEM

An arithmetic concept which uses two levels, instead of ten, but operates on the same logic is called the binary system. The binary system uses two symbols '0' and '1', known as bits, to form numbers. The base of this number system is 2. The system is called binary because it allows only two symbols for the formation of numbers. Binary numbers can be constructed just like decimal numbers except that the base is 2 instead of 10.

For example,

$$523 \text{ (decimal)} = 5 \times 10^2 + 2 \times 10^1 + 3 \times 10^0$$

Similarly,

$$111 \text{ (binary)} = 1 \times 2^2 + 1 \times 2^1 + 1 \times 2^0 = 7 \text{ (decimal)}$$

Thus, in the example, we see that in the decimal system, the first place is for 1s, 2nd place is for 10s and the 3rd place is for 100. On the other hand, in the binary system, the factor being 2 instead of 10, the first place is still for 1s but the 2nd place is for 2s, the 3rd for 4s, the 4th for 8s and so on.

Decimal to Binary Conversion: A positive decimal integer can be easily converted to equivalent binary form by repeated division by 2. The method works as follows:

Start by dividing the given decimal integer by 2. Let R_1 be the remainder and q_1 the quotient. Next, divide q_1 by 2 and let R_2 and q_2 be the remainder and quotient respectively. Continue this process of division by 2 until a 0 is obtained as quotient. The equivalent binary number can be formed by arranging the remainders as

$$R_k \, R_{k-1} \, ... \, R_1$$

where R_k and R_1 are the last and the first remainders respectively, obtained by the division process.

Illustration 1

Find the binary equivalents of 26 and 45.

Solution: Table for conversion of 26 into its Binary equivalent:

Number to be divided by 2	Quotient	Remainder
26	13	0
13	6	1
6	3	0
3	1	1
1	0	1

Collecting the remainders obtained in the above table we find that

$$26(\text{decimal}) = 11010 \text{ (binary)}$$

or

$$(26)_{10} = (11010)_2$$

Similarly, we can find the binary equivalent of 45 as under:

Table 15.1

Number to be divided by 2	Quotient	Remainder
45	22	1
22	11	0
11	5	1
5	2	1
2	1	0
1	0	1

Thus, we have $(45)_{10} = (101101)_2$

i.e., the binary equivalent of 45 is 101101.

Alternative method: Another simple method for decimal to binary conversion is to first express the given integer as a sum of powers of 2, written in ascending order. For example,

$$26 = 16 + 8 + 0 + 2 + 0 = 1 \times 2^4 + 1 \times 2^3 + 0 \times 2^2 + 1 \times 2^1 + 0 \times 2^0$$

Then collect the multipliers of the powers to form the binary equivalent. For 26, we get, from the above mentioned expansion 11010 as the binary equivalent. This alternative method is convenient for converting small decimal integers by hand.

Binary to Decimal Conversion: A simple method for converting a binary number to its decimal equivalent is known as double-babble method. This can be described as follows:

Begin the conversion process by doubling the leftmost bit of the given number and add to it the bit at its right. Then again double the sum and add to it the third bit from the left. Proceed in this manner till all the bits have been considered. The final sum obtained by repeated doubling and adding is the desired decimal equivalent.

Illustration 2

Convert 1101 to its decimal equivalent using the double-babble method.

Solution:

1. Doubling the leftmost bit we get 2.
2. Adding to it the bit on its right we get $2 + 1 = 3$
3. Doubling again the number obtained we get 6
4. Adding to it the next bit we get $6 + 0 = 6$
5. Again doubling we get 12
6. Finally adding the last bit we get $12 + 1 = 13$

 Thus, we have $(1101)_2 = (13)_{10}$

 In other words, the decimal equivalent of binary 1101 is 13.

(Conversion of real number to binary number is also possible but it involves little bit more complicated conversion process. Those interested may read any binary system book.)

Computations in Binary System

(a) *Binary addition:* Binary addition is just like decimal addition except that the rules are much simpler. The binary addition rules are as shown below:

0	0	1	1
+ 0	+ 1	+ 0	+ 1
0	1	1	10

Note that sum of 1 and 1 is written as '10' (a zero sum with a 1 carry) which is the equivalent of decimal digit '2'. We can now look at two examples of binary additions which make use of the above rules.

Illustration 3

Add 1010 and 101.

Solution:

Binary	Decimal equivalent
1010	(10)
+101	+(5)
1111	(15)

Illustration 4

Add 10111000 and 111011.

Solution:

	Carry 111		Carry 11
	10111000		184
	+ 111011		+ 59
	11110011		243

In Illustration 4, we find a new situation $(1 + 1 + 1)$ brought about by the 1 carry. However, we can still handle this by using the four combinations already mentioned. We add the digits in turn. $1 + 1 = 10$ (a zero sum with a 1 carry). The third 1 is now added to this result to obtain 11 (a 1 sum with a 1 carry).

The computer performs all the other arithmetical operations (viz. ×, −, +) by a form of addition. This is easily seen in the case of multiplication, e.g., 6×8 may be thought of as essentially being determined by evaluating, with necessary carry overs, $8 + 8 + 8 + 8 + 8 + 8$. This idea of repeated addition may seem to be a longer way of doing things, but remember that computer is well suited to carry out the operation at great speed. Subtraction and division are handled essentially by addition using the principle of complementing.

(b) *Complementary subtraction:* Three steps are involved in this method:

Step 1. Find the ones complement of the number you are subtracting;

Step 2. Add this to number from which you are taking away;

Step 3. If there is a carry of 1 add it to obtain the result; if there is no carry, add 0, recomplement and attach a negative sign to obtain the result.

Following two examples illustrate this method.

Illustration 5

Subtract 10 from 25.

Solution:

Decimal number	Binary number		According to complementary method	
25	11001		11001	
Subtract 10	01010	Step 1	+ 10101	(Ones complement of 01010)
15		Step 2	101110	
		Step 3	⌐→ 1	(add the carry of 1)
		Result	1111	Its decimal equivalent is 15.

Illustration 6

Subtract 72 from 14.

Solution:

Decimal number	Binary number		According to complementary method
14	0001110		0001110
Subtract 72	1001000	Step 1.	+0110111 (ones complement of 1001000)
−58		Step 2.	01000101
		Step 3.	⌐→ 0 (add 0 as no carry)
			1000101
		Result	−0111010 (recomplement and attach a negative sign). Its decimal equivalent is −58.

The computer performs the division operation essentially by repeating this complementary subtraction method. For example, $45 \div 9$ may be thought of as $45 - 9 = 36 - 9 = 27 - 9 = 18 - 9 = 9 - 9 = 0$ (minus 9 five times).

Binary Fractions

Just as we use a decimal point to separate the whole and decimal fraction parts of a decimal number, we can use a binary point in binary numbers to separate the whole and fractional parts. The binary fraction can be converted into decimal fraction as shown below:

$$0.101 \text{ (binary)} = (1 \times 2^{-1}) + (0 \times 2^{-2}) + (1 \times 2^{-3})$$
$$= 0.5 + 0.0 + 0.125$$
$$= 0.625 \text{ (decimal)}$$

To convert the decimal fraction to binary fraction, the following rules are applied:

   (i) Multiply the decimal fraction repeatedly by 2. The whole number part of the first multiplication gives the first 1 or 0 of the binary fraction;
   (ii) The fractional part of the result is carried over and multiplied by 2;
   (iii) The whole number part of the result gives the second 1 or 0 and so on.

Illustration 7

Convert 0.625 into its equivalent binary fraction.

Solution:

Applying the above rules, this can be done as under:

$$0.625 \times 2 = 1.250 \rightarrow 1$$
$$0.250 \times 2 = 0.500 \rightarrow 0$$
$$0.500 \times 2 = 1.000 \rightarrow 1$$

Hence, 0.101 is the required binary equivalent.

Illustration 8

Convert 3.375 into its equivalent binary number.

Solution:

This can be done in two stages. First $(3)_{10} = (11)_2$ as shown earlier. Secondly, $(0.375)_{10} = (0.011)_2$ as shown above. Hence, the required binary equivalent is 11.011.

From all this above description we find how computer arithmetic is based on addition. Exactly how this simplifies matters can only be understood in the context of binary (not in decimal). The number of individual steps may indeed be increased because all computer arithmetic is reduced to addition, but the computer can carry out binary additions at such great speed that this is not a disadvantage.

COMPUTER APPLICATIONS

At present, computers are widely used for varied purposes. Educational, commercial, industrial, administrative, transport, medical, social financial and several other organisations are increasingly depending upon the help of computers to some degree or the other. Even if our work does not involve the use of computers in our everyday work, as individuals, we are affected by them. "The motorists, the air passenger, hospital patients and those working in large departmental stores, are some of the people for whom computers process information. Everyone who pays for electricity or telephone has their bills processed by computers. Many people who are working in major organisations and receive monthly salary have their salary slips prepared by computers. Thus, it is difficult to find anyone who in some way or the other does not have some information concerning them processed by computer".[1] "Computers can be used by just about anyone: doctors, policemen, pilots, scientists, engineers and recently even house-wives. Computers are used not only in numeric applications but also in non-numeric applications such as proving theorems, playing chess, preparing menu, matrimonial match-making and so on. Without computers we might not have achieved a number of things. For example, man could not have landed on the moon nor could he have launched satellites. We might not have built 100 storied buildings or high speed trains and planes."[2]

The following table depicts some of the important applications and uses of computers:

Table 15.2

Applications in	Some of the various uses
1. Education	(i) Provide a large data bank of information;
	(ii) Aid to time-tabling;
	(iii) Carry out lengthy or complex calculations;
	(iv) Assist teaching and learning processes;
	(v) Provide students' profiles;
	(vi) Assist in career guidance.

Contd.

[1] N. Subramanian, *"Introduction to Computers"*, Tata McGraw-Hill Publishing Company Ltd., New Delhi, 1986, p. 192.

[2] *Ibid.*, p. 192–93.

Applications in	Some of the various uses
2. Commerce	(i) Assist the production of text material (known as word processing) such as reports, letters, circulars etc.
	(ii) Handle payroll of personnel, office accounts, invoicing, records keeping, sales analysis, stock control and financial forecasting.
3. Banks and Financial institutions	(i) Cheque handling;
	(ii) Updating of accounts;
	(iii) Printing of customer statements;
	(iv) Interest calculations.
4. Management	(i) Planning of new enterprises;
	(ii) Finding the best solution from several options;
	(iii) Helpful in inventory management, sales forecasting and production planning;
	(iv) Useful in scheduling of projects.
5. Industry	(i) In process control;
	(ii) In production control;
	(iii) Used for load control by electricity authorities;
	(iv) Computer aided designs to develop new products.
6. Communications and Transportation	(i) Helpful in electronic mail;
	(ii) Useful in aviation: Training of pilots, seat reservations, provide information to pilots about weather conditions;
	(iii) Facilitate routine jobs such as crew schedules, time-tables, maintenance schedules, safety systems, etc.;
	(iv) Helpful to railways, shipping companies;
	(v) Used in traffic control and also in space flight.
7. Scientific Research	(i) Model processing;
	(ii) Performing computations;
	(iii) Research and data analysis.
8. The homes	(i) Used for playing games such as chess, draughts, etc.;
	(ii) Can be used as an educational aid;
	(iii) Home management is facilitated.

COMPUTERS AND RESEARCHERS

Performing calculations almost at the speed of light, the computer has become one of the most useful research tools in modern times. Computers are ideally suited for data analysis concerning large research projects. Researchers are essentially concerned with huge storage of data, their faster retrieval when required and processing of data with the aid of various techniques. In all these operations, computers are of great help. Their use, apart expediting the research work, has reduced human drudgery and added to the quality of research activity.

Researchers in economics and other social sciences have found, by now, electronic computers to constitute an indispensable part of their research equipment. The computers can perform many statistical calculations easily and quickly. Computation of means, standard deviations, correlation coefficients, 't' tests, analysis of variance, analysis of covariance, multiple regression, factor analysis and various nonparametric analyses are just a few of the programs and subprograms that are available at almost all computer centres. Similarly, canned programs for linear programming, multivariate analysis, monte carlo simulation etc. are also available in the market. In brief, software packages are readily available for the various simple and complicated analytical and quantitative techniques of which researchers generally make use of. The only work a researcher has to do is to feed in the data he/she gathered after loading the operating system and particular software package on the computer. The output, or to say the result, will be ready within seconds or minutes depending upon the quantum of work.

Techniques involving trial and error process are quite frequently employed in research methodology. This involves lot of calculations and work of repetitive nature. Computer is best suited for such techniques, thus reducing the drudgery of researchers on the one hand and producing the final result rapidly on the other. Thus. different scenarios are made available to researchers by computers in no time which otherwise might have taken days or even months.

The storage facility which the computers provide is of immense help to a researcher for he can make use of stored up data whenever he requires to do so.

Thus, computers do facilitate the research work. Innumerable data can be processed and analyzed with greater ease and speed. Moreover, the results obtained are generally correct and reliable. Not only this, even the design, pictorial graphing and report are being developed with the help of computers. Hence, researchers should be given computer education and be trained in the line so that they can use computers for their research work.

Researchers interested in developing skills in computer data analysis, while consulting the computer centers and reading the relevant literature, must be aware of the following steps:

(i)   data organisation and coding;

(ii) storing the data in the computer;

(iii) selection of appropriate statistical measures/techniques;

(iv) selection of appropriate software package;

(v)   execution of the computer program.

A brief mention about each of the above steps is appropriate and can be stated as under:

First of all, researcher must pay attention toward data organisation and coding prior to the input stage of data analysis. If data are not properly organised, the researcher may face difficulty while analysing their meaning later on. For this purpose the data must be coded. Categorical data need to be given a number to represent them. For instance, regarding sex, we may give number 1 for male and 2 for female; regarding occupation, numbers 1, 2, and 3 may represent Farmer, Service and Professional respectively. The researcher may as well code interval or ratio data. For instance, I.Q. Level with marks 120 and above may be given number 1, 90–119 number 2, 60–89 number 3, 30–59 number 4 and 29 and below number 5. Similarly, the income data classified in class intervals such as Rs. 4000 and above, Rs. 3000–3999, Rs. 2000–2999 and below Rs. 2000 may respectively be represented or coded as 1, 2, 3 and 4. The coded data are to be put in coding forms (most systems call for a maximum of 80 columns per line in such forms) at the appropriate space meant for each variable. Once the researcher knows how many spaces each variable will occupy, the variables can be assigned to their column numbers (from 1 to 80). If more than 80 spaces are required for each subject, then two or more lines will need to be assigned. The first few columns are generally devoted for subject identity number. Remaining columns are used for variables. When large number of variables are used in a study, separating the variables with spaces make the data easier to comprehend and easier for use with other programs.

Once the data is coded, it is ready to be stored in the computer. Input devices may be used for the purpose. After this, the researcher must decide the appropriate statistical measure(s) he will use to analyse the data. He will also have to select the appropriate program to be used. Most researchers prefer one of the canned programs easily available but others may manage to develop it with the help of some specialised agency. Finally, the computer may be operated to execute instructions.

The above description indicates clearly the usefulness of computers to researchers in data analysis. Researchers, using computers, can carry on their task at faster speed and with greater reliability. The developments now taking place in computer technology will further enhance and facilitate the use of computers for researchers. Programming knowledge would no longer remain an obstacle in the use of a computer.

In spite of all this sophistication we should not forget that basically computers are machines that only compute, they do not think. The human brain remains supreme and will continue to be so for all times. As such, researchers should be fully aware about the following limitations of computer-based analysis:

1. Computerised analysis requires setting up of an elaborate system of monitoring, collection and feeding of data. All these require time, effort and money. Hence, computer based analysis may not prove economical in case of small projects.

2. Various items of detail which are not being specifically fed to computer may get lost sight of.

3. The computer does not think; it can only execute the instructions of a thinking person. If poor data or faulty programs are introduced into the computer, the data analysis would not be worthwhile. The expression "garbage in, garbage out" describes this limitation very well.

Questions

1. What is a computer? Point out the difference between a digital computer and analogue computer.
2. How are computers used as a tool in research? Explain giving examples.
3. Explain the meaning of the following terms in context of computers:
   (a) Hardware and Software
   (b) The binary number system
   (c) Computer generations
   (d) Central Processing Unit.
4. Describe some of the important applications and uses of computers in present times.

5. "The advancement in computers is astonishing". Do you agree? Answer pointing out the various characteristics of computers.

6. Write a note on "Computers and Researchers".

7. "Inspite of the sophistication achieved in computer technology, one should not forget that basically computers are machines that only compute, they do not think". Comment.

8. Add 110011 and 1011. State the decimal equivalent of the sum you arrive at.

9. Explain the method of complementary subtraction.

   Subtract 15 from 45 and 85 from 68 through this method using the binary equivalents of the given decimal numbers.

10. Workout the decimal equivalents of the following binary numbers:

    (a) 111.110

    (b) 0.111

    and binary equivalents of the following decimal numbers:

    (a) 4.210

    (b) 0.745

11. Convert 842 to binary and 10010101001 to decimal. Why binary system is being used in computer?

12. What do you understand by storage in a computer and how is that related to the generations?

Appendix
(Selected Statistical Tables)

Table 1: Area Under Normal Curve

An entry in the table is the proportion under the entire curve which is between $z = 0$ and a positive value of z. Areas for negative values for z are obtained by symmetry.

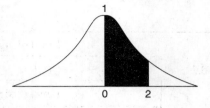

Areas of a standard normal distribution

z	.0	0.01	.02	.03	.04	.05	.06	.07	.08	.09
.0	.0000	.0040	.0080	.0120	.0160	.0199	.0239	.0279	.0319	.0359
.1	.0398	.0438	.0478	.0517	.0557	.0596	.0636	.0675	.0714	.0753
.2	.0793	.0832	.0871	.0910	.0948	.0987	.1026	.1064	.1103	.1141
.3	.1179	.1217	.1255	.1293	.1331	.1368	.1406	.1443	.1480	.1517
.4	.1554	.1591	.1628	.1664	.1700	.1736	.1772	.1808	.1844	.1879
.5	.1915	.1950	.1985	.2019	.2054	.2088	.2123	.2157	.2190	.2224
.6	.2257	.2291	.2324	.2357	.2389	.2422	.2454	.2486	.2517	.2549
.7	.2580	.2611	.2642	.2673	.2903	.2734	.2764	.2794	.2823	.2852
.8	.2881	.2910	.2939	.2967	.2995	.3023	.3051	.3078	.3106	.3133
.9	.3159	.3186	.3212	.3238	.3264	.3289	.3315	.3340	.3365	.3389
1.0	.3413	.3438	.3461	.3485	.3508	.3531	.3554	.3577	.3599	.3621
1.1	.3643	.3665	.3686	.3708	.3729	.3749	.3770	.3790	.3810	.3830
1.2	.3849	.3869	.3888	.3907	.3925	.3944	.3962	.3980	.3997	.4015
1.3	.4032	.4049	.4066	.4082	.4099	.4115	.4131	.4147	.4162	.4177
1.4	.4192	.4207	.4222	.4236	.4251	.4265	.4279	.4292	.4306	.4319
1.5	.4332	.4345	.4357	.4370	.4382	.4394	.4406	.4418	.4429	.4441
1.6	.4452	.4463	.4474	.4484	.4495	.4505	.4515	.4525	.4535	.4545
1.7	.4554	.4564	.4573	.4582	.4591	.4599	.4608	.4616	.4625	.4633
1.8	.4641	.4649	.4656	.4664	.4671	.4678	.4686	.4693	.4699	.4706
1.9	.4713	.4719	.4726	.4732	.4738	.4744	.4750	.4756	.4761	.4767
2.0	.4772	.4778	.4783	.4788	.4793	.4798	.4803	.4808	.4812	.4817
2.1	.4821	.4826	.4830	.4834	.4838	.4842	.4846	.4850	.4854	.4857
2.2	.4861	.4864	.4868	.4871	.4875	.4878	.4881	.4884	.4887	.4890
2.3	.4893	.4896	.4898	.4901	.4904	.4906	.4909	.4911	.4913	.4916
2.4	.4918	.4920	.4922	.4925	.4927	.4929	.4931	.4932	.4934	.4936
2.5	.4938	.4940	.4941	.4943	.4945	.4946	.4948	.4949	.4951	.4952
2.6	.4953	.4955	.4956	.4957	.4959	.4960	.4961	.4962	.4963	.4964
2.7	.4965	.4966	.4967	.4968	.4969	.4970	.4971	.4972	.4973	.4974
2.8	.4974	.4975	.4976	.4977	.4977	.4978	.4979	.4979	.4980	.4981
2.9	.4981	.4982	.4982	.4983	.4984	.4984	.4985	.4985	.4986	.4986
3.0	.4987	.4987	.4987	.4988	.4988	.4989	.4989	.4989	.4990	.4990

Table 2: Critical Values of Student's *t*-Distribution

d.f.	Level of significance for two-tailed test					d.f.
	0.20	0.10	0.05	0.02	0.01	
	Level of significance for one-tailed test					
	0.10	0.05	0.025	0.01	0.005	
1	3.078	6.314	12.706	31.821	63.657	1
2	1.886	2.920	4.303	6.965	9.925	2
3	1.638	2.353	3.182	4.541	5.841	3
4	1.533	2.132	2.776	3.747	4.604	4
5	1.476	2.015	2.571	3.365	4.032	5
6	1.440	1.943	2.447	3.143	3.707	6
7	1.415	1.895	2.365	2.998	3.499	7
8	1.397	1.860	2.306	2.896	3.355	8
9	1.383	1.833	2.262	2.821	3.250	9
10	1.372	1.812	2.228	2.764	3.169	10
11	1.363	1.796	2.201	2.718	3.106	11
12	1.356	1.782	2.179	2.681	3.055	12
13	1.350	1.771	2.160	2.650	3.012	13
14	1.345	1.761	2.145	2.624	2.977	14
15	1.341	1.753	2.731	2.602	2.947	15
16	1.337	1.746	2.120	2.583	2.921	16
17	1.333	1.740	2.110	2.567	2.898	17
18	1.330	1.734	2.101	2.552	2.878	18
19	1.328	1.729	2.093	2.539	2.861	19
20	1.325	1.725	2.086	2.528	2.845	20
21	1.323	1.721	2.080	2.518	2.831	21
22	1.321	1.717	2.074	2.508	2.819	22
23	1.319	1.714	2.069	2.500	2.807	23
24	1.318	1.711	2.064	2.492	2.797	24
25	1.316	1.708	2.060	2.485	2.787	25
26	1.315	1.706	2.056	2.479	2.779	26
27	1.314	1.703	2.052	2.473	2.771	27
28	1.313	1.701	2.048	2.467	2.763	28
29	1.311	1.699	2.045	2.462	2.756	29
Infinity	1.282	1.645	1.960	2.326	2.576	Infinity

Table 3: Critical Values of χ^2

Degrees of freedom	Probability under H_0 that of $\chi^2 >$ Chi square						
	.99	.95	.50	.10	.05	.02	.01
1	.000157	.00393	.455	2.706	3.841	5.412	6.635
2	.0201	.103	1.386	4.605	5.991	7.824	9.210
3	.115	.352	2.366	6.251	7.815	9.837	11.341
4	.297	.711	3.357	7.779	9.488	11.668	13.277
5	.554	.1145	4.351	9.236	11.070	13.388	15.086
6	.872	1.635	5.348	10.645	12.592	15.033	16.812
7	1.239	2.167	6.346	12.017	14.067	16.622	18.475
8	1.646	2.733	7.344	13.362	15.507	18.168	20.090
9	2.088	3.325	8.343	14.684	16.919	19.679	21.666
10	2.558	3.940	9.342	15.987	18.307	21.161	23.209
11	3.053	4.575	10.341	17.275	19.675	22.618	24.725
12	3.571	5.226	11.340	18.549	21.026	24.054	26.217
13	4.107	5.892	12.340	19.812	22.362	25.472	72.688
14	4.660	6.571	13.339	21.064	23.685	26.873	29.141
15	4.229	7.261	14.339	22.307	24.996	28.259	30.578
16	5.812	7.962	15.338	23.542	26.296	29.633	32.000
17	6.408	8.672	16.338	24.769	27.587	30.995	33.409
18	7.015	9.390	17.338	25.989	28.869	32.346	34.805
19	7.633	10.117	18.338	27.204	30.144	33.687	36.191
20	8.260	10.851	19.337	28.412	31.410	35.020	37.566
21	8.897	11.591	20.337	29.615	32.671	36.343	38.932
22	9.542	12.338	21.337	30.813	33.924	37.659	40.289
23	10.196	13.091	22.337	32.007	35.172	38.968	41.638
24	10.856	13.848	23.337	32.196	36.415	40.270	42.980
25	11.524	14.611	24.337	34.382	37.652	41.566	44.314
26	12.198	15.379	25.336	35.363	38.885	41.856	45.642
27	12.879	16.151	26.336	36.741	40.113	44.140	46.963
28	13.565	16.928	27.336	37.916	41.337	45.419	48.278
29	14.256	17.708	28.336	39.087	42.557	46.693	49.588
30	14.953	18.493	29.336	40.256	43.773	47.962	50.892

Note: For degrees of freedom greater than 30, the quantity $\sqrt{2\chi^2} - \sqrt{2 \text{d.f.} - 1}$ may be used as a normal variate with unit variance i.e., $z_\alpha = \sqrt{2\chi^2} - \sqrt{2 \text{d.f.} - 1}$.

Table 4(a): Critical Values of *F*-Distribution (at 5 per cent)

v_2 \ v_1	1	2	3	4	5	6	8	12	24	∞
1	161.4	199.5	215.7	224.6	230.2	234.0	238.9	243.9	249.1	243.3
2	18.51	19.00	19.16	19.25	19.30	19.33	19.37	19.41	19.45	19.50
3	10.13	9.55	9.28	9.12	9.01	8.94	8.85	8.74	8.64	8.53
4	7.71	6.94	6.59	6.39	6.26	6.16	6.04	5.91	5.77	5.63
5	6.61	5.79	5.41	5.19	5.05	4.95	4.82	4.68	4.53	4.36
6	5.99	5.14	4.76	4.53	4.39	4.28	4.15	4.00	3.84	3.67
7	5.59	4.74	4.35	4.12	3.97	3.87	3.73	3.57	3.41	3.23
8	5.32	4.46	4.07	3.84	3.69	3.58	3.44	3.28	3.12	2.93
9	5.12	4.26	3.86	3.63	3.48	3.37	3.23	3.07	2.90	2.71
10	4.96	4.10	3.71	3.48	3.33	3.22	3.07	2.91	2.74	2.54
11	4.84	3.98	3.59	3.36	3.20	3.09	2.95	2.79	2.61	2.40
12	4.75	3.88	3.49	3.26	3.11	3.00	2.85	2.69	2.51	2.30
13	4.67	3.80	3.41	3.18	3.02	2.92	2.77	2.60	2.42	2.21
14	4.60	3.74	3.34	3.11	2.96	2.85	2.70	2.53	2.35	2.13
15	4.54	3.68	3.29	3.06	2.90	2.79	2.64	2.48	2.29	2.07
16	4.49	3.63	3.24	3.01	2.85	2.74	2.59	2.42	2.24	2.01
17	4.45	3.59	3.20	2.96	2.81	2.70	2.55	2.38	2.19	1.96
18	4.41	3.55	3.16	2.93	2.77	2.66	2.51	2.34	2.15	1.92
19	4.38	3.52	3.13	2.90	2.74	2.63	2.48	2.31	2.11	1.88
20	4.35	3.49	3.10	2.87	2.71	2.60	2.45	2.28	2.08	1.84
21	4.32	3.47	3.07	2.84	2.68	2.57	2.42	2.25	2.05	1.81
22	4.30	3.44	3.05	2.82	2.66	2.55	2.40	2.23	2.03	1.78
23	4.28	3.42	3.03	2.80	2.64	2.53	2.38	2.20	2.01	1.76
24	4.26	3.40	3.01	2.78	2.62	2.51	2.36	2.18	1.98	1.73
25	4.24	3.38	2.99	2.76	2.60	2.49	2.34	2.16	1.96	1.71
26	4.22	3.37	2.98	2.74	2.59	2.47	2.32	2.15	1.95	1.69
27	4.21	3.35	2.96	2.73	2.57	2.46	2.31	2.13	1.93	1.67
28	4.20	3.34	2.95	2.71	2.56	2.45	2.29	2.12	1.91	1.65
29	4.18	3.33	2.93	2.70	2.54	2.43	2.28	2.10	1.90	1.64
30	4.17	3.32	2.92	2.69	2.53	2.42	2.27	2.09	1.89	1.62
40	4.08	3.23	2.84	2.61	2.45	2.34	2.18	2.00	1.79	1.51
60	4.00	3.15	2.76	2.52	2.37	2.25	2.10	1.92	1.70	1.39
120	3.92	3.07	2.68	2.45	2.29	2.17	2.02	1.83	1.61	1.25
∞	3.84	2.99	2.60	2.37	2.21	2.10	1.94	1.75	1.52	1.00

v_1 = Degrees of freedom for greater variance.

v_2 = Degrees of freedom for smaller variance.

Table 4(b): Critical Values of *F*-Distribution (at 1 per cent)

v_2 \ v_1	1	2	3	4	5	6	8	12	24	∞
1	4052	4999.5	5403	5625	5764	5859	5982	6106	6235	6366
2	98.50	99.00	99.17	99.25	99.30	99.33	99.37	99.42	99.46	99.50
3	34.12	30.82	29.46	28.71	28.24	27.91	27.49	27.05	26.60	26.13
4	21.20	18.00	16.69	15.98	15.52	15.21	14.80	14.37	13.93	13.45
5	16.26	13.27	12.06	11.39	10.97	10.67	10.29	9.89	9.47	9.02
6	13.75	10.92	9.78	9.15	8.75	8.47	8.10	7.72	7.31	6.88
7	12.25	9.55	8.45	7.85	7.46	7.19	6.84	6.47	6.07	5.65
8	11.26	8.65	7.59	7.01	6.63	6.37	6.03	5.67	5.28	4.86
9	10.56	8.02	6.99	6.42	6.06	5.80	5.47	5.11	4.73	4.31
10	10.04	7.56	6.55	5.99	5.64	5.39	5.06	4.71	4.33	3.91
11	9.65	7.21	6.22	5.87	5.32	5.07	4.74	4.40	4.02	3.60
12	9.33	6.93	5.95	5.41	5.06	4.82	4.50	4.16	3.78	3.36
13	9.07	6.70	5.74	5.21	4.86	4.62	4.30	3.96	3.59	3.17
14	8.86	6.51	5.56	5.04	4.69	4.46	4.14	3.80	3.43	3.00
15	8.68	6.36	5.42	4.89	4.56	4.32	4.00	3.67	3.29	2.87
16	8.53	6.23	5.29	4.77	4.44	4.20	3.89	3.55	3.18	2.75
17	8.40	6.11	5.18	4.67	4.34	4.10	3.79	3.46	3.08	2.65
18	8.29	6.01	5.09	4.58	4.25	4.01	3.71	3.37	3.00	2.57
19	8.18	5.93	5.01	4.50	4.17	3.94	3.63	3.30	3.92	2.49
20	8.10	5.85	4.94	4.43	4.10	3.87	3.56	3.23	2.86	2.42
21	8.02	5.78	4.87	4.37	4.04	3.81	3.51	3.17	2.80	2.36
22	7.95	5.72	4.82	4.31	3.99	3.76	3.45	3.12	2.75	2.31
23	7.88	5.66	4.76	4.26	3.94	3.71	3.41	3.07	2.70	2.26
24	7.82	5.61	4.72	4.22	3.90	3.67	3.36	3.03	2.66	2.21
25	7.77	5.57	4.68	4.18	3.85	3.63	3.32	2.99	2.62	2.17
26	7.72	5.53	4.64	4.14	3.82	3.59	3.20	2.96	2.58	2.10
27	7.68	5.49	4.60	4.11	3.78	3.56	3.26	2.93	2.45	2.13
28	7.64	5.45	4.57	4.07	3.75	3.53	3.23	2.90	2.52	2.06
29	7.60	5.42	4.54	4.04	3.73	3.50	3.20	2.87	2.49	2.03
30	7.56	5.39	4.51	4.02	3.70	3.47	3.17	2.84	2.47	2.01
40	7.31	5.18	4.31	3.83	3.51	3.29	2.99	2.66	2.29	1.80
60	7.08	4.98	4.13	3.65	3.34	3.12	2.82	2.50	2.12	1.60
120	6.85	4.79	3.95	3.48	3.17	2.96	2.66	2.34	1.95	1.38
∞	6.64	4.60	3.78	3.32	3.02	2.80	2.51	2.18	1.79	1.00

v_1 = Degrees of freedom for greater variance.
v_2 = Degrees of freedom for smaller variance.

Table 5: Values for Spearman's Rank Correlation (r_s) for Combined Areas in Both Tails

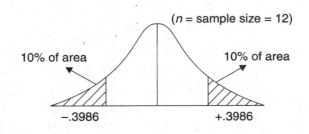

(n = sample size = 12)

10% of area   10% of area

−.3986   +.3986

n	.20	.10	.05	.02	.01	.002
4	.8000	.8000	—	—	—	—
5	.7000	.8000	.9000	.9000	—	—
6	.6000	.7714	.8236	.8857	.9429	—
7	.5357	.6786	.7450	.8571	.8929	.9643
8	.5000	.6190	.7143	.8095	.8571	.9286
9	.4667	.5833	.6833	.7667	.8167	.9000
10	.4424	.5515	.6364	.7333	.7818	.8667
11	.4182	.5273	.6091	.7000	.7455	.8364
12	.3986	.4965	.5804	.6713	.7273	.8182
13	.3791	.4780	.5549	.6429	.6978	.7912
14	.3626	.4593	.5341	.6220	.6747	.7670
15	.3500	.4429	.5179	.6000	.6536	.7464
16	.3382	.4265	.5000	.5824	.6324	.7265
17	.3260	.4118	.4853	.5637	.6152	.708
18	.3148	.3994	.4716	.5480	.5975	
19	.3070	.3895	.4579	.5333	.5825	
20	.2977	.3789	.4451	.5203	.5684	.55
21	.2909	.3688	.4351	.5078	.5545	.6318
22	.2829	.3597	.4241	.4963	.542	.6186
23	.2767	.3518	.4150	.4852	.5	.6070
24	.2704	.3435	.4061	.4748		.5962
25	.2646	.3362	.3977	.4654		.5856
26	.2588	.3299	.3894	.4564		.5757
27	.2540	.3236	.3822	.4481		.5660
28	.2480	.3175	.3749	.44		.5567
29	.2443	.3113	.3685			.5479
30	.2400	.3059	.3620			

Table 6: Selected [illegible]es of Wilcoxon's (Unpaired) Distribution $[W_s - \text{Min } W_s]$ or $[\text{Max. } W_l - W_l]$

s	l	Min W_s	Max W_l	0	1	2	3	4	5	6	7	8	9	10	11	12	13	14	15	16	17	18	19	20
				[illegible]	.190																			
		3	7	.071	.143																			
2	2	3	18	.056	.111																			
	3	3		.022	.044	.089	.133																	
	4			.100																				
	5		15	.050	.100																			
			22	.029	.057	.114																		
		6	30	.018	.036	.071	.125																	
		6	39	.012	.024	.048	.083	.131																
	7	6	49	.008	.017	.033	.058	.092	.133															
	8	6	60	.006	.012	.024	.042	.067	.097	.139														
4	2	10	11	.007	*																			
	3	10	18	.029	.057	.114																		
	4	10	26	.014	.029	.057	.100																	
	5	10	35	.008	.016	.032	.056	.095	.143															
	6	10	45	.005	.010	.019	.033	.057	.086	.129														
	7	10	56	.003	.006	.012	.021	.036	.055	.082	.115													
	8	10	68	.002	.004	.008	.014	.024	.036	.055	.077	.107												
5	3	15	21	.018	.036	.071	.125	*																
	4	15	30	.008	.016	.032	.056	.095	.143															
	5	15	40	.004	.008	.016	.028	.048	.075	.111														
	6	15	51	.002	.004	.009	.015	.026	.041	.063	.089	.123												
	7	15	63	.001	.003	.005	.009	.015	.024	.037	.053	.074	.101											
	8	15	76	.001	.002	.003	.005	.009	.015	.023	.033	.047	.064	.085	.111									

(*Contd.*)

s	l	Min W_s	Max W_l	0	1	2	3	4	5	6	7	8	9	10	11	12	13	14	15	16	17	18	19	20
6	3	21	24	.012	.024	*																		
	4	21	34	.005	.010	.019	.033	.057	.086	.129	*													
	5	21	45	.002	.004	.009	.015	.026	.041	.063	.089	.123												
	6	21	57	.001	.002	.004	.008	.013	.021	.032	.047	.066	.090	.120										
	7	21	70	.001	.001	.002	.004	.007	.011	.017	.026	.037	.051	.069	.090	.117								
	8	21	84	.000	.001	.001	.002	.004	.006	.010	.015	.021	.030	.041	.054	.071	.091	.114						
7	4	28	38	.003	.006	.012	.021	.036	.055*															
	5	28	50	.001	.003	.005	.009	.015	.024	.037	.053	.074	.101											
	6	28	63	.001	.001	.002	.004	.007	.011	.017	.026	.037	.051	.069	.090	.117								
	7	28	77	.000	.001	.001	.002	.003	.006	.009	.013	.019	.027	.036	.049	.064	.082	.104						
	8	28	92	.000	.000	.001	.001	.002	.003	.005	.007	.010	.014	.020	.027	.036	.047	.060	.076	.095	.116			
8	4	36	42	.002	.004	.008	.014*																	
	5	36	55	.001	.002	.003	.005	.009	.015	.023	.033	.047	.064*											
	6	36	69	.000	.001	.001	.002	.004	.006	.010	.015	.021	.030	.041	.054	.071	.091	.114						
	7	36	84	.000	.000	.001	.001	.002	.003	.005	.007	.010	.014	.020	.027	.036	.047	.060	.076	.095	.116			
	8	36	100	.000	.000	.000	.001	.001	.001	.002	.003	.005	.007	.010	.014	.019	.025	.032	.041	.052	.065	.080	.097	.117

* Indicates that the value at head of this column (add those values that are larger) are not possible for the given values of s and l in this row.

Table 7: Critical Values of *T* in the Wilcoxon Matched Pairs Test

	Level of significance for one-tailed test		
	.025	.01	.005
	Level of significance for two-tailed test		
n	.05	.02	.01
6	0	—	—
7	2	0	—
8	4	2	0
9	6	3	2
10	8	5	3
11	11	7	5
12	14	10	7
13	17	13	10
14	21	16	13
15	25	20	16
16	30	24	20
17	35	28	23
18	40	33	28
19	46	38	32
20	52	43	38
21	59	49	43
22	66	56	49
23	73	62	55
24	81	69	61
25	89	77	68

Table 8: Cumulative Binomial Probabilities: P $(r \gtrless r|n, p)$

n	r_0	.10	.25	.40	.50
1	0	.9000	.7500	.6000	.5000
	1	1.0000	1.0000	1.0000	1.0000
2	0	.8100	.5625	.3600	.2500
	1	.9900	.9375	.8400	.7500
	2	1.0000	1.0000	1.0000	1.0000
5	0	.5905	.2373	.0778	.0313
	1	.9185	.6328	.3370	.1875
	2	.9914	.8965	.6826	.5000
	3	.9995	.9844	.9130	.8125
	4	.9999	.9990	.9898	.9687
	5	1.0000	1.0000	1.0000	1.0000
10	0	.3487	.0563	.0060	.0010
	1	.7361	.2440	.0463	.0108
	2	.9298	.5256	.1672	.0547
	3	.9872	.7759	.3822	.1719
	4	.9984	.9219	.6330	.3770
	5	.9999	.9803	.8337	.6230
	6	1.0000	.9965	.9452	.8281
	7	1.0000	.9996	.9877	.9453
	8	1.0000	1.0000	.9983	.9892
	9	1.0000	1.0000	.9999	.9990
	10	1.0000	1.0000	1.0000	1.0000
12	0	.2824	.0317	.0022	.0002
	1	.6590	.1584	.0196	.0031
	2	.8891	.3907	.0835	.0192
	3	.9740	.6488	.2254	.0729
	4	.9963	.8424	.4382	.1937
	5	.9999	.9456	.6652	.3871
	6	1.0000	.9857	.8418	.6127
	7	1.0000	.9972	.9427	.8064
	8	1.0000	.9996	.9847	.9269
	9	1.0000	1.0000	.9972	.9806
	10	1.0000	1.0000	.9997	.9977
	11	1.0000	1.0000	1.0000	1.0000
	12	1.0000	1.0000	1.0000	1.0000

(Contd.)

n	r_0	.10	.25	.40	.50
20	0	.1216	.0032	.0000	.0000
	1	.3917	.0243	.0005	.0000
	2	.6768	.0912	.0036	.0002
	3	.8669	.2251	.0159	.0013
	4	.9567	.4148	.0509	.0059
	5	.9886	.6171	.1255	.0207
	6	.9975	.7857	.2499	.0577
	7	.9995	.8981	.4158	.1316
	8	.9999	.9590	.5955	.2517
	9	1.0000	.9861	.7552	.4119
	10	1.0000	.9960	.8723	.5881
	11	1.0000	.9990	.9433	.7483
	12	1.0000	.9998	.9788	.8684
	13	1.0000	1.0000	.9934	.9423
	14	1.0000	1.0000	.9983	.9793
	15	1.0000	1.0000	.9996	.9941
	16	1.0000	1.0000	1.0000	.9987
	17	1.0000	1.0000	1.0000	.9998
	18	1.0000	1.0000	1.0000	1.0000
	19	1.0000	1.0000	1.0000	1.0000
	20	1.0000	1.0000	1.0000	1.0000

Table 9: Selected Critical Values of S in the Kendall's Coefficient of Concordance

Values at 5% level of significance

k	N					Some additional values for $N = 3$	
	3	4	5	6	7	k	s
3			64.4	103.9	157.3	9	54.0
4		49.5	88.4	143.3	217.0	12	71.9
5		62.6	112.3	182.4	276.2	14	83.8
6		75.7	136.1	221.4	335.2	16	95.8
8	48.1	101.7	183.7	299.0	453.1	18	107.7
10	60.0	127.8	231.2	376.7	571.0		
15	89.8	192.9	349.8	570.5	864.9		
20	119.7	258.0	468.5	764.4	1158.7		

Values at 1% level of significance

k	3	4	5	6	7	k	s
3			75.6	122.8	185.6	9	75.9
4		61.4	109.3	176.2	265.0	12	103.5
5		80.5	142.8	229.4	343.8	14	121.9
6		99.5	176.1	282.4	422.6	16	140.2
8	66.8	137.4	242.7	388.3	579.9	18	158.6
10	85.1	175.3	309.1	494.0	737.0		
15	131.0	269.8	475.2	758.2	1129.5		
20	177.0	364.2	641.2	1022.2	1521.9		

Table 10: Table Showing Critical Values of *A*-Statistic for any Given Value of *n* – 1, Corresponding to Various Levels of Probability

(*A* is significant at a given level if it is ≲ the value shown in the table)

n – 1*	Level of significance for one-tailed test				
	.05	.025	.01	.005	.0005
	Level of significance for two-tailed test				
	.10	.05	.02	.01	.001
1	2	3	4	5	6
1	0.5125	0.5031	0.50049	0.50012	0.5000012
2	0.412	0.369	0.347	0.340	0.334
3	0.385	0.324	0.286	0.272	0.254
4	0.376	0.304	0.257	0.238	0.211
5	0.372	0.293	0.240	0.218	0.184
6	0.370	0.286	0.230	0.205	0.167
7	0.369	0.281	0.222	0.196	0.155
8	0.368	0.278	0.217	0.190	0.146
9	0.368	0.276	0.213	0.185	0.139
10	0.368	0.274	0.210	0.181	0.134
11	0.368	0.273	0.207	0.178	0.130
12	0.368	0.271	0.205	0.176	0.126
13	0.368	0.270	0.204	0.174	0.124
14	0.368	0.270	0.202	0.172	0.121
15	0.368	0.269	0.201	0.170	0.119
16	0.368	0.268	0.200	0.169	0.117
17	0.368	0.268	0.199	0.168	0.116
18	0.368	0.267	0.198	0.167	0.114
19	0.368	0.267	0.197	0.166	0.113
20	0.368	0.266	0.197	0.165	0.112
21	0.368	0.266	0.196	0.165	0.111
22	0.368	0.266	0.196	0.164	0.110
23	0.368	0.266	0.195	0.163	0.109
24	0.368	0.265	0.195	0.163	0.108
25	0.368	0.265	0.194	0.162	0.108
26	0.368	0.265	0.194	0.162	0.107
27	0.368	0.265	0.193	0.161	0.107
28	0.368	0.265	0.193	0.161	0.106
29	0.368	0.264	0.193	0.161	0.106
30	0.368	0.264	0.193	0.160	0.105

(Contd.)

1	2	3	4	5	6
40	0.368	0.263	0.191	0.158	0.102
60	0.369	0.262	0.189	0.155	0.099
120	0.369	0.261	0.187	0.153	0.095
∞	0.370	0.260	0.185	0.151	0.092

* n = number of pairs

Source: *The Brit. J. Psychol*, Volume XLVI, 1955, p. 226.

Selected References and Recommended Readings

1. Ackoff, Russell L., *The Design of Social Research,* Chicago: University of Chicago Press, 1961.

2. Ackoff, Russell L., *Scientific Method,* New York: John Wiley & Sons, 1962.

3. Allen, T. Harrell, *New Methods in Social Science Research,* New York: Praeger Publishers, 1978.

4. Anderson, H.H., and Anderson, G.L., *An Introduction to Projective Techniques and Other Devices for Understanding the Dynamics of Human Behaviour*, New York: Prentice Hall, 1951.

5. Anderson, T.W., *An Introduction to Multivariate Analysis,* New York: John Wiley & Sons, 1958.

6. Bailey, Kenneth D., *"Methods of Social Research,"* New York, 1978.

7. Baker, R.P., and Howell, A.C., *The Preparation of Reports,* New York: Ronald Press, 1938.

8. Bartee, T.C., *"Digital Computer Fundamentals,"* 5th Ed., McGraw-Hill, International Book Co., 1981.

9. Barzun, Jacques, and Graff, Henery, F., *The Modern Researcher,* rev. ed., New York: Harcourt, Brace & World, Inc., 1970.

10. Bell, J.E., *Projective Techniques: A. Dynamic Approach to the Study of Personality,* New York: Longmans Green, 1948.

11. Bellenger, Danny N., and Greenberg, Barnett A., *Marketing Research—A Management Information Approach,* Homewood, Illinois: Richard D. Irwin, Inc., 1978.

12. Berdie, Douglas R., and Anderson, John F., *Questionnaires: Design and Use,* Metuchen N.J.: The Scarecrow Press, Inc., 1974.

13. Berelson, Bernard, *Content Analysis in Communication Research,* New York: Free Press, 1952.

14. Berenson, Conard, and Colton, Raymond, *Research and Report Writing for Business and Economics,* New York: Random House, 1971.

15. Best, John W., and Kahn, James V., *"Research in Education,"* 5th Ed., New Delhi: Prentice-Hall of India Pvt. Ltd., 1986.

16. Bhattacharya, Srinibas, *Psychometrics & Behavioural Research,* New Delhi: Sterling Publishers Pvt. Ltd., 1972.

17. Boot, John C.G., and Cox, Edwin B., *Statistical Analysis for Managerial Decisions,* 2nd ed. New Delhi: McGraw-Hill Publishing Co. Ltd., (International Student Edition), 1979.

18. Bowley, A.L., *Elements of Statistics,* 6th ed. London: P.S. King and Staples Ltd., 1937.

19. Burgess, Ernest W., "Research Methods in Sociology" in Georges Gurvitch and W.E. Moore (Ed.), *Twentieth Century Sociology,* New York: New York Philosophical Library, 1949.

20. Chance, William A., *Statistical Methods for Decision Making,* Bombay: D.B. Taraporevala Sons & Co. Pvt. Ltd., 1975.

21. Chaturvedi, J.C., *Mathematical Statistics,* Agra: Nok Jhonk Karyalaya, 1953.

22. Chou, Ya-Lun, *Statistical Analysis with Business and Economic Applications,* 2nd ed. New York: Holt, Rinehart & Winston, 1974.

23. Clover, Vernon T., and Balsley, Howard L., *Business Research Methods,* Columbus, O.: Grid, Inc., 1974.

24. Cochran, W.G., *Sampling Techniques,* 2nd ed. New York: John Wiley & Sons., 1963.

25. Cooley, William W., and Lohnes, Paul R., *Multivariate Data Analysis,* New York: John Wiley & Sons., 1971.

26. Croxton, F.E., Cowden, D.J., and Klein, S., *Applied General Statistics,* 3rd ed., New Delhi: Prentice-Hall of India Pvt. Ltd., 1975.

27. Dass, S.L., *Personality Assessment Through Projective Movie Pictures*, New Delhi: S. Chand & Co. (Pvt.) Ltd., 1974.

28. Davis, G.B., *"Introduction to Computers,"* 3rd ed., McGraw-Hill International Book Co., 1981.

29. Deming, W. Edwards., *Sample Design in Business Research,* New York: John Wiley & Sons., Inc., 1960.

30. Dennis, Child, *The Essentials of Factor Analysis,* New York: Holt, Rinehart and Winston, 1973.

31. Denzin, Norman, *The Research Act,* Chicago: Aldine, 1973.

32. Edwards, Allen, *Statistical Methods,* 2nd ed., New York: Holt, Rinehart & Winston, 1967.

33. Edwards, Allen L., *Techniques of Attitude Scale Construction,* New York: Appleton-Century-Crofts, 1957.

34. Emory, C. William, *Business Research Methods*, Illinois: Richard D. Irwin, Inc. Homewood, 1976.

35. Ferber, Robert (ed.), *Handbook of Marketing Research,* New York: McGraw-Hill, Inc., 1948.

36. Ferber, R., and Verdoorn, P.J., *Research Methods in Economics and Business,* New York: The Macmillan Company, 1962.

37. Ferguson, George A., *Statistical Analysis in Psychology and Education*, 4th ed., New York: McGraw-Hill Book Co., Inc., 1959.

38. Festinger, Leon and Katz, Daniel (Eds.), *Research Methods in the Behavioral Sciences,* New Delhi: Amerind Publishing Co. Pvt. Ltd., Fourth Indian Reprint, 1976.

39. Fiebleman, J.K., *Scientific Method*, Netherlands: Martinus Nijhoff, The Hague, 1972.

40. Fisher, R.A., *Statistical Methods for Research Workers,* 13th ed., New York: Hafner Publishing Co., 1958.

41. Fisher, R.A., *The Design of Experiments,* 7th rev. ed., New York: Hafner Publishing Co., 1960.

42. Fox, James Harold, *Criteria of Good Research,* Phi Delta Kappa, Vol. 39 (March 1958).

43. Freedman, P., *The Principles of Scientific Research,* 2nd ed., New York: Pergamon Press, 1960.

44. Fruchter, Benjamin, *Introduction to Factor Analysis,* Princeton, N.J.: D. Van Nostrand, 1954.

45. Gatner, Elliot S.M., and Cordasco, Francesco, *Research and Report Writing*, New York: Barnes & Noble, Inc., 1956.

46. Gaum, Carl G., Graves, Harod F., and Hoffman, Lyne, S.S., *Report Writing*, 3rd ed., New York: Prentice-Hall, 1950.

47. Ghosh, B.N., *Scientific Methods and Social Research,* New Delhi: Sterling Publishers Pvt. Ltd., 1982.

48. Gibbons, J.D., *Nonparametric Statistical Inference,* Tokyo: McGraw-Hill Kogakusha Ltd., (International Student Edition), 1971.

49. Giles, G.B., *Marketing,* 2nd ed., London: Macdonald & Evans Ltd., 1974.

50. Glock, Charles Y., *Survey Research in the Social Sciences,* New York: Russell Sage Foundation, 1967.

51. Godfrey, Arthur, *Quantitative Methods for Managers,* London: Edward Arnold (Publishers) Ltd., 1977.

52. Good, Carter V., and Douglas, E. Scates, *Methods of Research—Educational, Psychological, Sociological,* New York: Appleton-Century-Crofts, Inc., 1954.

53. Goode, William J., and Hatt, Paul K., *Methods in Social Research,* New York: McGraw-Hill, 1952.

54. Gopal, M.H., *An Introduction to Research Procedure in Social Sciences,* Bombay: Asia Publishing House, 1964.

55. Gopal, M.H., *Research Reporting in Social Sciences,* Dharwar: Karnatak University, 1965.

56. Gorden, Raymond L., *Interviewing: Strategy, Techniques and Tactics,* rev. ed., Homewood, Ill.: Dorsey Press, 1975.

57. Green, Paul E., *Analyzing Multivariate Data,* Hinsdale, Ill.: Dryden Press, 1978.

58. Green, Paul E., and Carmone, F.J., *Multidimensional Scaling in Marketing Analysis,* Boston: Allyn & Bacon, Inc., 1970.

59. Guilford, J.P., *Psychometric Methods,* New York: McGraw Hill, Inc., 1954.

60. Harnett, Donald L., and Murphy, James L., *Introductory Statistical Analysis,* Philippines: Addison-Wesley Publishing Co., Inc., 1975.

61. Hillway, T., *Introduction to Research,* 2nd ed., Boston: Houghton Mifflin, 1964.

62. Hollander, Myles, and Wolfe, Douglas A., *Nonparametric Statistical Methods,* New York: John Wiley, 1973.

63. Hunt, R., and Shelley, J., *"Computers and Common Sense,"* 3rd ed., New Delhi: Prentice-Hall of India Ltd., 1984.

64. Hyman, Herbert H., et al., *Interviewing in Social Research,* Chicago: University of Chicago Press, 1975.

65. John, Peter W.M., *Statistical Design and Analysis of Experiments,* New York: The Macmillan Co., 1971.

66. Johnson, Ellen, *The Research Report: A Guide for the Beginner,* New York: Ronald Press, 1951.

67. Johnson, Rodney D., and Siskin, Bernard R., *Quantitative Techniques for Business Decisions,* New Delhi: Prentice-Hall of India Pvt. Ltd., 1977.

68. Kahn, Robert L. and Cannell, Charles F., *The Dynamics of Interviewing*, New York: John Wiley & Sons, 1957.

69. Karson, Marvin J., *Multivariate Statistical Methods*, Ames, Iowa: The Iowa State University Press, 1982.

70. Kendall, M.G., *A Course in Multivariate Analysis,* London, Griffin, 1961.

71. Kerlinger, Fred N. and Pedhazur, Elazar J., *Multiple Regression in Behavioral Research,* New York: Holt, Rinehart and Winston, 1973.

72. Kerlinger, Fred N., *Foundations of Behavioral Research,* 2nd ed., New York: Holt, Reinhart and Winston, 1973.

73. Kish, Leslie., *Survey Sampling,* New York: John Wiley & Sons, Inc., 1965.

74. Kothari, C.R., *Quantitative Techniques,* 2nd ed., New Delhi: Vikas Publishing House Pvt. Ltd., 1984.

75. Lastrucci, Carles L., *The Scientific Approach: Basic Principles of the Scientific Method,* Cambridge, Mass.: Schenkman Publishing Co., Inc., 1967.

76. Lazersfeld, Paul F., *"Evidence and Inference in Social Research,"* in David Lerher, *Evidence and Inference,* Glencoe: The Free Press, 1950.

77. Leonard Schatzman, and Anselm L. Strauss, *Field Research,* New Jersey: Prentice-Hall Inc., 1973.

78. Levin, Richard I., *Statistics for Management,* New Delhi: Prentice-Hall of India Pvt. Ltd., 1979.

79. Levine, S. and Elzey, Freeman F., *A Programmed Introduction to Research,* California: Wods Worth Publishing Co., 1968.

80. Maranell, Gary M. (ed.), *Scaling: A Source Book for Behavioral Scientists,* Chicago: Aldine, 1974.

81. Maxwell, Albert E., *Analyzing Qualitative Data,* New York: John Wiley & Sons, 1961.

82. Meadows, R., and Parsons, A.J., *"Microprocessors: Essentials, Components and Systems,"* Pitman, 1983.

83. Meir, Robert C., Newell, William T., and Dazier, Harold L., *Simulation in Business and Economics*, Englewood Cliffs, N.J: Prentice Hall, Inc., 1969.

84. Miller, Delbert C., *Handbook of Research Design & Social Measurement*, 3rd ed., New York: David Mckay Company, Inc., 1977.

85. Moroney, M.J., *Facts from Figures,* Baltimore: Penguin Books, 1956.

86. Morrison, Donald F., *Multivariate Statistical Methods,* New York: McGraw-Hill, 1967.

87. Nagel, Stuart S., and Neef, Marian, *Policy Analysis in Social Science Research*, London: Sage Publications, 1979.

88. Nie, N.H., Bent, D.H., and Hull, C.H., *Statistical Package for the Social Sciences,* New York: McGraw-Hill, 1970.

89. Noether, G.E., *Elements of Nonparametric Statistics,* New York: John Wiley & Sons, Inc., 1967.

90. Nunnally, Jum C., *Psychometric Theory,* 2nd ed., New York: McGraw-Hill, 1978.

91. Odum, H.W., and Jocher, Katharine, *An Introduction to Social Research*, New York: Henry Holt and Co., 1929.

92. Oppenheim, A.N., *Questionnaire Design and Attitude Measurement,* New York: Basic Books, 1966.

93. Ostle, Bernard, and Mensing, Richard W., *Statistics in Research*, 3rd ed., Ames Iowa: The Iowa State University Press, 1975.

94. Payne, Stanley, *The Art of Asking Questions,* Princeton: Princeton University Press, 1951.

95. Pearson, Karl, *The Grammar of Science,* New York: Meridian Books, Inc., 1957.

96. Phillips, Bernard S., *Social Research, Strategy and Tactics*, 2nd ed., New York: The Macmillan Company, 1971.

97. Piaget, Jean, *Main Trends in Interdisciplinary Research*, London: George Allen and Unwin Ltd., 1973.

98. Popper, Karl R., *The Logic of Scientific Discovery,* New York: Basic Books, 1959.

99. Rajaraman, V., *"Fundamentals of Computers,"* New Delhi: Prentice-Hall of India Pvt. Ltd., 1985.

100. Ramchandran, P., *Training in Research Methodology in Social Sciences in India,* New Delhi: ICSSR 1971.

101. Redman, L.V., and Mory, A.V.H., *The Romance of Research*, 1923.

102. Roscoe, John T., *Fundamental Research Statistics for the Behavioral Sciences,* New York: Holt, Rinehart and Winston, Inc., 1969.

103. Runyon, Richard P., *Inferential Statistics,* Philippines: Addison-Wesley Publishing Company, Inc., 1977.

104. Sadhu, A.N., and Singh, Amarjit, *Research Methodology in Social Sciences,* Bombay: Himalaya Publishing House, 1980.

105. Seboyar, G.E., *Manual for Report and Thesis Writing,* New York: F.S. Crofts & Co., 1929.

106. Selltiz, Claire: Jahoda, Marie, Deutsch, Morton, and Cook, Stuart W., *Research Methods in Social Relations,* rev. ed. New York: Holt, Rinehart and Winston, Inc., 1959.

107. Sharma, B.A.V., et al., *Research Methods in Social Sciences,* New Delhi: Sterling Publishers Pvt. Ltd., 1983.

108. Sharma, H.D., and Mukherji, S.P., *Research in Economics and Commerce, Methodology and Surveys,* Varanasi: Indian Biographic Centre, 1976.

109. Siegel, S., *Nonparametric Statistics for the Behavioral Sciences,* New York: McGraw-Hill Publishing Co., Inc., 1956.

110. Subramanian, N., *"Introduction to Computers,"* New Delhi: Tata McGraw-Hill Publishing Co. Ltd., 1986.

111. Summers, Gene F., (Ed.), *Attitude Measurement,* Chicago: Rand McNally & Co., 1970.

112. Takeuchi, K., Yanai, H. and Mukherjee, B.N., *The Foundations of Multivariate Analysis,* New Delhi: Wiley Eastern Ltd., 1982.

113. Tandon, B.C., *Research Methodology in Social Sciences,* Allahabad: Chaitanya Publishing House, 1979.

114. Thorndike, Robert L. and Hagen, Elizabeth P., *Measurement and Evaluation in Psychology and Education,* 4th ed., New York: John Wiley & Sons, 1977.

115. Thurstone, L.L., *The Measurement of Values,* Chicago: University of Chicago Press, 1959.

116. Torgerson, W., *Theory and Methods of Scaling,* New York: John Wiley & Sons, 1958.

117. Travers, Robert M.W., *An Introduction to Educational Research,* 4th ed., New York: Macmillan Publishing Co., Inc., 1978.

118. Tryon, R.C., and Bailey, D.E., *Cluster Analysis*, New York: McGraw-Hill, 1970.

119. Ullman, Neil R., *Elementary Statistics,* New York: John Wiley & Sons, Inc., 1978.

120. Whitney, F.L., *The Elements of Research,* 3rd ed., New York: Prentice-Hall, 1950.

121. Wilkinson, T.S. and Bhandarkar, P.L., *Methodology and Techniques of Social Research*, Bombay: Himalaya Publishing House, 1979.

122. Willemsen, Eleanor Walker, *Understanding Statistical Reasoning*, San Francisco: W.H. Freeman and Company, 1974.

123. Yamane, T., *Statistics: An Introductory Analysis,* 3rd ed., New York: Harper and Row, 1973.

124. Young, Pauline V., *Scientific Social Surveys and Research,* 3rd ed., New York: Prentice-Hall, 1960.

Author Index

Subject Index